INSIDERS' GUIDE® TO YOSEMITE

THIRD EDITION

HELP US KEEP THIS GUIDE UP TO DATE

Every effort has been made by the authors and editors to make this guide as accurate and useful as possible. However, many things can change after a guide is published—phone numbers change, facilities come under new management, etc.

We would love to hear from you concerning your experiences with this guide and how you feel it could be improved and be kept up to date. While we may not be able to respond to all comments and suggestions, we'll take them to heart and we'll also make certain to share them with the authors. Please send your comments and suggestions to the following address:

The Globe Pequot Press
Reader Response/Editorial Department
P. O. Box 480
Guilford, CT 06437

Or you may e-mail us at:

editorial@GlobePequot.com

Thanks for your input, and happy travels!

INSIDERS' GUIDE® SERIES

INSIDERS' GUIDE® TO YOSEMITE

THIRD EDITION

KAREN MISURACA
AND
MAXINE CASS

GUILFORD, CONNECTICUT
AN IMPRINT OF THE GLOBE PEQUOT PRESS

The prices and rates in this guidebook were confirmed at press time. We recommend, however, that you call establishments before traveling to obtain current information.

INSIDERS' GUIDE®

Text design by LeAnna Weller Smith
Maps by XNR Productions Inc. © Morris Book Publishing, LLC

ISSN 1535-5683
ISBN-13: 978-0-7627-4050-5
ISBN-10: 0-7627-4050-7

Manufactured in the United States of America
Third Edition/First Printing

CONTENTS

CONTENTS

Directory of Maps

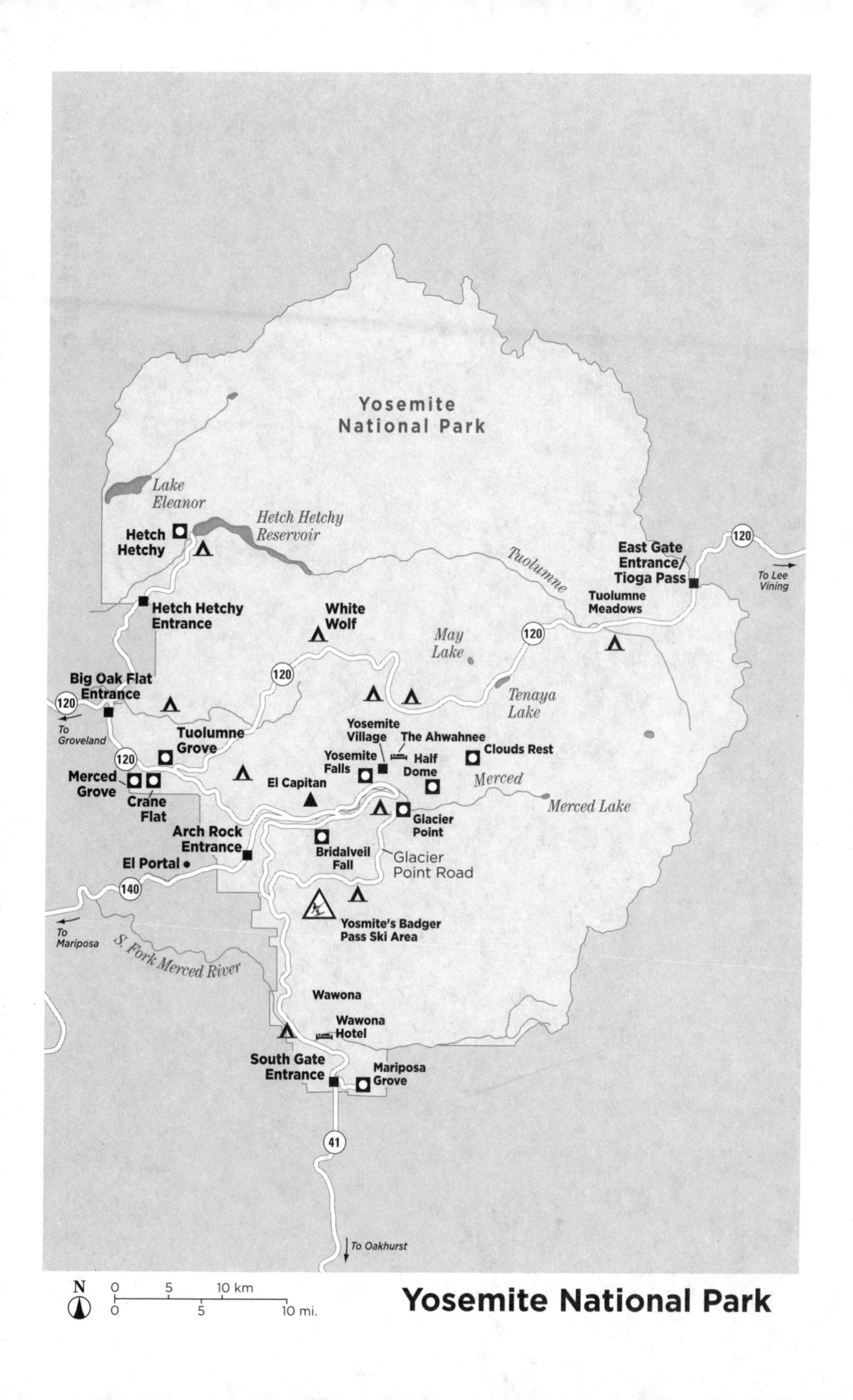

Yosemite National Park
Lake Eleanor
Hetch Hetchy Reservoir
Hetch Hetchy
Tuolumne
120
East Gate Entrance/ Tioga Pass
To Lee Vining
Hetch Hetchy Entrance
White Wolf
Tuolumne Meadows
May Lake
120
Big Oak Flat Entrance
120
To Groveland
Tenaya Lake
Tuolumne Grove
Yosemite Village
The Ahwahnee
Clouds Rest
120
Yosemite Falls
Half Dome
Merced Grove
Merced
El Capitan
Crane Flat
Merced Lake
Glacier Point
Arch Rock Entrance
Bridalveil Fall
Glacier Point Road
El Portal
140
To Mariposa
Yosmite's Badger Pass Ski Area
S. Fork Merced River
Wawona
Wawona Hotel
South Gate Entrance
Mariposa Grove
41
To Oakhurst
N
0 5 10 km
0 5 10 mi.
Yosemite National Park

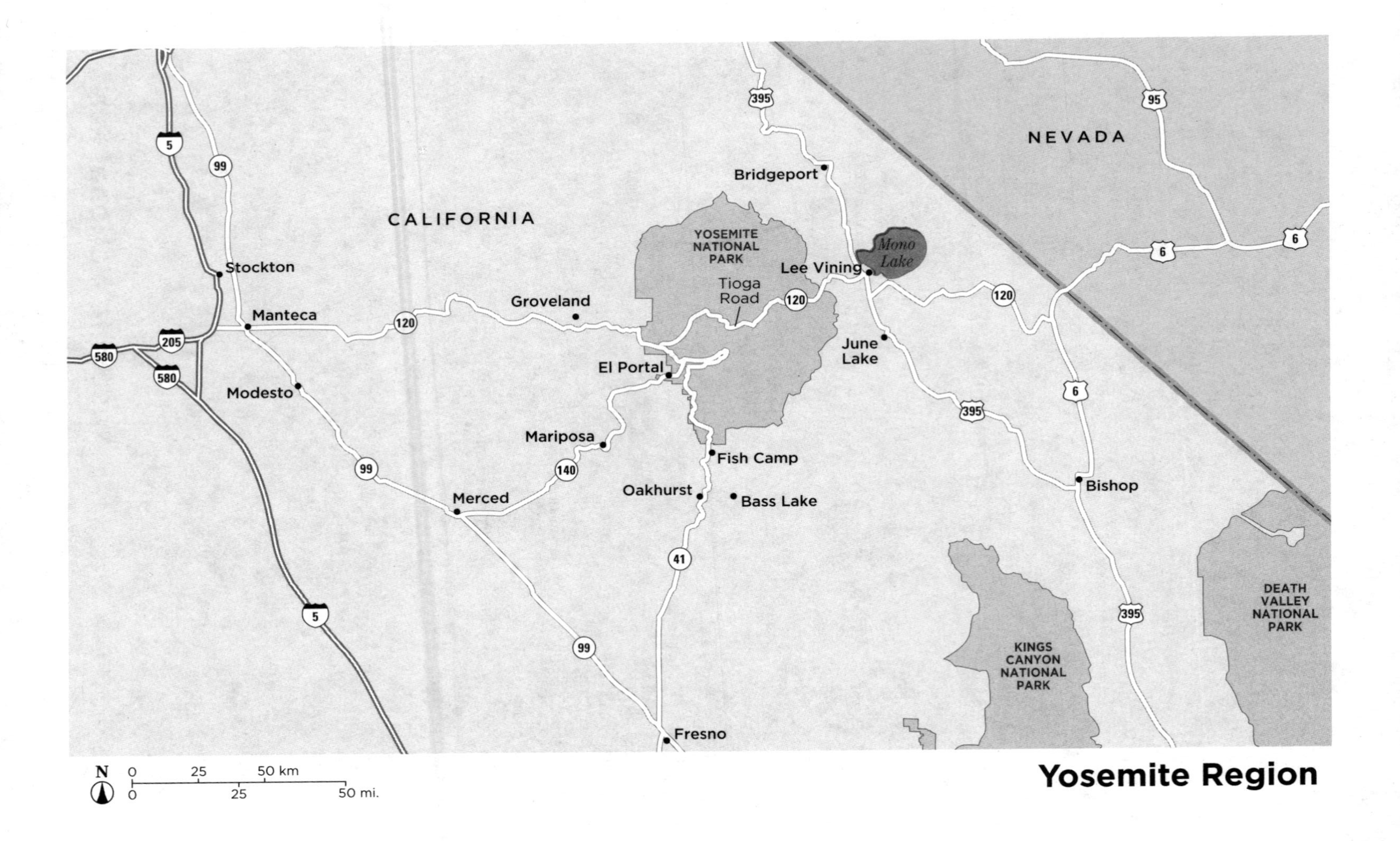

Yosemite Region

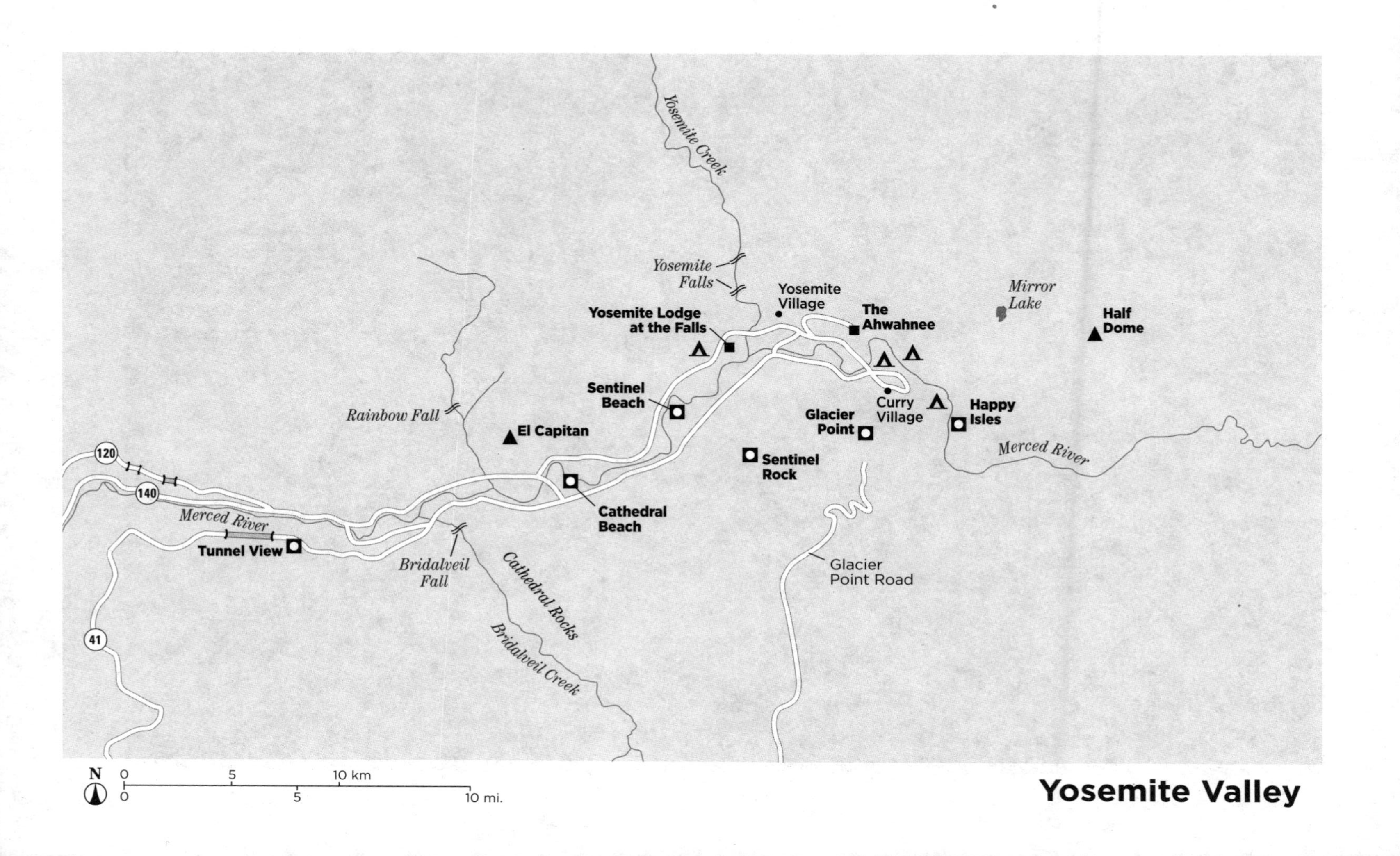

Yosemite Valley

Spray from Vernal Falls cools hikers on the Mist Trail. MAXINE CASS

ACKNOWLEDGMENTS

The perspectives of many insiders who are passionate about *their* Yosemite and their own Sierra Foothill communities enhance this *Insiders' Guide*. Support, encouragement, attention to detail, and enthusiasm were unflagging from both Ken Karst of Delaware North Companies Parks & Resorts, Inc. at Yosemite and Julie Miller, DNC's ever-smiling Interpretive Services Manager. Adrienne Freeman, National Park Service Ranger and doyenne of park information, willingly shared her knowledge.

As he has many times before, John Poimiroo of Poimiroo & Partners stepped up to represent his Yosemite gateway community tourism clients and then generously granted permission to use his fine photography to illustrate the spirit and excitement of the Yosemite region.

Abundant thanks are given to Susan Crain and Becky Rodriguez, Mariposa County Visitors Bureau; Dan Carter, Executive Director, Yosemite Sierra Visitors Bureau; Lorraine Moore, Geiger & Associates, for the Tuolumne County Visitors Bureau; Dan Lyster, Director, Mono County Economic Development; Catherine Boire; Fred Sater, Fred Sater Communications; Dan Marengo, The Fontayne Group; and to Steve Frisch of the Sierra Business Council. Linda Kundell of Kundell Communications enriched this edition by sharing her many years of personal experiences and impressions while she explored Yosemite National Park for the sheer pleasure of doing it.

My thanks continue to this book's original writer, Karen Misuraca, who encouraged me to update her fine work for this edition. I'm eternally grateful to Yosemite's original advocate and booster, John Muir, who wrote elegantly and lobbied eloquently for a Yosemite National Park.

No writer can survive without a support system: My thanks to Fred Gebhart for his love and for graciously providing some of this edition's photographs. Many purrs are due to my half-bobcat Mendo and to my silky Chocolate Panther, the steady cats who made sure I never wavered in checking details and writing new material. To the many friends who love the high and wild places, thank you!

—Maxine Cass

Snow-dusted El Capitan's reflection shimmers in the Merced River. MAXINE CASS

HOW TO USE THIS BOOK

Some of us have cherished memories of childhood vacations in Yosemite, and of visits to the park throughout our lives. If you are looking forward to your first visit, go ahead and indulge yourself in high expectations. The spectacular visions of Yosemite etched in your mind from postcards, books, and films are even more breathtaking in person. The more often you visit, the more you will be seduced by the ethereal beauty and drama of this unique part of the earth.

You will not be alone. Yosemite is the fourth most visited national park in the United States, welcoming nearly 3,281,000 visitors in 2004. As the main attractions are packed into a mere 7-mile-long, ½-mile-wide valley, this park requires the most advance planning to guarantee an enjoyable stay.

In decades past, families might just jump in the car and head for Yosemite, unworried about finding a campsite or a tent cabin. These day, lodgings and campgrounds throughout the park are booked months ahead, especially in summer. Yet, Yosemite is glorious in early spring, late fall, and during the winter, when visitor numbers are low. The Yosemite in Winter chapter will reveal a magical world that is surprisingly accessible, even if you hate to be cold and wouldn't think of skiing or snowshoeing.

If you are new to Yosemite, the value of this guidebook will be in the comprehensive details and basic information. Your only challenge will be choosing between the wide range of options, beginning with your choice of gateway highways. The most popular, lowest-elevation route is Highway 140 from Merced; however, you will find in the book good reasons to enter the park via the other three highways, each of which is a scenic route with great places to stay and plenty of outdoor recreation and historic attractions.

Take a look at the Getting Here, Getting Around chapter for information on easy, affordable public transportation that now makes it entirely unnecessary for you to drive your vehicle at all.

If you have been to Yosemite many times, this book will open your eyes to new ways of enjoying the park and environs, seeing it through the eyes of some interesting characters, past and present. The more often you return to the park, the more the rich geologic and human history of Yosemite will mean to you. The Area Overview and History chapters take a quick dip into how the park has grown and developed since the early 1800s.

Practical matters are laid out first—a general summary of the entire national park and surrounding geographical area; how to get to the park conveniently; and some interesting geological and human history.

Throughout this book we give you Insiders' Tips (indicated by i) for quick insights. Close-ups reveal information that is particularly interesting, unusual, and distinctly Yosemite.

The park falls into three geographical areas, each with its own natural attributes and man-made infrastructure (or lack of it). The main attractions are described in three separate chapters—Yosemite Valley, Wawona, and the Tuolumne and Hetch Hetchy—to help you determine where to spend most of your time. You will find that the roads, paved and unpaved trails, buildings, historic sites, access to natural attractions, and other infrastructure are designed for all ages and all physical abili-

The **Yosemite Road Guide** *is an essential reference—it is the key to the numbered roadside markers throughout the park and to those noted in this guide. Pick up a copy at the Yosemite Visitor Center or other retail outlets in the park or order it from The Yosemite Store, (209) 379-2648; www.yosemite.org.*

ties to enjoy. For toddlers and elders, for those who ride wheelchairs or bikes, for mountain climbers, backpackers, and couch potatoes, Yosemite promises memorable adventures in the wilderness.

Accommodations within the park are an important issue. From your own tent in a campground to a rented cabin, a motel-like room, or a luxurious hotel suite, there are decisions to be made based on cost, comfort, and availability. The Lodging and Rentals chapter, and the chapters describing the main highway routes, include lodgings in all price ranges and interests, for couples on romantic getaways, families, campers, and hard-core minimalists looking to save a buck. You can even rent a fully equipped, privately owned home within the national park.

Year after year, thousands of people camp in Yosemite Valley with their friends and family, making reservations a year ahead for their favorite sites. If you are not able to do that and arrive to find the valley campgrounds full, keep in mind that campgrounds may be available elsewhere in the park and in the national forests around Yosemite. Consult the Campgrounds chapter.

The Restaurants chapter describes the park's wide variety of restaurants, including ambience, cost, and type of food. More restaurants are reviewed in the chapters on gateway areas. Eating out three meals a day in the park can be expensive, so consider bringing some food from home, picnicking, and munching on healthy snacks before you head for a restaurant.

Visitors are often astonished to find out how many activities are scheduled in Yosemite every day of the year. You can sign up for an art class, hike with a park ranger, enjoy a play or a campfire sing-along, take a tour by moonlight, learn to take great photos, and a lot more. Delaware North Companies Parks & Resorts at Yosemite, Inc. (DNC), the main concessionaire, and other organizations are steadily expanding their schedules of activities—see the Events, Activities, and Tours chapter.

Several chapters clue you in to favorite hiking trails and outdoor recreation opportunities in and around the park, from river rafting and bicycling to fishing. If you are so inclined, check out the Hiking and Backpacking chapter.

Kids are V.I.P.s in Yosemite. The Kidstuff chapter suggests how to keep a gaggle of children busy, happy, and learning while they make vacation memories.

If you are considering moving to a community around Yosemite National Park, the final chapter on Relocation shares the practical details of what it is *really* like to live here.

Please let us know how the Insiders' Guide to Yosemite is working out for you. We would love to hear about your experiences and discoveries. Did you come across a dynamite barbecue restaurant on the way to the park? How about sharing the location of your favorite hidden swimming hole on the Merced River? Write to us at Insiders' Guide to Yosemite, Globe Pequot Press, P.O. Box 480, Guilford, CT 06437-0480, or visit our Web site at www.InsidersGuide.com.

AREA OVERVIEW

A jagged dragon's back of peaks and ridges running almost half the length of California, the Sierra Nevada range rises gradually from foothills to heights of 14,500 feet, dropping off on the east side in a nearly vertical escarpment.

A Spanish missionary traveling in 1772, Fray Pedro Font, saw the snowy peaks from a distance and named them *una gran sierra nevada,* "a great snowy range." Seeing the Sierra for the first time in 1868, the tireless explorer and conservator of Yosemite, John Muir, wrote, "And along the eastern shore of this lake of gold rose the mighty Sierra, miles in height, in massive, tranquil grandeur, so gloriously colored and so radiant that it seemed not clothed with light, but wholly composed of it, like the wall of some celestial city. Then it seemed to me the Sierra should be called, not the Nevada or Snowy Range, but the Range of Light."

Midway in the 430-mile wave of the Sierra, Yosemite National Park is a treasure-house of alpine peaks, gleaming granite domes and spires, vast meadows, and deep river canyons in a densely forested, true wilderness.

The jewel of the park is Yosemite Valley, astonishing in its array of geological formations created by millions of years of glacial activity. Granite monoliths form such a spectacular view corridor that its sentinels claim their own names—Half Dome, El Capitan, Cathedral Spires, Sentinel Rock, and Royal Arches. Plunging over the valley's rim out of a series of hanging valleys are some of the highest waterfalls in the world. From the day of its discovery by nonnatives in 1833, Yosemite became famous for its heart-stopping natural beauty, so remarkable that it was the first significant tract of land protected by American law, a bold move made by President Abraham Lincoln during the Civil War. Like the Grand Canyon and the Washington Monument, Yosemite is one of those places that must be seen by every American at least once in a lifetime.

A 4,733-foot-tall bulwark defining the eastern end of 7-mile-long Yosemite Valley, Half Dome guards the secret entrances into the Tenaya, the Illilouette, and the

Medical Assistance

Twenty-four-hour emergency care and limited pharmaceutical service are available at the Yosemite Medical Clinic (209-372-4637). Drop-in and urgent care services are offered between 8:00 A.M. and 7:00 P.M. (see the "Health Care" section of the Relocation chapter). You can make an appointment for emergency dental care; call (209) 372-4200. The clinic is located on Ahwahnee Drive to the east of the Yosemite Store.

Automated external defibrillators have been installed in public areas, including the Village Store parking lot entrance, the visitor center, at lodgings, and at the Crane Flat store in winter and Tuolumne Meadows store in summer.

What about Fido?

If your dog is more than 10 pounds and over six months old, you can make arrangements to have him or her cared for at the park kennel, a rather spartan, open-air facility with just nine kennels, located at the stables in Yosemite Valley at shuttle stop 18 near Curry Village (209-372-8348). Do have proof of shots and a license with you. The kennel is open on a first-come, first-served basis, Memorial Day to Labor Day, weather permitting. Cost is $8.00 a day, including one daily feeding and no exercise.

Dogs on their leashes may accompany their humans on paved trails in Yosemite Valley and not elsewhere in the park; pets are not allowed on unpaved trails or winter ski trails.

Some privately owned lodgings near the park allow dogs in guest rooms. See "Rentals" in the Lodging and Rentals chapter. For an additional charge, some "Canine Companion" rooms at the posh Tenaya Lodge at Yosemite in Fish Camp, are available for dogs and their owners, including a dog bed and some amenities. Dog-sitting and walking services give you both time away.

Merced River canyons, whose cascades rush from their birthplaces in the Sierra's crest. Fed by snowmelt and a living glacier on Mount Lyell, an even more powerful torrent, the Tuolumne River, leaps in cataracts and foaming rapids across the northern reaches of the park.

Rugged backcountry terrain comprises 94.5 percent of Yosemite National Park, which ranges in altitude from 2,000 to more than 13,000 feet. Near the southern and western entrances to the park, three groves of giant sequoias—the largest living things on earth—have been major tourist attractions since their discovery in 1852. It is no wonder that well over three million tourists visit annually.

GEOLOGIC HISTORY

Most of the Sierra Nevada is pale, gray granite, created from molten rock that bubbled up for millions of years. In later eons, upthrust occurred when earthquakes tilted the mass in a long slope from west to east, with an abrupt drop-off on the eastern side. At 430 miles long and 75 miles wide, the great wall of the Sierra reaches its zenith on Mount Whitney at 14,496 feet. More than 500 Sierra peaks rise beyond 12,000 feet above sea level.

Recently, only two or three million years ago, came a long Ice Age when the primitive wildlife withdrew and the giant sequoias and other evergreen and deciduous trees died. A great white winter descended in near silence, the only sound the low rumble and scrape of glaciers grinding down the granite blocks into spectacular gorges and deep valleys, spires, and cirques, cleaving and polishing the stone landmarks that we snap photographs of today. The Sierra ice cap was about 275 miles long and 20 to 40 miles wide.

In a process called exfoliation, the movement of the glaciers created rounded, smooth domes and knobs, as seen throughout the higher elevations of the park. Hikers scramble over Lembert Dome in the High Country, a "sheepback" formation, elongated and buffed in the direction of the ice flow. Somehow, as the glaciers wreaked havoc in the landscape, half of Half Dome's rounded mass cracked away.

Glacial exfoliation broke off horizontal layers of stone, leaving rounded sheets and strips parallel to the earth. Royal Arches, behind The Ahwahnee, and North Dome,

Monolithic Half Dome dominates the east end of Yosemite Valley. DNC

Many Web site URLs use the word "yosemite." Here are important sites that offer information, not an advertising pitch:
www.nps.gov/yose (National Park Service: Yosemite National Park)
www.yosemitepark.com (DNC in-park activites, lodging, dining, tours)
www.yosemite.com (Merced County Yosemite information & YARTS transportation)
www.yosemite.org (Yosemite Association)
www.yosemitefund.org (Yosemite Fund: nonprofit facility restoration projects)
www.yosemitethisyear.com (Yosemite Sierra Visitors Bureau/Madera County)

just above, are perfect examples of these singular geologic formations that are found throughout this national park.

When the glaciers melted about 10,000 years ago, the valley filled with water, a vast lake that gradually silted over and disappeared, leaving hanging valleys with rivers plunging off the edges of the steep granite walls in magnificent waterfalls. About 2,000 alpine and subalpine lakes in the Sierra, thousands of streams, and 15 major river systems remain, mostly flowing west into California's Central Valley.

While moisture generated off the Pacific Ocean was deflected to the west side of the mountain range, the eastern side of the Sierra went dry, becoming the desert of the Great Basin.

Abraded by the masses of ice, the formerly V-shaped Yosemite and Hetch Hetchy Valleys became flattened into U-shaped valleys. Pushed ahead of the advancing glaciers and remaining when the ice melted are gravelly moraine and erratics—huge boulders—still very much in evidence in Yosemite Valley, quite obvious in Bridalveil Meadow. As visitors drive into the park on Highway 41, thousands of building-size boulders in the riverbed and along both sides of the valley floor give the illusion of having recently fallen into place.

As temperatures moderated and vegetation returned, the seasons, as we know them, began again. Sixty-five glaciers still existed by the time John Muir wandered the High Country in the mid-1880s. Now, in the 21st century, more than 50 glaciers still exist in the Sierra, slowly moving on their rocky beds, and the mountains are ever-so-slowly continuing to push upwards. Living glaciers can still be seen on Mount Lyell and Mount McClure, within the park.

Yosemite Valley is in what is known as the Transition Zone, a lower montane forest life zone determined by altitude, wherein a mixed evergreen forest of ponderosa pines and aromatic incense cedar resides, along with a woodland of black oaks and bigleaf maple in the meadows, and sycamore and willows along the riverbanks. Most of the park is within the Canadian Zone, where upper montane forest red fir, Douglas fir, and Jeffrey, Western, white, and lodgepole pine are the predominant tree species. Above 9,000 feet in the Hudsonian Zone, subalpine mountain hemlocks and whitebark pines survive in treacherous climate throughout much of the year. Above the tree line in the Alpine Zone, a few small pines are ghostly figures, their bark pale against the silvery stone outcroppings.

The largest subalpine meadow in the Sierra—the idyllic Tuolumne Meadows on the eastern side of the park—is accessed, for only about 150 days a year, by the highest vehicle pass in the state, reaching 9,945 feet at Tioga Pass. A hub for backpacking trails and backcountry campgrounds and lakes, the meadows are bordered by the Tuolumne River and entirely surrounded by a breathtaking panorama of peaks and glacier-polished domes. The boiling waters of two forks of the river come together here, then drop into a wild canyon, and finally, into Hetch Hetchy Reservoir miles below, the drinking fountain for San Francisco.

CLOSE-UP

Teddy Roosevelt and John Muir

In 1903 President Theodore Roosevelt stood on Glacier Point and exclaimed, "I wouldn't miss this for anything . . . this is bully!"

Accompanied by the legendary explorer of Yosemite, John Muir, Roosevelt was on a three-day horseback expedition and camping trip that started at the Mariposa Grove under the Grizzly Giant, with the president bedding down in a pile of about 40 wool blankets. The second night was spent near Sentinel Dome during a snowstorm, and the third night they camped at Bridalveil Meadow in Yosemite Valley.

Muir regaled his captive audience with tales of the Yosemite wilderness and the urgent need to set aside, in perpetuity, this area and other precious tracts of land—posing the idea of a national park system. Following his hugely enjoyable campout with Muir, Roosevelt took a major role in the movement to add the Yosemite Valley and the Mariposa Grove to the National Park, which he signed into law in 1906.

Through the president's personal attention and during his term of office, together with the efforts of Muir, the Sierra Club, and others, five national parks, 18 national monuments, 55 national bird sanctuaries and wildlife refuges, and 148 million acres of national forests were designated.

President Theodore Roosevelt and John Muir admire the view at Glacier Point in 1903. DNC

Look for the sign in Bridalveil Meadow commemorating the Roosevelt–Muir meeting. The sign reads, "On this site President Theodore Roosevelt sat beside a campfire with John Muir on May 17, 1903, and talked forest good. Muir urged the President to work for preservation of priceless remnants of America's wilderness. At this spot one of our country's foremost conservationists received great inspiration."

Keep a weather eye open all year in the Sierra Nevada, where mountain weather is changeable. Afternoon thunderstorms are not uncommon, even in midsummer, and savvy park visitors are always prepared with lightweight ponchos or jackets.

FOUR GATEWAYS TO THE PARK

Beyond the eastern border of the National Park, the Ansel Adams Wilderness, the Hoover Wilderness, and the Inyo and Toiyabe National Forests are vast, undeveloped tracts of densely forested lands, wild rivers, canyons, and mountain peaks. In fact, the park is encircled by eight national forests. Along the four main access routes into the park—Highways 140, 120 east and west, and 41—the countryside is nearly as spectacular as the park itself.

Winding along beside the Wild and Scenic Merced River, Highway 140 is gently interrupted by the historic Gold Rush town of Mariposa. White-water rafters and anglers ply the river, while campers and hikers head into the Sierra National Forest.

Driving in on Highway 41 toward the southern entrance to the park, travelers stop in Oakhurst for antiques shopping and art galleries. They launch their Jet Skis and speedboats into the warm waters of Bass Lake and cross-country ski at Goat Meadow.

On the way to the Big Oak Flat gate into Yosemite, Highway 120 passes right through the tiny town of Groveland, where the oldest saloon in California and a grand Victorian hotel are reasons to linger awhile. Seeking the solitude that Yosemite Valley no longer provides, except in the wintertime, some explorers turn north to the Hetch Hetchy Valley, sometimes called "the other Yosemite Valley," hiking past 1,000-foot waterfalls into the lesser-known wilderness of the northwestern corner of the park.

In 1984 Yosemite National Park was declared a UNESCO World Heritage Site, one of about 20 in the United States. World Heritage Sites are deemed to be worthy of protection for their "natural and cultural properties of outstanding universal value against the threat of damage in a rapidly developing world," in the words of UNESCO. For more information about World Heritage Sites, go to whc.unesco.org.

ONLY ONE DAY

It's unbelievable, really, but some people have just a day to spend in Yosemite. Here are the top sights to see in a day, including the most accessible of the famous landmarks and views. Begin your day by parking at Yosemite Village. Stop in at the visitor center to pick up a map of the park and watch the film, *Spirit of Yosemite.*

The easiest and most relaxing way to see the valley and other attractions of the park in a day is to take the "Grand Tour," an eight-hour narrated excursion in a big, comfy, air-conditioned motorcoach. While your park ranger interpretive guide spins stories of old Yosemite and fills you in on the famous landmarks and historical sites, the bus tours the valley, drives up to Glacier Point and to the Mariposa Grove of Giant Sequoias, stopping at the Wawona Hotel at lunchtime, and makes stops along the way for stretching legs and taking photos (209-372-1240).

For touring on your own, hop on the free valley shuttle for these first four stops, then climb back into your car to explore the rest.

Lower Yosemite Fall
Road marker V19, V3, or shuttle stop 6

Walk 15 minutes on a paved trail from the visitor center or take shuttle bus 6 to one of two paved paths 500 yards to the base of the fall, which drops in a mighty plunge 320 feet from the base of the upper fall. The lower and upper falls together leap

The Sentinel Dome Pine

Carleton Watkins photographed it in 1867. Ansel Adams photographed it early in the 20th century. The striking, ruggedly simple form of a Jeffrey pine, perched on the summit of Sentinel Dome against a backdrop of Sierra peaks, was one of the most photographed icons of Yosemite. The pine died in the severe drought of 1976–77, although people tried to save it by bringing buckets of water. And, finally, in August of 2003, the tree fell over, likely due to severe storms earlier in the month.

out of a hanging valley 2,425 feet in two monumental cataracts, making this the tallest waterfall in North America. In late spring and early summer, the tremendous force of the falls vibrates in the ground at your feet.

Mist Trail
Shuttle stop 16, Happy Isles
From Happy Isles, it's 7⁄10 of a mile on a paved trail to the Vernal Fall bridge for views of Vernal Fall, which drops over a 317-foot cliff in a wide, mighty stream encircled by rainbows at its base (with more time, continue on a steep, ½-mile trail to the top of the fall). Bring a parka for the cold, drenching spray. There are restrooms and a water fountain located here.

Mirror Lake
Shuttle stop 17
An easy, very popular ½-mile walk on a paved path to a small lake named for its glassy reflection of Mount Watkins, this is a good vantage point for photos of Half Dome. A famous sight in the valley in decades past when it was a shallow, rockfall-dammed pool, now the lake is mostly a boggy meadow, reflective only in spring and early summer when there is some water. Among the live oaks and Douglas firs, dogwood blooms in creamy white clouds in the spring, and maples flame in the fall.

The Ahwahnee
Shuttle stop 3
At this architectural icon of Yosemite Valley, take a look at the vintage photos and paintings in the hotel lobby. Walk into the main dining room, a two-story, trestle-beamed hall with floor-to-ceiling windows looking onto a forest scene and Royal Arches. Sit a spell in the museum-like Great Lounge beneath the stained-glass windows and look at the king-size old photos and the Western and Indian regalia. Walk behind the Great Lounge to see a fine collection of Native American basketry and the wood-paneled Mural Room, Winter Club Room, and Solarium.

Bridalveil Fall
At the junction of Highways 140 and 41 in the park is a parking lot where a short, ½-mile paved trail leads to the base of the fall. Look up to a sheet of water flowing 620 feet to the valley floor. This fall never disappoints, as it flows year-round and is often decorated by rainbows. In the springtime turn around to get a view of 1,612-foot-high Ribbon Fall, the highest single fall in the park after 2,000-foot-high Sentinel Fall.

Tunnel View
Just east of the Wawona Tunnel, park at the turnout to see a classic panoramic view of the valley framed by famous mighty monoliths, El Capitan and Cathedral Rocks, with Half Dome, Sentinel Rock, and Cloud's Rest in the distance.

Glacier Point Road
Make the 32-mile drive to Glacier Point, stopping at pullouts along the way to

snap photos of dazzling alpine scenery, then get ready for the heart-stopping view from Glacier Point, 3,200 feet above the valley with peaks, spires, domes, and massive granite walls in a dizzying array at your feet and as far as you can see into the distance.

THE SEASONS OF YOSEMITE

Unlike much of California, which slides through the year in a blur of perfectly wonderful, monotonous weather, Yosemite experiences four distinct seasons. At altitudes of 2,000 feet at Arch Rock, to 4,000 feet on the valley floor and 13,114 feet on Mount Lyell, the weather changes rapidly, creating marvelous skies and cloud formations, with a pageant of shifting light against the cliffs and on the Merced River. It is no wonder that some photographers fall so deeply in love with Yosemite that they never recover.

In the valley, temperatures range from the high 90s in midsummer to glorious, clear spring and fall days in the 70s. Winters are generally moderate. Although snow can fall sporadically as early as September, most of the precipitation comes in January, February, and March, with just dustings of snow in the lower elevations. In the High Country, the Tioga Road closes and winter sets in hard from about the first of November through March, a time eagerly awaited by intrepid snow campers and skiers.

Spring in Yosemite means waterfalls, when snowmelt fills the Merced and Tuolumne Rivers, roiling recklessly down the canyons and dropping over the clifftops into Yosemite Valley. You can hear it thundering from Nevada, Vernal, and Yosemite Falls, stand in a rainbow at the foot of Bridalveil, and lean over a bridge, watching the Merced River splash and tumble over the boulders, the budding willows and cottonwoods reflected in quiet eddies. The sound and sight of water is one of the great pleasures of Yosemite, from its shining waterfalls to boggy meadows, trout streams, ferny seeps, vernal pools, and misted forest glens. Spring begins in the foothills in late February, when wildflowers burst into bloom along the highways into the park. Masses of color appear in Yosemite Valley in April and May. Left from old homesteads, apple trees turn into clouds of pink. Among the sequoias and the pines, dogwoods are a tracery of white against the dark branches, and the translucent, new green of the oak and willow leaves float in the chilly air. Dogwood trees bloom throughout the valley between late March and the end of May. Some of the best places to see them are on the trail to Mirror Lake, at Happy Isles, and in the Tuolumne Grove in late May—a magical sight among 25 giant sequoias and a forest of incense cedar, sugar pine, and white fir.

Sierra summers are typically very warm and dry, and spectacular afternoon thunderstorms are common. April and November are transition months, when sunny days can suddenly turn blustery.

Along about mid-September, when most campers and day-trippers are long gone, the days are sunny, and a snap in the crystalline mountain air seems to catch fire in the brilliant red and gold maples, oaks, and aspens. The Merced River and the waterfalls relax and leaves fall from the black oaks, turning them to stark silhouettes against the pale crags. Bigleaf maples seem littered with gold coins in the late afternoon sun, their treasure reflected in the water. Meadows are as tawny as mountain lions and rimmed with crunchy carpets of rust-colored pine needles and fernrows gone yellow. Crisp breezes rustle hauntingly through the sequoia groves.

WILDLIFE VIEWING

Preserving the environment results in an abundance of wildlife. In Yosemite Valley and throughout the park, you are likely to

Fabulous Facts about Yosemite National Park

Yosemite Valley and the Mariposa Big Trees together became the first state park in America in 1864.

Congress established Yosemite National Park on October 1, 1890.

Total square miles: 1,169 (about the size of Rhode Island)

Wilderness: 94.5 percent of the park

Highest of 10 major peaks: Mt. Lyell, 13,114 feet; Mt. Dana, 13,057 feet; Rodgers Peak, 12,978 feet

Developed trails: more than 800 miles

Streams: more than 1,600 miles

U.S. Wild and Scenic Rivers: Merced, Tuolumne

Elevation: 2,000 to 13,114 feet

Park visitation in 2004: 3,280,911

Three highest waterfalls in North America: Yosemite Falls, 2,425 feet; Sentinel Fall, 2,000 feet; Ribbon Fall, 1,612 feet

Highest pass in the Sierra Nevada: Tioga Pass, 9,945 feet

Wildlife Species

Amphibians and reptiles: 31
Fish: 11, 6 of which are endemic
Mammals: 89
Birds: 247

Threatened and Endangered Species

California bighorn sheep (t) (CA)
California wolverine (t) (CA)
Giant garter snake (t) (CA)
Great gray owl (t) (CA)
Limestone salamander (t) (CA)
Peregrine falcon (e) (US)
Sierra Nevada red fox (t) (CA)
Southern bald eagle (e) (US)
Willow flycatcher (e) (CA)
Congdon's woolly sunflower (t) (US) and (e) (CA)
Congdon's lewisia (t) (US) and (e) (CA)
Thompson's sedge (e) (CA)
Yosemite onion (e) (CA)
Yosemite woolly sunflower (e) (US)

see chipmunks, yellow-bellied marmots, ground squirrels—a black bear or two if you make the mistake of leaving food out—coyote, and mule deer.

Rarely seen residents of the High Country are the pine marten, fisher marten, wolverine, mountain lion, and Sierra Nevada red fox. You may catch a glimpse of an endangered southern bald eagle or a peregrine falcon circling a meadow, hunting for prey. Designated as threatened in California, the great gray owl nests in the valley and elsewhere in the park.

California bighorn sheep were declared extinct in Yosemite in 1914 and were reintroduced in 1986. Nonnative beaver and white-tailed ptarmigan were also introduced, as were German brown trout in the Merced River. Grizzly bears and probably the gray wolf disappeared from the area in the late 1800s and early 1900s.

At the timberline, 9,600 feet, spring begins later in the year—the Tioga Road to Tuolumne Meadows usually opens in late May, just in time for a veritable explosion of flowers in the alpine meadows that peaks in midsummer and fall, only to be blanketed with snow by November.

When the snow flies in Yosemite, the number of visitors drops dramatically and activities center around Yosemite's Badger Pass Ski Area and Yosemite Valley. Rangers lead snowshoe walks and ski tours at Crane Flat in the Mariposa Grove of Giant Sequoias. With icicle-clad Half Dome looking on, skating is fun at the outdoor rink in Curry Village. Winter brings a new perspective to Yosemite, when rain curtains and mists clothe the peaks. Bare black cottonwood branches shiver in their crystal coats beside streams almost covered with ice. From the top of Badger Pass, clouds billow 10 miles into the sky, and thunder rolls down the valley, pounding the canyon walls like an Indian beating a drum. Beneath the sheets of ice and snow blanketing the upper meadows, spring sleeps.

Few visitors enter the wondrous winter world of Yosemite, making it all the more enchanting for those who do. There is nothing cozier than sitting in front of a fireplace in The Ahwahnee or by blazing logs in the Yosemite Lodge at the Falls, while snowflakes scatter softly on the evergreens.

Miles from cities and traffic congestion, the skies over Yosemite are as relentlessly blue as the vibrant azure sky pilot flower that springs out of bare granite above 11,000 feet. Despite some human development on the valley floor and scattered here and there in the national park, Yosemite remains a stunningly beautiful, wild place, as John Muir said, ". . . the great fresh unblighted, unredeemed wilderness."

GETTING HERE, GETTING AROUND

About 3.3 million visitors enter Yosemite National Park each year, and most arrive in their own vehicles. One million arrive in July and August alone.

Advance planning will smooth your journey to Yosemite and within the park. The Yosemite Association will send you a Visitor Kit containing *The Complete Guidebook to Yosemite National Park;* a map and guide to Yosemite Valley, Tuolumne Meadows, and Wawona; the *Yosemite Road Guide;* the *Yosemite Magazine,* an annual Park Service guide to basic information and news; and *Yosemite Today,* which lists seasonal events and daily activities and tours. The kit is sold online for $19.95 at www.yosemitestore.com/merchant/index.html. The maps and guides are sold separately at the visitor center in Yosemite Valley.

If you drive in at the height of the summer season, or on weekends and holidays, you may experience delays and heavy traffic. To maximize your time and protect your state of mind, consider carefully the many transportation options. Weather and road conditions in the Sierra change quickly, so be prepared with tire chains from late fall through early spring.

For those who take public transportation, getting conveniently and quickly into and out of the park is a cinch, any day of the year in any weather. Keep in mind that public transportation is not subject to delays that may occur at park gates and riding in a bus transfers the responsibility of driving on icy winter roads to a professional.

Once at your lodgings, ask about the free shuttle buses that zip around the valley and the bus tours up to Tuolumne Meadows and Glacier Point and to Wawona. For reasonable fees, narrated bus tours are offered throughout most of the park.

At the park entrance gates, you will receive the free *Yosemite Today,* a seasonal tabloid published 15 times a year, filled with all the basic information anyone could need, from shuttle bus stops to the locations of attractions, lodgings, restaurants, and information kiosks, and schedules of daily activities and seasonal events.

After perusing *Yosemite Today,* the next step is to stop at the Yosemite Valley Visitor Center in Yosemite Village, west of the main post office. Walk into the center of the village facilities from the parking lot.

Yosemite Valley Visitor Center
Yosemite Village, shuttle stop 5, 9, or Road marker V1
(209) 372–0200 ext. 6

Here you will find trail maps, guidebooks, and campground information. And you can submit a wilderness permit application for High-Country hiking and backpacking and get well-informed advice and suggestions for recreational activities. The center is open from 9:00 A.M. to 5:00 P.M. every day.

If you plan to drive, hike, or bike around the park, the Yosemite Road Guide is one of the best publications to pick up in the bookstore here. The booklet clearly locates natural and man-made attractions in the

---

i

The park is open year-round, 365 days a year, 24 hours a day. Reservations are not required to enter the park. Private vehicles are always welcome.

A free lifetime Golden Access Passport for permanent U.S. residents is available for medically blind or disabled individuals. It admits the passholder and immediate family or caregiver, with a 50 percent discount on in-park camping. Although Yosemite National Park doesn't have braille publications, the Yosemite Valley Visitor Center does have a magnifying half-globe for map perusal. Other accessible facilities are detailed at www.nps.gov/yose/pphtml/accessibility.html.

park with numbered road markers and explains their significance and history. You will find these road markers mentioned in many guidebooks, including this one.

PARK ENTRANCE FEES

Vehicle and all occupants: $20, valid for seven days. Credit cards, cash, personal checks, and travelers checks are accepted.

Individual: $10 foot, bicycle, motorcycle, horse, or bus. (YARTS bus fee includes entrance fee, valid for seven days.)

Yosemite Pass: $40, valid for one year in Yosemite; includes all vehicle passengers.

National Parks Pass: $50, valid for one year, unlimited entry to all NPS sites; includes all vehicle passengers.

Golden Eagle Pass: $65, valid for one year in all national parks, plus all Forest Service, Bureau of Land Management, and Fish and Wildlife Service fee areas; includes all vehicle passengers.

Golden Age Passport: $10, for U.S. citizens or permanent residents age 62 and over; valid for the life of the holder. See www.nps.gov/parks/passes_fees.htm for details.

Golden Access Passport: free for blind or permanently disabled U.S. citizens or permanent residents. See www.nps.gov/parks/passes_fees.htm for details.

Park entrance is free every year on August 25, Founders Day. This is a tradition at all national parks in the country.

BY AIR

Fresno Yosemite International Airport
5175 East Clinton Way, Fresno
(559) 621-4500
www.fresno.gov/flyfresno/

Just 90 miles from the South Gate of Yosemite, major airlines and commuter airlines fly in, including Allegiant, America West, American Eagle, Horizon, Delta, United Airlines, United Express/Skywest, Alaska, Northwest, Continental, Frontier, Mesa, and Hawaiian Airlines, with connections to San Francisco and Los Angeles. Rental cars are available.

Mariposa-Yosemite Airport
(209) 966-2143

Land your private plane here on the 3,310-foot-long runway. Rental cars are available by advance reservation; call the airport for more information and reservations.

Merced Municipal Airport
20 Macready Drive, Merced
(209) 385-6873

Just 73 miles from Yosemite, this private service airport is served by Scenic Airlines' 13-hour tours from Las Vegas.

BY CAR

Depending on which of the four park entrances you choose, it is about a four-hour drive from San Francisco and a six-hour drive from Los Angeles to the park entrances. Along the four gateway highways to the park are charming, historic, foothill communities that are well worth a visit: Oakhurst, Mariposa, Groveland, and Lee Vining, each of which is described in detail in the four chapters near the end of this book. Each of the gateway highways winds through undeveloped, rural areas; the population surrounding the park is sparse, less than 100,000.

Highway 120/Big Oak Flat Entrance: about four and a half hours from San Francisco, 88 miles from Manteca, through Groveland and Big Oak Flat. From the park gate, it is about one hour to midvalley, with a fluctuation in elevation from 3,000 to 6,000 feet.

Highway 140/Arch Rock Entrance: 80 miles from Merced, through Mariposa and El Portal. From the park gate, it is about 30 minutes to midvalley. This is the lowest-elevation route, making it the best choice for wintertime.

Highway 41/South Entrance: about four and a half hours from San Francisco, 64 miles from Fresno, through Oakhurst and Fish Camp. From the park gate, it is about one hour to midvalley, with a change in elevation from 3,000 to 6,000 feet.

Highway 120/East Entrance: 10 miles from Lee Vining to the entrance, from the park gate, it is about two hours to midvalley; closed in winter. The elevation reaches 9,945 feet. The East entrance and the Tioga Road into the park are closed from sometime in late October or early November to May or June, depending on snowfall.

Glacier Point Road closes November to mid-December and the Mariposa Grove Road may also be closed in wintertime. All other park roads are open throughout the year, although chains may be required at times. Yosemite Valley roads are seldom closed, at least, not for long.

Road conditions in the Sierra can change from hour to hour, any month of the year, and particularly from late fall through the winter into early spring. Besides checking recorded highway information by phone, a good idea is to call lodgings in the park and ask the staff about the roads. See below for sources of road condition updates.

Distance from Yosemite Valley

El Portal	14 miles
Mariposa	45 miles
Oakhurst	50 miles
Fresno	105 miles
San Francisco	214 miles
Los Angeles	320 miles

Car Rental

There is no car rental availability in the national park.

In Fresno, rent a vehicle from Avis (800) 831-2847, Budget (800) 527-0700, Dollar (800) 800-4000, Enterprise (800) 736-8222, Hertz (800) 654-3131, or National (800) 227-7368.

In Modesto Avis, Budget, and Hertz have rental locations. For Merced or Oakhurst rentals, contact Enterprise or Hertz.

Road Conditions

For road information outside the park, call the Caltrans Highway Information Network: (800) 427-7623. Inside the park, call (209) 372-0200, ext. 1, or check out the National Park Web site: www.nps.gov/yose/now/conditions.htm for information on current road and weather conditions, waterfall and river flows, wildflowers, fire and bear updates, lodging and campground status, trail conditions and closures, and a link to wilderness conditions. All of this information is updated frequently, some on an hourly basis.

Fill up on gas before you enter the park. Gas is available in El Portal outside the Arch Rock entrance (including diesel); at Crane Flat, 15 miles inside the Big Oak Flat entrance; at Wawona near the hotel (also diesel and propane); and during the summer only at Tuolumne Meadows (propane, too). No gas is available in Yosemite Valley. For car trouble and towing, call (209) 372-8320.

BY BUS

Yosemite Area Regional Transportation System (YARTS)
(877) 989-2787, (209) 388-9589
www.yarts.com, www.yosemite.com

There is a comfortable way to get to the national park that can make your vehicle entirely unnecessary. An energy-saving and environmentally sensitive scenic alternative to driving into Yosemite National Park, YARTS provides economical, comfortable, and convenient bus service. YARTS serves the Highway 140 corridor from Merced and Mariposa counties with air conditioning, reclining seats, large windows, restrooms, roomy baggage compartments, and frequent daily departures, year-round.

From June through September, YARTS also runs on Highway 120 East between Yosemite Valley and Mammoth Lakes in Mono County with stops at June Lake and Lee Vining. Highway 120 East YARTS service is convenient for hikers and backpackers who want to hike one way and leave their cars in more developed areas.

Find schedules for YARTS transit service, routes, prices, and frequently asked questions on the Web site or by phone. In Merced, YARTS makes stops at the AMTRAK station, the Merced Transportation Center, and the Merced Municipal Airport.

Tickets are available from local lodgings, visitor bureaus, or from the YARTS driver. Fares are based on the distance traveled and cost from $5.00 to $20.00 round trip. You are not required to pay an additional entrance fee to enter the park. Ask about discounts for kids and for seniors (62 years and over). On the Highway 140 corridor, one child under 16 rides free with a paying adult.

BY TRAIN

You can get to Yosemite by AMTRAK train from all over the state. Arrivals from northern California are in Merced, with free connections to the park by bus; the drivers keep up a steady commentary about sights along the way. From Emeryville in the San Francisco Bay Area, you leave at about 7:30 A.M. and arrive in the park just after 1:00 P.M., for about $50 one-way. AMTRAK from Southern California arrives in Merced for bus connections. Call AMTRAK at (800)

Getting to Yosemite on the Cannonball Express

Operated by the Yosemite Stage and Turnpike Company in the 1870s, the "Cannonball" stagecoach brought travelers from the train station in Raymond to Wawona on a narrow, winding, bumpy, 72-mile road, a dusty trip that took about 12 hours. At the peak of its success, the company owned a dozen stables, 700 horses, and 25 stages. They called it the Cannonball because it promised to "shoot you through in one day" behind teams of horses that were changed every 7 or 8 miles, trotting at an even, fast pace uphill and down. Stop in at the Pioneer Yosemite History Center in Wawona to see some of the original Yosemite stagecoaches. The original wagon "The Cannonball Express" still runs the original route over Chowchilla Mountain Road from Wawona into the Fairgrounds in Mariposa during the second week in June as part of the four-day Pioneer Wagon Train Ride.

The Yosemite Plan

In 1999 Interior Secretary Bruce Babbitt announced the release of the Final Yosemite Valley Plan and Supplemental Environmental Impact Statement, a document avidly awaited, researched, and argued about for many years.

The intention of the plan is to conserve natural and cultural resources in the park for future generations, while providing access and ensuring a quality visitor experience. To be implemented over the next 10 to 15 years, the plan provides a framework for restoring degraded ecosystems and reducing human development; in other words, returning as much of the park as possible to its original state.

Visitors who are worried that they will be turned away from the park should rest assured that Yosemite will always be open to the public, every day of the year.

Some of the main mandates of the plan:

- Nonindigenous vegetation will be replaced with native flora.
- 176 acres of land will be restored to a natural state by removing roads and buildings.
- To diminish vehicle congestion and air pollution, some parking will be relocated and expanded in outlying areas within the park and outside the park.
- Upper and Lower River campgrounds have been closed and will be restored to meadow, riparian, and oak woodlands.
- Valley lodging will be cut from 1,260 to 961 rooms by removing cabins at Curry Village and Housekeeping Camp.
- Valley campsites will be increased to 500.
- Free public transportation within the park will be expanded.
- Public transportation to and from the park has been expanded and more choices will be offered in the future.
- A 3.2-mile section of Northside Drive, a main artery, will be replaced with paved foot and bike trails.
- A 150-foot-wide protection zone will be established along most of the Merced River.

Detailed explanations of the Yosemite Plan, along with interesting graphics, are on display in the visitor center, and more information on implementation or holds on projects is available at www.nps.gov/yose/planning.

USA-RAIL or visit www.amtrak.com. Ask about off-season discounts and special fares for children and seniors.

Through AMTRAK, you can sign up for a sight-seeing tour of the valley and lodging packages, or a Yosemite-in-a-Day tour.

SHUTTLE BUSES AROUND THE PARK

Complimentary shuttle bus service throughout the valley is provided year-round on a 21-stop route, running every 15 minutes, accessing trailheads, the visitor center, campgrounds, lodgings, museums, all public facilities, and many natural attractions. In summer, shuttles also run from Wawona to the Mariposa Grove, and between Tenaya Lake, Tuolumne Meadows Lodge, and the Tioga Pass. In winter, buses run twice daily from valley lodgings to Yosemite's Badger Pass Ski Area. In 2005, Yosemite became the first national park to operate a hybrid technology bus fleet, putting into service 18, 40-foot-long diesel-electric hybrid buses. Emissions and noise levels, along with gas consumption, immediately dropped. Handy shuttle-stop maps are available in most public buildings throughout the park.

Narrated, special bus and tram tours operate daily to major attractions in the valley and seasonally to Tuolumne Meadows, Glacier Point, Wawona, and the Mariposa Grove of Giant Sequoias. For fees, reservations, and information, call (209) 372-1240 or ask at hotel tour desks.

HISTORY

Smoke was likely rising from campfires in Yosemite Valley when the Joseph Walker party looked down from the north rim in 1833. The first non-natives to see the valley, they were exploring routes across the Sierra Nevada. Whether because of the sheer, 3,000-foot drop or fear of the resident tribe, Walker decided to ride on. It was nearly two decades later when Euro-Americans actually set foot in the valley for the first time.

Various Native American tribes lived in Yosemite as long as 10,000 years ago. Those inhabiting the valley in the 1800s were a Miwok tribe who referred to themselves as the Ahwahneechee. Their name for the valley was "Ahwahnee," which is believed to mean "place of the gaping mouth" or "deep, grassy valley."

Living in cone-shaped, incense cedar bark houses, the Ahwahneechee harvested acorns in the black oak woodlands and piñon nuts in the High Country. They hunted for deer, waterfowl, and rabbits and fished for rainbow trout in the rivers of the Yosemite and Hetch Hetchy Valleys and below in the Merced River canyon. In the summertime, they climbed into the eastern mountains and traded their fine baskets and obsidian implements with the Mono Lake Paiutes. Some 1,000 designated archaeological sites have been recorded during systematic surveys. Yosemite is viewed as a boundary zone between the two major cultural provinces of central California and Great Basin, principally the Miwok and Paiute Indians.

Around 1850 when gold was discovered in the foothills and hundreds of miners began to invade the Miwoks' homeland, Native Americans retaliated by robbing settlements and a trading post on the Fresno River. The miners put together the Mariposa Battalion, which was authorized by the state of California and commanded by James D. Savage. On March 27, 1851, the soldiers entered Yosemite Valley, camped at the foot of Bridalveil Fall, and planned the rout of the Ahwahneechee, an attack that was easy to accomplish with guns and horses. They captured the Yosemite chief, Tenaya, and in spite of his efforts to secure a peaceful compromise, they killed some of his tribe and rounded up the rest, moving them to loosely organized reservations in the Central Valley, whereupon some of the Native Americans fled east to the Mono Lake area and a few hid in Yosemite Valley, only to be chased out. Chief Tenaya died a violent death in 1853. Some historians believe he was stoned to death by eastern Sierra Indians from whom the Ahwahneechees had stolen horses, while others believe white settlers killed him.

Triumphant, the soldiers chose their own name for the valley—*u-zu-ma-te*—based on the Indian word for grizzly bear, and they told tales of the spectacular geological sights and waterfalls they had seen. By 1855 the first tourists visited Yosemite on horseback, led by an English-born gold-seeker, James Mason Hutchings. Entranced more with Yosemite than with the hard life of mining, Hutchings wrote of the glories of the place in his own publication, the *Hutchings' Illustrated California Magazine*. A few years later he built three drafty, barnlike hotels in Yosemite Valley, located at what is now the Yosemite Chapel parking area.

Pick up the* Guide to the Yosemite Cemetery *at the visitor center and take a walk through history in the Yosemite Cemetery (across the street from and just west of the Yosemite Museum) where Galen Clark, Native Americans, pioneers, and other early residents are buried.

CLOSE-UP

The Artists of Yosemite

Among sightseers who began arriving in 1855, Thomas Ayres was the first artist to sketch Yosemite Valley. Published in *Hutchings' Illustrated California Magazine,* Ayres' dramatic lithograph of "The Yo-Hamite Falls" was the first widely seen image of the valley, and together with the tales of other visitors, it resulted in public notice of the astounding scenic treasures of Yosemite. Six years later, Carleton Watkins made the first images of the valley and the Mariposa Grove with a camera. His prints were shown in New York to great interest and acclaim.

By 1863, the artist Albert Bierstadt, already known for immortalizing the West, began painting scenes of Yosemite in his inimitable, lit-from-within, melodramatic style.

Landscape painter Thomas Hill was the resident artist at Wawona from 1884 until his death in 1908. He lived in the Wawona Hotel and maintained a gallery and art studio nearby. Among the steady flow of visitors was President Theodore Roosevelt, to whom Hill gave a painting of Bridalveil Fall. The charming, restored studio is a museum and tourist information station today, open spring through fall.

The best-known modern artist associated with Yosemite National Park is the landscape photographer Ansel Adams, who photographed this and other national parks for more than 60 years. He lived for years in the park and married the daughter of painter Harry Best, who was the founder, in 1902, of the park's "Best's Studio."

In the 1940s, along with legendary photographer Edward Weston, Adams began the tradition of teaching photography in Yosemite, which continues today as the Ansel Adams Gallery Photography

About the same time, a homesteader in the Wawona area, Galen Clark, explored the Mariposa Grove of Giant Sequoias. Recognizing the timeless beauty of the big trees, he began a crusade to protect the sequoias and Yosemite Valley from loggers, cattle ranchers, sheepherders, and settlers who were making claims on the land. Yosemite was becoming famous, due not only to Clark's lobbying efforts but also from the early photographs, sketches, and paintings made by artists who accompanied groups of tourists, explorers, and the U.S. Army.

Another early visitor, Thomas Starr King, a Unitarian minister, spread the word about Yosemite in the *Boston Evening Transcript.* His words attracted the attention of Abraham Lincoln.

In the midst of the Civil War in 1864, President Lincoln signed the Yosemite Grant, which drew the Mariposa Grove and Yosemite Valley under the protection of the state, the first time any government in the world had set aside land based solely on its unique natural splendors. The establishment of Yosemite as the first state park paved the way for America's national parks. Frederick Law Olmsted, the landscape architect who designed New York's Central Park, became the newly established California Yosemite Commission's first chief. In 1866, he wrote the first public lands' environment preser-

Artists from around the world find Yosemite inspiring. DNC

Workshops, (209) 372-4413, www.ansel adams.com.

Today, the Ansel Adams Gallery in Yosemite Village displays the works of William Neil, Michael Frye, and other notable photographers.

For visitors inspired by the natural surroundings, free outdoor art classes are available through the Yosemite Art Center in Yosemite Village. For more information call (209) 372-1442.

vation statement, mandating that Yosemite's natural wonders had to be protected from development in favor of popular recreational access.

In 1875 a jolting, two-day stagecoach or horseback journey over unpaved, corkscrew roads brought visitors into Yosemite from train depots in the Central Valley, and when they arrived, they stayed awhile. In 1879 the Wawona Hotel, the first resort hotel in California, opened to accommodate travelers, including Ulysses S. Grant, on their way to Yosemite Valley.

When they got their first views of the valley from the Wawona Road and descended on the bumpy, dusty byway to the refreshment of the river and the dazzling waterfalls, visitors were as breathless in their amazement as the tourists of today. As Ralph Waldo Emerson said, "this valley is the only place that comes up to the brag and exceeds it."

Yosemite's sheer, vertical cliffs, snow-capped peaks, and fascinating spires were irresistible to climbers, even then. The history of mountain climbing here began in 1871, when J. B. Tileston ascended Mount Lyell, the highest mountain in Yosemite. George Anderson made the first ascent of Half Dome in 1875, long before the later installation of ropes and cables. (It wasn't until 1946 that someone reached the tip-top of Lost Arrow Spire.) Rising 3,593 feet above Yosemite Valley, El Capitan is one

Natural Disasters

Surrounded by a rugged wilderness of granite cliffs and wild river gorges in the High Sierra, Yosemite is subject to the effects of snowpack that may melt into torrents in the spring; lightning storms that occasionally set off forest fires; and the perpetual eroding and breaking off of boulders and rocks from the cliffsides. Park infrastructure such as buildings, parking lots, campgrounds, and other facilities are located in areas that remain safe from these natural disasters except when Mother Nature flexes her muscles. For park visitors, inconvenience is usually the only result. The park itself may take years to recover.

The Merced River raged over its banks in the winter of 1997, destroying Upper and Lower River campgrounds, some cabins at Yosemite Lodge, and Lower Yosemite Fall Bridge. The high waters flooded roads, meadows, and parking lots throughout the valley, and the heavy snowmelt created boulder and rock slides, closing Highway 140 into the park. Take a look at photos of the devastation at www.yosemite.org/vryos/pages/views/floodindex.htm.

On July 10, 1996, a huge section of cliff fell from Washburn Point into the north end of the valley, creating a gust of wind and debris that uprooted hundreds of trees and blanketed a large area with thick granite dust; one person was killed. You can see the tremendous rockfall behind the Nature Center at Happy Isles, and a series of photos online at www.yosemite.org/vryos/pages/views/rockfall.htm.

of the largest unbroken blocks of granite in the world, and Warren Harding was the first to climb it in 1958.

By the 1880s, although only about 2,500 people were touring Yosemite annually, some visionaries foresaw a dim future of commercialization. In 1881 the Wawona Tunnel Tree in the Mariposa Grove, a massive, centuries-old sequoia, was hollowed out, wide enough for a horse and wagon to ride through (although dead, the Tunnel Tree stood until 1969). In the mid-1890s, the last grizzly bear was shot in Yosemite at Crescent Lake. Orchards were planted, fragile meadows were plowed under, and pioneers erected cabins in Yosemite Valley.

John Muir, known as the father of environmentalism in the West, together with the editor of *Century* magazine, Robert Underwood Johnson, the Southern Pacific Railroad, and a group of influential Californians, lobbied the U.S. Congress vigorously until, on October 1, 1890, they established federal jurisdiction over greater Yosemite, including much of the High Country; Yosemite Valley and the Mariposa Grove remained as state parklands.

Meanwhile, tourism thrived in the valley. A private concessionaire opened a simple, nicely maintained encampment, Camp Curry, which opened to nine guests on July 1, 1899. Stepping off their stagecoaches, exhausted and grimy, guests were greeted by camp staff who whisked away the road dirt with feather dusters. For $2.00 a day, guests got three meals and a clean napkin and slept in tents with canvas roofs and wood floors. By the summer of the next year, stages and wagons shared the toll roads with a few automobiles.

CLOSE-UP

Robert Redford and Yosemite

Actor and producer Robert Redford has loved Yosemite since his childhood. As a 10-year-old, he became ill with polio, and upon his recovery, his mother took him to Yosemite for the first time. He said, "When I went through the tunnel that leads to Inspiration Point, it so rocked me. My immediate impulse . . . was that I wanted to be in it. I wanted to be a part of it."

He returned to the park to work as a waiter in the Yosemite Lodge in 1951; his first art show was held there at the lodge. And he spent many days hiking and climbing in the Yosemite High Country.

In 1989 Redford produced and narrated *The Fate of Heaven,* a documentary film that combines words from the journals of early explorers with those of park visitors and rangers. Stunning images of the park are the backgrounds for thoughtful, moving testimony to the timeless value of nature and national parks. Of interest to those who remember the legendary ranger of Tuolumne, Carl Sharsmith, is the interview with him in his last years.

In 1903 a troupe of about 400 African-American soldiers in the U.S. Cavalry made a two-week trek on horseback and in wagons from the Presidio of San Francisco to Yosemite for a three-year posting. The "Buffalo Soldiers," as they were called, protected the park from wildlife poachers, illegal farm animal grazing, and loggers. Park ranger Shelton Johnson performs a living-history program and has developed a multimedia Web site at http://shadowsoldier.wilderness.net/ to elucidate the soldiers' adventures and their admirable guardianship of Yosemite. Johnson leads a free, one- to two-hour narrated walk titled "Yosemite Through the Eyes of a Buffalo Soldier, 1904." See *Yosemite Today* for days and times.

In the late spring of 1903, the intrepid outdoorsman President Theodore Roosevelt was persuaded to meet John Muir and to explore Yosemite. Together, they rode horseback and tramped around, camping out on Glacier Point, in the Mariposa Grove, and near Bridalveil Fall. The president slept between 40 army blankets and got caught in a brief snowstorm. In the glow of campfires, he listened to Muir, who warned that Yosemite would be changed forever by sheep grazing, mining, and logging.

When someone asked him about his visit to Yosemite, Roosevelt exclaimed, "I had the time of my life . . . three of the most delightful days in my life." Greatly moved by his experience, he became instrumental in making Yosemite Valley and the Mariposa Grove part of the National Park in 1906. A year later, the completed Yosemite Valley Railroad from Merced to El Portal offered passengers a rapid, comfortable ride to the western edge of the park.

Another American president is known not for helping to preserve Yosemite but, in the opinion of some, for helping to destroy part of it. In 1913 President Woodrow Wilson signed the Raker Act,

Yosemite National Park Time Line

1833 General Joseph Walker crosses the Sierra Nevada and is the first non-native to see Yosemite Valley.

1851 Commander of the Mariposa Battalion, James D. Savage, and his soldiers enter Yosemite Valley to pursue the resident Ahwahneechees, a Miwok Tribe.

1852 Discovery of the Mariposa Grove of Giant Sequoias.

1853 Chief Tenaya, leader of the Yosemite Tribe, dies.

1855 The first tourists arrive in Yosemite, led by James Hutchings. One member of the group, Thomas Ayres, is the first artist to sketch the Yosemite Valley.

1856 Galen Clark opens Clark's Station, a way station for visitors in transit between Yosemite Valley and the town of Mariposa.

1859 C. L. Weed is the first person to create photographic images of Yosemite.

1864 President Abraham Lincoln signs a bill on June 30 ceding Yosemite Valley and the Mariposa Big Trees to the state of California as a permanent preserve, making it the first state park in America. Frederick Law Olmsted becomes the California Yosemite Commission's first chief.

1868 John Muir first visits Yosemite.

1875 George Anderson makes the first ascent of Half Dome.

1879 The Wawona Hotel opens, the first resort hotel in California.

1881 The book *Discovery of the Yosemite* is published, detailing the chronicle of the Mariposa Battalion's expedition of 1851, as recorded by a private in the battalion, Lafayette Bunnell.

1890 Congress establishes Yosemite National Park on October 1. The park does not include Yosemite Valley or the Mariposa Grove, which remain as state parklands, but does include much of the High Country above the valley.

1899 David and Jennie Curry open Camp Curry in Yosemite Valley.

1903 President Theodore Roosevelt camps out in Yosemite with John Muir.
About 400 African-American "Buffalo Soldiers" enter park for a three-year posting to protect its natural resources.

which allowed the city of San Francisco to build the O'Shaughnessy Dam within the National Park in the Hetch Hetchy Valley. Said to be a twin of Yosemite Valley, the Hetch Hetchy Valley was immortalized by John Muir and other explorers, who waxed poetic about the gleaming assemblage of granite cliffs, peaks and domes, and many waterfalls lining the great valley into which the mighty Tuolumne River drained from the Sierra Nevada. Between 1914 and 1938, despite ardent opposition by John Muir, the Sierra Club, and others nationwide, the Hetch Hetchy Valley was drowned behind a 364-foot-high dam; the dam was raised to its current 430-foot height in 1938. Today, it remains a reservoir that provides water and power for San Francisco. Muir's friends and family believed that when he died, a year after the dam was approved, it was of a broken heart.

Two years after Muir's death, the official National Park System was born in 1916. Within a few years, the Park Service

1906 Yosemite Valley and the Mariposa Grove are ceded to the federal government and become part of Yosemite National Park.

1913 President Woodrow Wilson signs the Raker Act, allowing San Francisco to build the O'Shaughnessy Dam at Hetch Hetchy, within the national park.
Automobiles are officially admitted to the park (autos first entered the park in 1900).

1914 John Muir dies at age 76.

1915 Yosemite Lodge opens to the public.

1916 Having protected the park from 1872 to 1916, the U.S. Army turns operations over to the National Park Service.

1917 The Wawona Golf Course opens.

1927 The Ahwahnee Hotel opens on July 14.

1930 Carl Sharsmith begins his career as a Yosemite park ranger; he died in 1994 at age 90 as the oldest ranger in the National Park Service.

1932 The Wawona Basin, including the Wawona Hotel and golf course, are purchased and included in the national park.

1935 Badger Pass Ski Area opens, establishing the first ski school in California.

1954 Total visitors in the park top one million.

1958 Warren Harding makes the first ascent of El Capitan.

1961 The Tioga Road opens for travelers seeking a route through the park and over the Sierra Nevada.

1964 The federal government passes The Wilderness Act to retain wilderness areas "without permanent improvements or human habitation."

1984 Yosemite is named as a World Heritage Site.
89 percent of the park is designated as wilderness by the California Wilderness bill.

1990 As major forest fires rage in the park, Yosemite National Park celebrates its centennial.

1995 Visitor total tops four million.

1997 A devastating winter flood destroys campgrounds, bridges, and public facilities along the Merced River in Yosemite Valley; two campgrounds and some infrastructure are allowed to return to nature; extensive riparian and meadow restoration begins.

1999 The Department of the Interior releases the Final Yosemite Valley Plan and Supplemental Environmental Impact Statement.

2005 Yosemite Falls restoration complete.

began interpretive activities, with naturalist guides leading visitors on nature walks and teaching the value of preserving Yosemite's scenic beauty and wildlife habitat in their natural state, a program that might have soothed Muir's spirit if he had lived to see it.

In 1926 Highway 140, an all-year-round, paved road, connected Merced to El Portal and continued into the valley. By 1927 well-heeled tourists could stay at the castle-like Ahwahnee Hotel, standing like an apparition at the foot of a geologic landmark, the Royal Arches. Massive stone fireplaces and soaring, log-beamed ceilings, Native American artifacts, and stained-glass windows still maintain the impressive and museum-like atmosphere the hotel presented in the Roaring Twenties.

In contrast, during the Great Depression of the 1930s, the government looked the other way while homeless Americans lived in the valley in their cars and in makeshift shelters, eating fish from the

Merced River. During the 1930s, the Works Progress Administration constructed a number of trails, stone bridges, and buildings in the park.

In 1932 the Wawona Basin, including the Wawona Hotel and golf course, were added to the national park to bring it to its current size of 1,169 square miles. The beautiful, 9-hole, seasonal golf course is one of only a few within a national park. The Merced and Wawona Airline flew passengers, mail, and supplies from San Francisco to the hotel, every day, in biplanes. In 1941 after it was declared dangerous to humans and disruptive to wildlife, the airfield was closed.

The first ski school in California opened at Badger Pass in 1935, outfitted with rope tows and a T-bar. To drum up business, instructors conducted dry-land ski lessons in Fresno every fall for more than 30 years.

To open the rugged Yosemite High Country and spectacular Tuolumne Meadows to public use and provide a shortcut over the Sierra, the newly paved Tioga Road opened in 1961. Winding through stunning mountain scenery, this segment of Highway 120 runs 45 miles from Crane Flat to Tioga Pass at 9,945 feet and is the highest vehicle pass in the state.

Major forest fires raged in the park in 1990, as the national park celebrated its centennial. In 1995 the annual visitor total topped four million. That fact, and the devastating Merced River flood in 1997, resulted in a new look at infrastructure and park management.

Wiped out by the raging flood waters, Upper and Lower River Campgrounds, a bridge, and some accommodations at Yosemite Lodge were either relocated or abandoned. Much riparian habitat and meadowlands are being restored, as mandated by the Yosemite Valley Plan.

The result of nearly 20 years of study and wrangling over the implementation of the original General Management Plan, the Final Yosemite Valley Plan and Supplemental Environmental Impact Statement was released by the Department of the Interior in 1999. Although media attention focused on transportation-related issues that may or may not impact future visitor experience in the park, today's visitors with campground or lodging reservations will always be able to drive into the park in their own vehicles.

In 2004, 3,280,911 people enjoyed the great outdoors of Yosemite National Park. Unlike visitors of the 19th and early 20th centuries, who encountered a relatively untouched wilderness in solitude, those of the 21st century bask in the scenic glories of Yosemite from the comfort of their RVs and automobiles. They tour the valley in open-air tram cars and air-conditioned buses and watch big-screen TV in the pizza parlor at Curry Village. They sleep in snug tent cabins at Housekeeping Camp and in luxurious hotel rooms at The Ahwahnee. Redone guest rooms and a food court at Yosemite Lodge at the Falls replace a dreary old cafeteria, and the Victorian-era Wawona Hotel decor is right out of yesteryear. Gourmet food aficionados and famous chefs gather annually for gala celebrations. Wine lovers, artists, and writers meet for yearly confabs in the park. Climbers congregate, ski racers compete, and couples take wedding vows. All in all, the national park is a busy place.

Although the granite monoliths, the waterfalls, and the breathtaking views remain the same, the true wilderness lies in the Yosemite High Country, beyond Tuolumne Meadows, where old Native American trails wander into the mountains and down the Grand Canyon of the Tuolumne, where John Muir once mused, "into this one mountain mansion nature had gathered her choicest treasures, to draw her lovers into close and confiding communion with her."

YOSEMITE VALLEY

Yosemite Valley is a holy place to some people, a Shangri-la floating in pristine beauty in their memories. Like besotted lovers, they return, year after year, decade after decade, to regain the glow of summer vacations past, to feel again that catch in the throat at the first sight of the stunning portal to the valley at Tunnel View, framed by the bastion of El Capitan and the soaring pyramids of Cathedral Rocks, with Bridalveil Fall's wispy fingers beckoning a welcome.

A startling phenomenon of nature, Yosemite Valley is like no other. Just 7 miles long and barely a half-mile at its widest point, it is lined by an astonishing array of bare granite cliffs and spires, domes, and towers. Luminous in the clear mountain air, the monoliths thrust up out of the valley floor, their feet in flowers and aromatic evergreens, their peaks in heaven. Dozens of waterfalls plunge off the ramparts into a silvery river tumbled with boulders and reflective of the sky and the stone crags above—a photographer's dream.

A visit to Yosemite Valley is for many people the ultimate American experience, one of the legendary sites in the West where pioneers sought the promise of the virgin wilderness. The first nonnatives to see Yosemite Valley in the mid-1800s were overwhelmed. Their drawings, paintings, rhapsodic writings, and later their photographs, set off a longing in Americans that has never diminished. Even today, as millions of visitors pass into the valley, and a few escape into the vast reaches of the High Country, Yosemite continues to work its magic.

Below the mountain peaks on the valley floor, higher than it seems at 3,000 to 4,500 feet in elevation, is a mosaic of meadows awash in wildflowers and flowering shrubs, black oak woodlands, and mixed-conifer forests of Ponderosa pine, incense cedar, and Douglas fir. Meadows of this size are rare in the Sierra Nevada, which is primarily a sea of granite with pockets of forest and little topsoil.

Visible from within the valley are some of the park's many thrilling waterfalls, some of the highest in the world. Bridalveil, Nevada, Vernal, and Yosemite Falls are among Yosemite's booming, miraculous water curtains. Thundering in the springtime, the largest can be heard from as far as 2 miles away. On the hottest summer days, the air around the falls is cool and misty, even windy, and full of rainbows.

You will wax poetic when a setting sun paints a shining swath across the face of Half Dome and glitters like a crown on snowcapped peaks above the lush river valley. Native Americans called it "deep, grassy valley." John Muir saw it as a "great temple lit from above." The best vantage point for photos of the monumental valley entrance is at "Valley View," at road marker V11 on the Merced River. At sunset

---

i

In Yosemite, early morning is the best time to see wildlife, hear the birds and waterfalls, and beat the crowds. From June through August, plan to arrive at popular destinations between dawn and 9:30 A.M. or in the early evening. Between 9:30 A.M. and midafternoon, parking lots are full, shuttles and buses are crowded, and the main roads are clogged with traffic.

In Yosemite Valley, chase the light to get fabulous photographs. Go downriver in the morning, upriver in the afternoon. To darken the dazzling Sierra sky, use a polarizing filter to get more cloud detail; use a graduated, neutral-density filter in bright sun.

and other times of day, golden light floods the cliffsides and fills the river with reflections. In spring, Western azalea blooms snowy white. Fall is a good time to be here, when kids are back in school and the Merced River turns to molten gold, with bright maples reflected in its chilly stream. And a winter weekend at Yosemite can be unforgettable, whether you cross-country ski on a silent forest trail or gaze, enraptured, at a white wonderland through the tall windows of The Ahwahnee hotel. The average annual snowfall is 29 inches, and that generally means just enough of a dusting to turn the valley into a postcard.

At least three or four days are required to see the main natural attractions and to enjoy some outdoor recreation in the valley. You can explore hiking and biking trails, fish and wade in the river, take a dip in one of the swimming pools, and get in on some of the many seminars, lectures, theater presentations, and tours offered throughout the year.

Eighty percent of visitors to Yosemite National Park spend their time in Yosemite Valley, which comprises just 1 percent of the park and is where most of the public facilities and the best-known geologic features and dazzling views are found. Hot, dry, dusty, and throbbing with rumbling RVs and cars heading for thousands of campsites, the valley can look like a long parking lot in midsummer. Crowded campgrounds and traffic glut may spoil your family's Yosemite experience unless you opt for an off-season trip or take care to make your forays around the park in the very early mornings and early evenings, when most visitors are either slumbering or resting up from their day outdoors.

The lower, westernmost 4 miles of the valley are mostly undeveloped and are an enchanted world of grassy meadows, riverside trails, and boulder fields. Clustered around Yosemite Village in midvalley, you'll find lodgings, campgrounds, historical museums, theaters, retail outlets, and attendant infrastructure. On the far end of the valley, east from Upper Pines Campground and Happy Isles, the backcountry trails begin and roads are closed to all vehicles, except for shuttles and bikes.

Yosemite Valley is not the wilderness, although it may seem so to city dwellers. More like a small town in a spectacular location, the valley offers every human convenience. To orient yourself to the valley and the park, and to locate natural and man-made attractions, pick up a copy of the *Yosemite Road Guide*, a key to road markers used in this book and in many guidebooks to the park. Rather than viewing wonders from your car, sightseeing is best done on foot, on 12 miles of bike trails, on a tour, or by hopping on and off the free shuttle buses. Via a 21-stop route, the shuttles serve the eastern end of the valley year-round, accessing trailheads and all public facilities.

In more than a dozen retail outlets, you can buy groceries and deli foods, gifts, souvenirs and art, clothing, sporting goods, and outdoor equipment—just about anything you might need for a day or a month in Yosemite.

And now, here are the superstars of Yosemite Valley—the views, the geological miracles, the historic sites, the waterfalls, and the touch of man.

The Ahwahnee
Shuttle stop 3, road marker V23

One of the world's great hostelries, The Ahwahnee stands in a meadow at the foot of Royal Arches. Designed by the architect of Hearst Castle, Julia Morgan, and completed in 1927, the massive stone, con-

A couple explores a grassy meadow in Yosemite Valley. JOHN POIMIROO

Wildflowers on Display

In the vast meadows and in the forest glades of Yosemite, a flower show begins in March in the valley, gradually moving up the slopes into the alpine regions and continuing until the snow flies. A good reference for wildflower viewing is *Wildflowers of Yosemite* by Lynn and Jim Wilson and Jeff Nicholas. The book has terrific color photos and suggestions for flowery walks.

Look for sheets of blue, yellow, and white iris in El Capitan Meadow in late April and early May and rose-pink bleeding heart in the cedar forest at Bridalveil Fall. Ginger and buttercups grow rampant around Mirror Lake, while a rainbow of wildflowers is seen across the road from the Yosemite Chapel. Tuolumne Meadows at midsummer is a riot of lavender shooting stars, red paintbrush, and magenta penstemons, among other alpine flowers. Here are some of the best places to see seasonal displays:

- In Stoneman Meadow, Western azaleas along the Merced River burst into bloom early in the spring, followed by yarrow and golden monkey flowers. Black-eyed Susans crowd in beside sprigs of white yarrow, stalks of lavender-blue field mint, pale yellow evening primrose, and lacy cow parsnip.
- From mid-April through September in Cook's Meadow, masses of flowers are on parade. See more about this meadow in this chapter.
- A half-hour drive out of the valley, 1.2 miles past the Badger Pass turnoff on Glacier Point Road, Summit, McGurk, and Westfall Meadows are subalpine fields gloriously abloom throughout the summer. Right by the road there are restrooms and picnic tables at Summit Meadow, awash with tiny pale green Sierra Rein orchids, purple Alpine shooting stars, corn lilies, and more wildflowers. Another 1.6 miles along the road is a trailhead for a 1-mile walk to McGurk Meadow and a 1-mile walk to Westfall Meadow, both equally efflorescent.

crete, and redwood edifice is the architectural symbol of Yosemite and a living museum, every bit as popular a sight-seeing attraction as Glacier Point or Yosemite Falls.

Cavernous beamed ceilings notwithstanding, the public rooms evoke a cozy, vintage lodge feeling, with richly colored Native American–design rugs, basketry, art, and artifacts, and fabulous old photos, all glowing with natural light through two-story windows that look onto a lyrical setting of forest and meadows. The design is a masterful combination of German gothic and California Craftsman styles. In the Great Lounge, the focal point of the hotel, wide-eyed visitors wander around with their mouths open, agog at the tremendous walk-in fireplaces and wrought-iron chandeliers big enough for a castle. The other pièce de résistance is the colossal dining room, ready for King Arthur's entire court.

Those who cannot afford the pricey room rates at The Ahwahnee enjoy the Great Lounge and the lobbies for hours at a time while they read and warm their toes by the fires. Free guided tours of the hotel are conducted daily. (For more details, see the Lodging and Rentals chapter.)

Ansel Adams Gallery
Yosemite Village, shuttle stops 5 and 9
Road marker V1
(209) 372-4413
www.anseladams.com

The best-known artist associated with Yosemite National Park is the landscape photographer Ansel Adams, who photographed this and other national parks for more than 60 years. In his career, Adams created more than 40,000 photographs, most in California and thousands in Yosemite.

Adams's images of Yosemite, such as "Moon and Half Dome" and "Clearing Winter Storm," define Yosemite National Park and are as familiar to Americans as the classic paintings of George Washington. An American hero, Adams received the Presidential Medal of Freedom, in addition to having Mount Ansel Adams and the vast, spectacular Ansel Adams Wilderness named for him. He died in 1984 at the age of 82.

In the 1940s, along with legendary photographer Edward Weston, Adams pioneered photography workshops in Yosemite, which continue today as the Ansel Adams Gallery Photography Workshops. They continue to be the benchmark against which all other photo workshops are measured. Originally taught by Adams himself, the sessions are now presented by a slate of top-notch experts and have included Ruth Bernard, Ernst Hass, and Annie Leibovitz.

Adams invented the Zone System, which enables photographers to determine light levels, a fundamental contribution to creative photography. Over his long lifetime, he taught extensively, wrote, and produced many books and was outspoken in his views of conservation and politics as they related to preservation of the wilderness. Armed with dazzling photographs, he was instrumental in soliciting the U.S. Congress for the establishment of Kings Canyon National Park.

Here in the Ansel Adams Gallery, you'll find a charming collage of photos of Adams, from his childhood through his Yosemite years. The gallery is owned and operated by Adams's son, Michael, a fine landscape photographer in his own right. Original photographs, printed and signed by Ansel Adams, are available here, along with books and posters, boxed note cards, calendars, and inexpensive prints of the famous images of Yosemite. You can also find images by a few other outstanding photographers, including William Neill and Michael Frye. In the shop, look for the photo of Adams standing on top of a "woodie" station wagon, taking pictures. On Sunday, watch the free documentary film about Adams's career and his lifelong love affair with Yosemite. The Ansel Adams Gallery is open daily from 9:00 A.M. to 5:00 P.M.

The gift shop is the best in the park; see the Shopping chapter. Free photography walks with knowledgeable experts are offered most days, Walks are based at the gallery; reservations are advised.

There is also an Ansel Adams Gallery at the Mono Inn at Mono Lake, 4 miles north of the town of Lee Vining, about 30 minutes north of Mammoth Lakes on U.S. Highway 395, (760) 647-6581.

Cathedral Spires and Cathedral Rocks
Road marker V15

Located opposite El Capitan on the south rim of Yosemite Valley, these twin pinnacles rise nearly 2,000 feet, connected at their bases. The two granite columns are named for their resemblance to the towers of a Gothic cathedral. Climbers do attempt to climb the spires; few are successful.

An elongated pyramid rivaling those in Egypt, Cathedral Rocks forms an impressive backdrop to Bridalveil Fall.

Cook's Meadow

Take a stroll across the boardwalk over this vast wetland, glorious in the winter and springtime, lush with grasses 2 feet high and scattered with wildflowers. Western azaleas are a dazzling white background for lavender shooting stars and yellow-gold sneezeweed. As picturesque and as cooling as Monet's water gardens are the dinner plate-size floating leaves

CLOSE-UP

Curry Village

The original log sign at the entrance to Camp Curry stands today, and in the parking area is a gnarled tree from the old apple orchard, planted in 1859 by a homesteader. Nine guests came the first night the camp was open, on July 1, 1899, stepping off a stagecoach after a torturous trip over bumpy, corkscrew, dirt roads. Legend has it that camp staff greeted the guests with feather dusters to help clean off the thick dust.

At the end of the first year, Camp Curry had grown to 25 tents. For $2.00 a day, guests got three meals and a clean napkin. They slept in tents with canvas roofs and wood floors, which they still do today. The patriarch of the camp, David Curry, was famous for raising a ruckus at sunrise by yelling out, "Those who do not rise for breakfast will have to postpone it until tomorrow. At eight o'clock, the cook gets hot and burns the breakfast!" At night when all were snuggled under their blankets, he called, "All's well!" And when guests climbed back aboard the stagecoach for their departure, he boomed, "Farewell!"

Unexpectedly, David Curry died in 1917 of food poisoning. His wife Jennie, affectionately called "Mother Curry," carried on the traditions of hospitality at the camp. In her 60s she climbed the steep Ledge Trail to Glacier Point. At 70 she learned to drive and to play golf. She moved into the Ahwahnee Hotel for her waning years and died at age 87 in 1948. Until her death, she was a lively and

and yellow flowers of the Indian pond lily. In midsummer cow parsnips stand tall with lacy white flower heads a foot wide.

In recent years, 35-acre Cook's Meadow and all of the larger meadows in the valley have been fenced and boardwalked. Nonindigenous flora have been removed and old roadbeds eliminated, resulting in improved water flows. This protection of the habitat has encouraged the reemergence and flourishing of indigenous trees, such as black oaks, which support flora and fauna and are currently in decline throughout California.

Meadows are important in the Sierra Nevada due to their species diversity. Comprising less than 10 percent of the total vegetation in the Sierra and less than 4 percent of the park, the meadows contain nearly 40 percent of the park's flora, providing food and shelter for a wide variety of animals and birds. The great gray owl is directly dependent on several meadow systems within the park, and deer, bighorn sheep, and other mammals forage in the meadows.

Curry Village Guest Lounge
Shuttle stops 13A, 13B, and 14

Even if you are not staying at Curry Village, stop in here to see the great old Guest Lounge, a bit of old Yosemite circa 1912–1918. Take a slow stroll around the room to see display cases full of charming artifacts from early days in the park and the dozens of vintage photos on the walls. The early-20th-century letters from campers are fun to read and match the outdoor spirit of the furniture in the lounge—hickory branch rockers, birchbark tables, and Adirondack chairs on the porch. Get a beer from the bar across the

Curry Village's welcome sign hearkens back to its origins as Camp Curry. JOHN POIMIROO/DNC

important participant in the daily doings at Camp Curry.

Three hundred campers were accommodated at Camp Curry during the first season, as the 20th century began. Today, several thousand people spend their summer vacations here at Curry Village, in more than 600 tent cabins and lodge rooms.

way, sit on the porch and enjoy a summer evening, or sit inside by the fireplace and play at one of the game tables. The Curry Village Guest Lounge is open from 8:00 A.M. to 10:00 P.M., but closed in winter.

El Capitan
Road markers V8 and V9

Nearly every day of the year, except during storms, climbers can be seen making their ascents to the dizzying summit of "El Cap," clinging to the vertical mass of silver-white granite, four times as large as the Rock of Gibraltar, and said to be the largest single block of exposed granite in the world.

Topping 3,500 feet, El Cap is the guardian at the entrance to Yosemite Valley, a memento of an Ice Age when glaciers tore off and ground into little pieces great sections of mountain. Just past El Cap on the left, an apron of rocky moraine is left from the last of the valley's glaciers. A strenuous 8-mile trail attains the summit via the Yosemite Falls Trail.

For a good photo of El Cap, stand at Cathedral Beach on the Merced River, near El Capitan Bridge.

Fern Spring
Road marker V12

Near Pohono Bridge on the south side of the river, next to the road, a natural spring emerges from the talus slope, bubbling to the surface in little waterfalls just before entering the river. When the temperature soars, this is a cool, shady spot under a canopy of trees, making a lovely photograph when creamy-white Pacific dogwood are in bloom in early May, and in the fall when the bigleaf maples turn bright gold.

Dogwood trees bloom throughout the

It is not unusual to see animals on park roads, particularly the Wawona Road. It is okay to stop to watch them, but do not lower your windows. They hang out near roads because people feed them. Feeding wild animals—coyotes, deer, raccoons, squirrels, birds—is dangerous. Park visitors have been gored and bitten. And the wildlife can get accustomed to human food during good weather months and may starve to death in the wintertime. Don't feed them!

valley between late March and the end of May. Some of the best places to see them are on the trail to Mirror Lake, at Happy Isles, and in the Tuolumne Grove in late May—a magical sight among giant sequoias and a forest of incense cedar, sugar pine, and white fir.

Glacier Point
Glacier Point Road, road marker G11
Early morning and late afternoon are the best times for the 32-mile road trip from the valley up to Glacier Point, when vehicle traffic is less of an issue and the light is most dramatic on the mountain peaks. Give yourself an hour to get there, not counting stops along the way. From the valley, take Highway 41 for 14 miles to the Chinquapin junction, and turn left onto Glacier Point Road, which ends at Glacier Point. In winter the road is plowed as far as Yosemite's Badger Pass Ski Area, and Glacier Point can only be reached on skis or snowshoes.

The mesmerizing view from this rock outcropping—which hangs 3,214 feet above the valley—is a peek back through millions of years of geologic history. You can see how the unique, U-shaped valley was carved out by powerful glaciers that inched along, cracking the granite domes and grinding mountains to smithereens, leaving high walls, spires, domes, and "hanging valleys" from which the rivers pour over the sheer cliffs, creating the waterfalls that we see today.

Carry a flashlight after dark. Lighting in the park is kept at a bare minimum to maintain a natural environment for wildlife and visitors. A headlamp works well, too.

Looking down into the chasm, with the help of the plaques provided, it's fun to search for landmarks. The Ahwahnee is easy to locate at the foot of Royal Arches. Vernal and Nevada Falls are visible, Happy Isles is right below your feet, and the Clark Range looms beyond. At this elevation of 7,214 feet, looking eastward, one can study the detail of the distant High Sierra with its rugged ridges, glaciated canyons, and serrated summits. The rising and setting sun illuminate endless rows of snowcapped peaks that seem to glitter like a crown.

The historic stone-and-timber Glacier Point Ski Hut has been restored to grandeur with massive beams in a high cathedral ceiling and a big stone fireplace. In summer the ski hut turns into Glacier Point Lodge gift shop and snack bar and is jammed with tourists. In 1998 the park added new viewing terraces and a 150-seat granite amphitheater, the gathering place for campfire programs and ranger talks. Ranger-narrated programs include walks to Taft Point and Sentinel Dome, sunset talks, an alpenglow photo walk, and many more. In the wintertime, the building becomes a twenty-bed bunkhouse for cross-country skiers.

At Glacier Point and off Glacier Point Road, you'll find trailheads for popular day hikes into the less-traveled wilderness in southern Yosemite. The road, generally open from late May to early November, in winter months serves as a groomed cross-country ski track from Yosemite's Badger Pass Ski Area.

A relaxing way to get to Glacier Point is on a narrated bus tour that runs three times a day from the valley. You can also

take the bus one-way up and walk down to the valley, a 4.8-mile, 3.5-hour hike for the super-fit.

On some summer evenings, photographers will enjoy the "Alpenglow Photo Shoot" at Glacier Point, led by experts from the Kodak company; see *Yosemite Today* for dates and times.

Half Dome

With half its enormous dome chopped off as if by a tomahawk, Half Dome is the icon of Yosemite Valley, and it fills up half the sky to the east. Rising 4,733 feet above the valley floor, the 87-million-year-old monolith seems to lure shifting clouds and mist to its nearly vertical northwest face.

The missing half is believed to have fallen away when the glaciers receded. Gleaming in the sun and the moonlight, Half Dome and the many cliff faces, domes, and arches throughout the valley and the park were polished into giant mirrors by the moving ice.

One of the best locations for a photo shoot is from Sentinel Bridge, where the unusual shape of Half Dome is often reflected in the river, along with a belt of trees—golden in the fall, dark green in the summer, and lacy with ice in the wintertime. Sunsets turn the dome into a portrait in gold, orange, and pink. When the forest and the river are clothed in ice and snow, the scene looks as if it were caressed by the gods. See classic photos of Half Dome at www.yosemite.org/vryos/pages/views/hd.htm.

Happy Isles
Shuttle stop 16, road marker V24

Happy Isles is named for a pair of small islands surrounded by rapids where the Merced River enters the valley. It is fitting that the Nature Center here caters to children, as an enchanted forest surrounds this corner of the park. Full of streams perfect for wading and scattered with moss-covered boulders, the open forest just begs for a game of hide-and-seek.

Exhibits in the Nature Center elucidate the natural features of the park and the wildlife, and this is the headquarters for many children's activities, including the Junior Ranger program. See more about Happy Isles in the Kidstuff chapter. Happy Isles is also home to the trailheads for the famed John Muir Trail and for popular routes to Vernal and Nevada Falls, Merced Lake, and Half Dome.

The huge talus pile at the base of Glacier Point behind Happy Isles is from the 1996 rock fall, when a humongous piece of granite cracked off the wall and smashed to the earth with such force that it flattened several hundred trees. Miraculously, no one was hurt.

Every clear night at Glacier Point, the stars put on a show that most city dwellers have never seen. The spectacular Perseid meteor shower, a dramatic display of shooting stars, fireballs, comets, and trajectories peaks in August and is clearly visible with the naked eye. The National Park Service's one-hour-long Starry Skies Over Yosemite summer program happens three times a week in Yosemite Valley and once per week at Wawona. Call (209) 372-0299, ask at park lodging desks, or check **Yosemite Today** ***for schedules.***

Indian Cultural Exhibit and Yosemite Museum
Yosemite Village, shuttle stops 5 and 9
Road marker V1
(209) 372-0282

The cultural history of Yosemite's native Miwok and Paiute hunter-gatherers from 1850 to the present is featured in photos; stunning, priceless baskets; feather capes; and many other artifacts. Local Native American artisans demonstrate basket weaving, beadwork, and traditional games. Rotating exhibits of historic and contemporary works from the Yosemite Museum Collection are on view intermittently. The wonderful, early-times photos and books located in the upstairs research library are worth a look. The library is open to all. The museum, located next to the Yosemite Valley Visitor Center, is open daily 9:30 A.M. to 5:00 P.M. Admission is free.

A descendant of the Yosemite Indians and a historian and artisan, Lucy Parker teaches "Southern Miwok Miniature Burden Basketmaking," a two-day event at the museum. Lucy and her mother Julia demonstrate weaving techniques and help students start their own baskets while discussing Native American history and traditions. Short walks in the valley are included, and materials are provided. Call (209) 379-2321 or go to www.yosemite.org for more information.

The National Park and local tribes are cooperating in the planning of a new Indian cultural center, which will be built in the park.

Indian Village of Ahwahneechee
Yosemite Village, shuttle stops 5 and 9
Road marker V1

In a pine-and-oak forest, a self-guided trail introduces the daily life, history, and language of the Southern Miwoks in a reconstructed Miwok-Paiute village of 1872, 20 years after first contact with non-Native Americans. The exceptional basketry, food preparation, and arts of the Ahwahneechee people of Yosemite are on display in the model village, and rangers lead frequent talks and walks. The village is located behind the Yosemite Valley Visitor Center.

Le Conte Memorial Lodge
Shuttle stop 12, road marker V21
(209) 372-4542
www.sierraclub.org/education/leconte

Built by the Sierra Club in 1904, and a National Historic Landmark, this charming, Tudor-style, rough-hewn wood-and-stone building houses changing displays and a library focusing on the natural and human history of Yosemite and the Sierra and on conservation issues. A daily schedule includes such programs as "Our National Park System," "Animals and Their Senses," "Trees of Yosemite," "Flowers and Pollinators in the Meadow," "All About Bears," and many more. Among the displays are those highlighting John Muir, Joseph Le Conte, Ansel Adams (who was the lodge caretaker in 1919), and the early history of the Sierra Club in the park. Also showcased are the battle for Hetch Hetchy, early exploration, and trail building.

A professor of geology and natural history, Joseph Le Conte wrote about his ramblings in Yosemite and the High Sierra while on a five-week horseback journey in 1890 with some members of the first class of the University of California. From then until his death in 1901, he worked with the Sierra Club to promote conservation of Yosemite.

The building itself is an architectural landmark, with rough-hewn granite block walls under a steep wood-shingled roof and California Craftsman-style chandeliers. A wood stove rests on an immense hearth beneath a plaque honoring Le Conte: SCIENTIST AND SAVANT, DIED IN THIS VALLEY, JVLY VI MCMI.

A special corner for children is stocked with books and offers planned activities. The lodge is open Wednesday through Sunday from 10:00 A.M. to 4:00 P.M. from May through September and for evening presentations, usually at 8:00 P.M. Check *Yosemite Today* for schedules.

Merced River

El Rio de Nuestra Señora de la Merced—the River of Our Lady of Mercy, the Merced River originates at more than 11,000 feet above the valley in Sierra snows and drops over Nevada and Vernal Falls, tumbling down into a sinuous, wide stream and tributaries along the main roads and through campgrounds. Lively and fast-flowing most of the year, the course is lined with a glorious array of willows, alders, bigleaf maples, and other riparian flora, with the granite monoliths reflected in the waters.

Early settlers deepened and widened the river with boulder dams. Today, due to the tumultuous nature of the Merced, which tends to reclaim its birthright during winter flooding, the park service is allowing the river to resume its wild, natural state by removing man-made barriers, campgrounds, and buildings.

The Merced exits the valley on the western side of the park, plunging into a steep-sided canyon and flowing on to water and beautify the San Joaquin Valley. After the rush of the spring thaw has calmed somewhat in midsummer, kayaking, canoeing, inner tubing, and rafting are popular. Sunbathers gather on the few narrow sandbars and beaches. With pools and riffles purely translucent, fishing is not easy, as the fish can see the angler.

An easy walk along the river follows a trail, about 2.5 miles, from Yosemite Lodge at the Falls to El Capitan Bridge. In the spring newly green, budding willows and cottonwoods are reflected in the water, and you may dodge patches of snow in the shady spots.

Royal Arches
Road marker V23

Behind The Ahwahnee hotel, this striking mountain face shows how glaciers broke off layers of granite in a process called exfoliation, leaving rounded sheets and strips parallel to the valley floor. A 1,000-foot waterfall to the left of the arches adds to the beauty in springtime, while skyscraper-like Washington Column stands 1,920 feet high on the right. High above, North Dome echoes the arches' geologic formations. This is a spectacular scene from the north-facing windows of rooms in The Ahwahnee.

Three Brothers
Road marker V16

Just to the east of El Capitan, the Three Brothers are three sloping, bare granite peaks, each rising above the other, pitched at the same dramatic angle. Named for the three sons of Chief Tenaya who were taken prisoner in 1851 by the Mariposa Battalion, the Brothers are best seen and photographed from Leidig Meadow by the river, reached by the easy trail running west from Yosemite Lodge at the Falls.

While exploring the Merced River, watch for a delightful denizen of Yosemite, the belted kingfisher. A striking, bright blue and white bird, about a foot long with a long bill and a jagged crest on its head, the kingfisher perches on the outer edges of tree limbs over the river and swoops low over the water, spearing fish. When you hear a loud clicking rattle, that's the kingfisher.

The Cathedral picnic area near El Capitan Bridge is another prime site for viewing and photographing the Brothers. A branch of the El Capitan Trail leads to Eagle Peak, the tallest of the trio.

From the east face of the middle peak, a tremendous rockfall occurred in 1987, creating the heaps of boulders and rocks you see today. The rocks of that one slide are estimated to have weighed 1.4 million tons; giant boulders ripped out huge trees and even ended up in the river, hundreds of yards away.

On the opposite side of the valley, you'll find similar "stepped" formations, such as Sentinel Rock, produced by the major glacier- and water-caused cracks and fractures that are common throughout the park. In spring Sentinel Creek drops into Sentinel Falls, beside the 3,068-foot-tall, watchtower-like spire.

Tunnel View
Highway 41, road marker W2

Entering the park on Highway 41, you get your first breathtaking look at Yosemite Valley from the turnout at Tunnel View, one of the most famous "photo ops" in the world. Carpeted thickly by an evergreen forest, the flat, narrow valley winds into the distance, heralded by the mass of El Capitan on one side and Cathedral Rocks on the other, with Bridalveil the first waterfall in sight, and Half Dome, Sentinel Rock, and Cloud's Rest in the distance.

When spectacular cloud formations wreathe the scene, many viewers sense a certain familiarity. This is the same, almost theatrical setting immortalized by Ansel Adams in his "Clearing Winter Storm" and other photographs.

For a wider, even more dazzling vista, walk up the switchback trail on the opposite side of the highway to the old Wawona Road and walk left for about a half mile; this is called Inspiration Point. This is where the Mariposa Battalion began its descent into Yosemite in 1851 and went on to banish the Native Americans forever from their villages on the valley floor.

Visitor Center
Yosemite Village, shuttle stops 5 and 9
(209) 372-0200
Surprisingly small for the number of visitors served and easy to use, the main National Park Visitor Center is accessed on foot a short distance from shuttle stops and parking lots. The center is not easy to find: When you see the Village Store, you're getting warm. From the parking lot, walk through the store, turn right, and keep going.

Come here for information and good advice from park service rangers and interpreters, and for multilingual assistance. Make reservations for guided walks, hikes, classes, live theater, musical programs, and exhibits. You can watch slide shows and films, peruse dioramas and exhibits, and browse the excellent bookstore for guidebooks, posters, videos, maps, and books for children.

Ask about live presentations and films scheduled in the auditorium here, such as the *The Spirit of Yosemite,* which presents an overview of the seasonal glories and the natural and human history of the park. *One Day in Yosemite* is a short video offering advice to visitors with limited time to spend in the park. And you will find a handy courtesy phone with which to make lodging reservations and for obtaining information about DNC-offered tours and activities (see the Events, Activities, and Tours chapter for more about DNC tours). The center is open daily 9:00 A.M. to 7:00 P.M. in summer, with more limited hours seasonally.

Wilderness Center
Yosemite Village, shuttle stop 2
Road marker V1
(209) 372-0740
www.nps.gov/yose/wilderness/
Get complete information, maps, accessories for hikers, bear-proof containers, and advice here regarding more than 800 miles of hiking trails, backpacking, campgrounds, and winter trekking in the High Country. Permits are required for overnight wilderness users. In the wintertime when the Wilderness Center is closed, check in at the visitor center.

See more about wilderness permits in the Hiking and Backpacking chapter.

Yosemite Chapel
Shuttle stop 11, road marker V20
(209) 372-4831
Many weddings are held in this sweet, simple chapel in the heart of the valley. Built in 1879 with a slender spire, it is the oldest building still occupied in the park. Check the *Yosemite Guide* for a schedule of services, which are primarily interdenominational.

The Waterfalls of Yosemite Valley

Bridalveil Fall
Road marker V14
The whirling mistiness of Bridalveil Fall prompted Yosemite's original residents, the Miwoks, to call it "the fall of the puffing winds." At its peak in early spring, the fall roars from 620 feet above into creek cascades and sprays, half falling, half floating, over a wide area, making rainbows that are beautiful to see but elusive in photographs.

An elongated pyramid rivaling those in Egypt, Cathedral Rocks forms an impressive backdrop to the scene. The fall descends out of a classic "hanging valley," a geologic phenomenon seen throughout the valley.

A hiker passes by Nevada Fall. MAXINE CASS

i

If a waterfall drops in one continuous downpour, it is a "fall," as in Nevada Fall. If it drops in more than one cascade, it is known as "falls," as in Yosemite Falls, which has two main cataracts. Watch a short video of the valley's famous waterfalls at www.yosemitefund.org.

For the best photo of Bridalveil, drive or walk to the opposite side of the river to road marker V10, between El Capitan and the Three Brothers. In late afternoon until just before sunset, the light on the cliffs and the fall can be golden and ethereal.

Below the fall, Bridalveil Creek flows into several beautiful channels under three stone bridges. Just east of the parking lot beneath the cedars, look for displays of rose-pink, heart-shaped, Western bleeding-hearts between March and July.

The first group of non-Native Americans in the valley, the Mariposa Battalion, camped in Bridalveil Meadow in 1851 while they hunted the Ahwahneechee tribe in order to rout them from the Yosemite area. President Theodore Roosevelt and John Muir also camped here together in 1903. Today Bridalveil Meadow is a beautiful, 65-acre open space bordered by oak woodlands.

The Fire of Horsetail Fall
1.7 miles west of Yosemite Lodge at the Falls on the north side of the valley

Horsetail Fall creates a curious phenomenon that occurs only during the last two weeks of February. The setting sun blazes in a brilliant red-orange light behind the fall, making the cascade seem as if it is on fire. Photographers line up every clear-sky evening just before sunset to get the shot of a lifetime. For your best opportunity, walk about 200 yards east of the picnic area to a small clearing. Although you can see it easily with the naked eye, you will need a 200- or 300mm lens to capture a superior image.

Nevada Fall/Vernal Fall
Shuttle stop 16, road marker V24

From high in the Sierra, the Merced River empties onto the upper step of the "Giant's Stairway," the 594-foot Nevada Fall. Nevada feeds Vernal Fall, which plunges 317 feet in a wide, white curtain encircled by rainbows at its base. In the springtime, you can hear the low boom of the falls as far as 2 miles away, and they remain active throughout the summer months. Vernal Fall can be reached from Happy Isles on the Mist Trail, a slippery, spray-drenched route in spring and early summer. The trail includes a strenuous climb of huge granite stairs but is a more gradual climb via the John Muir Trail (see the Hiking and Backpacking chapter).

Ribbon Fall
To the west of El Capitan

The highest single fall in Yosemite and one of the highest in the world, Ribbon Fall descends 1,612 feet in a narrow stream from the northwest rim of the valley, near El Capitan. As it is partially hidden by the rocks, many people miss the sight of this fall, which is best viewed in spring and early summer; by August, it will likely be dry. Watch for it as you drive into the valley.

Yosemite Falls
Shuttle stop 6, road marker V3

As if directly from the sky, Yosemite Creek drops out of a hanging valley 2,425 feet in two monumental cataracts into the Merced River, making it the tallest waterfall in North America and the fifth highest in the world. Niagara Falls is only 167 feet high.

One of the easiest and most popular valley walks is to the base of the lower fall, which drops 320 feet (from shuttle stop 6, road marker V3). It is a very strenuous, 3.6-mile hike to the top section, which plunges 1,430 feet, cascades across a 675-foot ledge, and drops again. You can get one of the best views of the upper fall from the footbridge called Swinging Bridge.

In late spring and early summer, the tremendous force of the falls vibrates in

Everyone Comes to Yosemite, Sooner or Later

If you arrive in Yosemite Valley in July or August, you may mistake the valley for Grand Central Station or an L.A. freeway. A million people visit Yosemite during these months. Just think of the noise and dust and exhaust fumes! Hot, dry, and throbbing with rumbling RVs and cars heading for thousands of campsites, the valley becomes a 7-mile-long, 1-mile-wide parking lot.

Fortunately for you, 80 percent of these visitors remain within the valley, which is just 1 percent of the park and where most of the man-made development is found.

To avoid crowded campgrounds and the high-season glut, opt to come between October and March. If you came here once a year in the off-season, it would take a lifetime to discover all the glories of Yosemite.

If summer is your only choice, come on weekdays and stick to the two quieter but no less attractive areas of the park, Wawona and Tuolumne. The southern section of the park, Wawona, is loaded with historic architecture, riverside walking trails and campsites, and some of the tallest and oldest trees in the world.

You can get away from people and midsummer heat by heading for the Tuolumne High Country, accessed by scenic Tioga Road, which leads to campgrounds, lakes, the roaring Tuolumne River, and wildflower-bedecked Tuolumne Meadows at 8,600 feet.

Even though well over three million people visit the park each year, it is still relatively easy to find yourself alone on the more than 800 miles of trails winding their way through 750,000 acres of park land. Even midsummer at the height of the crush you can get away from people within a few minutes on foot or a bike. Plan to set out early in the mornings to be first on the trails and to experience the valley at its sparkling, pristine best. Ask employees where they go for solitude—Yosemite staffers are usually full of inside information. Most of them work here not for the pay, which is low, but because they are strongly attracted to Yosemite and love the outdoors.

If all else fails and you find yourself here on an August weekend, just look up. Above the parking lots and traffic jams, the buses, RVs, and the tykes on bikes, the spectacular granite monoliths that line the valley, the thundering falls, and the empty, wild beauty of the High Country remain as they were when the Ahwahneechee were the only people here to see them.

the ground at the base of the lower fall. By August, the avalanche of water has usually dried to a whisper. In midwinter, ice cones as large as 300 feet high, covering four acres, form on the ledge and can be easily seen. When the sun warms the air, the ice often cracks into huge boulders, thundering across the valley as it bursts and falls.

Look on the left side of the falls for the light patch of granite left by a huge piece of rock that fell off the cliff face in the early 1980s.

The nonprofit Yosemite Fund

(www.yosemitefund.org) in cooperation with the National Park Service, worked with world-renowned landscape architect Larry Halprin to develop a new design for the 52-acre area at the base of Yosemite Falls. It took 10 years and $13.5 million dollars to reduce congestion along the approach to the base of Lower Yosemite Fall. The loop trail opened in spring 2005, with east and west paved walkways to spread crowds out as visitors marvel at the water plunging earthward. The eastern side is flat-graded for wheelchair access. The shuttle bus stop was moved further from the trail, bridges were replaced to allow more natural flow of streams, forest and streamside habitat was restored, and benches and alcoves were added along the loop trail for folks who want to soak up the view without being distracted by crowd flow. Open space and a picnic area replaced a parking lot that was infamous for tour bus fumes and noise.

WAWONA

The southern part of Yosemite, called Wawona, is about 35 miles from Yosemite Valley by way of Highway 41 and 2 miles from the South Gate entrance of the park. Once a Native American encampment, Wawona was later the site of a hotel built by Galen Clark—the original guardian of the park—for travelers who journeyed to Yosemite in stagecoaches and on horseback. In 1875 the Washburn brothers took over the place and built the Wawona Hotel, a charming, early-Victorian-style vacation resort that is still in operation today.

Because of the relatively low elevation at 4,000 feet, Wawona is accessible year-round for camping, sight-seeing, hiking, and Nordic skiing. Many skiers make Wawona their base camp for skiing at Yosemite's Badger Pass Ski Area, a half-hour drive up the Glacier Point Road.

The Mariposa Grove of Giant Sequoias is a main attraction in the Wawona area. Families love Wawona for the quieter, less commercial atmosphere than the valley and for the campground on the banks of the South Fork of the Merced River. The area's numerous hiking trails, beaches, and swimming holes are all less frequented than those in other parts of the park. And, a surprise—there's a 9-hole golf course.

The lush open meadows and spring and summer wildflower displays are heroic, from blue and white lupines to lavender elephant's heads, foxgloves, red-orange fuschias, and yellow-gold monkey flowers.

Adjacent to the Pioneer Yosemite History Center and the Wawona Information Station at Hill's Studio, you'll find a small grocery store, gift shop, and the post office.

In the Wawona Campground, rangers come to the campfire nightly to tell stories and talk about Yosemite's history, flora, and fauna; program topics are posted at the campground. Junior Rangers meet with the ranger on Thursday and Sunday. (For more information on Junior Rangers, check out the Kidstuff chapter.)

Everyone is welcome to gather in the Wawona Hotel lobby, Tuesday through Saturday evenings, to hear Tom Bopp, Wawona's legendary pianist and singer. On some summer weekday evenings, programs are conducted at the hotel with slides, narration, and music. Morning and afternoon nature walks are offered in the summer. For all events, watch for postings in the campground, ask at the hotel, and check *Yosemite Today.*

Campfire Programs

Meet park rangers and gather with other campers at 8:00 P.M. for campfire songs, stories, educational talks, and family fun at the Wawona Campground amphitheater. Free.

Exploring Wawona History
(209) 379-2321
www.yosemite.org

A Yosemite ranger for nine years, historian and naturalist Fred Fisher leads an in-depth, daylong walking tour of Wawona, from the Pioneer Yosemite History Center to the giant sequoias and the Thomas Hill Studio, while recounting early history. Fee is $80.

The Mariposa Grove of Big Trees

The largest of three sequoia groves in Yosemite, the Mariposa Grove is one of the unforgettable natural phenomena in the national park. More than 200 giant sequoias live here, many of them 2,000 to 3,000 years old.

The grove has two main sections—the upper grove, where the Mariposa Grove Museum is located, and the lower grove, which shelters the Grizzly Giant and other behemoths. Tall firs and sugar pines that would be impressive in any other setting are dwarfed by the big sequoias.

CLOSE-UP

The Big Trees

Possessors of the earth for thousands of years, through lightning storms, snow, torrential rain, earthquakes, and fires, the giant sequoias have been a magnetic attraction for tourists in Yosemite since the middle of the 19th century. For some people, they represent a certain spiritual connection with the earth. Certainly, their astonishing size and regal beauty never fail to elicit a catch in the throat.

Related to the California redwoods and descendants of huge evergreens that grew during the age of the dinosaurs, sequoias—*Sequoiadendron giganteum*—thrive in a few pockets in Kings Canyon, Sequoia, and Yosemite National Parks, with scattered specimens in nearby parks. These are the largest living things on earth.

Sapless, cinnamon-brown bark, as much as 2 feet thick, gives the sequoia its distinctive fluted appearance and contains tannin, which successfully resists pests, diseases, fire, and floods. Reaching maturity at 1,000 to 3,000 years, the tree grows slowly and massively wide. At least one specimen, the Grizzly Giant, is 34 feet across, has a circumference at the base of 96.5 feet, and weighs hundreds of tons.

Melting snow engorges their roots, and in the dryer months, they draw moisture from the air through their boughs, one molecule at a time, an adaptation that explains, to a degree, why they are able to live so long. Given their tremendous height, their root systems are surprisingly shallow—only 8 to 10 feet deep—with no taproot. Massing together in groves, they are able to withstand high winds, attaining 200 to 300 feet in height. The trunks are largely bare, with twisted, muscular arms, close to the trunk, sparsely covered in fine needles.

Called the "Big Trees," the sequoias in Yosemite National Park are clustered in three groves, the largest of which is the Mariposa Grove in the southern section of the park. The Tuolumne Grove is near Crane Flat on the Tioga Road, and the Merced Grove is off the Big Oak Flat Road between Crane Flat and the Big Oak Flat Entrance. The easiest access is in the Mariposa Grove, where you can drive to a parking area and walk or take a tram ride to the trees. There are also a few in Yosemite Valley, planted by early settlers.

These 200 sequoias survive in immense dignity, providing vital homes for dozens of species of animals and birds who chatter, hoot, and squawk in the windy treetops.

Beginning in the 19th century, the virgin stands of sequoias were largely decimated, primarily by clear-cutting that not only destroyed the trees but also damaged the creeks and hillsides that served as wildlife habitat. The giant sequoias are currently off limits to logging, although the Forest Service has proposed logging them in Sequoia National Park.

In February 2003, two giant sequoias fell in the Mariposa Grove. Believed to be 300 to 750 years old, the two had been surrounded by foot traffic, which may have damaged the root systems and caused the collapse. Although the fallen beauties block a path through the grove, there are no plans to cut or move them. Over time in their deterioration, they will contribute to the ecosystem.

Visitors explore a fallen giant sequoia in the Mariposa Grove. DNC

Did you know that privately owned homes are available to rent in the Wawona area within the national park? For more information, see "Rentals" in the Lodging and Rentals chapter.

Of the walking trails throughout the grove, the most popular starts at the parking lot and gradually climbs through a beautiful mixed forest corridor, including notable sequoia specimens—called the Bachelor and the Three Graces—on the way to the Grizzly Giant, at the 0.8-mile point.

The 209-foot, 300-ton Grizzly Giant, with a diameter of more than 34 feet and a circumference at the base of 96.5 feet, is the biggest tree in Yosemite and the fifth largest living thing on the planet. Standing at its foot, it is difficult to grasp the scale of this tree, as high as a 22-story skyscraper. One branch of the Grizzly is more than 6 feet in diameter. A hundred yards behind the Grizzly, the California Tree is one of two sequoias in the grove that have been tunneled, this one in 1895. More than 200 feet tall, the Wawona Tunnel Tree was hollowed out in 1881 by the Yosemite Stage and Turnpike Company, who paid loggers $75 to enlarge a burn scar to 8 feet wide, 9 feet high, and 26 feet long. Under a heavy snow load in 1969, the tree fell.

The sight of this tree on the ground does give an idea of its immense girth and height and reminds us that when mature sequoias do occasionally fall over due to natural causes, they continue to act as nursery trees, providing sustenance and shelter for small animals and birds. This is an aspect of old-growth forests that is missing in tree plantations and in logged-over, replanted forests. After many decades, sometimes as long as a hundred years, the toppled trees decay completely, becoming rich soil from which new sequoias are born.

In the cool stillness of the early morning, and in late afternoon when tourists have departed, you will hear only bustling chickarees in the arms of the big trees and the prattle of Steller's jays. Trillium and wild iris spring from ferny carpets. Not really flowers, and phenomenal in their vibrant color, are the red snow plant and pinedrops that emerge in May and June.

A narrated, open-air tram tour begins every 15 to 20 minutes in the parking lot and stops frequently so you can hop on and off to wander the nature trails; you can also stay onboard, visit the museum, walk around a bit, and ride back down. One trailhead leads to a vista point at 6,810 feet, overlooking the vast Wawona forest basin. Rather than taking the tram back down, many people walk the 2.5-mile, easy downhill path. Tickets for the Big Trees Tram Tour are $16 for adults, $14 for seniors, $10 for children 5 to 13, and free for kids under 5. Call (209) 375-1621 for departure times; (209) 372-1240 for reservations up to seven days in advance for tours offered May through October.

Free, ranger-led, narrated, 90-minute walks are offered Wednesdays and Fridays at 10:00 A.M. and 2:00 P.M. in the lower grove. Meet the ranger at the tram boarding area to walk up to the Grizzly Giant and back. The 90-minute Photo Walk starts at the gift shop and introduces you to the challenges of photographing huge and tall Big Trees. A professional photographer leads the Mariposa Grove of Giant Sequoias Photo Walk and it's free!

The small museum and gift shop and a snack bar selling sandwiches and drinks are all open May through October. In wintertime, you can park at the bottom of the hill and snowshoe or ski up to the grove, a relatively easy, absolutely beautiful route.

When the parking lot is full, which is often in midsummer, take the free shuttle from the Wawona Store and the South Gate entrance to the park.

An easy, comfortable way to see the Mariposa Grove and visit Wawona is on the six-hour, narrated Grand Tour by motorcoach to the grove from Yosemite

Valley. You will not be bored. The drivers are fun and well informed about the park's flora, fauna, history, and geology. There is plenty of time to take the Big Trees Tram Tour, stroll around under the giant sequoias, and have lunch at the Wawona Hotel. The Grand Tour departs from Yosemite Lodge at the Falls at 8:45 A.M., late May to early November, weather permitting, stopping at Tunnel View, Glacier Point, Wawona, and the Big Trees. Cost, not including lunch at the Wawona Hotel, is $60 for adults and $33 for children. For more information and reservations, call (209) 372-1240. You can bring your own picnic or buy lunch at the Wawona Store.

Pioneer Yosemite History Center
Highway 41, near the Wawona General Store
(209) 375-9531

A covered bridge built in the 1870s, old stagecoaches and wagons, mining machinery, authentic furnished cabins and houses, a jail, a Wells Fargo bank, and history exhibits create a major destination for history buffs and Yosemite lovers. The center is always open for self-guided tours, with the aid of explanatory signs and brochures. The walking tour is easy for all ages and abilities, except during extreme snow conditions, which are rare.

The charming George Anderson log cabin was built in the 1870s. A Scottish sailor, Anderson immigrated to the Sierra during the Gold Rush. He was one of the first trailbuilders of Yosemite and a local blacksmith and is said to be the first person to scale Half Dome. After his ascent, he then charged a few dollars to guide others to the top.

The two-story log Hodgdon Cabin was built by homesteaders who claimed summer pastures in Yosemite, in spite of protests from John Muir and others who favored complete protection of park lands. The Blacksmith Shop, Degnan Bakery, Ranger Patrol Cabin, and the Powderhouse and Jail Building show how park residents and law enforcers dealt with practical details.

A few hundred yards upstream from the covered bridge at the Pioneer Yosemite History Center are swimming and wading pools in the Merced River, the warmest waters in the park. You can park on the side of the road and wade across to big, flat boulders warmed by the sun, and picnic or just loll.

Viewing the stagecoaches brings to mind the arduous journey that the first tourists made. They arrived by train from San Francisco and boarded stages in Raymond, then held on for the bumpy, dusty, two-day ride over the corkscrew Wawona Road into Yosemite Valley; Wawona was a way station along the way. For $3.00 ($2.00 for kids), you can climb on board a horse-drawn wagon in the summertime and ride around the History Center and surrounding area for a half hour, while the wagon driver recounts Wawona history. Saturday night barn dances are held in the summertime, too.

Wawona Golf Course
across Highway 41 from the Wawona Hotel
(209) 375-6572

You will not find a golf course in many national parks, and certainly not one on which you might occasionally call "fore" to a family of mule deer. Opened in 1917, this lovely, 3,050-yard 9-holer comes as a surprise to most visitors. Relatively easy on rolling terrain, it does have some tricky spots, with ball-grabbing rough and tons of water, depending on the time of year. No pesticides are used on this golf course that is also a designated Audubon Cooperative Sanctuary.

Call ahead for tee times; green fees are $18.50 for 9 holes and $29.50 for 18 holes. Two tee positions provide an 18-hole format. The course and putting green are open daily mid-April through October

A deer is a common sight on the Wawona golf course. FRED GEBHART

(weather permitting). Amenities include electric and caddie-cart rentals and good quality club rentals, available from the small pro shop, which is stocked with golf apparel and accessories.

Located near the pro shop is a snack stand serving hot dogs, sandwiches, and beverages.

After golf, come back with your fishing rod to try for the brown trout in the crystalline stream on holes 1, 6, and 9; remember, it's strictly catch-and-release.

Wawona Hotel
Highway 41, 7 miles from the South Gate entrance of the park
(209) 375-6556

For the mood and the look of early days in Yosemite, the Wawona Hotel is the place to stay. Founded in 1856 and now a National Historic Landmark, the absolutely charming, 104-room Victorian hotel compound in a tall pine glade beckons vacationers back, year after year. Guests rock in their rockers on the covered verandas. They luxuriate in their antiques-filled, comfy rooms; take dips in the small swimming pool; play tennis; sunbathe on the sweeping lawns; gather by the fireplace in the lobby; and stroll Wawona Meadow. The hotel is described in detail in the Lodging and Rentals chapter of this book.

If you are camping at Wawona or driving through, do stop in for an excellent meal in the beautiful, light-filled dining room and take advantage of the music and history programs offered in the evenings (see *Yosemite Today* for days and times).

Stay to enjoy Tom Bopp Tuesday through Saturday evenings. He has been playing a restored 1906 grand piano and singing in the Wawona Hotel parlor for more than a decade. Invited to play for a week at the hotel, he stayed for a second week and has been delighting guests ever since. He regales his audience with stories of the old days in Yosemite and plays everything from Beethoven to ragtime and improvisational jazz, with an emphasis on popular music from the first half of the 20th century.

Over the years, Tom has collected historic music of Yosemite, including campfire ditties, marches, cowboy songs, and ragtime tunes. Tom recorded Vintage Songs of Yosemite on five CDs; clips can be heard on Tom's Web site, www.yosemitemusic.com.

Besides his regular gig at the Wawona Hotel, Tom often tickles the ivories during the winter at The Ahwahnee and at the Tenaya Lodge at Yosemite in Fish Camp.

A Saturday night summertime tradition on the Wawona lawns is old-fashioned barbecue, open to all, that can be the highlight of a family vacation, as it has been for decades. Have a glass of lemonade, sit on the porch, and watch the red-checked tablecloths get spread out and the burgers, steak, chicken, and fish sizzle on the grills. All-you-can-eat salads, corn on the cob, beans, dessert, and nonalcoholic beverages make this a bargain at $7.95 to $18.95 for adults and $5.25 to $6.75 for children. When the sun goes down in the summertime, everyone is welcome for the Saturday night barn dance at the nearby Pioneer Yosemite History Center—it's free.

Every December the Victorian-era Wawona Hotel is draped and decorated in elaborate style to celebrate a Pioneer Christmas. Brought from outside the park, natural materials are combined with vivid ribbons and fripperies. The scent of cedar, juniper, pine, and eucalyptus is heady, as visitors view the garlands and arrangements of flowers, pinecones, berries, pomegranates, oak leaves, and lichen balls. The lobby Christmas tree is lit in midmonth at a special occasion calling for hot chocolate, cider, and cookies, while pianist and singer Tom Bopp leads guests in Christmas caroling.

Live music and caroling is planned for other holiday evenings, too, and the Wawona Store and Pioneer Gift Shop stays open for last-minute holiday shopping. You can bring gifts to the front desk on Christmas Eve for Santa to present that afternoon before he reads Christmas stories and sits for photos with the kids. Special holiday dishes are featured in the dining room. Make your reservations early, even months ahead, as Christmas at Wawona is a treasured tradition of many families.

A Dickens' Christmas at Wawona is the marketing theme for the definitively Victorian celebration, where a highlight is the Wawona Hotel fireside reading of* A Christmas Carol, *no doubt approvingly watched from the beyond by the spirit of Scrooge's creator.

Wawona Information Station at Hill's Studio
Adjacent to the Wawona Hotel
(209) 375-1416

Open 8:00 A.M. to 4:30 P.M. mid-May through early October, the Information Station at Wawona is the place to find out all you need to know about park activities, scheduled events, and trail conditions and to pick up maps, guidebooks, and wilderness permits.

Landscape painter Thomas Hill was a resident artist at Wawona from 1884 until 1908. His charming depictions of Yosemite scenes were beloved by such luminaries as Theodore Roosevelt. In the charming Victorian-era house in which he worked, which now functions as the Information Station, some of his paintings are on exhibit in the summertime, along with other Yosemite-related art.

Wawona Meadow
Highway 41, across the road from the Wawona Hotel

Even toddlers can manage all or part of this 3.5-mile, flat-loop trail around the meadow, and they like watching the herds of grazing deer. During the winter, Wawona Meadow and several more open meadows in the Wawona area are popular for cross-country skiing.

Wawona Stable
Chilnualna Falls Road
(209) 375-6502

Like Wawona's early pioneers, take a two-hour mule ride that follows the historic

CLOSE-UP

Galen Clark, the Guardian

One of Yosemite's earliest explorers, Galen Clark arrived in the valley in the early 1850s, when the campfires of the vanquished Native Americans were barely cold. Widowed and seriously ill, he hoped the undefiled beauty of the wilderness and the fresh, clean air would help him recover his body and spirit. In fact, Clark became the park's first public guardian and a legendary tour guide, protecting and promoting Yosemite throughout his life. He studied the geography, geology, and botany of the region and taught many people to love and fight for the place as he did.

In 1857 he homesteaded 160 acres and built a log cabin, which he called "Clark's Station," and welcomed overnight travelers. The local Native Americans called it Pallahchun, meaning "A Good Place to Stop," and it turned out to be the predecessor of today's Wawona Hotel.

Struggling to make a meager living, he realized the unique value of the Mariposa Grove of Giant Sequoias as a tourist attraction and a national treasure, and he helped to bring about the establishment of the Yosemite Grant in 1864, which set aside the valley and the grove for the state.

Knowledgeable about natural history, ever hospitable, and motivated to take part in the burgeoning movement to preserve Yosemite, he was named the park's first official resident superintendent, serving from 1866 to 1880 during the early days of disputes over private use of the valley for agriculture, livestock, and logging.

Unpaid for years, he maintained trails and bridges, acted as a mediator, and enforced regulations banning tree cutting, all the while introducing visitors to the glories of Yosemite by offering them tours in his nine-seat buggy to the landmarks and vistas that were to become world famous.

There are numerous old photographs of Clark, affectionately called "Mr. Yosemite," an old man with a long, white beard and disheveled suit, posing by the Grizzly Giant in the Mariposa Grove, which he named for the Mariposa lily.

Clark continued to hike and ride horseback throughout Yosemite into his 90s, charming and lobbying everyone he met, including his good friend and occasional hiking buddy, John Muir. He died in 1910 at the age of 95 and is buried in the Yosemite Valley Cemetery beneath a sequoia that he planted, under a granite stone upon which he chiseled his own name.

wagon road—the original route into Wawona over Chowchilla Mountain—around the Wawona Meadow and golf course. The flat, even terrain is great for beginning riders getting accustomed to the saddle.

The half-day, five-hour ride rambles on a nice, long climb through a pine and cedar forest to picturesque Chilnualna Falls, where you can take a dip in an icy swimming hole and take pictures of the spectacular, cascading waterfalls and scenic views (see more about Chilnualna Falls in the Hiking and Backpacking chapter).

The all-day trail ride is for experienced riders in top physical condition. Destinations are the Grove of Giant Sequoias and Johnson Lake. This is a challenging ride, but the spectacular views make it worth the effort.

Departing several times a day, the two-hour ride costs $51. The half-day trip, departing at 8:00 A.M. and 1:00 P.M. is $67, and the daylong ride is $94. See more about horseback riding in the park and beyond in the Outdoor Recreation chapter.

TUOLUMNE AND HETCH HETCHY

TUOLUMNE AND THE TIOGA ROAD

Most of Yosemite National Park lies above 7,500 feet in the High Country, a rugged, dramatic landscape of jagged, snow-capped peaks, glacial lakes, rocky moraines, and a deep river canyon. From Crane Flat, 45 miles to Tioga Pass at the East Gate of the park, the Tioga Road winds across this stunning part of the Sierra, through some of the most spectacular scenery in the world. At an elevation of 9,945 feet, Tioga Pass is the highest vehicle pass in California. Opened in 1882 as a wagon trail for hauling silver from local mines, it wasn't until 1961 that the state rebuilt the national park section of the road for vacationers seeking a shortcut over the Sierra. The road now carries nearly a quarter-million visitors annually.

Along the way, you'll see subalpine lakes and tarns, meadows full of wildflowers, glacier-polished granite domes, and forests stretching to distant mountain ranges. Motorists stop at the many turnouts and vista points to gasp and gape at the breathtaking sights. Just pull into the Olmsted Point parking area and look across to Half Dome, Tenaya Canyon, and Clouds Rest to see what the fuss is all about.

As the road nears the summit of Tioga Pass, the temperature drops as much as 15 to 20 degrees. The road is normally open for about 150 days a year, from late May or early June until the first big snowstorm, about November 1; it may be open for as little as two months or as much as half the year. Snow showers can occur as late as June and as early as September. Mount Dana, Mount Lyell, and other peaks remain snowcapped throughout the summer. For current conditions and opening and closing dates for the Tioga Road, go to www.nps.gov/yose/now/conditions.htm.

In the brief, sweet season of crystal-clear summer days, hikers trod hundreds of miles of backcountry hiking trails, seeking the healing, invigorating powers of the wilderness as exalted by John Muir in his book *Our National Parks:* "Keep close to Nature's heart . . . and break clear away, once in awhile, and climb a mountain or spend a week in the woods. Wash your spirit clean."

Once the road closes for the season, the ungroomed road itself and ungroomed backcountry trails are accessible to experienced cross-country skiers, snowshoers, and snow campers.

Strenuous backpacking trips afford access into the northern-most reaches of the national park and to extended trans-Sierra routes such as the John Muir Trail and the Pacific Crest Trail. For more information on hiking and backpacking in the High Country, see the Hiking and Backpacking chapter of this guidebook.

Early Tuolumne History

The name Tuolumne may be derived from the Taulamnell, Tahualamne, or Yokuts Indians living near Knights Ferry, and it may have meant "cave people" or "stone wigwams." Another theory is that Tuolumne is a Miwok word—*talmalmne,* with an unclear meaning.

The Tuolumne River drainage was the southern boundary of the range of the Central Sierra Miwok Indians, and it served as a main artery for travel, trade, and communications between tribal members.

The Miwok thrived along the river in its deep, steep canyon and dense forests, protected from wind, snow, and summer heat. They used the tremendous rock outcroppings for grinding traditional foods—in particular, their staple, acorns.

When the gold miners arrived in the 1840s, the Miwok began to relocate and disappear. Miners' camps liberally spread over the riverbanks and meadows until the winter of 1861, when tremendous rainstorms flooded the river, destroying the camps and villages.

In 1916 the fledgling National Park Service wanted to attract visitors to Yosemite's High Country with the goal of educating the public that there was value in protecting the wilderness from animal grazing, logging, and development. To make hiking and horseback riding convenient, mountain chalets were built in scenic locations, and they are still in use today as the High Sierra Camps. The Merced Lake camp was built in 1916, Vogelsang and Glen Aulin in the mid-1920s, May Lake in the late '30s, and Sunrise camp in 1961. See the Hiking and Backpacking chapter for information about hiking between the High Sierra camps.

Tuolumne Meadows

The main destination on the Tioga Road is Tuolumne Meadows; at 8,775 feet, it is actually a network of subalpine wetlands and grassy clearings below a dramatic surround of glacier-polished domes, high peaks, and granite outcroppings. So numerous and unique are the stone formations that avid rock climbers set up camp and stay all summer. The largest open, subalpine meadow in the Sierra, Tuolumne Meadows is 2.5 miles long and bordered by the snow-fed Tuolumne River. From early summer through fall, the meadow seems a boundless ocean of tall grass and wildflowers, freshened by water channels and boggy creeks. It may sparkle with frost or be awash in purple nightshade, golden monkey flowers, and riots of magenta-colored lady slipper orchids.

Driving on the Tioga Road? You'll see signs on Highway 120 East with a bright red outline of a bear on all fours facing you. It's the park's "Red Bear, Dead Bear" pilot program to slow down drivers at spots where several bears have been hit in the past, thereby saving the lives of bears, as well as deer and other animals crossing the road in High Country.

Watering the meadows, two forks of the Tuolumne River begin their westward plunge into a rugged canyon to emerge 25 miles below in the Hetch Hetchy Reservoir. Hiking trails follow the river much of the way.

You'll find a number of public facilities at Tuolumne Meadows, including the Tuolumne Meadows Visitor Center, a restaurant, a fast-food grill, a general store, a mountaineering and wilderness center, a post office, the ranger station, stables, a gas station, and the largest campground in the park. Tent cabins are available at Tuolumne Meadows Lodge, (559) 253-5635. Everything is open from late spring through early fall.

Park rangers lead narrated walks and hikes, talking about geology, birds, wildflowers, Native American history, and more. Kids can participate in the educational Junior Ranger program and get in on evening campfires and family lunch walks. Star parties and moonlight walks are among the wide variety of scheduled activities and programs. The Night Prowl is an after-dark caravan around the meadow, when you'll encounter the nocturnal denizens of the High Sierra, including great gray owls and spotted bats.

From Tuolumne Meadows, it is just a few minutes to the eastern entrance of the park, called the Tioga Pass entrance. Beyond are the Ansel Adams Wilderness, the Hoover Wilderness, the Toiyabe and Inyo National Forests, and Mono Lake.

Tuolumne Meadows Hiker's Bus
(209) 372-1240

To avoid the hassle of driving up the

The free Tuolumne Meadows shuttle bus runs throughout the Tuolumne Meadows area between the Tuolumne Meadows Lodge and Olmsted Point (including Tenaya Lake) during the summer, usually mid-June through early September.

sometimes-congested Tioga Road from July through Labor Day and parking at Tuolumne Meadows, hikers and backpackers take the Hiker's Bus from Yosemite Valley to High Country trailheads, with drop-offs at Crane Flat, White Wolf, and Tuolumne Meadows Lodge. From the lodge, you can also switch to a free shuttle bus to Pothole Dome, Tenaya Lake, and Olmsted Point trailheads. The bus departs Yosemite Lodge at the Falls, the Village Store, and Curry Village around 8:00 A.M. daily in the summer. See the Hiking and Backpacking chapter for details.

Tuolumne Meadows Ranger Station
Highway 120 East/Tioga Road, road marker T30
(209) 372-0450
www.yosemite.org/diary/tuolumne.html
Stop in here, call, or check the Web site for current trail and weather information, which is updated frequently.

Tuolumne Meadows Visitor Center
Highway 120 East/Tioga Road, road marker T30
(209) 372-0263
This is the clearinghouse for information on where to picnic and take day hikes, obtain a campsite, and plan a backpacking trip. Sign up here for a wide variety of ranger-guided walks and presentations. Exhibits explain geology, alpine and subalpine ecology, bears and other wildlife, wildflowers, and human history. Open daily 9:00 A.M. to 5:00 P.M. when Tioga Road is open.

Dog Lake
Highway 120 East/Tioga Road, Lembert Dome parking area, road marker T32
This is the closest lake to Tuolumne Meadows and the warmest of the chilly lakes at this altitude, offering good swimming and fishing. It is a 1.5-mile, one-way hike from the parking area, a little steep at first, but easy enough for all ages.

Evening Activities at Tuolumne Meadows
(209) 372-0263
Dana Campfire Circle at Tuolumne Meadows Campground is a favorite gathering place for after-dark sing-alongs, ranger talks, storytelling, and a chance to ask questions and visit with rangers and other campers. A schedule of programs is posted at the campground, at the visitor center, and at Tuolumne Meadows Lodge. Children's programs are scheduled on Wednesday evenings at the Conness Circle in the C loop of the campground. Junior Ranger programs are on Tuesdays and Thursdays.

Olmsted Point
Road marker T24, 2.5 miles west of Tenaya Lake
This is one of Yosemite's "must see" viewpoints. Park in the turnout by the road, or walk a quarter-mile to the small dome to see Tenaya Lake and the granite walls of Tenaya Canyon with the back side of Half Dome, Mount Conness, Clouds Rest, and more domes and peaks. Interpretive signs explain the fascinating glacier-caused geological features. Massive granite slabs were deeply scarred and split by the moving glaciers. The scattered boulders you see are erratics, which were pushed ahead of the advancing glaciers and remained, like handfuls of marbles, when the ice melted.

The best time of day to photograph this extraordinary panorama is later in the day, particularly at sunset. Please do not approach the marmots or feed them.

Parsons Memorial Lodge
Road marker T32
Take an easy, 1-mile walk from the Tuolumne Meadows Visitor Center or a half-mile walk from the Lembert Dome parking area to this historic lodge, built in 1914 by the Sierra Club. Afternoon one-

hour talks include topics such as "A Way Across the Mountains: Joseph Walker's 1833 Traverse of the Sierra Nevada" and "Miwok Women." The lodge, a robust stone cabin, is usually open 11:00 A.M. to 4:00 P.M. Restrooms are nearby.

A tributary of the river and groves of evergreens and aspens run through the meadows here, with Lembert Dome in the near distance, making this a photogenic spot. You will also find an upwelling of carbonated mineral water, called Soda Springs, a few steps below the lodge. Where John Muir and Robert Underhill Johnson discussed the creation of a Yosemite National Park, near sunrise or sunset you'll see birds and deer visiting the springs. And from here, you set off on the Glen Aulin Trail.

Photography in the High Country
Tuolumne Meadows Lodge
(209) 379-2321

The magnificent landscapes and dramatic geologic formations of the Sierra are the subjects of this three-day, two-night, color workshop for intermediate to advanced photographers. The small group will enjoy multiple opportunities to capture High Country habitats—close-up to panoramic—from shallow subalpine lakes and wet meadows littered with shooting stars to the rocky environs of the Olmsted Point overlook. Instructor Howard Weamer is a Yosemite veteran and noted photographer of the park. You must be in excellent physical condition for the moderate hikes of up to 3 miles over rough terrain at more than 10,000 feet in elevation, and you will be camping out. Fee is $225.

Tenaya Lake
31.9 miles east of Crane Flat, road marker T25, on Tioga Road

Carved by a branch of the Tuolumne Glacier, beautiful Tenaya Lake was named for Chief Tenaya, who desperately tried to mediate peace and ultimately defended his tribe against the Mariposa Battalion in 1851. During a surprise attack, his tribe was captured on the shores of the lake.

A great place to swim in the summertime is in the Tuolumne River at the Tuolumne Meadows Campground. The water will be chilly, very chilly—a delightful experience when daytime temperatures rise into the 90s.

At 8,149 feet, 1 mile long and ½-mile wide, the lake is adjacent to the road and surrounded by stunning glacier-polished domes and granite mounds. Across the road, rock and mountain climbers are often in evidence on the dramatic, uprising granite faces, cliffs, and on the route up to Tenaya Peak.

Although the waters are frigid, this is one of the most popular sites in the High Country and crowded in the summertime with swimmers, sunbathers, picnickers, sailboarders, sailors, and windsurfers. Many visitors congregate on the beach on the northeast shore. Swimming is best on the southwest side, where frequent winds are the calmest. The easy hike around the lake is just over 3 miles. There are restrooms and picnic tables. A popular, walk-in campground is located at the west end, near parking. Bring mosquito repellent in midsummer.

Tuolumne Meadows *En Plein Air*
Tuolumne Meadows Lodge
(209) 379-2321

Capture the essence of the ethereal High Sierra in oils with the aid of an acclaimed artist and teacher. Through demonstrations, critiques of your work, and discussions, you will learn the language of painting and how to translate what you see into art through composition, color, texture, and brushwork; both novice and experienced painters will benefit. Tuolumne Meadows is a spectacular setting for this artists' retreat. Lodging is in dorm-style, permanent tents, and short walks are involved. Fee is $360.

A Yosemite Favorite

A common sight in the streams of the High Country, the water ouzel—also called the American dipper—was described by John Muir and is beloved by Yosemite hikers. A small, dark gray, short-tailed bird, the ouzel makes a "zeet-zeet" call as it scoots along the gravel in shallow water, appearing to walk on the surface. One of the few birds that seem to swim, it sometimes dives into the water and runs along the bottom with half-open wings, browsing for insects.

Mosquitoes can be maddening in July and August at Tuolumne Meadows. Come prepared with DEET-enhanced insect repellent.

Tuolumne Meadows Stable
(209) 372-8427

The perspective of the High Country from the back of a sturdy mule is the same as that of the pioneer explorers of Yosemite a century ago. Sign on for a two-hour Tuolumne Meadows trail ride for a trek to Tuolumne View on the Young Lakes Trail, an ideal lookout point for incredible vistas of the Cathedral Range, Johnson Peak, and Mammoth Peaks.

The half-day group ride goes to Twin Bridges on the Tuolumne River just above Tuolumne Falls. The all-day, 18-mile ride, with a 1,200-foot elevation drop, usually goes to Waterwheel Falls, one of the most spectacular sights in the Sierra (see the Hiking and Backpacking chapter). Only experienced riders in top physical shape will be up for the all-day expedition. And on this ride, you can request a specific itinerary.

From the Tuolumne River in the High Country of Yosemite, water flows into the Hetch Hetchy Reservoir, and by gravity from there, well over 200 miles to San Francisco. The reservoir is the primary source of water for the city.

Cost for the two-hour ride, which departs several times daily in the summertime, is $51; the four-hour ride, departing at 8:00 A.M. and 1:00 P.M. is $67. Cost for the eight-hour trip is $94.

Tuolumne Tours and Activities

The Yosemite Association offers guided day hikes and multiexpeditions in the Tuolumne High Country, including photography, advanced backpacking, sketching along the rivers, and more. Call (209) 379-2321 or go to www.yosemite.org for more information.

Summer or fall birding, investigating the wildflowers in Tuolumne Meadows, and geology tours are among the many courses offered in Yosemite's High Country. There may be a writer, poet, philosopher, or artist to help guide your interests or hone your craft. Most instructors and leaders have won awards and acclaim for their subjects and the enthusiasm shows.

Yosemite naturalist and author Michael Ross leads a fall day hike through forest, meadow, and water habitats in search of songbirds, raptors, and other avian habitants of the High Sierra. The 4-mile expedition is easy to moderate.

You can also sign on for "Yosemite with an Artist's Eye: Quick Sketching in Watercolor," with artist Chris Van Winkle. It consists of five days of walking through meadows, streams, forests, and the mountains to capture the scenic inspiration around Tuolumne Meadows. Both budding and advanced watercolorists are welcome.

White Wolf
Road marker T9
(559) 252-4848

Right off the Tioga Road, 30 miles from Yosemite Valley, White Wolf is a summer-only headquarters for backcountry trails and a favorite campground for those who like the cooler daytime temperatures at 7,900 feet and easy access to nearby lakes and streams. The atmosphere here is much more serene than the valley and quieter than the Tuolumne Meadows area. The camp lies in a beautiful subalpine meadow abloom with wildflowers from late spring through fall, fringed by towering lodgepole pines and bordered by the middle fork of the Tuolumne River.

The complex consists of 24 canvas cabins, a bathhouse, four cabins with private baths, a small general store, a 74-site campground open July through early September, and stables. Hearty meals are served in a central dining room in a quaint wooden building with a porch overlooking the forest. You can order box lunches at the front desk the night before you go off to explore High Country. Dinner reservations are required and can be made by calling (209) 372-8416.

From White Wolf, it is an easy 3-mile walk to Harden Lake. From 1.8 miles east of the White Wolf intersection, you walk a mile to Lukens Lake for fishing and picnicking.

HETCH HETCHY

Once, the mighty Tuolumne River streamed across the Hetch Hetchy Valley beneath a startling array of granite cliffs, peaks, and domes, and many waterfalls. Created by the same geological processes as Yosemite Valley, and said to have been as spectacular, Hetch Hetchy was drowned behind the O'Shaughnessy Dam, built between 1914 and 1938. A half hour's drive from the Big Oak Flat entrance to the park, today's 8-mile-long reservoir behind the 430-foot-high, 910-foot-long dam lies in a quiet, wild region of the park.

Lesser-known by most Yosemite visitors and less-traveled, by far, than the Yosemite Valley, Wawona, and the Tuolumne areas, Hetch Hetchy offers quiet charms. Short hikes lead to beautiful waterfalls, including the lively Tueeulala and Wapama on the north rim and Rancheria Falls beyond. Lakes and small valleys are popular hikers' destinations within 15 miles of the reservoir, and some people head as far as Tuolumne Meadows and beyond.

You can fish in the reservoir, but swimming and boating are not allowed.

John Muir and the Sierra Club vigorously opposed the building of the O'Shaughnessy Dam, and nationwide opinion was against it. The dam was erected nonetheless. Many people still believe that alternative sources for water and power were available, and some continue to argue for removal of the dam.

Muir's friends and family believed he died of a broken heart, the year construction of the dam began. In Muir's unpublished journals from 1913, before the battle was lost, he wrote:

"A great political miracle this of 'improving' the beauty of the most beautiful of all mountain parks by cutting down its groves, and burying all the thicket of azalea and wild rose, lily gardens, and ferneries two or three hundred feet deep. . . . we are promised a road blasted on the slope of the north wall, where nature-lovers may sit on rustic stools or rocks, like frogs on logs, to admire the sham dam lake, the grave of Hetch Hetchy. Never for a moment have I believed that the American people would fail to defend it for the welfare of themselves and all the world."

To reach the Hetch Hetchy area from Highway 120 West, 1 mile west of the Big Oak Flat entrance to the park turn north on Evergreen Road. After 16 miles, the paved road ends at the dam. The Hetch Hetchy entrance station (209-379-1922) is

CLOSE-UP

To Restore Hetch Hetchy?

From O'Shaughnessy Dam at the west end of Hetch Hetchy Reservoir, the scenery is pretty but not unusual in a park noted for dramatic cliffs, waterfalls, and meadows. At the reservoir's east end is the Grand Canyon of the Tuolumne River, hinting at what the Hetch Hetchy Valley must have looked like before it became the Yosemite Valley's northern lost twin when the dam was constructed in the early 20th century.

Hetch Hetchy Reservoir and its drainage supplies drinking water to 2.4 million residents of the San Francisco Bay Area and hydropower to agricultural areas of California. This bland fact belies the outcry that flooding the Hetch Hetchy Valley caused initially from John Muir, advocate of the national park and Sierra Nevada and the first Sierra Club president. After decades of occasional talk about undamming the reservoir to return Hetch Hetchy Valley to its rugged rises, plunging waterfalls, and wildflower-filled meadows, proposals to turn back time and geography have gotten serious. Draining the valley could cost from $500 million to $8 billion.

Watch the news for the ongoing debate balancing local water rights and California's agricultural needs with the economic, social, and environmental impact of undamming the dam to restore Hetch Hetchy.

A view of Hetch Hetchy near O'Shaughnessy Dam. FRED GEBHART

Coming Back: California Bighorn Sheep

More than a century ago, hundreds of bighorn sheep roamed the Sierra. Hunting, disease, and competition for food by domestic sheep destroyed the bighorn population. Now that the bighorns are officially endangered, there is an effort under way to reestablish them in the Yosemite area. One dozen sheep were reintroduced to Yosemite from the southern Sierra in 1986, and today they are occasionally sighted along the eastern edge of the park beside Highway 120 East, beyond Tuolumne Meadows, and outside the park on the east side. Keep your eyes peeled for bighorns—short and stocky, weighing up to 220 pounds—above 10,000 feet. For more information, contact Sierra Nevada Bighorn Sheep Foundation, P.O. Box 1183, Bishop, CA 93514; www.sierrabighorn.org.

open 7:00 A.M. to 9:00 P.M. during the summer, 8:00 A.M. to 7:00 P.M. in the fall, and 8:00 A.M. to 5:00 P.M. in the winter. The road is closed at all other times to protect San Francisco's water supply. It may sometimes be closed due to snow in midwinter, and vehicles more than 25 feet are prohibited at all times, due to the narrowness of the road.

At 3,900 feet, Hetch Hetchy is quite hot in the summertime and delightful for hiking in spring and fall. Spring wildflower displays are among the most beautiful in the entire park, and you can hike here very early in the season, when the Tioga Road trailheads are still under a blanket of snow. May is the best month for purple larkspur, the gauzy-pink farewell-to-spring, and harlequin lupine. The Hetch Hetchy Valley's first inhabitants, the Ahwahneechee and Paiute tribes, referred to a certain species of grass with edible seeds as Hatchatchie.

The reservoir is ringed with granite formations and high cliff faces, and you can easily view waterfalls from a footpath on top of the dam. Anglers hook excellent rainbow and brook trout on the Tuolumne River on the stretch above Hetch Hetchy. Each day you can catch and release rainbows and keep five brown trout.

Author, teacher, and longtime Yosemite explorer Suzanne Swedo leads an in-depth, three-day wildflower seminar at Hetch Hetchy in mid-May, including daily walks, botany and flower identification instruction, and enjoyment of the lush, colorful countryside when wildflowers are their best; dorm accommodations and meals are at a nearby camp. Call the Yosemite Association at (209) 379-2321; www.yosemite.org. Cost for the seminar is $165.

CAMPING

There is a walk-in campground at Hetch Hetchy, with a one-night maximum or both before and after a wilderness trip, and no developed, drive-in campgrounds or lodgings. Nearby at Big Oak Flat, you can camp at Hodgdon Meadow Campground, and there are two Forest Service campgrounds on Evergreen Road. See more about camping at Hetch Hetchy in the Campgrounds chapter.

Big Oak Flat Information Station
Highway 120 West and Big Oak Flat Road
(209) 379-1925

This information station issues wilderness permits for overnight camping. You can also come here to make campground reservations and pick up guidebooks, maps, and good advice on exploring the entire national park. There are restrooms here, too.

Crane Flat
Road marker B7

Inside the Highway 120 West entrance to the park, called the Big Oak Flat Entrance, Crane Flat is near the junction with Tioga Road. At 6,200 feet elevation, this is a pretty, forested area with a complex of meadows full of flowers in the summertime. It is a 16-mile drive from here to Yosemite Valley.

There is a campground here open June through September. Nearby you'll find the Tuolumne and Merced Groves of giant sequoias, as well as hiking trails and picnic sites. During the winter in good snow years, this is a great spot for cross-country skiing and snowshoeing. Ranger-led walks and talks are conducted in the summertime. See *Yosemite Today* for days and times.

Fire Lookout

You can visit national park rangers at the Crane Flat Fire Lookout from May through October to see where they used to scan the Hetch Hetchy area for signs of smoke. The lookout buildings' 1931 rustic architecture earned the fire lookout a spot on the National Register of Historic Places. About a mile north of Crane Flat on Highway 120, watch for a dirt road going east. The loop walk is about 3 miles and is moderately strenuous, with a tremendous reward of views at the top. So as not to be disappointed if they are absent, give the rangers a call first: (209) 379-1911. This is also a good cross-country ski trail in wintertime.

Merced Grove of Giant Sequoias
3.5 miles north of Crane Flat off Big Oak Flat Road/Highway 120, road marker B10

In a lovely glade in Moss Creek Valley, accessible only on foot on a 4-mile dirt-road loop, this grove of 20 or so giant sequoias was visited by more people in the 1800s than it is now, as it was once on the main route into Yosemite. This is one place in Yosemite where you can usually get away from people and enjoy a quiet walk in a magnificent forest.

Strawberry Music Festival

Twice a year over the Memorial Day and Labor Day weekends, the popular Strawberry Music Festival happens at Camp Mather near Hetch Hetchy. On the main stage, performers have included Arlo Guthrie, Mark O'Connor, Queen Ida, Leon Redbone, Kathy Mattea, Asleep at the Wheel, Beausoleil, blues and bluegrass bands, zydeco, string quartets, gospel groups, and many more. Notable musicians and performers in the acoustic music world conduct workshops for instruments, vocals, and dance.

At Birch Lake a variety of activities takes place, such as music, storytelling, and arts and crafts for children, and there is a Sunday revival on the lakeside. Literally hundreds of the attendees bring their own instruments to participate in Strawberry Jams. Call or check out the Web site for the schedule of events, lodging, and camping information (209-984-8630, www.strawberrymusic.com).

Tuolumne Grove of Giant Sequoias
Just north of the intersection of Big Oak Flat and Tioga Roads, road marker O1

Within a beautiful old-growth mixed forest, 25 humongous, gorgeous giant sequoias are worth the 2-mile round-trip walk from the parking lot, even with the 600-foot gain in elevation on the return trek. In late spring, Pacific dogwoods light up the grove with oceans of creamy-white blooms, and in the fall their leaves and those of bigleaf maples turn golden and red.

Many of the massive trees are more than 5 feet in diameter and 15 are more than 10 feet across. Look for the super-tall Siamese Twins, joined at their huge base, and the King of the Forest, 114 feet

The Tuolumne Grove of Giant Sequoias protects the tallest and largest trees on Earth.

JOHN POIMIROO

CLOSE-UP

The Great Gray

Yosemite is home to the rare and, in California, the threatened great gray owl, *Strix nebulosa,* one of the most dramatic of the more than 200 species of birds found in the park. At 2 feet long and longer, with a wingspan that can reach 60 inches, this is the largest owl in North America. It has a large, pale, round face, pale yellow eyes, and a curved, sharp beak.

In California the species is primarily restricted to the Yosemite area, where it nests in forests surrounding montane meadows or other forest openings. When quietly observing in mid-elevation west-side meadows, you may hear the distinctive, deep-toned owl's hoot in early mornings, at dusk, and after dark, when the bird hunts.

According to park biologist Les Chow, "Great gray owls in Yosemite can most reliably be viewed at Crane Flat meadow. The owls hunt by establishing a perch near the edge of a meadow and listening for mice as they move through the grass. This requires absolute quiet. Any disturbance forces them to reestablish a new perch and start the process all over again. Consequently, the park does not divulge nesting locations. The best way to see a great gray owl is to wait quietly near the edge of a medium-size to large meadow at dusk. With a little luck and patience, anyone has a reasonably good chance of seeing a great gray."

The owls' diet consists almost entirely of small rodents. The bird can detect prey under the snow by sound alone and will dive into the snow for hidden prey.

The great gray population has been estimated to include fewer than 150 individuals, with a handful of pairs in the national park. A study is under way to document the status, distribution, numbers, habits, and health of the park population of this noble species.

around at the bottom, with bark 20 inches thick. A tunnel tree cut in 1878, the Dead Giant stands in dignity, growing no longer.

The walking path through 25 acres of forest is an old road closed to vehicles. And there is a half-mile, signed nature trail, too.

Camping and Lodging

Dorm-style tent cabins are located at five High Sierra Camps, which can all be reached on foot or horseback. The rustic Tuolumne Meadows Lodge and the Tuolumne Meadows Campground can be reached by car. Along the Tioga Road are four campgrounds: Tamarack Flat, White Wolf, Yosemite Creek, and Porcupine Flat. For more information, see the Campgrounds chapter of this guidebook.

HIKING

From the top of the dam, take the flat trail through the tunnel and along the north edge of the water, about 2 miles, to Tueeulala Fall and Wapama Falls, which both drop a thousand feet, the latter so enthusiastic that it sometimes washes out the trail. Between the falls are two stone monuments—Kolana Rock and Hetch Hetchy Dome—that are reminiscent of those in Yosemite Valley. At 6.5 miles farther on the trail, Rancheria Falls are misty and refreshing. For more on hiking at Hetch Hetchy, see the Hiking and Backpacking chapter of this guidebook.

YOSEMITE IN WINTER

The familiar and intimate aspects of the Sierra that one has learned to love during the long summer days are not obscured by winter snows. Rather the grand contours and profiles of the range are clarified and embellished under the white splendor; the mountains are possessed of a new majesty and peace. There is no sound of streams in the valleys; in place of the far-off sigh of waters is heard the thunder-roar of avalanches, and the wind makes only faint and brittle whisper through the snowy forests. . . ."
—Ansel Adams, *Sierra Club Bulletin,* 1931

Whether you live an hour's drive from the national park or a long airline flight away, nothing will make your cares seem so distant as the winter world of Yosemite. The lush forest cover along the Merced River becomes a lacy, crystalline corridor, the bare trees glazed in ice. With boundless visibility in the brisk, effervescent air, visitors enjoy more opportunities to view wildlife, including coyotes, mule deer, and raccoons. Brushed with snow and ice, granite cliffs and crags glitter in the sun, turning pink when the sun sets. Snow pillows and ice sheets line the riverbanks, soft footings for Half Dome, reflected in the slow-moving water. El Capitan is the Snow King, an immense iceberg glowering beneath the azure bowl of sky.

Waterfalls range from wispy to completely dry. When the winter sun melts the ice dams on Yosemite Falls in the mornings, they break with a haunting, soft boom, and for a few seconds, the falls are gorged with water, as if in spring.

An exciting time to tour and photograph the valley is just as a storm is clearing. Some of the most famous photos and paintings of Yosemite were created when clouds and mist wreathed the famous monoliths, such as in Ansel Adams' photograph "Clearing Winter Storm," which was taken from the road at the Wawona Tunnel.

Winter is the coziest time of year, indoors. You can sip a hot buttered rum while toasting your toes at the fireplace in the Yosemite Lodge at the Falls Mountain Room Lounge, with the namesake falls a whisper beyond the tall windows. The glow of stained glass warms contented guests in the Great Lounge of The Ahwahnee as they gaze at the blazing logs in one of the giant-size fireplaces. Lanternlight gleams in the tents of Curry Village. Lodging rates are the lowest of the year in the winter, and Ski & Stay packages at Yosemite Lodge at the Falls, The Ahwahnee, the Wawona Hotel, and Curry Village are money-savers.

With moderate winter temperatures and at 4,000 feet in elevation, the valley receives about 29 inches of snow through the season, just enough to lightly decorate the landscape. It is a rare winter day when valley roads are impassable. The average daytime temperature at this elevation is in the low 50s in midwinter, and skies are often sparkling and sunny. You will find that the winter sun shines on the northern walls of the valley, warming the trails and making that side more comfortable for midday walks and even picnics on the boulders.

At 7,200 feet, Yosemite's Badger Pass Ski Area gets about 180 inches annually, and the road to the ski area there is nearly always plowed and passable. At Badger, five lifts take skiers to the 8,000-foot summit for downhill skiing, and there is cross-country skiing, snowboarding, snow tubing, and snowshoeing. A skier's bus makes it unnecessary for you to drive your own vehicle.

The national park is open all year, and when the snow flies, the number of visitors

Winter Driving in Yosemite

Winter weather in Yosemite Valley is generally mild, although there are days when chains are required on one or more of the gateway highways. On one snowy evening in the Sierra, I skidded off the road and was stuck on the roadside for an hour or so in a blizzard, waiting for a tow truck. Fortunately, I had warm clothes, a flashlight, and road flares because my car was on a sharp turn, not too visible from the road, and not safe to sit in. I waited in the wintry weather. Not fun, but a good lesson in being prepared. Before you leave home, check the antifreeze, battery, brakes, lights, emergency flashers, tires, and wiper blades. Always carry chains and a basic kit of emergency tools and supplies, including:

- November 1 through March 31, carry tire chains that fit your tires, even with 4WD
- Tool kit, road flares, battery booster cables, small shovel, flashlight
- Extra clothing, blankets or sleeping bags, water, protein bars
- A bag of sand or kitty litter (to get your car out of slush and snow banks)
- Ice scraper and antifreeze window-washing solution
- Lock de-icer and extra car key

Remember to take your time in the wintertime. Driving to and within the park may take longer in stormy conditions and on icy roads. Take care to give yourself extra time, and check road conditions before you leave and along the way. Travel with a full tank of gas in case you find it necessary to change routes or you encounter a traffic delay. Stop frequently at safe turnouts to clean your windshield and windows. If snow or ice is on the roadway, drive slower than the speed limit and stay well back of vehicles ahead. Or relieve yourself of the stress of winter driving by taking YARTS (see Getting Here, Getting Around chapter).

—Karen Misuraca

drops dramatically and outdoor activities center around Yosemite's Badger Pass, Yosemite Valley, Crane Flat, and the Mariposa Grove. With icicle-clad Half Dome looking on, skating is fun to try or to watch at the outdoor rink in Curry Village. Stay warm on motorcoach tours, or take a brisk, guided nature walk or photography walk. A wide variety of indoor talks, shows, tours, and events takes place all winter long; see *Yosemite Today*.

The lowest elevation, driest highway into the park in winter is Highway 140 from Merced to the Arch Rock entrance. Highways 120 (on the west side of the Sierra) and 41 are often open, too, although they may require chains. The eastern entrance to the park on Highway 120, over the Tioga Road, is closed all winter.

If you are nervous about driving on icy roads, take the two-hour narrated winter sight-seeing tour of Yosemite Valley in a comfortable motorcoach with large windows. You can also get from the valley to Wawona and Badger Pass by bus.

Dress in layers for outdoor expeditions. As you get steamed up, you'll peel off hats and jackets. When clouds hide the sun and it starts to snow, you'll put them back on. It's a good idea to carry a daypack or backpack in which to store extra clothing, water, a trail map, and snacks.

Before setting out to explore the park in the wintertime, call (209) 372-0200 for current road and weather information; for ski conditions, call (209) 372-1000.

BACKCOUNTRY TOURING

Tioga Pass Resort
P.O. Box 7, Lee Vining, CA 93541
(209) 372-4471
www.tiogapassresort.com

Guests return year after year to this, their favorite rustic wilderness lodge, located 1 mile from the East Gate (Tioga Pass) Entrance of the park. At 9,641 feet elevation, the place is popular with cross-country skiers who ski throughout the region from here, from the Saturday before Christmas until the last Sunday in April. Fit, experienced skiers love the endless vertical feet of chutes and bowls throughout the Ansel Adams Wilderness, the lakes basin, and around Mount Dana.

In midwinter, when the road to the lodge is snowed in, you may have to ski with your pack about 6 miles to the resort. Conditions permitting, lodge staff will meet you at the gate and haul you and your pack to the snow line.

The resort consists of cabins with kitchens, motel units, and dorms, and there is a restaurant and a little grocery store. Think about crackling woodstoves, deep comfy chairs, books, games, and a video library, with home-cooked meals. In the winter, rates per person in cabins start at $145; dorm accommodations are $140, with discounts for multidays and midweek, with hearty meals included.

Yosemite Guides
P.O. Box 650, El Portal, CA 95318
(209) 379-9111
www.yosemiteguides.com

Some of the region's best-known and most-experienced High Sierra guides lead Nordic, alpine, snowshoeing, and snowboarding wilderness tours for all ages and abilities. Lodging, equipment, and meals are included, plus instruction in backcountry survival skills, avalanche avoidance, route-finding, and emergency shelters. These are custom, small-group tours in the Tioga Pass and Mount Hoffman areas of the park, with expeditions also to Rock Creek Canyon on the east side of the park. Ask about the hot tubs!

Call well ahead to reserve space in the annual Memorial Day Classic backcountry ski tour on the east side of Yosemite, with great descents and glorious late-winter scenery in spring conditions. Guides work with skiers of varying abilities on technique improvement, avalanche awareness, snow shelters, and route selection, so that everyone has an awesome time. You join up with the group on Friday night in Bridgeport or Saturday morning in Lee Vining, departing for home in the late afternoon on Monday.

CROSS-COUNTRY SKIING

In and around the national park are enough scenic ski trails for a lifetime of winters. Within the park are 350 miles of accessible trails and roads, more than 90 miles of marked trails with 25 miles of machine-groomed trails and skating lanes, with no trail fees. Track and skating lanes are groomed from Badger Pass to Glacier Point (a 21-mile round-trip); a 1.8-mile track runs to scenic Old Badger Summit.

You can also join a small group and a ranger for a guided trek to Glacier Point for an overnight. Just outside the South Gate entrance to the park, Goat Meadow and Beasore Road are favorite Nordic ski areas.

The Yosemite Cross-Country Ski Center and Ski School offers Learn-to-Ski packages, with two-hour lessons and equipment rental, for $31. For $53 you can sign up for a Tuesday, Thursday, or Saturday guided, half-day ski tour from Badger Pass to a variety of spots, depending on interest and weather conditions. Telemark and cross-country skating lessons are also available.

A cross-country skier has Glacier Point Road to himself near Yosemite's Badger Pass Ski Area.

JOHN POIMIROO

Crane Flat to Tuolumne Grove and Gin Flat
Big Oak Flat Road/Highway 41 and the Tioga Road

The relatively easy trail follows the old Big Oak Flat Road 2 miles downhill to the Tuolumne Grove of giant sequoias; it is a 500-foot gain in elevation on the return. Ski another mile from the grove to the wide-open, beautiful meadow at Gin Flat. Often, you can walk this snowy trail easily in waterproof boots.

Glacier Point Hut Overnight
(209) 372-8444

For a winter adventure of a lifetime, sign up for the guided, two-day ski tour to Glacier Point. The terrain is flat and easy, and guides provide instruction for all ages and abilities, although some experience is necessary. As long as everyone is of at least intermediate ability, if your family or group is of various levels of expertise and fitness, this is a nice choice. And your guide will be keeping track of each participant. This is a popular adventure for many people, so reserve well in advance.

Guides provide trail snacks and prepare dinner and breakfast for you at the hut. After a day of skiing, stay in dorm-style bunks in the historic hut that has been restored to grandeur with massive beams in a high cathedral ceiling and a big stone fireplace (in summer, it's the Glacier Point Lodge gift shop and snack bar).

You can carry your own sleeping bags or rent the ones already at the hut; liners are provided. Cost is $160 to $192 per person per night, including meals and wine; $240 to $288 for two nights. A package, including an all-day lesson at Yosemite's Badger Pass, a preparatory day of touring, equipment rental, and the overnight, is $245.50.

Glacier Point Trail
From Badger Pass, head out on 10.5 miles of machine-groomed track, one-way, to spectacular Glacier Point, and/or take one or more of the groomed and ungroomed loops along the way. It takes the average skier about four to five hours, one-way.

Mariposa Grove of Giant Sequoias
36 miles south of Yosemite Valley via Highway 41, 2 miles from the South Gate Entrance
Obtain a wilderness permit to ski or snowshoe through and/or camp among the magnificent sequoias. The trail from the parking lot to the grove is 2 miles, one-way, and moderately strenuous.

Ostrander Hut
Ostrander Hut Reservations
P.O. Box 545, Yosemite, CA 95389
(209) 372-0740
www.ostranderhut.com
At 8,500 feet in an idyllic glacial cirque on the edge of beautiful Ostrander Lake stands a two-story stone chalet built in 1941 by the Civilian Conservation Corps to shelter cross-country skiers. A 10-mile ski from Badger Pass, the building provides basic overnight accommodations and cooking facilities, sleeping 25 people in bunks. You bring your own sleeping gear (mattresses are provided), food, a water filter, and be prepared to haul water from the lake in buckets.

On a given day, ski conditions can be fine for intermediates, or it may be a heck of a hard way to go; be advised that only experienced, hardy skiers should make the trek, either on skis or snowshoes. Although a ranger lives at the hut in the wintertime, solely for the purpose of rescuing stranded skiers, the ranger takes on the attitude of a bear awakened from hibernation when called upon to brave a snowstorm to find you.

The cost is $20 per person per night, and a drawing is held for reservations in early November; you can start calling December 1. Check out the Web site for detailed descriptions and personal stories. If you are up for it, the ski to Ostrander through the spectacular, surrounding wilderness is a trip you won't ever forget. The hut is open from late December to early April, depending on snow conditions.

A wonderful book was written by Howard Weamer, the ranger who has spent nearly three decades guarding Ostrander Hut and aiding skiers. Look for *The Perfect Art: The Ostrander Hut and Ski Touring in Yosemite* in retail stores in the park, or order it from the Yosemite Bookstore. Weamer leads fine-art photo workshops and guides photo backpacker trips.

Tuolumne Meadows Ski Hut
(209) 372-8444
On a first-come-first-served basis, you can bunk at this ski hut; during peak months it may be full, so be prepared to spend the night out. The Yosemite Cross-Country Ski Center and Ski School offers a six-day Tuolumne Meadows Ski Hut Tour package with day touring around Tuolumne Meadows, lodging at the hut, a guide, and meals for $800. A wilderness permit is required for overnight winter travel; you can register at the hut.

DOWNHILL SKIING AND SNOWBOARDING

Yosemite's Badger Pass Ski Area
6 miles from the Chinquapin turnoff on Highway 41, 22 miles from Yosemite Valley
(209) 372-8430
www.badgerpass.com
The oldest ski resort in the state, Yosemite's Badger Pass opened in 1935 and is still one of the best ski mountains in the country for adult beginners and intermediates, and especially for kids learning to ski. It is a good idea to take the comfortable, free shuttle buses from your

The Legendary Badger Pass Booster

When he arrived here from French Canada in 1947 as a 28 year old, Nic Fiore spoke little English. He came for one winter to teach skiing and forgot to go home. The patriarch of Yosemite's Badger Pass and its most avid promoter of skiing, Fiore taught an estimated 100,000 people to ski. Grandchildren and even great-grandchildren of his early students are now Badger Pup ski schoolers.

When Fiore first set eyes on Yosemite, Badger had only rope tows and a T-bar. It was nearly 20 years before chairlifts were installed. Helping to develop steady clientele for the ski area, he conducted dry-land ski lessons on a football field in Fresno every fall for more than 30 years. During the summers, he was director of the High Sierra Camps in the Tuolumne High Country, running 8 to 10 miles between the camps just because he liked to run.

He took over as director of the ski school at Badger Pass in 1956 and by the 1970s was a prominent figure in the sport nationwide. The Professional Ski Instructors of America voted him the Most Valuable Ski Instructor, and he was elected to the U.S. National Ski Hall of Fame, among other awards.

Fiore loves to tell of one night in the 1970s when Badger Pass got snowed in, making it impossible for skiers to head home at the end of the day. All of them, about 200 people, stayed overnight, drinking up all the hot chocolate, singing songs into the night, and finally sleeping on the floor in their ski clothes.

Fiore is an official "Ski Ambassador," and always says, "Yosemite is absolutely the best place in the world to learn to ski."

accommodations up the (sometimes icy) hill to Badger Pass.

Five lifts take skiers to 10 runs, topping out at 8,000 feet; 85 percent of the slopes are designed for beginner and intermediate skiers. The emphasis is on friendly, non-intimidating instruction at both the downhill and the cross-country ski schools. Snowshoeing is another popular activity.

Except on holiday weekends, you won't wait in lift lines. The dining decks and all facilities are just steps away from the lifts and school meeting places. There are also a general store, a bar, restaurants, and a sundeck overlooking the action. Yosemite's Badger Pass is open daily from 9:00 A.M. to 4:30 P.M., mid-December through late March, depending on weather and snow.

i

Baby-sitting in the Badger Pups Den is available for kids three to nine years old for $8.00 per hour or $50.00 per day; children must be toilet trained. Parents are required to lunch with their kids. Nutritious snacks are provided midmorning and midafternoon (209–372–8430).

Compared to most ski resorts in the Sierra, prices for everything at Yosemite's Badger Pass are reasonable. All-day adult lift tickets are $38, or $28 for a half-day (noon to 4:00 P.M.). A child's lift ticket costs $15 for a full day; $11 for a half-day. For 24-hour ski conditions, call (209) 372–1000, ext. 1. The Guaranteed Learn to

Ski package includes beginner lessons, equipment rental, and lift ticket—what a deal for $59, or $49 for a child! Private lessons for a group of four are just over $28 per person an hour. The Guaranteed Learn to Snowboard Package includes two group lessons, equipment, and a lift ticket for $69, and $59 for a child. If you still can't hack it after a second lesson, come back for more instruction for free.

You can arrive in nothing but your parka, hat, and gloves (and maybe some ski pants) and rent everything, including cross-country telemark boots, skating skis, downhill skis, boots, poles, snowboards and boots, and sleeping bags for snow camping. Wilderness permits for overnight travel from Badger Pass can be acquired at the A-Frame building.

Badger Pass Ski Bus

A free shuttle bus to Yosemite's Badger Pass Ski Area departs twice each morning from Curry Village, The Ahwahnee, Yosemite Village, and the Yosemite Lodge at the Falls, starting at 8:00 A.M. Return buses leave Yosemite's Badger Pass at 2:00 and 4:00 P.M. Allow at least one hour for the one-way trip.

Badger Pups

This is the best place in the world for kids ages four to six to learn to downhill ski. Since the day it opened decades ago, Badger has hired instructors who love kids and love to teach them to ski. For $39 little kids get a one-hour group lesson, equipment rental, and Turtle Rope Tow ticket; two-hour group lessons are $59, with a Bruin Chair Lift ticket.

Badger Pass Restaurants

Sliders Grab-N-Go on the main floor of the day lodge is where you get fast snacks and lunches to take outside, including pizza, hamburgers, deli sandwiches, salads, soups, and chili. In the Snowflake Room, sit down for the same menu, plus wine, beer, and cocktails. Check out the great photos of old-time skiers and their vintage equipment.

ICE-SKATING

Since 1928, the Curry Village Ice Rink in the shadow of Glacier Point has been a fun place to be from mid-November through March. While taking in the view of Half Dome in its icy winter coat, you can sidle into the warming hut, hang out at the fire pit, have a hot drink and a snack, or rent skates and waltz around the rink.

Daily skating sessions (subject to weather conditions) are offered from 3:30 to 6:00 P.M. and 7:00 to 9:30 P.M. weekdays. On weekends the rink is open for a morning session from 8:30 to 11:00 A.M. and an afternoon session from noon to 2:30 P.M. Skating is $6.50 per adult, per session, and $5.00 for children. Skate rental is $3.25, including free helmets. For more information, call (209) 372-8341.

SLEDDING

Sledding, except for child-pull sleds, is not allowed at the Badger Pass Ski Area. Saucer rentals are available for free snow play at the Curry Village toboggan hill. There is a free, developed snow play area, and rentals are available at Crane Flat on Highway 120 and at another snow play area at Goat Meadow, a half mile outside the South Gate/Highway 41 entrance to the park. See sidebar for safe sledding tips.

SLEIGH RIDES

On weekends and during the winter holidays, horse-drawn sleighs depart hourly from near the Tenaya Lodge at Yosemite, just outside the south entrance to the national park. Bells jingle and you can see your breath as the white-maned horses pull the sleigh down forest-lined Jackson Road. Call (559) 683-7611 for reservations, or go to www.yosemitetrails.com; cost is $20 for adults, $15 for kids. There are no sleighs at Yosemite's Badger Pass.

Skaters at the Curry Village Ice Rink enjoy a breathtaking view of Half Dome. JOHN POIMIROO

Safe Sledding

- Choose a snow play area with a long, gentle slope.
- Slow down! The faster you go, the less control you have.
- Stop or slow down by leaning or falling to the side. If you stick a foot or an arm into the snow, you may end up with a broken or dislocated limb.
- Hit the slope one at a time. The more people on a saucer, sled, or toboggan, and the more people on the slope, the higher the danger of injury.
- Small children riding in front or in the laps of others are vulnerable to injury during stops or spills.

SNOW CAMPING

Four campgrounds in the park are open during the winter: Upper Pines, Camp 4, Wawona, and Hodgdon Meadow. Call (800) 436-7275 for reservations at Upper Pines; the others are first-come, first-served in the winter.

To learn the fundamentals of snow camping and winter survival, spend a day and a night near Badger Pass with experienced guides. For more information, go to the Cross-Country Ski Center and Ski School at Yosemite's Badger Pass, or call (209) 372-8444.

SNOW TUBING

A snow tubing area at Yosemite's Badger Pass, near the Turtle Rope Tow, is a winter playground offering a safe, fun experience for kids and nonskiing adults. The 100-yard tubing hill has a slope of 20 degrees, with a generous run-out and stopping berm at the bottom. Snow grooming machines ensure a smooth ride.

Snowshoe and hike, if you like, on snowy roads and groomed trails, but take care not to walk or snowshoe in the carved Nordic ski tracks—this will ruin the tracks for skiers.

Two-hour tubing sessions are scheduled twice daily: at 11:30 A.M. and 2:00 P.M. Each session is $11 per person, including equipment; you are not permitted to use your own tubes or sliding devices, and a parent must accompany children aged 10 and younger.

SNOWMOBILING

Whisky Snowmobile Trail, on Whisky Ridge above North Fork, on the south side of the park, is a 35-mile, USDA Forest Service marked trail through the forest following existing roads. For more information, call (559) 297-0706. Other roads accessing the national forest provide good starting points for snowmobiling and other winter sports. You can rent snowmobiles at Pines Village at Bass Lake and drive out Beasore Road to the snow line, where the fun begins. Keep in mind that there is no snow removal on national forest roads.

SNOWSHOEING

A popular mode of winter transport in Yosemite since the 19th century, snowshoeing is a delightful way to get into the spectacular wintertime landscape. And it's easier than you might imagine. If you can walk, you can snowshoe, with the new, high-tech, streamlined, lightweight equip-

ment. The best areas for snowshoeing are in Yosemite Valley, at Crane Flat, in the Mariposa Big Trees, and at Badger Pass.

Full Moon Snowshoe Walks

From December through March, during the four days preceding and the night of the full moon, a naturalist ranger leads small groups on a winding, 2.5-mile trail through a sparkling pine forest to a ridge to watch the moon rise over a flotilla of mountain peaks—quite a breathtaking vista. The wintertime activities of animals are described, and tales of moony folklore are told. The snowy landscape is lit up almost as bright as day, and the heavens are scattered with stars right down to the horizon.

You can be a first-time snowshoer on this trek, although the walk is moderately strenuous and is not recommended for children under the age of eight; it takes about two hours. Cost is $14.75 including rental of snowshoes. Sign up at the Yosemite Lodge at the Falls Tour Desk or call (209) 372-1240. Check *Yosemite Today* for dates and times, which depend on the moonrise.

Guided Snowshoe Walks

The daily ranger-led, interpretive snowshoe walks at Yosemite's Badger Pass (from mid-December through early April) move at the pace of the slowest person. The cost is a $5.00 "maintenance donation" that goes to provide the equipment that is included for snowshoers on these walks. Tours take about two hours, and you can just show up. Wear warm clothes that can be peeled off and any kind of waterproof boots for this moderately strenuous trek. Although snowshoes are provided, the sizes available are not recommended for children under 10 years of age (209-372-8430).

Head Out on Your Own

You can rent snowshoes from the Yosemite Cross-Country Ski School Center at Badger Pass or from the Yosemite Mountaineering Center at Curry Village, when snow conditions are appropriate.

i

If you are just moderately fit or a beginning snowshoer, stick to the groomed trails. Breaking your own trail into the wilderness may be an adventurous notion, but it will take the stuffing right out of you, pronto.

Maps of the marked trails are available, and staff members will help you select a trail that suits your abilities. The cost is $15.00 for all day and $10.50 for half-day rental (209-372-8444).

WINTER EVENTS AND TOURS

California's longest-running citizens' cross-country race is run from Badger Pass in March, and the just-for-fun "Ancient Jocks Race" for skiers older than age 30 features a beverage stop halfway. In December at the Pioneer Yosemite History Center in Wawona, costumed docents recount early Yosemite winters, and there is caroling by candlelight and hot cider and cocoa in the old barn.

If your family likes storytelling, face painting, crafts, winter ecology walks, and hot cocoa, you will want to join national park interpretive staff for "Open House for Families," a free afternoon of activities scheduled on winter holidays. You can drop by anytime during the three-hour open house at the Curry Village Guest Lounge. The low-key event is geared for families with children ages fourteen and younger, accompanied by at least one adult. See *Yosemite Today* for dates and time.

An expert photographer leads small groups on winter photography walks in Yosemite Valley. On an easy walk, you will photograph snow-dressed pines and icy waterfalls, dramatic bare aspens and cottonwoods, and the reflection of the silvery monoliths in the Merced River (209-372-4413, www.anseladams.com).

The end of the season is heralded by a big ski carnival in early April, Yosemite's

Badger Pass Springfest, with novelty races for all ages, snow sculpting, a barbecue, a costume contest, and snow sculptures. Fun races include the kids' obstacle and slalom courses, a dual slalom race, and the annual "dummy" race (209-372-8430, www.badgerpass.com).

WINTER SKI AND STAY PACKAGES

Special winter lodging and ski packages, as low as $68 per person per day, make Yosemite's Badger Pass one of the least expensive ski resorts in the state. Most packages include two nights lodging, two all-day lift tickets, and a full breakfast. Kids under six stay, ski, and have breakfast free. Call (559) 253-5635 or visit www.yosemitepark.com.

Winter Ski and Stay package prices are based on two nights, adult double occupancy. At the Wawona Hotel, the packages start at $477.50 with bath, $335.50 without in-room bath; at Yosemite Lodge at the Falls, from $337; and at The Ahwahnee, from $911.55. For Curry Village Ski and Stay, a cabin with bath starts from $289.80 or $287.80 without bath; tent cabins, the economical option, are $249.80, or from $253.80 if heated. For reservations, call (559) 252-4848 or visit www.yosemitepark.com.

WINTER WALKS

Most valley trails are open and relatively dry during the winter. Usually, just a dusting of snow remains on the ground, so with boots, you can get around on foot just fine. After a few days of dry weather, the Yosemite Falls Trail is a great winter hike. Fit hikers carry their snowshoes up the John Muir Trail to Little Yosemite Valley and trek around, enjoying the incredible views.

The low elevation of Wawona, about 4,000 feet, means that walking trails in that area of the park are usually quite accessible.

LODGING AND RENTALS

Delaware North Companies Parks & Resorts at Yosemite, Inc. (DNC) manages 1,253 guest units in the park, from rustic tent cabins in the High Country to luxurious suites in The Ahwahnee. Most of these accommodations are sold out a year in advance for July and August and for weekends and holidays other months of the year. The average stay is two nights, and some accommodations are so popular that reservations are doled out by lottery, such as those for the High Sierra Camps.

Rates range from about $70 per night for a basic tent cabin with nearby bathroom, to $379 per night for a room at The Ahwahnee. The least requested are the tent cabins; the most difficult to get in high season are the rooms at The Ahwahnee.

The best time to get a reservation for a specific date is one year and one day ahead; the reservations office opens at 8:00 A.M., Pacific Standard time, seven days a week; you can also check availability and make bookings on the Web site. Try for cancellations at 30, 21, 15, and 7 days out from your desired date. Your best bet may be during the off-season months: November, January, February, and March. Upon your arrival in the park, you may be able to get an upgrade on your lodging type if cancellations have come in.

Many visitors have no idea that more than 100 privately owned cabins and homes are available to rent within the southern section of the park near Wawona. See the end of this chapter for information. For more lodging information, see the four chapters on gateway highways.

DNC Parks & Resorts at Yosemite, Inc.
Central Reservations Office
6771 North Palm Avenue
Fresno, CA 93704
(559) 252-4848
www.yosemitepark.com

PRICE CODE

The average nightly rates for two adults at the lodgings listed are indicated in this section by a dollar sign ($) ranking, according to the following chart. High-season, summer rates may vary from winter rates. Unless otherwise noted, lodgings accept credit cards.

$	$49–$75
$$	$76–$124
$$$	$125–$175
$$$$	$176 and up

LODGING

The Ahwahnee **$$$$**
Shuttle stop 3
(559) 252-4848 (room reservations),
(209) 372-1489 (dining reservations),
(209) 372-1407 (front desk)

A stunning masterpiece of Art Deco and California Craftsman architecture, The Ahwahnee hotel opened July 14, 1927, and has been one of the icons of Yosemite Valley ever since. This is a "must-see" tourist attraction and a fabulous place to stay. Those who have not stayed here after 1996 will be delighted with the complete redecoration of the rooms and cottages. Priceless Native American baskets and artifacts, historic photos and artworks, and Persian and American Indian rugs create a museum-like atmosphere (notice the three Swedish watercolors near the front desk and the large vintage photos of cowboys and Native Americans in the Great Lounge). The landscaping was originally designed by the famous architect Frederick Law Olmsted.

Most of the 99 guest rooms have glorious views through big windows and are done up in "mountain lodge" style, with oakleaf-motif draperies and upholstery, Native American designs, comfy sofas and chairs, interesting original art, and nice, if small, bathrooms. Some are parlor rooms with separate sitting rooms. Some boast north-facing views of Royal Arches, a striking, striated slab that shows how glaciers broke off layers of granite in a process called exfoliation, leaving rounded sheets and strips parallel to the valley floor. A 1,000-foot waterfall to the left of the arches adds to the beauty in the fullness of springtime, but is dry in summer, while skyscraper-like Washington Column looms, 1,920 feet high, on the right. Behind the column in the near distance, North Dome echoes the arches' geologic formations. Room rates start at $379; ask about special event and ski packages.

On the grounds of The Ahwahnee are 24 spacious cottages in a grove of tall pines near the river. Insiders know that the cottages rent for the same nightly rate as the hotel rooms. Fireplaces, Native American-themed accessories, and elegant, yet rustic, country-style interiors make the cottages the top accommodations in the park.

Among thoughtful amenities are honor libraries, in-room coffee makers, newspapers at your door, refrigerators, bathrobes, concierge service, valet parking, turn-down service, and room service. Outdoors in a lyrical meadow and forest setting, guests enjoy a swimming pool and tennis courts.

An interpretive historian conducts free tours of The Ahwahnee, relating the architecture, art, famous guests, and historic role of the hotel. You and the kids can listen to evening fireside storytelling in the Great Lounge, too. See **Yosemite Today** *for days and times.*

With a 34-foot-high ceiling and baronial chandeliers, the 130-foot-long dining room is world famous for its impressive size, massive sugar pine log beam structure, and views of the landscape through the sky-high windows. A pianist plays at dinner, and the food is better than it has ever been in the history of the hotel—top-notch American fare with local ingredients when possible, and a good wine list. The elaborately decorated dining room glows with candles and merriment every Christmas season during the old-English-style Bracebridge Dinners. Yosemite's Vintners' Holidays and Yosemite's Chefs' Holidays are popular in the wintertime (209-372-5635). The average employee on the wait staff is an 18-year veteran, and the service is exceptionally friendly.

The Ahwahnee Bar, in rich fabrics and warm colors, has booths in a cozy alcove and historic photographs and art. Light meals are served in the bar, and the Sunday "carvery" brunch buffet is a bargain. Light meals are also served on the outdoor terrace, and guests enjoy afternoon tea in the Great Lounge.

The large gift shop is a good place to get souvenirs and books. You can walk or bike on myriad trails from the front door of the hotel, or hop on a shuttle bus to tour the park.

The Bracebridge Dinner

Based on Washington Irving's 1820 tale, "The Sketch Book," about Christmas Day at Bracebridge Hall in Yorkshire, England, the three-hour Bracebridge Dinner re-creates the lively, colorful holiday entertainments of an English squire of the 17th century. Each year since 1927, during the Christmas season, the merriment, the music, the lavish feast, and even the dress are re-created in a series of December evenings at The Ahwahnee Dining Room.

Guests enjoy an elaborate seven-course banquet, and entertainers perform in old English costume. Dr. Donald B. Tresidder, then president of the Yosemite Park and Curry Co. and later president of Stanford University, played the first Squire Bracebridge, the pageant's main character. Famed Yosemite photographer Ansel Adams and others later rewrote the original program, which remains to this day true to Adams's score of classic carols, old English traditions, and music of the Middle Ages.

The eight individual dinners are often sold out a year in advance, and reservation is first-come, first-served by phone (unlike the lottery system of the past). Call (559) 253-5676 or (559) 253-5604 in early February for the following December. The Bracebridge Dinner tickets are $330 per person. Ask for the Bracebridge Dinner lodging packages at The Ahwahnee and Yosemite Lodge at the Falls.

Curry Village **$-$$**
Shuttle stops 13B (registration office), 13A (Curry Village Recreation Center), 14 (Curry Village parking lot)
(209) 252-4848 (reservations), (209) 372-8333, (209) 372-8334

Sprinkled for a half-mile under incense cedars, Kellogg oaks, and Jeffrey pines in the eastern end of the valley at the foot of Glacier Point, Curry Village is the coolest spot in the valley in the summertime and the coldest in the winter. Established in 1899, this is the camp that thousands of people remember from their childhoods. In the summertime expect lots of people; a busy, fun, lively, not-very-quiet atmosphere; and plenty of things to do within walking distance, perfect for families. The village is open spring to fall, and weekends and holidays in the winter.

Scattered strategically under shade trees are 628 units, including 18 standard, very nicely decorated motel rooms with sleeping lofts, 103 wooden cabins with private bath, 80 wooden cabins with central bath, and 427 canvas tent cabins with a central bathhouse. Tent cabins have wood

"Please be Bear Aware" says the warning you'll sign and date when you check into national park lodging. Store scented items, food, snacks, toothpaste, laundry detergent, and chewing gum in your room—or in a "bear box" if you're staying in a Curry Village tent cabin or Housekeeping Camp unit. Each year 600 to 800 vehicles are trashed by bear break-ins.

floors, electricity (but no outlets and no phones), screened windows, and nearby shared restroom/shower facilities. Only half of the tent cabins have wood-burning stoves; the rest have no heating. Linens, blankets, and pillows are provided in all tent cabins. Ask about winter discounts, usually available between November 1 and March 15.

Curry Village is headquarters for outdoor recreation in the valley, including the Yosemite Mountaineering School (September through June); the Mountain Shop, selling and renting state-of-the-art outdoor sports equipment and clothing; bicycle and river raft rental stands in the summer; cross-country ski rentals; and an ice-skating rink in winter. Free shuttle buses and tour buses stop at the Village, and trailheads are nearby.

There are several food outlets (see the Restaurants chapter for details), a gift shop and general store, a large swimming pool with lifeguards, and a post office. Almost daily, interpretive programs and/or entertainment are presented in the Curry Village Amphitheater. And the historic Curry Village Guest Lounge is a wonderful place to sit by the fire or on the porch, reading or making new friends. Take a look at the vintage photos and artifacts around the room.

Housekeeping Camp **$**
Shuttle stop 12
(559) 252-4848

For tent cabins with cooking facilities, see information about Housekeeping Camp in the Campgrounds chapter.

CLOSE-UP

The Quiet Side of The Ahwahnee

The Great Lounge is the immense parlor of The Ahwahnee, where three-story stained-glass windows, a walk-in fireplace, and chandeliers as big as Volkswagens create an impressive, castlelike atmosphere. Guests who happen to wander behind the Great Lounge are delighted to find a clutch of quiet, snug, charming rooms.

The Solarium, where crystalline light streams through the windows, framing views of Yosemite Falls, pristine meadows, and specimen conifers, is an ideal setting for weddings. At the small tables by the windows, play cards or soak up the sun. Notice the beautiful wrought-iron, Art Deco–era floor lamps with parchment shades.

The Winter Club Room recalls the halcyon days of skiing and sledding in the 1930s and 1940s in the old photos displayed around the room; antique skis and snowshoes complete the theme. The view of Half Dome and deer grazing or wandering in the forest meadow may distract you from your armchair reading.

The Lobby, a small museum and gathering place, houses old books on the mantel above a huge fireplace and a display of priceless Paiute baskets.

The snug Mural Room is decorated with a brass fireplace and a wall-length painting by Robert Boardman Howard that depicts local flora and fauna in a style reminiscent of medieval tapestries. Two armchairs sit in front of a window with a view of Upper Yosemite Fall and a grassy clearing where deer graze in the wild strawberries.

In the Great Lounge, large photographs on the walls are fascinating historical documents. The cowboy from the late 1890s is Jim Helm, who was in charge of the stables once located where The Ahwahnee now stands. The Native American man is Chief Leemee (also known as Chris Brown) in a photo taken in the mid-20th century. Taken in 1899, the photo of mother and child shows Yosemite Falls and a traditional packboard used for babies. The same

Tuolumne Meadows Lodge $
Tioga Road, road marker T30
(559) 252–4848 (reservations),
(209) 372–8413 (front desk)

In a lyrical forest setting by the river, summer-only accommodations are in 69 canvas-sided cabins sleeping up to four people, with concrete floors, woodstoves, and no electricity, phones, or plumbing. Showers and restrooms are centrally located; soap and towels are provided. Daily maid service and linens are available for a small fee.

Within walking distance of the lodge are a grocery store, stables, and a tented restaurant serving substantial American fare (see Restaurants chapter). The facilities are basic, the atmosphere is friendly and fun, and the High Country is at your door. You can access the lodge by shuttle bus from Yosemite Valley.

The Ahwahnee shines during the December holiday season. DNC

photographer, Ralph Anderson, took the photo of the Yosemite Indian making a basket and grinding corn. Another image, taken in the late 1800s, is Chief Francisco Jeorgley, with a deerskin around his waist and carrying a bow and arrow.

The ultimate vantage point from which to shoot photos of the Great Room is on the mezzanine at the west end of the room. There is an interesting collection of art, kilim and other rugs, and photos on the walls and a wide opening where you can set up your tripod. On the east mezzanine is another wide opening.

Wawona Hotel **$$-$$$**
Highway 41, 7 miles from the South Gate entrance
(559) 252-4848 (reservations),
(209) 375-6556 (front desk),
(209) 375-1425 (dining reservations)
www.yosemitepark.com.

Riding above Wawona Meadow like an aging, but still glistening, white ocean liner, the oldest resort hotel in the state was built in the 1870s and is in fabulous shape. In an enchanted pine and cedar forest setting are eight white, Victorian-style buildings with wraparound verandas. There is a beautiful small pool, sweeping lawns, a 9-hole golf course, walking trails, tennis, horseback riding, and the Merced River nearby for swimming and fishing. Or you can just sink into a rocker on the covered porch; in the wintertime, the hotel provides blankets to bundle you up while you enjoy the snowy scene. Evenings by the fireplace in the lobby are sweet, while a pianist plays and spins tales of old

At the Wawona Hotel, "Little White" is a small cottage with a porch and three adjoining rooms, perfect for a big family. In the Annex upstairs, room #137 has three beds—a queen-size, a double, and a single. And several rooms in the Annex are connected with baths.

Yosemite. Ask for the printed, self-guided tour of the vintage photos in the lobby, which show the early days when guests arrived on horseback and in stagecoaches on their way to Yosemite Valley and huge sequoias were cut with handsaws. Check the Restaurants chapter for a description of the excellent restaurant.

Families return, year after year, and many family reunions are held here. You can arrange for as many as five connecting rooms. More than a hundred rooms in the vintage buildings and cottages vary in size, and many have been redone with sumptuous fabrics, armoires, new furnishings, and nice bathrooms with amenities, even clawfoot tubs. Some of the 104 rooms are done up in simple, country style, some are rich with Victorian elegance; some have private baths, some are shared. The 16-room Washburn Cottage has some of the nicest rooms. Fortunately, rooms contain no TVs or telephones. Unfortunately, the hotel is open only on weekends and holidays in the off-season; the good news is that winters are mild and beautiful at this elevation. Ask about ski packages and off-season rates.

Within walking distance are a general store, stables, historic attractions, biking and walking trails, and a gas station. Give your car a rest and jump on the free shuttle mid-spring through late fall that goes between the Wawona Store and Pioneer Gift Shop and the Mariposa Grove of Giant Sequoias Big Trees parking lot.

The hotel and the restaurant are closed from December through late March, although they are open during the Christmas holidays. Call to confirm available dates.

On the Fourth of July, the charming, white-painted Wawona Hotel is festooned with red, white, and blue bunting to welcome all comers for old-fashioned fun. Kids love the games—potato sack races, an egg toss, and more—with prizes for all. Parents lounge on the porches in Adirondack chairs while the barbecue heats up. You can choose from hot dogs early in the day or wait for the chuck wagon barbecue served on the lawns in the early evening; the menu offers everything from burgers to steak, chicken, and fish; salads; corn on the cob; beans; dessert; and nonalcoholic beverages. Reservations are not taken, although early arrival is advised (559-252-4848). Most folks stay on for the square dance in the barn of the Pioneer Yosemite History Center.

White Wolf Lodge **$-$$**
1 mile off Tioga Road, between Tuolumne Meadows and Yosemite Valley, road marker T9
(559) 252-4848, (209) 372-8416 (front desk)

This summertime-only headquarters for backcountry trails offers 28 rustic tent cabins and four more cabins with private bath, all in a lovely meadow and forest setting. There is a small general store, stables, and a great old clapboard dining hall that serves simple meals all day. Ranger-led programs and events are scheduled, from nature walks to campfires with storytelling and music, lunch hikes, and, once a week, an "Earth Walk," just for families and kids. Look for the schedules posted at the campgrounds and the lodge. Showers and restrooms are centrally located; soap and towels are provided. The lodge is accessible by shuttle bus from Yosemite Valley.

Yosemite Lodge at the Falls **$$-$$$**
Shuttle stop 8, road marker V4
(559) 252-4848 (reservations),
(209) 372-1240 (tour desk),
(209) 372-1274 (front desk)

If you haven't been here for a few years, you will find it more mountain lodge-like, fresher and nicer, with redecorated rooms and a more developed aesthetic link to the outdoors. There are 245 units, from motel-type rooms with balconies or small patios to rustic cabins, with or without baths. The compound includes a cafeteria, two restaurants, a bar, a post office, gift shops, a swimming pool, a bike rental stand, and an outdoor theater. The lodge is 90 percent booked year-round.

After the devastation of the 1997 flood, buildings within 250 feet of the river were removed and will not be replaced; plans call for a new, 60-room building. Nonnative landscaping is being replaced with native flora.

Near the base of Yosemite Falls in midvalley, the lodge is conveniently located for all valley activities and sights, with shuttle bus and tour bus service at the door, a tour desk, and free nightly programs, from slide shows to historical presentations to entertainment. Just a few hundred yards away are some nice swimming holes in the river, and walking and biking trails start right here.

See the Restaurants chapter for a description of the food outlets.

RENTALS

The Redwoods **$$-$$$$**
P.O. Box 2085, Wawona Station, Yosemite National Park, CA 95389, Chilnualna Falls Road, off Highway 41, Wawona
(888) 225-6666, (209) 375-6666
www.redwoodsinyosemite.com
Choose from more than 125 privately owned cabins and houses to rent in a wooded setting near the river. Homes are in a wide variety of sizes and qualities, all fully furnished and equipped. Rates are from about $117 per night for a small cabin in the off-season to about $662 nightly for a large house sleeping 8 or 10 people in the high season. The Web site shows interior and exterior views, most of which are simple and attractive, although not luxurious. Make reservations for holidays several months ahead; as The Redwoods is just a few miles from Yosemite's Badger Pass, Christmas vacation reservations are popular—call early in the year for the December holidays.

Scenic Wonders **$$-$$$$**
7421 Yosemite Park Way, Yosemite
(888) 296-7364
www.scenicwonders.com
One of several private home and condo rental companies just inside the national park boundary in Yosemite West, Scenic Wonders offers 16 completely furnished mountain homes and 6 condominiums, from $125 per night for two to more than $350 nightly.

Yosemite Peregrine Bed & Breakfast **$$$-$$$$**
7509 Henness Circle, Yosemite
(209) 372-8517
www.yosemitewest.com/peregrine.htm
In a dramatic forest setting, three bed-and-breakfast units have private baths, stone fireplaces, and decks. Cross-country skiing and hiking start from the front door. This is one of the nicest and most popular of the choices at Yosemite West (see below), with more of a bed-and-breakfast style, as guests share a living room and enjoy a complimentary continental breakfast. The largest unit has a double whirlpool tub in the bedroom.

Yosemite West **$$-$$$$**
(559) 642-2211
www.yosemitewest.com
A wide variety of rental accommodations, Yosemite West offers year-round vacation

There is no need to pay a reservation service charge to book accommodations within Yosemite National Park. Use DNC, Inc. the park's concessionaire (559-253-5635; www.yosemitepark.com) or book directly with property owners. You should be prepared, however, to pay state and local county taxes that may add as much as 10 percent to your bill.

A Bear at the Party

Shortly before one wedding at The Ahwahnee, a mother bear nudged her two cubs up into the apple tree and proceeded to teach them how to shake the tree to get the apples. The hotel staff gently urged them away by banging pots and pans and waving their arms, as wedding guests watched from the Solarium.

It is not uncommon for deer to strike elegant poses just beyond the wedding meadow and for coyotes to hide in the trees near the creek.

homes and condominiums in the Wawona area within the national park. The Yosemite West area is about 30 minutes from Yosemite Valley and 8 miles from Yosemite's Badger Pass Ski Area. The Web site shows details and photos of everything from studios to luxury lodge homes. Nightly rates range from $95 for a studio to more than $500 for a spacious, fully equipped home sleeping 10 people. Many of the homes and condos have sundecks with mountain or forest views, fireplaces or wood stoves, and hot tubs or spas; all have fully equipped kitchens. Linens are supplied, and a staff is available 24 hours a day.

Among the rentals available is Camins Log Retreat, a two-story house with log or knotty pine walls and lots of country charm. Cozy quilts warm up the three bedrooms—one with extra-long twin beds, one with a queen, and a master bedroom with king-size bed and private deck.

The Pine Arbor Retreat is a large contemporary home with a fireplace, separate dining room, and spacious, comfortable accommodations for up to 10 people.

WEDDINGS IN THE PARK

Some people have such a nostalgic love for Yosemite that they dream of getting married in the park. Hundreds of weddings are held here every year. The Yosemite Chapel, The Ahwahnee, and the Wawona Hotel are popular venues. Outdoorsy types may get hitched on Glacier Point or Half Dome, at the foot of a waterfall, or in the middle of a pristine alpine meadow in the High Country.

Wedding parties often stay in the park for three or four days, embarking on guided hikes, fishing expeditions, and other activities arranged in advance.

For weddings in the Yosemite Community Church, known to all as the Yosemite Chapel, or at the park's lodgings, wedding bookings are taken from 1 year to no less than 21 days in advance of the date. Call the NPS/Yosemite Office of Special Programs, (209) 379-1854, and DNC Special Functions Office at (559) 253-5673, for more information. You will need a permit to be married in the national park; available online, the application and permit cost $150. Check www.nps.gov/yose/trip/weddings.html, for the permit process, fees, a list of ministers who can officiate at Yosemite Chapel, a link to a number of possible locations within the park, and a link to DNC facilities.

The wedding is limited to three hours and not permitted on Memorial Day weekend, the Fourth of July, or the Labor Day weekend. Wedding parties of more than 50 outside of the DNC facilities require an Event Monitor, with an additional fee. Some unusual restrictions protect national park resources: no meadow or base of giant sequoia weddings, horse-drawn carriages, balloon or butterfly release, or throwing of rice or birdseed. Permits are also required for commercial filming and photography.

The Yosemite Chapel with a fresh dusting of snow is a romantic spot for a wedding. DNC

The Ahwahnee
(209) 372-1407

Most ceremonies are held outdoors in a heavenly grassy area between a century-old apple tree and a gorgeous cedar with Yosemite Falls as a backdrop. With dogwoods and wildflowers in bloom, or when bigleaf maples and oaks are golden, a simple wedding looks like a picture postcard.

Wedding parties of up to about 200 people use three rooms of the hotel tucked behind the Great Lounge. The Solarium has two-story windows overlooking the wedding meadow and is used for dining, receptions, and sometimes for the ceremony itself. The Winter Club Room has a view of Half Dome. And the Mural Room, a warm, wood-paneled space adorned with a beautiful mural and a corner fireplace, is a charming location for a very small wedding; with light streaming in from high windows and snow on the cedars, this is a stunning setting for a winter wedding. Also tucked behind the Great Lounge, the small lounge area, which is used as a reception area, has a huge fireplace. The upper lounge on the mezzanine can be a supervised play area for children who are guests at the wedding—it comes complete with games, videos, and no escape!

The castlelike atmosphere of The Ahwahnee has inspired some wedding parties to dress in elegant medieval costumes. At least one couple climbed Half Dome with their friends, family, and the minister and said their vows at the top before returning for a big hotel reception the following day. Some brides wear rhinestoned sneakers under their gowns, and some wear cowboy boots and Stetson hats.

On the mezzanine above the Great Lounge fireplace is a cupboard filled with albums of photos taken of weddings in all seasons of the year.

Wawona Hotel
(209) 375-6556
Casual and Victorian-theme weddings are popular at the Wawona Hotel, creating picturesque scenes against the quaint, white buildings. Often ceremonies are held on the lawn or at Clark Cottage between the Jeffrey pines, while guests look on from balconies above. Wedding parties and family gatherings at the hotel are limited to 150 guests.

Yosemite Chapel
(209) 372-4831 (church secretary)
Many weddings are held in this sweet, simple chapel in the heart of the valley. Built in 1879, with a slender spire, this chapel is the oldest building in the park still in use. Many couples have the ceremony here, and the reception or party elsewhere in the park.

Yosemite Lodge at the Falls
(209) 372-1274
With a glorious view of Yosemite Falls, the Mountain Room is a beautiful place for a small wedding or a reception, which can also be held outdoors on the small patio, usually in the morning or early afternoon.

CAMPGROUNDS

Every summer, miles of cars line up at dawn at Yosemite National Park's entrance gates, most heading for 1,445 campsites. Of the 13 campgrounds in the park, three of the four camps in Yosemite Valley are filled by reservation months in advance, from May through September, leaving a shortage of campground sites. High-season campers must plan well ahead, try campgrounds on a first-come, first-served basis, or hope for a cancellation. Either way, plan to arrive early in the morning to avoid disappointment.

You might also resort to alternatives in the surrounding region. The park is completely surrounded by national forests, whose lesser-known, often no less attractive and convenient campgrounds are good alternatives to the crowded sites in the park; most national forest campgrounds are first-come, first-served.

National Park Campground Reservations
P.O. Box 1600, Cumberland, MD 21502
(800) 436-PARK (7275),
(888) 530-9796 (TDD),
(301) 722-1257 (International)
http://reservations.nps.gov
Beginning the 15th of each month, you can make campground reservations up to five months in advance of your desired date by telephone (7:00 A.M. to 7:00 P.M. Pacific time), by mail, or on the Web site. For more information and campsite descriptions, call the National Park Campgrounds Office at (209) 372-8502. On the Web site, you can pull up maps of the valley campgrounds and get brief descriptions of individual sites.

You are allowed to camp for no more than 30 days in the park per year. In Yosemite Valley and Wawona, the camping limit is seven days between May 1 and September 15; outside the valley the limit is 14 days during the same months. And remember, you are allowed to park only two vehicles per site, and a maximum of six people, including children, are permitted per site.

If you are unable to obtain a campsite, do not make the mistake of parking overnight on the roadside in the park or setting up camp, even if it's only sleeping bags, in an undesignated spot; you will definitely be rousted out by a highly distressed ranger.

Pets are allowed on leash in all but a few campgrounds. When you make your reservations, take care to mention if you plan to bring a pet.

YOSEMITE NATIONAL PARK CAMPGROUNDS

Unfortunately for those who remember them fondly, Upper and Lower River campgrounds and a portion of Lower Pines Campground were destroyed by the flooding of the Merced River in January 1997. These campgrounds will not be replaced; the area is being restored to meadow, riparian, and oak woodlands. However, plans are under way to increase the number of park campsites.

North, Upper, and Lower Pines Campgrounds are crowded in high season. Although they can be noisy with road traf-

i

The maximum length for RVs is 40 feet, although few sites can accommodate lengths over 35 feet. No hookups are available at Yosemite campgrounds; sanitary dump stations are open all year in Yosemite Valley and in the summer at Wawona and Tuolumne Meadows. Generators may be used sparingly between 7:00 A.M. and 7:00 P.M. Do not connect extension cords to restroom outlets; leave your hair dryer at home!

Big Wall Climbers

Camp 4 Campground in Yosemite Valley was listed with the National Register of Historic Places in February 2003. Considered the birthplace of American big wall climbing, the campground, often called Sunnyside, was the center of rock climbing activity from 1947 to 1970 and today remains a popular gathering place for climbers. Technological advancements and skills developed here made significant contributions at the regional, national, and international levels within the sport. Using Camp 4 as a base, world-renowned pioneer climbers such as Tom Frost, Royal Robbins, and Yvon Chouinard developed modern equipment and techniques and forged new routes in Yosemite. Knowledge and skills were passed on by word of mouth and hands-on climbing expeditions, since few if any manuals or guidebooks were available in the early days, making the base camp a vital meeting ground for training, ascent planning, information and equipment design, and the comradeship that defined the history of the climbing movement. From time to time, some of the famous climbers present talks in Yosemite; see *Yosemite Today* for days and times. The National Park Service refers to it only as Camp 4.

fic and RV generators, they're conveniently located for walking and biking to most public places and trailheads. If your family is interested in the classes and the interpretive hikes and performances scheduled throughout the summer, a valley campground may be your best choice—if you can get a reservation. For quieter, pretty, cool places to camp outside the valley, consider Bridalveil Creek, Wawona, or Tuolumne Meadows Campgrounds.

Backpacker Walk-In Campground
Below Royal Arches at Sugarpine Bridge; shuttle stop 18

Accessed only on foot and offering a one-night stay for those with wilderness permits, this is a first-come, first-served campground for those heading into or out of the wilderness. Check in with rangers at the North Pines campground. The cost is $5.00 per night, and pets are now allowed.

Bridalveil Creek Campground
25 miles from Yosemite Valley on the Glacier Point Road, road marker G4

Give up the crowded valley for solitude and beauty by camping at 7,200 feet. Each of the 110 tent and RV sites here and at other higher elevation camps are provided with "bear lockers," secure boxes where your food can be kept safe from black bears. The overnight fee is $14, and leashed pets are allowed. The campground is open during the summer months on a first-come, first-served basis. Dress warmly in June, as snow may still be on the ground. For avid day-hikers, this is a perfect base camp for treks to Sentinel Dome, Taft Point, Ostrander Lake, and many more destinations within a few hours.

Camp 4 Campground
Shuttle stop 7

Behind Yosemite Lodge at the Falls at the base of the cliffs, Camp 4 is a walk-in campground open all year on a first-come, first-served, per person basis. This means that six people may be placed in each of 35 campsites regardless of the number of people in your party. The campground often fills up before 9:00 A.M. from May through September. In the heart of the action, within sight and sound of vehicles and lots of people, right on the popular walking trail to Lower Yosemite Fall, the camp is a favorite of rock and mountain climbers, a boisterous, young, often exclusive bunch. In fact, Camp 4 is the birthplace of big wall climbing in the United States. Families may feel out of place.

Parking is a few minutes away. The nightly camping fee is $5.00 per person, and pets are not allowed. In midsummer, many avid climbers base their camp in the High Country, at Tuolumne Meadows, while Camp 4 becomes a mecca for rock climbers and for those attempting El Capitan, Half Dome, and massifs in the valley.

Crane Flat Campground
Highway 120 near the Tioga Road Junction, road marker B7

At 6,200 feet altitude near the Tuolumne Grove of Giant Sequoias, about 20 minutes from Yosemite Valley, these 166 sites are open June to September by reservation. The overnight fee is $20 per site, with some RV sites, and pets are allowed on leash. A variety of scheduled, ranger-led programs and events include nature walks, campfires with storytelling and music, lunch hikes, and, once a week, an "Earth Walk" just for families and kids. Look for the posted schedule. The campground is located near a gas station.

Hetch Hetchy Backpackers Campground
Hetch Hetchy Reservoir

With a wilderness permit, you can camp at this 20-site campground for one night on your way into the Hetch Hetchy area and for one more night on your way out. Parking is conveniently nearby, and you will find running water and toilets. The cost is $5.00 per night per person. Travelers on horseback can also camp here.

High Sierra Camps
(559) 253-5674
www.yosemitepark.com

Five developed High Sierra Camps (plus the Tuolumne Meadows Lodge) are located in the Yosemite wilderness in a rough loop, 5.7 to 10 miles apart, at elevations between 7,150 and 10,300 feet. You can hike between them, arrange to take one of the four- or six-day saddle trips, or a five- or seven-day guided hike, all of which overnight at the camps.

Nightly campfire programs, a friendly atmosphere, and spectacular High Country settings make the camps so ideal that people return year after year.

Reservations through the concessionaire, Delaware North Companies Parks & Resorts at Yosemite, Inc. (DNC), must be made well in advance; in fact, they are sold out all summer, and bookings are made by lottery. Lottery application forms are accepted between October 15 and November 30 for the following summer; you get a reply by February 28. Although the High Sierra Camps are initially avail-

i

Hiking in the vicinity of the High Sierra Camps (HSC) and camping on your own? Lodging guests and nonresident hikers can order sack lunches the evening before. Those without HSC lodging may complete a dinner and breakfast "meals-only" lottery application available in early November by calling (559) 252-4848. A maximum of eight spaces (six for "meals-only") may be requested on one lottery application form. Cancellations are filled by a second lottery using applications left after the first round. You can book available spots after the HSCs open on April 1 on a first-come, first-served basis, by calling the High Sierra Camp desk at (559) 253-5674.

i

A fast way to check campsite availability year-round is on the Web site, www.yosemitesites.com. Independent from the National Park Service, this site charts, day by day, which campgrounds are open to reservation and which have no vacancies.

able only through the lottery, some dates will open up once the season begins.

There are 204 beds in 56 dorm-style tent cabins at the five camps. Each camp supplies beds with pillows, blankets, and comforters; bring your own sheets or sleep sacks and towels. Wood-burning stoves, central showers, and bathroom facilities are provided. Hearty breakfasts and dinners are included, to enjoy in heated dining tents. You can purchase bag lunches. The nightly fee is $126 per person, including two meals.

To reach May Lake Camp, hike in just over a mile from Snow Flat off Highway 120 (road marker T21), near Tenaya Lake, to this lovely sapphire blue lake bordered by forest at 9,270 feet at the foot of Mount Hoffman. It is too cold to swim and fishing is not so hot, but this is a beautiful spot from which to set off on day hikes.

Merced Lake Camp is the biggest High Country camp, great for groups, with 60 campers housed in 19 cabins at a relatively low and somewhat warmer 7,150 feet. Vogelsang Camp, at 10,300 feet, sleeps 42 people in 12 cabins.

From the Lembert Dome parking area on Highway 120 near Tuolumne Meadows, take the 5-mile, easy walk on the Pacific Crest Trail to Glen Aulin Camp, with beds for 32 in eight cabins. Sunrise Camp has a total of nine canvas cabins for up to 34 people.

Hodgdon Meadow Campground
Highway 120 near Big Oak Flat

Make reservations for mid-April through mid-October; the nightly fee is $20. It's first-come, first-served from mid-October to mid-April, with a $14 nightly fee. Some of the 105 sites accommodate RVs. Pets on leashes are allowed except in group campsites. The campground is ideally located on North Crane Creek near the Tuolumne Grove of Giant Sequoias at 4,900 feet, about a half-hour from Yosemite Valley. You can reserve one of the group sites for 13 to 30 people. A small grocery store is nearby.

Housekeeping Camp
Shuttle stop 12
(559) 252-4848

If you like to camp but are not ready to set up your own tent or sleep on the ground, Housekeeping Camp may be just right. With your own linens and sleeping bags, (or for $2.50 per night, rent a two-of-each bedpack that includes sheets, blankets, and pillows), cooking equipment, dishes, and food, you will be all set in a super-convenient location by the river in the heart of Yosemite Valley, within walking distance of all major attractions and on the valley shuttle route. The semi-bad news is that these are not your dream cabins in the woods. The 266 tent cabins are rather close together and unattractive, to say the least. Nonetheless, they offer an inexpensive, easy way to sort of camp out at Yosemite.

The tent cabins have concrete walls and floors and canvas roofs, and each has a fire ring. Each sleeps up to six people; a canvas curtain separates the sleeping area from a covered cooking and dining area with electricity, but no phones, TVs, or plumbing. Facilities include central restroom and shower facilities (soap and towels are provided), a laundry, and a small grocery store. The nightly rate is $67.00 for one to four people; $5.00 each additional person.

Lower Pines Campground
Shuttle stop 19

At this campground, the spaces near the river are the first to go. The 60 sites—some of which are wheelchair accessible and suited for RVs—are open March to October. The campsites are located midvalley, within walking distance of all public facilities and several trailheads. The nightly fee is $20 per site.

North Pines Campground
Shuttle stop 18

Many valley campers prefer North Pines as it is a little more isolated than others and is shaded by tall pines. The sites near

Housekeeping Camp in Yosemite Valley is simple, affordable, and close to facilities and trails. DNC

the Merced River are the first to go, so make your reservations well in advance. North Pines is within walking distance of most valley facilities and several trailheads. You can push a stroller or ride your bike right from here on a paved trail to Mirror Lake.

Eighty-one sites, including those for RVs up to 40 feet long, are open April through September. The nightly fee is $20 per site. You can bring your pet, keeping it on a leash.

Porcupine Flat Campground
off the Tioga Road, road marker T17

At 8,100 feet, west of Tenaya Lake, this simple campground among huge boulders and beneath tall pines is a great headquarters for hiking the High Country. Open July through early September on a first-come, first-served basis, these 52 sites include a few RV sites but have no piped water. The overnight fee is $10 per site. You are in the heart of the Yosemite wilderness here, with trailheads and landmark geologic sites nearby. The disadvantage may be road noise, depending where your site is located.

i

Hot showers are available 24 hours a day at Curry Village and when Housekeeping Camp is open, spring through fall. A small fee includes towel and soap. You will also find public showers at Tuolumne Meadows Lodge in summertime. This is not like high school—you will have complete privacy in the shower and a small dressing area. Bring an extra towel on which to stand in your bare feet. The sole Laundromat in the park, open yearround, is at Housekeeping Camp in Yosemite Valley.

Leave Only Footprints

- No bushwhacking: use only established campsites to minimize impact on the environment.
- Clean water: do not even think about pouring soapy water or soap of any kind, even biodegradable, into or near the rivers, lakes, or streams in the park.
- Choose campsites more than 200 feet from a clean water source to avoid pollution and erosion.
- Choose fuel wisely: use a butane or propane stove to help prevent air pollution. If you must build a fire, use the fire rings and grates that are provided, and confine your fires to between the hours of 5:00 and 10:00 P.M. Bring your own fuel or purchase it in the park; wood and pinecones may not be collected in Yosemite Valley. Wood may not be gathered at elevations above 9,600 feet or in sequoia groves, and you may not cut found wood with any tool.
- Litter is the least of it: besides packing out your trash, return rocks, logs, and other natural elements to where you found them. Scatter cold ashes, excess firewood, and brush, leaves, or needles over your site. Strive for zero impact.

Tamarack Flat Campground
4 miles east of Crane Flat off the Tioga Road

One of the first-come, first-served campgrounds, at 6,300 feet in elevation, Tamarack Flat is open summer through early fall. Fifty-two basic sites are popular with backpackers, with picnic tables, nearby vault toilets, and no running water. There is parking, but the access road is not appropriate for large RVs or trailers. You can camp here with an RV no longer than 24 feet, without pets. Nightly fee is $10.

Tuolumne Meadows Campground
1 mile off the Tioga Road, road marker T30, accessible by shuttle bus

This is the largest campground in the park, at 8,600 feet, with 304 sites in a picturesque high mountain setting. The most desirable sites are on the east side near the Tuolumne River. On most nights, rangers lead campfire programs with educational presentations, songs, and stories. This campground is close to a general store, stables, a rustic restaurant serving hearty American fare, and tent cabins. This is a busy place, located near many High Country trailheads, lakes, streams, and spectacular natural attractions.

Open July through September, half of the sites are available by reservation only and half on a first-come, first-served basis. There are some RV sites, and pets are allowed on leashes except in group campsites. The nightly fee is $20 per site. There are some RV sites for vehicles under 27 feet and a dump station. In addition to the regular campsites, there are a few walk-in, one-night-maximum sites for backpackers, requiring wilderness permits; cost $5.00, and a horse camp with four, six-horse sites, for $25.00 per night.

Upper Pines Campground
Shuttle stop 15

Within a short walk of waterfalls, ice cream, pizza, bike trails, and Happy Isles, Upper Pines is super-convenient for families with small children. Although you will not feel alone here, the back and outside edges of the campground are a little more private—site numbers 214, 216, 218, 220, etc. Stay at one of the 238 sites that are open year-round, and bring your pets, but be sure to keep them on a leash. The nightly fee is $20 per site.

Wawona Campground
2 miles from the South Gate entrance off Highway 41, near the Pioneer Yosemite History Center
Open year-round, this pretty, 93-site campground stretches for a mile along the banks of the South Fork of the Merced River, with river-view sites the most coveted. Every evening, rangers meet with campers around a bonfire to talk about the history of the park and its flora and fauna; a schedule of nightly topics is posted on the bulletin board. Make reservations for May through September; it's first-come, first-served from October to April; the camping limit here is seven days. There are wheelchair accessible as well as RV sites. The nightly fee is $20 in summertime, $12 in low season, and pets on leashes are allowed except in group campsites. A single horse campsite on Chilnualna Falls Road requires reservations (800-436-7275), and costs the same $40 per night as the group campsite that can accommodate 13 to 30 people per site. When the U.S. Army was the protector of the park, from 1891 to 1906, this was its headquarters.

White Wolf Campground
Between Tuolumne and Yosemite Valley off the Tioga Road, road marker T9
A summertime-only headquarters for backcountry trails, this campground is a favorite of campers who like the cooler daytime temperatures at 8,000 feet and easy access to nearby subalpine lakes and streams. The 74 sites are open June through early September on a first-come, first-served basis. RVs must be less than 27 feet long. The overnight fee is $14 per site. Pets are allowed on leash. Ranger-led programs and events are scheduled, from nature walks to campfires with storytelling and music, lunch hikes, and, once a week, an "Earth Walk" just for families and kids. You can walk from here to Lukens Lake, Grant Lakes, Harden Lake, and on into the Grand Canyon of the Tuolumne.

For your big family and lots of friends, there are four group campgrounds in Yosemite—at Wawona, Tuolumne Meadows, Hodgdon Meadow, and Bridalveil Creek, for a maximum of 30 people in each group. In regular campsites, a maximum of six people may stay together, including children.

Yosemite Creek Campground
Off the Tioga Road, between White Wolf and Porcupine Flat
Accessible by an unpaved, 5-mile-long road, these 75 sites at 7,700 feet are open during the summer months on a first-come, first-served basis. Overnight fee is $10 per site, with some RV sites, but no potable water. From here you can hike along the creek to where it rushes over Yosemite Falls, and continue on the trail into Yosemite Valley. Sites are available for RVs no longer than 24 feet, although the road is rough and RVs and trailers are not advised. Your pet is welcome, on a leash.

CAMPGROUNDS OUTSIDE THE NATIONAL PARK

The USDA Forest Service and the U.S. Army Corps of Engineers operate many campgrounds, seasonally, near Yosemite in the Inyo, Sierra, Stanislaus, and Toiyabe National Forests. Many are on a first-come, first-served basis; in some campgrounds, at least half of the sites may be reserved. To make reservations and get information, call (877) 444-6777 or check out the Web sites, www.reserveusa.com and www.fs.fed.us. You can also contact local district offices, listed at the end of this chapter. For more information on California campgrounds, check out the book *California Camping* by Tom Steinstra.

Big Sandy Campground
Oakhurst
(559) 877-2218
From Oakhurst, take Highway 41 north to Jackson Road, driving 5 miles north from there, onto Road 632 for another 20 miles, to beauty and solitude on the Big Creek in the Sierra National Forest. With a dozen tent sites and very few RV sites, at $14 per night, this campground has no running water but is not far from the South Gate entrance to the national park, at 5,800 feet. Big Sandy is open May through September.

Boulder, Big Bend, Moraine, and Aspen Campgrounds
Off Highway 120 East
(760) 647-3044
Fishermen fill up these first-come, first-served Inyo National Forest campgrounds that are laid out right along Lee Vining Creek—you can actually fish from some campsites. Tents and RVs are a little crowded together, although the sites, at 7,800 feet in elevation, are nicely shaded with hundreds of pines and aspens. The campgrounds are open from about the end of April through mid-October; daily fee is $15. At Big Bend Campground, the creek rushes into a smashing display of waterfalls.

Dimond O Campground
near Hetch Hetchy
(reserve), (877) 444-6777,
(209) 962-7825;
www.reserveusa.com
In the Stanislaus National Forest, this campground offers three dozen sites for tents and RVs for $16 a night in a nice setting on the Middle Fork of the Tuolumne River, at 4,400 feet. Dimond O, open mid-April through October, is located off Highway 120, off Evergreen Road, on the way to Hetch Hetchy.

Ellery Lake Campground
Lee Vining
(760) 647-3044
South of Lee Vining, drive west on Highway 120 about 10 miles to this small campground in a spectacular setting by the lake. At 9,500 feet in elevation and located in the Inyo National Forest, this is a prime spot when Tuolumne Meadows facilities are full. If you cannot get in here, try the Junction Campground (another pretty one nearby) or Tioga Lake (see below). Fishing here at 9,500 feet elevation is excellent for native brookies and browns, and the lake is regularly stocked with rainbow trout. The first-come, first-served campground at $15 per night is open from about early June through mid-October. RVs are welcome up to 30 feet long, and pets, too, on a leash.

Indian Flat RV Park
9988 Highway 140, El Portal
(209) 379-2339
www.indianflatrvpark.com
Just 4 miles north of El Portal and 10 minutes from the Arch Rock entrance to the national park, this is a popular strip of 50 sites and cottages along the Merced River. At 1,500 feet in elevation, it's open year-round. It can get hot in the summertime, but you can cool off in the swimming holes.

Lumsden Campground
Groveland
(209) 962-7825
Approximately 20 minutes from the Big Oak Flat entrance to the national park, in the Stanislaus National Forest, this is a favorite 10-site campground for white-water rafters on the Tuolumne River. The campground is located 10 miles east of Groveland off Highway 120, off Ferretti Road and is open all year and free.

Lundy Canyon Campground
Just north of Lee Vining, off Highway 395
(877) 444-6777
In a stunning, aspen-filled canyon near a great fishing lake, 40 campsites are nicely separated under the trees; the closer to the lake, the nicer the sites. Per-night cost is $8.00; no water is available.

CLOSE-UP

Save a Bear

In visitor's facilities around the park, you will see photos and videos of bears breaking car windows and climbing inside vehicles.

In 2004, there were 721 "bear incidents," where property damage occurred, food was taken, or the uncommon bear-injures-human scenario occurred. Since 1998, National Park Service statistics show that the number of incidents have decreased, probably because of decreasing numbers of Yosemite Valley visitors rather than a decrease in the fairly steady park-wide population of 300 bears. Approximately 30 black bears live in the valley. Those that roam around Little Yosemite Valley and Tuolumne Meadows are more active in seeking food. Along the Tioga Road, you will see outlines of bears, indicating spots where vehicles have struck them.

Each year black bears must be destroyed as a direct result of human carelessness and improper food storage. This is not a "bear problem," but a people problem. Yosemite's black bears recognize ice chests, packaging, and cans, and they can smell food in backpacks, tents, vehicles, and garbage cans. You can save a bear by properly handling your food throughout the park.

Black bears are not uncommon in Yosemite. If you see a bear, report it to the Save-a-Bear Hotline. DNC

- Seal food and food-related supplies in airtight containers and store in metal storage boxes where provided.
- Store grocery bags, garbage, and scented articles such as soap, sunscreen, hairspray, and toothpaste.
- Where storage boxes are not available, put all food and scented objects out of sight in your vehicle trunk.
- Never leave food unattended in a picnic area or campsite. Never throw food or food packaging into open dumpsters.
- When staying in a hotel room, bring all food items into your room, including bottled drinks, canned goods, empty ice chests, and all items listed above.

The National Park Service is testing a remote alarm system that uses radio telemetry to alert rangers when a bear appears in a developed area. Rangers will then "haze" the bear away, reducing the amount of human food the animals obtain and the amount of damage the bears may do to human property, and to better track the habits of bears.

Hazing is the use of loud noises, bright lights, beanbag bullets, and simply throwing small rocks in the vicinity of the bears to reeducate them and discourage them from remaining in developed areas.

After all these precautions, remember that the likelihood of seeing bears remains low, as they tend to avoid human contact. Often, visitors will see the results of bear activity and never see a bear.

Bear sightings, wildlife feedings, overflowing dumpsters, and other bear-related concerns can be reported by calling the Save-A-Bear Hotline at (209) 372-0200 (follow the prompts).

Merced River Recreation Area
Mariposa area
(209) 966-3638, (209) 966-3192
On an enchanted section of the Merced River are three campgrounds near a beautiful hiking trail and swimming holes, with not-bad fishing. Some of the 31 sites in the Railroad Flat, McCabe Flat, and Willow Placer campgrounds are walk-in; some are accessible by car and RV. The sites are open all year, with leashed pets allowed. To get here, at the Briceburg BLM Visitor's Center, turn left over the bridge and along the river (see more about the Visitor's Center in the Arch Rock chapter). These are first-come, first-served campgrounds with a $10 nightly fee.

Hikers, mountain bikers, and horseback riders like the Yosemite Railroad Grade along the north side of the river, an 18-mile route that ends up at the Highway 49 bridge at Bagby.

Nelder Grove Campground
Oakhurst
(559) 877-2218
From Oakhurst, drive on Highway 41 north to Sky Ranch Road, going northeast about 8 miles to this seven-site campground, an incredibly well-located spot in the Sierra National Forest within the Nelder Grove of Giant Sequoias, just a few minutes from the South Gate entrance to the national park. RVs are allowed but not recommended. The campground is open May to October.

Oh Ridge Campground
June Lake
(reserve), (877) 444-6777
(760) 647-3045
www.reserveusa.com
Just south of the town of June Lake, anglers congregate at this Forest Service campground, and families gather here in the summertime, late April through October. Although you will find little privacy for the 164 campsites, the development is convenient and includes a playground, picnic sites, volleyball, and a nice swimming beach. RVs up to 40 feet are accommodated; per-night cost is $15.

Saddlebag Lake Campground
Off Highway 120, 2.4 miles from the East Gate entrance of the national park, take the dirt road 2.5 miles
www.saddlebaglakeresort.com
At 10,087 feet, this is the highest lake in the state reachable by public road. You can rent a fishing boat, and/or get a boat ride to the trailhead for Twenty Lakes Basin of the Hoover Wilderness (see the East Gate Entrance chapter of this book).

Twenty small campsites, with little or no privacy, are available on a first-come, first-served basis for $15 a night. The scenery is fabulous, and there is a small store and cafe at the resort that serves anglers and hikers. The road and the area are generally accessible mid-June through October; call (760) 647-3044 for updates.

Silver Lake Campground
June Lake Loop
In an open field near the road, the 63 tent and RV sites in this Forest Service campground, open late May through October, are not particularly pretty or private, but fishermen don't care because the beautiful lake, at 7,200 feet in elevation, is loaded with trout, and the adjacent resort has a great cafe, a small grocery store, and boat rentals. RVs up to 40 feet are accommodated; per-night cost is $13.

The surrounding mountain setting is lovely, in the Inyo National Forest on the June Lake Loop, 6 miles from Lee Vining. From here you can horseback ride and hike into the Ansel Adams Wilderness.

Summerdale Campground
Fish Camp
(reserve), (877) 444-6777
(559) 877-2218, (559) 642-3212
www.reserveusa.com
Open from June to November, just 1 mile north of Fish Camp off Highway 41, 1.5 miles from the South Gate entrance to the park, this USDA Forest Service campground is in a nice, streamside setting on Big Creek, with 29 sites, including some sites for RVs up to 24 feet for $17 per night. A grocery store is a mile away, and

you can bring your pet on a leash. You'll find some good swimming holes here in the South Fork of the Merced River, at 5,000 feet in elevation.

Summit Campground
Off Highway 41, a mile south of Fish Camp
(559) 877-2218
The tiny, tents-only six-site campground in the Sierra National Forest is 6 miles down a gravel road, near good fishing on Big Creek. Open from June to October, the road is driveable by most vehicles with high clearance. Your pet is OK on a leash; no running water is available. Camping costs $12 per night.

Tioga Lake Campground
Lee Vining
(760) 647-3044
In the Inyo National Forest 2 miles from the Tioga Pass entrance to the national park, this 13-site small-tent and RV campground sits at 9,700 feet on a scenic lake and is located 6 miles west of Lee Vining adjacent to Highway 120. The rainbow trout fishing is very good by boat or from the shore during a season roughly from early June through mid-October. This is a popular, although often windy, camping spot, with no reservations necessary, at $15 per night.

Yosemite-Mariposa KOA Campground
6323 Highway 140, Midpines
(800) 562-9391, (209) 966-2201
www.koa.com
This KOA offers 49 RV sites with partial or full hookups, tent sites, cute, simple cabins, and a lodge beside a nice little lake, with beds and no linens plus central restrooms and showers. Amenities include a swimming pool and paddleboats, laundry, a small convenience store, recreation room, and a playground. Pets are welcome on a leash. Rates range from $29 to $50 for an RV, $21 to $31 for tents, $52 to $65 for a "kabin," and $140 to $165 for a lodge room. To get here, take Highway 140 for 5.5 miles east of Mariposa.

NATIONAL FOREST REGIONAL OFFICES

The rangers at the National Forest offices are the ultimate sources of information for the status of campgrounds. They will advise you as to the best campgrounds for your particular type of family and your interests in outdoor recreation; when each campground and the access roads open and close for the season; which ones require reservations; where pets and RVs are allowed; whether running water and other amenities are available; and the like. Call weeks or even months ahead to have printed material sent to you.

When you are traveling near the offices, stop in to browse and purchase maps, guidebooks, and souvenirs related to the national forests.

Highway 41
Sierra National Forest,
Oakhurst Ranger Station/
Yosemite Sierra Visitors Bureau
(559) 683-4636

Highway 120 East
Inyo National Forest,
Mono Lake Ranger Station
(760) 647-3044

Highway 120 West
Stanislaus National Forest,
Groveland Ranger Station
(209) 962-7825

Highway 140
Sierra National Forest,
Mariposa Ranger Station
(209) 966-3638

RESTAURANTS

Californians are "foodies." They are used to some of the finest fresh ingredients produced in the world, and they are used to paying the price. Thus, food and beverage outlets in the park are generally top quality and pricey. Hungry park visitors can expect a wide variety of pretty darn good food, and in some cases, fabulous food, from pizza to pasta primavera, rack of lamb, and portobello mushroom sandwiches with cabernet sauce, from barbecued burgers and hot dogs to fruit smoothies, from crème brûlée to ice-cream cones.

Since 1993, when Delaware North Companies Parks & Resorts (DNC) took over the 22 restaurants and food and beverage outlets throughout the park, quality has risen dramatically, and prices, somewhat. Families will save big-time by bringing their own food, at least for lunches and snacks. The Yosemite Lodge at the Falls Food Court and Curry Village Pavilion offer good, hearty American food at moderate prices. And there are groceries and convenience stores, fast-food cafes, and delis in several locations.

Yosemite has three restaurants with truly exceptional food, top-notch wine lists, and lovely surroundings—the dining rooms at The Ahwahnee and Wawona Hotel and the Mountain Room at Yosemite Lodge at the Falls.

The dress code throughout the park is very casual, with some partial exceptions. At the main dining room at The Ahwahnee, where gentlemen used to be required to don jackets, the dress code has relaxed to collared shirts and slacks; women are comfortable in a dress or a blouse with a skirt or slacks. There are special events in The Ahwahnee Dining Room—the Yosemite's Chefs' Holidays, Yosemite's Vintners' Holidays, and The Bracebridge Dinner—that call for a dressy look. For breakfast and lunch in the dining room, the hotel bar, and on the pool terrace, just about anything goes.

At the Wawona Hotel, guests are asked to dress tastefully to "preserve the traditional atmosphere" at dinner, meaning no play clothes or shorts; coats and ties for men are not required. In the Mountain Room at Yosemite Lodge at the Falls, although you can wear whatever you like, the decor, the menu, and the atmosphere deserve respect.

For groceries, see the Shopping chapter.

PRICE CODE

The follwing dollar sign ($) ranking is based on the price of two entrees from the dinner menu, not including appetizers, desserts, beverages, taxes, or gratuities.

$	**Less than $15**
$$	**$16–$25**
$$$	**$26–$35**
$$$$	**More than $35**

Ahwahnee Bar **$–$$$**
The Ahwahnee, shuttle stop 3
(209) 372-1289

Light meals, such as hot and cold sandwiches, soups, chili, wraps, and salads, are served in the bar and on the terrace at teak tables from 11:00 A.M. to 11:00 P.M. Stone and dark wood walls, rich fabrics, and warm colors create a nice atmosphere, and the terrace is lovely, with views of meadows, Half Dome, and Glacier Point. Weekend service can be quite slow, so settle in and enjoy the ambience.

Live piano music is played on the Steinway on most Friday and Saturday evenings. A special martini menu lists the following: French, Citrus, James Bond original, Cosmopolitan, Sapphire and Orange, plus four Classics, which are three-ounce martinis in an Ahwahnee-logo martini glass.

The Ahwahnee Dining Room $$$-$$$$
Just east of Yosemite Village, shuttle stop 3
(209) 372-1489

One of the most famous and impressive dining rooms in the world, this is a stunner—130 feet long, lined with tall windows looking onto a meadow and forest setting, with huge wrought-iron chandeliers hanging from a 34-foot-high ceiling crisscrossed with painted log beams. Just the walk into the glorious, light-filled or candlelit dining room, seating 450 people, is an experience in itself.

Breakfast in this sparkling environment can be memorable, with snow on the evergreens or wildflowers in the meadows. Expensive and worth it, the breakfast menu includes omelettes, frittatas, apple crepes, and traditional fare. Try the raisin brioche French toast or a flatiron steak and eggs.

For lunch, the homemade French onion soup, mountain trout, grilled portobello mushroom sandwich, and Dungeness crab cakes are great choices.

The dinner menu is legendary, featuring traditional and exotic seasonal choices such as diver scallop and shiitake mushroom Wellington, pan-roasted line-caught halibut, grilled peppered Angus beef filet mignon with Humboldt Fog Blue Cheese, and butter-braised Turlock Ranch rabbit. Save room for The Ahwahnee signature "s'mores" made with rich chocolate cake, peanut butter mousse, or the famous boysenberry and apple pies.

The dining room glows with candles and merriment every Christmas season during The Bracebridge Dinner. Also in the wintertime, the Yosemite's Vintners' Holidays and Yosemite's Chefs' Holidays feature prestigious winemakers and internationally known chefs, creating splendid multicourse dinners. Guests taste and sip, tour the kitchens, and rub elbows with the chefs and winemakers. For the gala dinners, guests enjoy ingredients flown in from around the world and rare vintage wines.

You can't go wrong with picnics in Yosemite. Either bring in your own food or find deli meats, cheeses, and a host of other picnic-perfect items at the Village Store or at convenience stores around the park (see the Shopping chapter).

Sunday Brunch at The Ahwahnee

A tradition for many returning guests, Sunday Brunch is a feast in the glorious, world-famous Ahwahnee Dining Room, with nine buffet stations offering traditional breakfast fare and exotic gourmet dishes. Among the cold choices are yogurt, fresh fruit, cheeses, and meats, plus several kinds of salad, prawns, oysters on the half shell, and smoked salmon. Hot entrees include quiche, potato and egg dishes, omelettes cooked to order, and carved roast beef, ham, and turkey. Do not pass up the bakery station with its platters of house-made pastries, muffins, and croissants and the several desserts. The Just For Kids station is filled with pint-size favorites. Brunch is served between 7:00 A.M. and 3:00 P.M. Cost is $32.00 for adults and $16.50 for children; ages three and under are free.

Curry Village Cocktail Lounge $-$$
Shuttle stop 14
(209) 372-8333

TVs are scarce in the national park, so on game days, the small, basic six-stool cocktail bar adjacent to the Dining Pavilion is a popular place—you will find two screens here. You can also sit outside at a tiny bar adjacent to the large, outdoor Pizza Deck area. Besides beer, wine, and cocktails, you can also order burgers and fries. Try the signature strawberry margaritas!

Curry Village Coffee Corner and Ice Cream Stand $
Shuttle stop 14

A great place to get fast take-out service for espresso drinks; pastries such as muffins, danish, and bagels; yogurt; juices;

Beer lovers will find a unique brew within the national park boundaries: Yosemite Falls Pale Ale is brewed by Snowshoe Brewery in Sonora and is sold exclusively in Yosemite National Park.

hand-dipped ice cream; and prepackaged sandwiches and snacks.

Curry Village Dining Pavilion **$-$$**
Shuttle stop 14
(209) 372-8303
This big, airy cafeteria with a very nice mountain lodge atmosphere serves good American food for breakfast and dinner at moderate prices. The pavilion is open from mid-May to November and weekends and holidays during other months. All-you-can-eat buffets offer a wide variety, from a salad bar, build-your-own tacos, and pastas to chicken strips and fries, meat and potatoes, veggie specials, and even macaroni and cheese.

The fireplace lobby has some of the widest, comfiest armchairs and sofas you'll ever lounge in!

Curry Village Pizza Deck **$**
Shuttle stop 14
(209) 372-8333
Choose custom toppings for really good pizza and enjoy it outdoors under the trees at an umbrella table, right in the bustle of Curry Village. If tables are full, head around the back of the building to more tables, or sit on benches in the adjacent amphitheater. You can get hot dogs and salads here, too, as well as burgers, grilled sandwiches, big orders of fries, snacks, and wine and beer on tap. Open spring through early fall, noon to 10:00 P.M.

Curry Village Taqueria **$**
Shuttle stop 14
Adjacent to the pizza place, get quick take-out service of burritos, tacos, nachos, soft-serve ice cream, and beverages. Open spring to early fall for lunch only.

Degnan's Deli **$**
Yosemite Village, shuttle stop 2
(209) 372-8454
Open year-round, Degnan's offers custom-made and premade deli sandwiches, zippy fresh salads, homemade soups, snacks, espresso drinks, and other beverages. The fancy sandwiches include winners such as roast chicken with cranberry mayonnaise. Gourmet coffees and soft-serve ice cream and yogurt are better than ever, and fresh pastries and desserts are baked here. Sit inside or out on the patio, or take away. Open 8:00 A.M. to 6:00 P.M.

Degnan's Pizza Loft **$-$$**
Yosemite Village, shuttle stop 2
Upstairs over Degnan's Deli, this lofty, roomy pizzeria with a central fireplace and valley views makes fresh pizza crusts and adds luscious toppings. Soups, salads, and desserts are also available. Open 11:00 A.M. to 8:30 P.M., mid-April through the end of October.

Dining Room at the Wawona Hotel **$$-$$$**
Highway 41, 2 miles from the South Gate entrance to the park
(209) 375-1425
Directed by a fabulous head chef, the menu is a cross between California cuisine and American comfort food, with numerous seasonal specials and an excellent wine list and full bar. Don't miss Clarence Washburn's Scarlet Trout, and French onion soup. Vegetarian choices are offered too. Among the dessert seductions are hot fudge and brownie sundaes, pine nut pie, boysenberry pie, and luscious cakes. Kids' menus are inexpensive and include peanut butter and jelly sandwiches; child-size portions of burgers, spaghetti, and chicken strips; and smaller dessert plates.

Redecorated in grand style, the Victorian-style dining room has views of the beautiful hotel grounds and glowing sunsets over Wawona Meadow. Take the time to peruse the historic old photos in the dining room and the parlors, and notice the wonderful, handmade sequoia cone light fixtures. The dining room is open 7:30 A.M. to 9:00 P.M.; no reservations, except for groups of 10 or more. Weather permitting, a few tables are set up on the porch.

Breakfast, buffet lunch, dinner, and Sunday buffet brunch are served from early spring to early December, and Thursday through Sunday in winter. In the summertime, the outdoor barbecues are great fun, with red-checked tablecloths, corn on the cob, steak, hamburgers, and all the trimmings.

Mountain Room Lounge $$
Yosemite Lodge at the Falls, shuttle stop 8
(209) 372-1035
Tall windows showcase views of Yosemite Falls, while a round Swedish fireplace adds coziness for afternoon and evening cocktail service and appetizers, chili and crackers, snacks, and s'mores you can roast over the open fireplace. The lounge is open year-round, and you can sit outside, spring through fall. Four TVs are tuned to major sporting events, family-oriented sitcoms, and national news. Kids are welcome, except at the bar, which is open noon to midnight daily.

Mountain Room Restaurant $$-$$$
Yosemite Lodge at the Falls, shuttle stop 8
(209) 372-1274
Blond wood paneling, low lights, and the killer view of Yosemite Falls make this a grand dinner house, not formal but with considerable panache. Scenic landscapes are featured in photos, art, and a mural. Among sophisticated appetizers are the smoked trout cake and rabbit rillette. For an entree, try the grilled chicken lasagna, mountain trout with San Joaquin Valley almonds, line-caught Pacific yellowfin tuna, mahi-mahi with ranchero sauce, or slow-roasted duckling. You can also choose from lighter fare, such as Caesar or spinach salad. On the wine list is a quite acceptable array of California wines, including a goodly choice of wines by the glass.

The restaurant is open all year. No reservations are accepted, and the wait can be considerable—come early. Open 5:00 to 9:30 P.M.

In midsummer, when the Tuolumne Meadows Lodge restaurant is overflowing with hungry campers, drive out of the park, east about 2 miles on Highway 120, to the Tioga Pass Resort, where you can get three meals a day of hearty American food and divine homemade pie (209-372-4471).

Tuolumne Meadows Grill $
Tuolumne Meadows off Tioga Road
(209) 372-8426
Located next to the post office, the Tuolumne Meadows Grill serves up burgers, sandwiches, snacks, hot breakfasts, full lunches, and light dinners. Sit at the counter or takeout. Opens in late spring when Tioga Road opens, through mid-September.

Tuolumne Meadows Lodge $-$$
Highway 120 East, Tuolumne Meadows
(209) 372-8413
A restaurant in a tent beside the river, Tuolumne Meadows Lodge serves substantial American fare family style for breakfast and dinner. You sit at tables with other campers and sightseers. Box lunches are available, as well as beer and wine. Dig into a Meadow Scramble in the morning, or the prime rib or veggie specialties for dinner. Reservations are necessary for dinner. Opens when Tioga Road opens in late spring, through mid-September.

Village Grill $
Yosemite Village, shuttle stop 10
Yosemite Grill offers pretty good fast food from a walk-up window: hamburgers, fries, onion rings, chicken strips, and the like.

Bringing your own food into Yosemite Village? The quietest, shadiest, nicest picnic tables are outside the Village Sport Shop at the east end of the village.

Eat at a table on the deck or take it away. Open spring through fall.

Wawona Golf Shop **$**
Highway 41, 2 miles from the South Gate entrance
(209) 375-1425
Conveniently located near the road, in the building on the right of the main hotel, the Wawona Golf Shop is a great place to stop for hot dogs, premade sandwiches, drinks, and snacks.

White Wolf Lodge **$-$$**
Highway 120 between Tuolumne Meadows and Yosemite Valley
(209) 372-8416
White Wolf Lodge, a great old clapboard dining hall with a covered dining porch, serves hearty, big American comfort food breakfasts and dinners; dinner reservations are recommended. Sit by the fireplace with a glass of wine or a beer. You can buy sandwiches at the adjacent store.

Yosemite Lodge at the Falls Food Court **$-$$**
Shuttle stop 8
(209) 372-1265
A million-dollar renovation has transformed the cafeteria of old into an attractive food court updated with fresh-looking green canvas awnings, decorative tiles, and a tree-shaded, enlarged patio with umbrella tables. Pass-through at food lines and check-out are faster than before, and lodging guests can charge their purchases to their rooms. Separate venues offer fast "to-go" snacks and prepacked lunches. Hot, made-to-order meals are focused on daily specials and healthy, varied choices. At entree stations, you can order vegetarian and meat-based entrees and a daily rotating menu of ethnic selections, such as Mexican on Fridays.

At the pasta station, specialty sauces range from traditional pesto, marinara, and Bolognese to roasted garlic and sun-dried tomato pesto, with daily specials such as spinach ravioli and tortellini. The deli station offers cold salads, chef and shrimp salads, cheese and fruit plates, wrap sandwiches, and deli-style sandwiches. The grill station is popular for Philly cheese steaks, with or without grilled onions, hamburgers, garden burgers, hot dogs, fries, and chicken and fish sandwiches. At the bakery-dessert station are muffins, bagels, danishes, cakes, pies, yogurt, and desserts; at the hot breakfast station, it's bacon and sausage, eggs, Eggs Benedict, hot cereal, and fresh fruit. George the Pancake Flipper has been doing so for over 15 years; kids can request a pancake with ears resembling those of a very famous mouse. A Coffee Corner is open all day for espresso drinks, hot chocolate, and juices. Open 6:30 A.M. to 9:00 P.M.

Yosemite's Badger Pass Cafeteria **$**
Badger Pass Ski Area
(209) 372-8430
The cafeteria serves hot and cold comfort food, soups, chili, barbecued burgers and sandwiches, snacks, drinks for chilly skiers, beer, and wine. This spot opens around December 15 and stays open 8:00 A.M. to 2:00 P.M. through the ski season.

EVENTS, ACTIVITIES, AND TOURS

Once in Yosemite, you can lie in a meadow and contemplate the shifting clouds. Walk alone in the forest, watch the reflection of Half Dome in the Merced River, or put your feet up in front of a fireplace at The Ahwahnee and read a book.

Or you can check out some of the hundreds of classes, talks, walks, hikes, slide shows, videos, and theater presentations offered year-round throughout the park. Rangers from the National Park Service (NPS) and Interpretive Specialists from Delaware North Companies Parks & Resorts at Yosemite, Inc. (DNC) are the experts on hand to enhance your Yosemite experience. They know where to find the spotted owl near El Capitan, how to recognize the constellations, and where to find the best fishing and swimming holes. They tell stories and recount history at traditional campfires in the campgrounds and help you identify and appreciate wildlife and wildflowers.

A nonprofit organization, the Yosemite Association also gives wonderful in-depth workshops and educational tours. An environmental organization, the Sierra Club, schedules events at Le Conte Memorial Lodge. Park rangers lead hikes from most of the campgrounds, and each of the lodgings in the park offers unique programs.

Narrated bus tours operate daily to major attractions in the valley and seasonally to Tuolumne Meadows, Glacier Point, Wawona, and the Mariposa Grove of Giant Sequoias.

For schedules of events and activities, check *Yosemite Today*, look for postings at the campgrounds, and ask at the main desk of your lodging.

EVENTS AND ACTIVITIES

Ansel Adams Gallery Photography Workshops
(209) 372-4413
www.anseladams.com

Since they began in 1940, these workshops have been open to all serious photographers, whether students, amateurs, or professionals. Demanding activities start early in the morning and can go well into the night. Along with scheduled events, there is frequent student/instructor contact during evening lectures and meals. Among the offerings are Platinum II: Gum Over Platinum; Crafting the Fine Black and White Creative Photograph; Women's Only Color Photography; Introduction to Color Landscape Photography; Large Format; and more in-depth subjects. Workshop fees range from $550 up.

Camera Walks
Ansel Adams Gallery
Shuttle stops 5, 9
(209) 372-4413
www.anseladams.com

Professional photographers from the Ansel Adams Gallery, DNC photographers, and Kodak experts lead free, educational, two-hour camera walks and show you how to best use your own camera equipment while shooting the natural landmarks in Yosemite Valley. Sign up three days in advance by phone or at the gallery and meet there. Walks depart, weather willing, five to six times a week from June through August, and two to three times a week the rest of the year. Summer is also the time for kids to grab a camera on a photo walk. Most of these photo walks are held early in the morning to take advantage of the most dramatic light; a few are in late afternoon and at sunset. Attendance is limited and reservations are required. E-mail the gallery, photowalks@anseladams.com, for more information.

Children's Story Time

Another free activity for kids 12 and under, the Story Time meets on varying days and times at either the Ansel Adams Gallery porch, the Curry Village Guest Lounge, or Degnan's Pizza Loft. Check *Yosemite Today* for times. Staff members may read to mesmerized kids from a great collection of books while the adults enjoy being close by, listening or reading. If Story Time is by the Ansel Adams Gallery, adults can browse the fine collection of photography books and cards, and peruse the fine art prints on the gallery walls.

Curry Village Ski Buffet

On three winter weekends; Martin Luther King Jr.'s birthday in mid-January, and the weekends preceding and following Presidents' Day in February, Saturday nights are lively at Curry Village Pavilion with dancing, a DJ or live music, and plenty to eat. Check *Yosemite Today* for information; you can also sign up at www.yosemitepark.com to receive an e-mail newsletter for updates on seasonal events.

Evening Programs

Nightly talks and multimedia shows cover a wide range of topics on the natural and cultural history of Yosemite. You may learn about the secret life of bats, experience Yosemite in the early 1900s through the eyes of a Buffalo soldier, or see award-winning photography documenting the extraordinary beauty of Yosemite. The hour-long programs are free, they require no preregistration, and they are held at the amphitheaters at Curry Village and Yosemite Lodge at the Falls, Lower Pines Campground, and the Le Conte Memorial Lodge. In the wintertime, they are held indoors at Yosemite Lodge at the Falls and at The Ahwahnee. Look in *Yosemite Today* for schedules and topics.

Yosemite lovers get the latest information on what's new in the park by receiving the* Yosemite Newsletter. *Log on to www.yosemitepark.com and register to receive e-mail newsletters about upcoming special events and seasonal lodging packages.

Explore Yosemite Family Program
Curry Village
Shuttle stop 16
(209) 372-1240

A three-hour morning program in summer introduces families to the natural and cultural world of Yosemite. You learn about wildlife, geology, Ahwahneechee Indian culture, and ecology, among other topics, and about 2 to 3 miles of easy walking is involved. The program is offered three or four times a week in the summertime, and the cost is $12.50 for the first child, $10.00 for each additional child, and two parents per child are free (at least one parent must accompany each family's kids). Children under age three are free with an older sibling, and you may wish to bring a stroller for little ones who may get tired out. Headquartered at the Curry Village Amphitheater, this unique, in-depth program is led by interpretive specialists who are knowledgeable and experienced with children. You can get tickets in advance at the Curry Village Tour Kiosk or the Yosemite Lodge at the Falls Tour Desk. This is a popular program and limited to 20 people. Bring water and simple snacks for your family.

Le Conte Memorial
Shuttle stop 12, road marker V21
(209) 372-4542
www.sierraclub.org/education/leconte

A National Historic Landmark built in 1904,

this charming, rustic building in midvalley is a museum of the Sierra Club and the site of numerous free talks and presentations from May through September. Subjects may range from "3-D Slides of National Parks and Mt. Diablo" to "Search and Rescue in Yosemite," "Watercolor Workshop," and "Hetch Hetchy Valley: Yosemite's Lost Twin." Most evening events are at 8:00 P.M. at the lodge; there are a few in the afternoons, meeting at locations around the valley. The lodge is open Wednesday through Sunday from 10:00 A.M. to 4:00 P.M. May through September for museum browsing. Check *Yosemite Today* and the Web site for days and times of events.

Old-fashioned Campfires
(209) 372-1240
Four to five times a week, May through October, families make memories together around a blazing campfire in a gorgeous setting beneath tall pines and silvery granite cliffs. The program includes family-friendly activities, songs, and stories; talks about Yosemite history, ecology, and geology; and a marshmallow roast. The campfires are limited to 65 people, and preregistration is required. You can purchase tickets at the Yosemite Lodge at the Falls Tour Desk or the Curry Village Tour Kiosk; tickets are not available at the campfire. Cost is $5.00 per person or $20.00 per family.

When you buy tickets, you will receive instructions regarding at which shuttle stop to gather and at what time; a special shuttle picks up participants. Bring along jackets or sweatshirts, a flashlight, water, and bug spray. Wooden benches are provided, and some families bring blankets so they can lie on the ground. This program is not easily accessible by wheelchair, but with prior notice to DNC, the physically challenged can arrange electric cart transportation to the campfire area. Outside of the valley within the park, ranger-led campfire programs are offered in some campgrounds; check schedules in *Yosemite Today*.

Photography in the Fall
(209) 379-2321
www.yosemite.org
During the peak of autumn color, plunge into a two- or three-day course focusing on nature and landscape photography. In various scenic locations in the valley and beyond, you will learn the fundamental concepts of successful composition while creating images with a strong sense of shape, form, and texture. The legendary Yosemite light contributes to an inspirational photographic experience, with brilliant fall hues as a palette. These are rare opportunities to work with famous photographers of Yosemite, including Keith S. Walklet. Courses are offered by the Yosemite Association.

Ranger Walks & Talks
Take a stroll with a park ranger as he or she talks about such topics as geology, Yosemite history, wildflowers, or fauna in the park. These free programs are offered throughout the park, departing from campgrounds, popular attractions, and lodgings, and you can just show up—no reservations required. Take a two-hour stroll along the Tuolumne River, learn about fire ecology at White Wolf Lodge, identify poisonous and edible plants, take a twilight trek to see nocturnal creatures, find out about the rivers and waterfalls of Yosemite, or take a nature walk near The Ahwahnee, among many other choices. Check *Yosemite Today* for locations and times.

Starry Skies Over Yosemite
With minimal night lighting throughout the park and no cities nearby, the Sierra skies are sparkling with more stars than most people have ever seen. Join a ranger and a member of a local astronomical society for an evening of stargazing. Dress warmly. Check *Yosemite Today* for days and times. The program is also held weekly during the summer and fall at Wawona and three times a week in Yosemite Valley. The cost is $5.00 per per-

CLOSE-UP

Photographing in Yosemite and the Wild Places

The temptation is to look up: up to the top of Half Dome from Yosemite Valley, up the crashing cascades of a waterfall, up the ruddy rough trunk of a giant sequoia, up at rock climbers clinging like human flies, or up to the full moon framed by cliffs in silhouette. When confronted with icons and classic scenery, the challenge is to make a photograph that is as unique as the moment it was created.

Follow in the footsteps of Ansel Adams, Galen Rowell, and other famous Yosemite region photographers who constantly watch what John Muir described as the Sierra Nevada's "Range of Light."

Start photographing as the first light brightens the morning sky. Flat monochromatic rock faces begin to have textured ridges and in winter, Yosemite Falls's frozen crystals' "V" form is suddenly visible. You might return to the same spot as the sun glows low and golden, as the sky turns streaky colors, or as peaks catch pink alpenglow at sunset. If you're lucky enough to have a storm, observe the cloud movements, how Half Dome and other peaks seem to lasso the clouds, and where alpine lakes reflect the sky color. Be there when early morning mists rise damply from the meadows, rivers, ponds, and streams to capture the otherworldly atmosphere. Listen for birds and animals rustling, chirping, piping, and even cruching the undergrowth, then raise your camera where the wildlife is visibly in action.

Be tempted to look down—at rocks, leaves, patterns of animal tracks crisscrossing in winter snow, and wildflowers. Go in close for the details or use a macro lens for an extreme close-up that becomes an abstract. Try a telephoto to bring a faraway detail close, blurring the background. Slow the camera speed to 1/30 of a second to freeze a waterfall's flow, a river's white water, or to blur the action when a skier glides by at Yosemite's Badger Pass or when a biker peddles by. Up the camera speed to catch the moment when a bird flies by or a deer bounds across a meadow. Use a strobe (flash) to light up people or subjects in shadow, or freeze the slight movement of a flower. Try an evening-time exposure of a waterfall—it may look like a richly colored daytime picture.

Arrange your gear compactly in a

son or $20.00 per family; purchase tickets at the Yosemite Lodge at the Falls Tour Desk, the Curry Village Tour Kiosk, or the Wawona Hotel front desk. Groups are limited to 65, so reservations are advised. You will be told the location when you purchase tickets, as it changes seasonally. The "light show" lasts an hour and a half.

The Yosemite Association also offers its own four-night, in-depth, *Starry Skies Over Yosemite* astronomy course at Glacier Point. From expert astronomers, you will learn about star lore and mythology; the motions of the sun, moon, and planets; finding direction using the sun and stars; and identification of heavenly bodies (209–379–2321, www.yosemite.org).

A photographer readies the camera by Mono Lake's tufa towers. FRED GEBHART

backpack, and practice getting to the essential lenses and other accessories like a polarizing filter that can darken the sky or a warming filter that makes scenics and portraits more cheerful and enticing. Stow water well away from equipment, film, or digital media, and pack snacks, a hat that doesn't interfere with camera operation, sunglasses, and sunscreen. Layer your clothing for warmth and protection against a sudden rain or snowstorm, and bring along gloves that leave fingers free to photograph with. Strap a lightweight tripod onto your pack where you can reach it quickly, but keep your hands free. Make a list of where you would like to be and when. You may be the only photographer there when Mono Lake's eerie tufa columns pick up the dawn's glow!

—Maxine Cass

Sunset at Glacier Point

Meet at the Glacier Point railing to enjoy the lengthening shadows in Yosemite Valley and the alpine glow on the Sierra High Country, and hear about the geological history of Yosemite. Closed in winter. Check *Yosemite Today* for days and times.

Yosemite Art Center
Shuttle stop 2 or 10
Yosemite Village next to the Village Store
(209) 372-1442

Many people are completely unaware that free outdoor art classes are available from spring to fall in the valley. It is amazing how the spectacular natural surroundings inspire kids and adults to create. The center is open from 9:30 A.M. to 5:00 P.M., and supplies are available to purchase. From 10:00 A.M. to 2:00 P.M., classes may include watercolor, sketching, Chinese brush painting, Mexican paper sculpture, and mixed media.

When the weather is wet or otherwise inclement, the class is limited to 15 students. Children older than 10 with long attention spans and a genuine interest in art may participate; those under 12 must be accompanied by a parent or guardian.

Yosemite Institute
P.O. Box 487, Yosemite, CA 95389
(209) 379-9511
yi@yni.org, www.yni.org
Working with 13- to 18-year-old students from July through August, this nonprofit organization offers experiential, multiday, hands-on programs, focusing on environmental education, ecology, history, culture, and the natural wonders of Yosemite. There is a Backpacking Adventure for 13- to 15-year-olds and for 15- to 18-year-olds there are Advanced Backpacking, an All-Girls Adventure, Advanced Wilderness Training, and Fly Fishing with Stream Biomonitoring. The Institute usually offers programs for adult and Elderhostel groups too.

Yosemite Outdoor Adventures
P.O. Box 230, El Portal, CA 95318
(209) 379-2321
www.yosemite.org
Your outdoor experience in Yosemite and those of your children and grandchildren will be greatly enriched by participation in one or more of the exceptional seminars offered by the Yosemite Association. Since 1971, the programs have grown and become exceedingly popular. The faculty consists of top experts, scientists, and naturalists, including rangers, longtime park researchers, wildlife and landscape photographers, teachers, and professors. The Yosemite Association is a nonprofit, educational organization whose profits go to the interpretive, museum, and research programs of the park.

The courses are college-level for adults and for teens age 16 and up, if accompanied by an adult; there are a few family courses open to younger kids. And in almost every seminar, you must be physically able to do at least some hiking.

The catalog is mailed in January, and courses fill up rapidly, with waiting lists established. Fees include park entrance fee and campground fees, and backcountry permit fees when applicable. Some of the programs last for several days, with lodging or camping included; some are day trips.

Among the enticing seminars that may be offered between mid-January and early November are Hetch Hetchy Wildflowers, Alpine Botany, Miwok Paiute Basketmaking and Ethnobotany, Winter Ecology, Moonrise Photography over Half Dome, Hawks & Hikes in Yosemite High Country, and Fall Photography. There are introductory, intermediate, and advanced backpacking trips, teen hikes, and family adventures.

Yosemite Theatre
Auditoriums at the Valley Visitors Center
Shuttle stops 5 and 9
Every night but Saturday from mid-May through September, there's live theater or a special presentation like "Return to Balance," a breathtaking film on Yosemite rock climbing with renowned climber Ron Kauk. In "Wild Stories with John Muir," Lee Stetson re-creates Muir's real-life adventures in a fun romp from arctic ice fields to climbing a tree in a thunderstorm and rattlesnake encounters. Stetson's exciting portrayal of John Muir, now in three different performances a week, brings to life Muir's famous adventures, conservation struggles, and joyous encounters with wildlife, and has enthralled Yosemite visitors for more than 20 years.

Connie Stetson spins tales of the pioneers from the journals, diaries, and other accounts of women who lived in wild California during the Gold Rush.

Tickets are reasonably priced and available at the door or at your lodging and activity kiosks. The professional productions are designed for all ages and especially for families. Check *Yosemite Today* for days and times.

TOURS

Sight-seeing Tours and Park Activities

- Curry Village Tour and Activity Desk
  Shuttle stop 14, Yosemite Valley
- Delaware North Companies Parks & Resorts at Yosemite, Inc. (DNC) Tour Desk
  Yosemite Lodge at the Falls, shuttle stop 8
  (209) 372-1240
  www.yosemitepark.com
- National Park Service Tour Desk
  Valley Visitor Center, Yosemite Village, Shuttle stops 5, 9
- Village Area Tour and Activity Desk
  In front of Village Store, shuttle stop 2
- Wawona Information Station
  Adjacent to the Wawona Hotel
  (209) 375-1621, for the Big Trees Tram Tour

A wide variety of park-wide bus tours and guided hiking and walking tours, talks, events, and activities are scheduled throughout the year; keep in mind that many options are seasonal, with most during summer.

Narrated tours operate daily to major attractions in the valley and during summer to Tuolumne Meadows, Glacier Point, Wawona, and the Mariposa Grove of Giant Sequoias. Children under age five generally ride free in the lap of an adult.

Start your planning by perusing *Yosemite Today*, the free tabloid available throughout the park and at park entrance stations, to check schedules and locations of activities. In all cases, call ahead to confirm details and/or stop at the tour desks to make reservations.

See the Yosemite in Winter chapter for wintertime walks and tours; browse through the Tuolumne and Wawona chapters for activities in those areas of the park.

Once a month from noon to 1:00 P.M., the National Park Service hosts the Yosemite Forum, an hour-long talk by expert government scientists, researchers, and academics on subjects ranging from Yosemite's spotted owls, Yosemite Falls archaeology, and Southern Sierra Miwok traditional culture to the reintroduction of Sierra bighorn sheep. Check www.nps.gov/yose/pphtml/events.html for dates of programs at the Yosemite Valley Visitor Center West Auditorium.

Big Trees Tram Tour
Shuttle to tram departs from Wawona Store and Pioneer Gift Shop
(209) 375-1621

The tram tour to the Mariposa Grove of Giant Sequoias runs from May through October, 9:00 A.M. to 5:00 P.M., but can be cancelled for bad weather. The tour includes special effects, music, and voices of scientists and fire fighters as part of the audio narration, in your choice of English, French, German, Japanese, and Spanish. There's also a narrated description for the visually impaired. The driver can answer questions, and the 1¼ hour-long tour allows lots of time for photos. Adults are $16, seniors pay $14, and children five and older are $10.

Design A Program Group Tours
Yosemite Groups Department
(559) 253-5600

Planning a family reunion or a group trip? Is your Boy Scout or Girl Scout troop coming to Yosemite? Would you like to arrange special outdoor activities for a wedding party?

The highly qualified interpretive staff at DNC will design a narrated walk, talk, climb, or hike and even overnights focusing on your chosen theme of flora and

Groups like the Yosemite Association and the Sierra Club provide support for park improvement or cleanup projects. If you have the inclination and time to lend yourself to cleanup or research projects, contact Yosemite National Park's Volunteer Coordinator, Tammie Parks, at (209) 379-1850.

fauna, park history, Native Americans, architecture, geology, astronomy, or other subjects, according to your desires.

Giant Sequoias
(209) 372-0299
Park rangers lead narrated nature walks in the Mariposa Grove of Giant Sequoias, interpreting the natural and human history and ecological dynamics of the giant sequoia community. Check *Yosemite Today* for days and times.

Glacier Point Tour
Yosemite Lodge at the Falls, shuttle stop 8
(209) 372-1240
Riding in a big, air-conditioned bus through the valley and up the Glacier Point Road, you climb up 3,214 feet, with zowie views all the way and many stops to breathe in the mountain air and snap photos. Much of the park and surrounding peaks, valleys, and mountain ranges can be seen from Glacier Point, and there are short hikes nearby. This is the most carefree, relaxing way to see the upper reaches of the park. Available from about late May to early November, weather permitting, the round-trip takes about four hours, departing Yosemite Lodge at 8:30 A.M., 10:00 A.M., and 1:30 P.M. daily. Round-trip fees: $32.50 adults, $26.00 children. over four years. You can also purchase a one-way ticket and hike back into the valley on the Four Mile Trail. Views from this trail are breathtaking, and coming down the trail is much easier than going up! One-way fees: $20 adults, $12 children.

Grand Tour
Yosemite Lodge at the Falls, shuttle stop 8
(209) 372-1240
A full-day, eight-hour excursion around the valley, up to Glacier Point, and to the Mariposa Grove of Giant Sequoias on the southern side of the park, this tour stops at the Wawona Hotel for you to have lunch if you want to and makes many stops along the way so you can stretch your legs and set up your tripod. If you have only one day at Yosemite and have never been here before, this is the tour for you. Well-informed, friendly drivers spin stories of old Yosemite and fill you in on all the famous attractions. Available from about late May to early November, weather permitting; the round-trip fee is $60 adults, $33 children. Lunch at the Wawona Hotel is available at your own expense or for an additional charge. Sunday Brunch at the Wawona adds $15 to the tour cost. You can also bring your own picnic or buy lunch at the Wawona Store.

Moonlight Tour
Yosemite Lodge at the Falls, shuttle stop 8
(209) 372-1240
Romantics snuggle together in a comfy open-air tram, cruising slowly through Yosemite Valley under a full moon and a zillion stars. If you've never taken this trip, treat yourself and your favorite person to an evening of dazzling beauty, watching the moon paint silver across the gleaming granite cliffs and the river. These two hours of enchantment are offered on full-moon nights from May through October, weather permitting. The cost is $22 adults, $17 children. Departure times vary depending on moon rise.

Night Prowl
(209) 372-1240
What happens to Yosemite's creatures at night? An easy, 90-minute, 1-mile guided hike helps families safely find out together

CLOSE-UP

Julie Miller, Yosemite Guide

Julie Miller came to Yosemite for the first time as a 16 year old, working with a trail restoration crew for a few weeks in the summertime. "We lived behind Yosemite Falls, and our mail and food was carried up to us on horseback," she said. "When we saw or heard the rider approaching, we would run to get the ice cream before it melted."

She studied science and outdoor education during her college years and returned to the park in 1988, working as a field instructor and a bear technician, including 10 years as a National Park Service Ranger. She is now the interpretive services manager for Delaware North Companies Parks & Resorts at Yosemite, Inc. Julie has recently produced a film titled *Yosemite in Winter: the Secret Season.*

Julie Miller leads a variety of guided tours and hikes in the National Park. DNC

Julie's passion is exploring Yosemite in the wintertime on skis and snowshoes and on foot all year long. "Over the years," she said, "individuals and families have come back to the park, some several times, to join my hikes and seminars. I believe that people return to the mountains of Yosemite for a variety of reasons, not the least of which is a kind of healing, a restoration of the spirit that only the wilderness can give."

Julie particularly loves to get visitors out into the park after dark. Among the favorite outdoor adventure programs that Julie personally conducts is the two-hour "Full Moon Snowshoe Hike" at Yosemite's Badger Pass Ski Area. A first experience on snowshoes combined with watching a huge moon rise above mountain peaks and cast its yellow glow on a palette of snow is pure magic for the participants, says Julie.

So are the old-fashioned campfire programs, star gazing, and "Night Prowls" that let guests in on the nightlife of Yosemite National Park. As an interpreter, she loves classic adventures in an outdoor setting. "To sing songs, laugh, and hear stories around a fire while roasting marshmallows. To lie on one's back in a valley meadow and look for meteors and pick out constellations or to hear bats zeroing in on an insect or an owl hooting in the distance are lifetime experiences that tie people intimately to natural places." Don't be surprised if you have Julie Miller, who gets out of the office into nature whenever she can, as *your* guide.

For your nature-loving friends and family, the perfect gifts may be Yosemite Gift Certificates. Available in increments of $25, $50, or $100, the certificates can be used for lodging, dining, touring, and in-park services offered by DNC; there are no expiration dates. Place your order by calling (559) 252-4848.

what is out there and how it survives in the dark. A naturalist will help you use your senses to detect nocturnal animals such as owls, bats, insects, and bears. Parents and kids can join in for $5.00 a person, or $20.00 per family. With an advance request to DNC's Interpretive Services, a wheelchair-accessible route can be chosen. Listening devices are available to assist hearing, and the blind are welcome with a sighted partner.

Sunset Walks
Yosemite Guides
(866) 922-9111, (209) 379-9111
www.yosemiteguides.com
The most popular hike of the many offered daily by Yosemite Guides is the Sunset Walk to Sentinel Dome, from the time the Glacier Point Road opens—usually around April—until it closes, about mid-October or so. All ages enjoy this relatively easy walk to see some spectacular Sierra Nevada scenery. When you reach Sentinel Dome, all man-made structures are out of sight and a 360-degree view of nature surrounds you. More than 90 percent of the park spreads out before you and on a clear day, you will be able to gaze west to the San Francisco Bay Area Naturalist guides talk about the plants, animals, and geologic features encountered along the trail and share the inspiring words of nature writers. A light, healthy, luscious picnic dinner is provided.

Earlier in the spring, the Sunset Walks are to the top of the Rostrum, a cliff overlooking the lower Merced River that gives spectacular views of Cascade Fall and down into the river canyon. The trail is about a half mile each way, on easy to moderate terrain. The north face of the cliffs is an active peregrine falcon aerie, where nests are sometimes inhabited by the endangered birds.

Tuolumne Meadows Tour
Curry Village, shuttle stop 20
Village Store, shuttle stop 2
Yosemite Lodge at the Falls, shuttle stop 8
(209) 372-1240
In a big, comfortable bus with camera-friendly windows, take the Tioga Road, the highest road in the Sierra Nevada on an eight-hour round-trip adventure to Tuolumne Meadows. Enjoy a short hike along the Tuolumne River or a relaxing picnic in the largest open subalpine meadow in the Sierra. Along the way are stunning views of mountains and lakes. Departures are daily at 8:00 A.M. or shortly after, July to Labor Day, weather permitting.

Round-trip fees: $23.00 adults, $11.50 children. See the Hiking and Backpacking chapter for information on the one-way hikers' bus along the Tioga Road.

Valley Floor Tour
Yosemite Lodge at the Falls, shuttle stop 8
(209) 372-1240
You will see and be able to stop and photograph the most famous and picturesque sights in the valley on this two-hour tour that departs several times a day starting at 10:00 A.M. This is the basic, never-been-here-before introduction to the glories of Yosemite Valley narrated by a park ranger, who describes the park's history, geology, and wildlife. Spring through fall, you ride in an open-air tram. Late October through April, the tour is conducted in a heated motorcoach with large windows allowing unimpeded views of the famous sights. Fees are $22 adults, $17 children; ask about family discounts.

Tour Companies

Yosemite Guides
P.O. Box 650, El Portal, CA 95318
Highway 140 at the Yosemite View Lodge
(866) 922-9111, (209) 379-9111
www.yosemiteguides.com

Call ahead for brochures or stop in at the lodge, two miles west of the Arch Rock entrance to the park. A group of highly experienced local naturalists, mountain guides, and fishing experts lead expeditions in the park and throughout the Yosemite region, offering a wide array of hikes and walks, fly-fishing, photo walks, birding, rafting trips, and easy wildflower walks and challenging wilderness backpacks, with all details, equipment, and food provided.

You can choose from half-day, full-day or multiday trips, and sign up by phone or at the office. The daily Valley Floor Tour, High Country Hike, the Rim Hike, the popular Sunset Hike, and others are in Yosemite National Park. Ask about custom tours for all ages and abilities and group tours for organizations and businesses.

Guides talk knowledgeably about plant and animal life and the geology of the region, and their programs have a high return-guest ratio. It is difficult to avoid hyperbole when describing the level of expertise and local experience of the Yosemite guides.

Don Bain has created 360-degree video panoramic views of more than 45 major points of interest in Yosemite National Park at http://virtualguidebooks.com/centralcalif/yosemite.html. Many spots have multiple views. It's a fine way to preview the trails and scenery before you go, and help you narrow down your list of must-sees.

Yosemite Sightseeing Tours
(559) 658-8687
www.yosemitetours.com

This company has been operating tours from the gateway communities on Highway 41 for more than a decade, with medium-size, air-conditioned coaches with big windows and experienced, knowledgeable drivers. Photo stops are made at all the important vistas, including Glacier Point, and the lunch hour at Yosemite Village is on your own. An easy nature walk is scheduled in the Mariposa Grove. Departures from lodgings at Bass Lake, Oakhurst, and Fish Camp are at about 8:00 A.M., with return in the late afternoon.

Rates for a full-day, eight-hour tour of Yosemite Valley and the Mariposa Grove are $86 adults, $82 seniors, and $43 children, ages 3 to 12; toddlers can sit on parents' laps. The company offers other guided Yosemite tours, too, including nature hikes and easy walks throughout the park.

ANNUAL EVENTS

Special events in a national park? You bet. Delaware North Companies Parks & Resorts at Yosemite, Inc. (DNC), the company that operates the lodgings and restaurants within the park, presents a variety of worthwhile and quite popular annual affairs, from a ski festival to cooking demonstrations by famous chefs and the traditional Bracebridge Dinner during the Christmas holidays. Do call months ahead to reserve for these events, and ask about package pricing that includes lodging (www.yosemitepark.com).

Surrounding the park on the four gateway highways, in the California Gold Country, are small picturesque towns that put on fairs, festivals, and exhibitions galore, complete with costumed players and re-creations of historic events, vintage boat and car shows, crafts and antiques expositions, and much more.

You may wish to schedule your drive to Yosemite to coincide with a fishing derby or a classic car show, an art tour or a county fair. Spring and fall are the best times for outdoor events, when the weather is sparkling clear and warm and not too hot.

Here is a sampling of annual events in and around Yosemite.

JANUARY

Yosemite's Chefs' Holidays
The Ahwahnee
(559) 253-5635
Ingredients are flown in from across the continent for some of America's most celebrated culinary titans, who demonstrate classic recipes in the Great Lounge of The Ahwahnee. Guests attend morning and afternoon presentations, taste the recipes, and hobnob with the chefs and fellow foodies. A gala multicourse banquet in the world-famous Ahwahnee Dining Room is included, as well as a private tour of The Ahwahnee kitchens.

A different slate of culinary luminaries participate each year; past chefs have included Cindy Pawlcyn of Mustards Grill in the Napa Valley; Michael Mina of Aqua in San Francisco; and Jerry Regester from the Lodge at Pebble Beach. Cost for a two-, or three-, or five-night package, including lodging at Yosemite Lodge at the Falls or The Ahwahnee, ranges from about $499 to $1,849, and the grand banquet may be attended as a separate event. Yosemite's Chefs' Holidays sell out, so advance reservations are highly recommended.

FEBRUARY

Wine and Chocolate Weekend
Madera Vintners Association
(800) 733-8068
Eight family wineries southwest of Yosemite National Park's South Entrance raise the winter cheer factor by pouring wine to go with individual chocolate desserts served at each winery.

Yosemite Renaissance Competition and Exhibition
Yosemite Museum Gallery at Yosemite Valley Visitor Center
(209) 372-0299
www.yosemiterenaissance.org
This annual exposition features juried displays of paintings, photography, sculpture, and more fine art, with the landscape, environment, wildlife, and people of Yosemite and the Sierra as themes. In addition to the fine-art competition, which features the works of more than 30 artists, a historic collection of rare vintage photos and paintings is displayed. The nonprofit Yosemite Renaissance organization also operates an Artists-in-Residence program in the park.

MARCH

Ahwahnee Heritage Holidays
The Ahwahnee
(559) 253-5676
Playing off The Ahwahnee's 1927 debut and art deco architecture, the Roaring Twenties comes alive for three days, with many free events. Many aficionados arrive in costume to listen to speakeasy performances in the Great Lounge; bone up on the fox-trot, tango, Charleston, and the waltz with lessons; dance to jazz, big band, and swing music at a tea dance and grand ball; attend a fashion show of period clothing; and soak up the atmosphere after taking a historic tour of The Ahwahnee. A five-course 1920s Gala Dinner menu in The Ahwahnee Dining Room is accompanied by music and interpretive commentary, and can be booked on its own or with a lodging package. Make reservations early, as both The Ahwahnee and Yosemite Lodge at the Falls sell out early for the Sunday through Tuesday event.

Mariposa Storytelling Festival
Mariposa
(800) 903-9936, (209) 966-3155
www.arts-mariposa.org/storytelling.html
Storytellers from around the country have convened in Mariposa in the spring since 1987. Cajun folktales, ghost stories, and myths, tales, and songs from Africa, Europe, and America are on the menu. Public events can be sold out; call early for reservations.

Nordic Holiday Race
Yosemite's Badger Pass Ski Area
(209) 372-8444
Skiers and spectators enjoy a 16K diagonal striding race, a telemark competition, and a 35K freestyle race to Glacier Point and back. All ages turn out in funny costumes for California's oldest Nordic ski race that began in 1972.

For dates and information about festivals and special events throughout the West, go to the* VIA *magazine Web site: www.viamagazine.com/events. You can search by place; the Yosemite region is in the Gold Country & Sierras section.

APRIL

Easter Sunday Celebration
Tenaya Lodge at Yosemite, Fish Camp
(888) 514-2167, (559) 683-6555
www.tenayalodge.com
A colossal Sunday brunch begins a day of family fun that includes photos with the Easter bunny, an egg hunt on the lawn, a petting zoo, and a pony carousel. Stay, if you are still hungry, for the special Easter dinner in the Sierra Restaurant. See more about Tenaya Lodge in the Lodging and Rentals chapter.

Oakdale PRCA Rodeo
Oakdale Saddle Club, Highway 120/108, Oakdale
(209) 847-4083
www.oakdalerodeo.com
Some call Oakdale the "Cowboy Capital of the World" because of the number of rodeo cowboys who live there. The first outdoor rodeo in the western United States, the Oakdale Rodeo has been held the second week of April since 1954, rain or shine. Besides watching world champion competitors ride and rope, buck and lasso all weekend, you will have fun at the Saturday morning parade and the Saturday night dance and barbecue. You can buy boots and a Stetson in town!

Driving through Oakdale, stop in at the charming Cowboy Museum in the historic Southern Pacific Railroad depot building at Sierra and 355 East F Street, adjacent to the visitor center, open weekdays 10:00 A.M. to 2:00 P.M. (209-847-5163; www.oakdalecowboymuseum.org).

Sonora Spring Festival
Sonora
(209) 532-7725
The Gold Country town has turned out at the end of April since 1975 to listen to music, watch artists at work, and enjoy historic downtown storefronts and what lies inside.

Yosemite Springfest
Yosemite's Badger Pass Ski Area
(209) 372-8430
The annual end-of-the-season snow carnival to celebrate the arrival of spring is a many-splendored event, with ski and snowboard racing, dual slalom and obstacle races, costume contests, entertainment, lessons, snowshoeing, demonstrations, a barbecue, snow sculpting, and more fun for all ages. Even if the snow is not at its absolute best by April, the Springfest is always a hoot.

MAY

Antique and Classic Wooden Boat Show
Bass Lake
(916) 922-3003
Since 1990 there's been an annual exhibition of fabulous vintage lake cruisers and yachts at the Pines Resort marina, with boat rides and entertainment.

Bass Lake Fishing Derby
Bass Lake, off Highway 41
(559) 642-3676
www.basslakechamber.org
You can win $10,000 for the biggest rainbow trout caught at the annual fishing tournament. A thousand trout are tagged for prizes up to $20 each—the cash totals $40,000 in all. Record catches at Bass Lake were a 22-pound catfish and a 14.48-pound bass. Barbecues, children's activities, and entertainment are part of the fun. For more information, fishing licenses, tackle, and bait, stop in at the Pines Market in Pines Village, (800) 350-7463.

Fire Muster
Columbia State Historic Park
(209) 536-1672
www.columbiagazette.com/muster.html
Volunteer firefighters from the western United States spend an early May weekend parading with antique fire equipment from the 1840s through the 1950s and practicing old-time techniques in this Gold Rush–era town and historic park. Watch the bucket brigade contest, horse-cart race, and a hand-pumper engine competition that displays brawn and stamina.

Jazz On the Lake
Ducey's, Bass Lake
(559) 642-3121
Memorial Day to Labor Day, a series of popular live concerts takes place on Friday evenings at poolside overlooking Bass Lake. You can have dinner at the excellent Ducey's restaurant, then head into the balmy outdoors and settle in for jazz, blues, country and western music, swing sounds, or the beat of a Caribbean steel drum band. Admission is $8.00 per person.

Mariposa County Indian Council Pow-Wow
Mariposa
(209) 742-2244
Native American tribes from throughout the region get together in early May at the Mariposa County Fairgrounds to celebrate their heritage with traditional artworks and crafts, food, and Miwok and Maidu dancing. The fantastic costumes, the dramatic music, and the dancing are stirring. This is a non-smoking, alcohol-free event, perfect for families.

Mother Lode Round-up and Fair
Sonora
(209) 984-4881
The second-largest high school band in the state sounds off at the annual parade kicking off the Mother Lode Round-up and Fair in Sonora in May. Since 1956 the Round-up Parade has had vintage autos putt-putt along, the sheriff's posse rein in their mounts, and the rodeo queen ride in elegance, watched by 50,000 spectators.

Four days of fun include a rodeo, a livestock auction, live entertainment, and a western dance.

Oakhurst Mountain Peddler's Fair
Oakhurst
(559) 683-7766
The southern Gold Country is famous for antiques shops. It is the rare Gold Rush-era town without a lineup of antiques emporiums on the main street. You can browse and buy all in one place at a large venue at Road 426 and Sierra Way, where hundreds of antiques dealers and vendors sell their wares on both the Memorial Day and Labor Day weekends. Book your lodgings early for this very popular fair.

JUNE

Buckin' Bash
Mariposa County Fairgrounds
(209) 382-0553
Wear your boots and wave your 10-gallon hat for the bull riding, mutton bustin', calf riding, stick horse racing, and freestyle bull fighting. Kick up your heels at the country western dance.

Mariposa County Pioneer Wagon Train
Mariposa
(209) 966-3620
http://mariposawagontrain.org
Starting at Goat Meadows on Highway 41 above Fish Camp, marchers, teamsters, performers, and horseback riders parade in Gold Rush- or pioneer-era costumes into Mariposa and through downtown, ending at the Mariposa County Fairgrounds, where daylong events are held. Don't miss the century-old Cannonball Stage, which once transported travelers from the Central Valley into Yosemite.

You can enjoy arts and crafts vendors and food booths selling things like Indian tacos. Living-history demonstrations include blacksmithing, a vintage ore crusher, and do-it-yourself panning for gold. Everyone in town gets involved one way or the other, and they warmly welcome visitors. You will see spinners, quilters, weavers, rag-doll makers, and basket weavers. Printers run an antique press in the old *Gazette* office.

Hang around for the chuck wagon dinner and the western dance, and don't miss the Cannonball Cowboy Poetry Reading.

Mariposa Evenings
Mariposa
(800) 903-9936, (209) 966-3155
www.arts-mariposa.org/meves.html
Bring a lawn chair or blanket to the turf or the natural amphitheater of the Mariposa County Arts Park on Highway 140 on a Friday or Saturday summer night to enjoy free live music.

Mono Basin Bird Chautauqua
Lee Vining/Mono Lake
(760) 647-6595
www.birdchautauqua.org; www.monolake.org
A Chautauqua is more than an academic event with lectures and workshops; it's participatory, and since 2002, this Friday-afternoon-through-Saturday gathering near the time of the summer solstice combines the unique scenery of Mono Lake and its vibrant shorebirds with fun, live music and picnics. There's serious education and a chance to meet some of the world's ornithology experts while being initiated into or helping others with birding skills. Birdwatching and bird walks especially for kids make this family-inclusive.

Spring Wine Trail Adventure Weekend
East side of Highway 99 near Madera
(800) 733-8068
www.maderavintners.com
A sprinkling of excellent, small, family-owned wineries puts on an annual open house. Such highly rated wineries as Ficklin and Quady roll out the wine-colored carpet to visitors, offering tastings, entertainment, gourmet food pairing, and artwork. Come early, as this is a popular

A country musician plays a banjo at a Sunday afternoon jam in Mariposa. JOHN POIMIROO

event. The wineries are located near each other, so you can tour in a couple of hours on your way to Yosemite—accompanied by your designated driver, of course!

JULY

Fourth of July Celebration
Mariposa Museum and History Center
Mariposa
(209) 966-2924
A day of old-fashioned fun, including a crafters fair, a gunfight reenactment, live music, food, and entertainment.

July Fourth Celebration and Rodeo
Bridgeport
(760) 932-7500 (July Fourth), (405) 235-6540 (rodeo)
Since the 1860s, Bridgeport has been whooping it up for the Fourth of July. These days, the holiday begins with a 6:00 A.M. pancake breakfast and ends with fireworks. In between, there's a parade with a string of mules, a full-dress Marine Corps color guard, a marching regiment, classic cars, fire engines, mounted riders, dogs, hogs (motorcycles), and a participatory atmosphere. Anyone can join the parade. The rest of the weekend is taken up with rides, a crafts fair, mud volleyball, a softball tournament, cowboy singers, a rubber duck race, and, to make sure everyone's still grounded in reality, a greased pole climb.

Mariposa Classic Car and Craft Show
Catheys Valley
(209) 966-5680, (209) 966-5112
Show your own vintage beauty or just come and see the fabulous cars and trucks from many eras. Food, arts and crafts, and auto accessory booths make a great day for those in love with wheels.

Yosemite National Park celebrates the anniversary of the founding of the National Park Service by admitting visitors free of charge every August 25. The free day is good only for admission to the park.

AUGUST

Native American Craft Days
Bridgeport
(760) 932-7500
Members of the Shoshone, Paiute, and Washoe Indian tribes gather on the lawns of the 1880-era courthouse to celebrate their heritage and welcome visitors to see demonstrations of traditional Native American crafts, dancing, and music and to try some delicious food. Fine arts and textiles are on sale.

Sierra Mono Indian Fair Days and Pow-Wow
North Fork
(559) 877-2115
A two-day celebration of Native American culture opens with the cleansing of "bad spirits" with eagle feathers and the smoke of burning sage. Events include traditional dancing, drumming, and singing. Vendors sell handmade jewelry, beadwork, baskets, and food. Storytelling, soap-root making, flint making, wood and soapstone carving, acorn processing, basket making, and other skills are demonstrated.

Yosemite Writers Conference
Tenaya Lodge at Yosemite, Fish Camp
(877) 849-0176
www.yosemitewriters.com
Publishers, editors, literary agents, and, of course, writers gather at the portal of the national park to learn, find inspiration, network, attend workshops, socialize, and make contacts over a late August weekend.

SEPTEMBER

Mariposa County Fair and Homecoming
Mariposa Fairgrounds
(209) 966-2432
www.mariposafair.com/annualfair.htm
A country-style, family-oriented fair with agricultural exhibits, livestock, a horse show, live entertainment, contests, a carnival, a rodeo, food, and fireworks. Good, clean fun, since 1939!

Mountain Heritage Days
Oakhurst
(559) 683-6470
An old-fashioned, hometown Saturday morning parade begins a weekend of events commemorating pioneer days and the Gold Rush in the Sierra. Marching bands, costumed riders on horseback and in covered wagons and vintage cars, a sluice box race, and floats are among the highlights. Don't miss the cycling clowns, the Wild Wonderful Women Kazoo Band, and the gun-totin' Chicken Gulch Posse, self-described as "citizen riders dedicated to truth, justice, and the mountain way of life." More events at Fresno Flats Historical Park include a championship horseshoe tournament, a petting zoo, children's games, and the Fabulous Faux Frog Flipping contest.

Oakhurst Classic Car Show and Oldies Weekend
(559) 877-6500
The fall weather is perfect for this gathering of vintage car enthusiasts. The fun begins Friday night at the barbecue and dance, and the fabulous vehicles line up in Oakhurst Community Park on Saturday—stick around for the live entertainment, raffles, and food. The "Cruise of Champions" parade of cars to the glitzy Chukchansi Gold Resort and Casino takes place at day's end, followed by a buffet dinner and headliner entertainment.

OCTOBER

Bass Lake Fall Festival and Craft Fair
(559) 877-3474
For more than two decades, artisans and crafters have assembled at Bass Lake to show and sell their wares. The weather is sparkling and brisk, and the aspens have turned to gold—a perfect time of year for browsing and Christmas shopping.

Mariposa-Yosemite Airport EAA Fly-In
Mariposa
(209) 966-7081
Fabulous classic and experimental aircraft and vintage cars are on display, and you can take an ultralight lesson, watch a radio-control demonstration, and stoke up at the food booths, pancake breakfast, and the tri-tip barbecue. Shuttle buses to and from town help you avoid the parking and traffic hassle.

North Fork Fall Festival
(559) 877-2244
The annual Grizzly Century Bicycle Run, with more than 600 participants, is the highlight of a multievent weekend of giant yard sales, a craft and fine art show and sale, an omelette breakfast, a barbecue dinner, an open house at the Sierra Mono Museum, and entertainment galore.

Tarantula Awareness Festival
Coarsegold
(559) 683-3900
In this country town, it's hard not to be aware of the large hairy spiders that emerge from dark places by the thousands in a month-long search for a mate starting in mid-October. Residents of Coarsegold, especially kids, catch the eight-legged creatures on the way to compete in a Tarantula Derby. There's a Best Tarantula Poem Contest and a human Hairy Leg Contest, all just a few days before Halloween.

NOVEMBER

Yosemite's Vintners' Holidays
The Ahwahnee
(559) 253-5635

Right after the fall wine grape harvest, distinguished winemakers from around the state assemble at The Ahwahnee to present in-depth two- and three-day seminars and wine tastings. Among the activities are panel discussions and tastings professionally moderated by nationally recognized wine authorities. The event ends with an impressive five-course dinner in the elegant Ahwahnee Dining Room, with fabulous wines paired with a custom gourmet menu. Yosemite's Vintners' Holidays, a tradition for nearly two decades, are popular and sell out well in advance; call early for reservations, and ask about two-, three-, and five-day accommodation packages.

DECEMBER

The Bracebridge Dinner
The Ahwahnee
(559) 253-5676
www.bracebridgedinner.com

The Bracebridge Dinner, now presented eight nights in December, is a glorious winter spectacle of drama, entertainment, food, and merriment. This splendid annual banquet re-creates a 17th-century English manor house Christmas, loosely based on a meal in Washington Irving's "The Sketch Book." Set in the magnificent Ahwahnee Dining Room, with professional costumed actors, period music, and fabulous food, it's no wonder this is such a popular event. Plan to book immediately when tickets become available in February. See the Lodging and Rentals chapter for more information.

A Dickens' Christmas at Wawona
Wawona Hotel
(559) 253-5676

Throughout December, the halls are decked with greenery and Christmas decor, and an array of special programs is held at the Victorian-era hotel, from caroling and candlelight tours to live musical performances, storytelling, holiday menus, and the festive lighting of the Christmas tree. Be sure to take a break from the activities and have a hot toddy in an armchair by one of the lobby fireplaces.

New Year's Eve Dinner Dances
The Ahwahnee, Yosemite Lodge at the Falls, and Wawona Hotel
(559) 253-5676

Make your reservations early for a glamorous evening with dancing to a swing band and a special multicourse banquet at The Ahwahnee, with Yosemite's spectacular snowy landscape as a backdrop. The lofty Ahwahnee Dining Room, the Mountain Room Restaurant at Yosemite Lodge at the Falls, and the Wawona Hotel are decorated in holiday finery for the romantic, festive evenings.

New Year's Eve Gala
Tenaya Lodge, Fish Camp
(888) 514-2167
www.tenayalodge.com

A grand buffet starts a long, elegant evening in the Grand Ballroom of the sprawling resort near the South Gate entrance to the national park. A live band plays until the wee hours for dancing. Ask about lodging packages that include the ball, party favors, dinner, and champagne.

Take a break from your revel to stroll around the lobby, a sparkling winter wonderland with a 34-foot-high white fir Christmas tree decorated with 5,000 white lights and whimsical ornaments. Around the resort are giant wreaths, prancing reindeer, and giant gingerbread houses.

Yosemite Christmas Crafts Bazaar
Curry Village Pavilion
(209) 372-4819
Local artisans sell original art, photography, gifts, clothing, gourmet foods, and decorative accessories. This is a unique opportunity to do all your Christmas shopping at one time and to meet the residents, park employees, and their families and friends.

Yosemite Winter Club Kick-Off Dinner Dance
Curry Village Pavilion
www.yosemitewinterclub.com
You can join the Winter Club and get discounts on rentals, retail items, and skiing, and celebrate winter sports in Yosemite at this fun, free evening. The Winter Club was established in Yosemite in 1928 to "encourage and develop all kinds of winter sports." In addition to this dinner, it puts on the annual Ancient Jocks Race and the February Silver Ski Race. (Open to skiers over 30 years old, the Jocks Race features a beverage stop halfway down the course, which gives you an idea of what the racers have on their minds.)

KIDSTUFF

American parents relive their own childhoods by bringing their kids to Yosemite, the most revisited national park in the country. Most of the old favorite campgrounds are still there, rangers still tell tall tales at evening campfires, and memories are made on hikes around Tuolumne Meadows. Those who have not been in the park for a decade or so will find that the Delaware North Companies Parks & Resorts, Inc. (DNC), the National Park Service, Sierra Club, and other organizations offer a wider variety of scheduled activities for kids and families. You can hightail it to the High Country, seeking solitude and family bonding at a wilderness campground, or hang out in the valley and sign the kids up for busy days of guided hikes and learning experiences.

The starting point for kids is Happy Isles Nature Center at the east end of the valley, where free, ranger-led walks, talks, and presentations are held throughout the day, spring through fall. Encourage your children to strike up conversations with the park rangers. They live and work in Yosemite because they love people and the outdoors, and they are great sources of insight into the natural and human history of the park.

Check out the ranger-guided hikes and activities based at some campgrounds, off the Tioga Road at the Lembert Dome parking area and at Tuolumne Meadows, and at Wawona and Crane Flat.

The *Yosemite Today* tabloid, available free at park entrances and throughout the park, lists a lively calendar of activities, classes, tours, talks, and live musical and dramatic performances (you can also access the tabloid online at www.nps.gov/yose/now/today.htm). Read the Events, Activities, and Tours chapter of this book for more things for kids to do.

Children ages 7 through 13 are the lucky ones who get to take part in the Junior Ranger program. For kids ages 3 through 6, the "Little Cubs" self-guided booklet helps discovery of Yosemite's natural charms and earns a Little Cubs button (www.nps.gov/yose/learn/jr.htm).

Enrich your family's experience by walking the signed, self-guided nature trails in the park; ask at the visitor center for a map. In Yosemite Valley, a mile-long path explores oak habitats. In the Mariposa Grove of Giant Sequoias, there are two self-guided walks through the trees, and there is also one in the Tuolumne Grove of Big Trees. In the Indian Village of Ahwahneechee, a self-guided trail winds through a re-created dwelling site with bark houses and tools used by Native Americans who lived in the valley in the 1800s. The self-guided trail through the Pioneer Yosemite History Center is open year-round at Wawona, in the southern part of the park; during the summer, costumed docents enact the daily life of pioneers.

As you explore the park with children, explain how off-trail hiking is destructive to habitat. Each time you break off a wildflower, nature's fragile ecosystem is interrupted. Each time you pick up leaves or cones or pieces of wood, the soil loses nutrients and animals lose potential homes. Encourage kids to walk quietly, so as to see and hear a few of the 247 species of birds and 89 species of mammals who call this park home. Give them

---

i

Bring your little ones along for the ride. Rent a bike and trailer (fits one little kid or two small toddlers or babies) for $13.50 per hour, $42.00 a day. Strollers and jogging strollers are $7.50 an hour or $11.00 a day. Rent equipment at the Yosemite Lodge at the Falls bike stand (209-372-1208) and at Curry Village (209-372-8319); helmets are included.

---

flower- and tree-identifying booklets and those disposable cameras for taking photos of wildflowers and cones, rather than collecting them. Tree- and flower-finder books, inexpensive and small enough to fit into a shirt pocket, are available from the Nature Study Guild Publishers, P.O. Box 10489, Rochester NY 14610-0489, (800) 954-2984; http://home.att.net/~nature books/finders.html.

Remember that Yosemite Valley is 3,000 to 4,800 feet above sea level, Glacier Point is 7,200 feet up, and Tuolumne Meadows is 8,600 feet in elevation. For the first day or two of your visit to Yosemite, everyone in the family and particularly the children may feel more tired than usual. If someone is nauseated, it may be altitude sickness. Extra rest and limited physical activity for a day or two are the cures. The ultimate cure is to descend to a lower altitude. Keep in mind that high altitude also means greater risk of sunburn. Use sunscreen every day, no matter how cold it feels outdoors, and stay hydrated.

Backpacking for Teens
(209) 379-9511
www.yni.org/programs/summer programs.html#yba

For more than 30 years, the private, nonprofit Yosemite Institute has provided educational adventures in the classroom of nature, inspiring young people to realize their connection with the natural world. The institute offers a nine-day backpacking program for 13- to 15-year-olds, and another for 15- to 18-year-olds; just 12 hikers are accepted for each trip. An All Girls Adventure takes the competition-with-boys factor out of learning backcountry skills, as girls 15 to 18 plan and execute peak ascents, cook tasty meals, and learn how to be leaders and doers in Yosemite's High Country.

The teens learn all about backcountry travel and survival, topographic map reading, wilderness safety, teamwork and group decision making, human and geologic history, and more, besides having the summer vacation of a lifetime!

Each trip is led by two experienced, highly qualified instructors who are Wilderness First Responder-certified. They lead these teen-oriented programs because they enjoy sharing their expertise and inspiring kids to appreciate wilderness ethics, natural and cultural history, and resource issues. The cost is $855.

> ***Your budding young scientist can learn about the park's geology in advance at www.nps.gov/yose/education on the Yosemite National Park Web site. While primarily designed for teachers with students, it's easy for your young computer-comfy scholar to answer the questions about types of rocks and how the landscape you'll be seeing together was formed.***

Badger Pups
Yosemite's Badger Pass Ski Area
(209) 372-8430
www.yosemitepark.com

Kids ages four to six learn to ski at one of the best family ski areas in the Sierra. For $39, they'll take a one-hour group lesson, including equipment rental, a rope-tow ticket, a place to rest, and supervised play. For $59, there's a Bruin Chair lift ticket and two group lessons.

Books for Parents and Kids

A longtime Yosemite resident, naturalist guide, and environmental educator, Michael Elsohn Ross is the author of a number of popular books for kids and parents, including *The Happy Camper Handbook: A Guide to Camping for Kids and Their Parents,* complete with a flashlight and a whistle, and *Family Nature Explorations: A Resource Kit.* Ross has also authored a number of excellent children's books on natural history, including *World of Small: Nature Explorations with a Hand Lens,* including the lens, and a delightful series of "Backyard Buddies" books, including *Spiderology, Wormology, and Ladybugology.* Look for the kits at Happy Isles.

Badger Pups gather at Yosemite's Badger Pass Ski Area. MAXINE CASS

Kids stay at no extra cost with their parents at the hotels and lodges in the park, and babysitting is available for children of guests at The Ahwahnee and the Yosemite Lodge at the Falls.

If you plan to try backpacking with little ones, get a copy of *Backpacking With Babies and Small Children: A Guide to Taking the Kids Along on Day Hikes, Overnighters and Long Trail Trips,* by Goldie Silverman.

Children's Corner
LeConte Memorial
Shuttle stop 12, road marker V21
(209) 372-4542
www.sierraclub.org/education/leconte
Since the turn of the 20th century, the Sierra Club has taken part in the preservation of the park and the education and enlightenment of visitors. Kids, in particular, are welcome at workshops, exhibits, and activities at the lodge. A corner in the rustic Sierra Club lodge is set aside for kids to spend quiet time coloring, leafing through nature books, and playing with hand puppets while their parents browse the library and displays. Free evening talks, slide shows, and programs are held on such topics as geology, history, Native Americans, flora, fauna, and the like. The curator, Bonnie Gisel, gives a talk that all ages seem to enjoy: "Good to Be Back Home in the Mountains: Stories of Pioneers and Friends in Yosemite Valley." Children too young to be interested in the presentations are usually found hanging out in the Children's Corner.

The lodge is open Wednesday through Sunday from 10:00 A.M. to 4:00 P.M. from May through September and for evening presentations, usually at 8:00 P.M. Check *Yosemite Today* for schedules.

From the Sierra Club Web site, your children can download a template and instructions for making a nature journal (www.sierraclub.org/education/nature_journal.asp).

Children's Story Time
Children 12 and under flock to the free 45-minute storytelling programs held in various locations in the summer. In winter, spring, and fall, The Ahwahnee Great Lounge fireplace is the cozy setting for stories about Yosemite's people, places, and natural history. Storytelling is free, and you can just show up. See *Yosemite Today* for listings.

Curry Village
Shuttle stop 14
Since 1899, families have spent their summer vacation at Curry Village, formerly called Camp Curry. This is a large complex of cabins and tent cabins and a few motel rooms. Facilities and rentals for just about every outdoor activity are based here, from river rafting to bicycling and ice-skating, plus swimming in the pool in summer. There is a cafeteria, pizza parlor, hamburger stand, ice-cream parlor, general store, and mountain sports store. Hiking trailheads start here, and the free shuttle bus stops here. The more kids you have, the better Curry Village will suit you and them, if you are up for sharing your Yosemite experience with a lot of other people. Amazingly, all of this infrastructure is nicely laid out and sheltered in a forest setting. See lodging details in the Lodging and Rentals chapter.

With secret maps, kids search for clues and explore the over-100-year history of Curry Village during children's scavenger hunts led by interpretive guides. It's free, and kids get a prize, too.

Explore Yosemite Family Program
Curry Village
(209) 372-1240
A three-hour morning program in the summertime introduces families to the natural and cultural world of Yosemite. See complete details in the Events, Activities, and Tours chapter.

Words for Wilderness Around the World

Visitors to the LeConte Memorial in Yosemite are invited to add their words to the Sierra Club–sponsored Words for Wilderness Around the World "necklace" program. Your 50 words about your own wilderness experiences or about the need to preserve wilderness will become a link in a chain of words and art that will eventually circle the earth on a pathway that begins with the John Muir Trail. You and your children can also submit drawings or poems. Learn more about Words for Wilderness at www.sierraclub.org/education/leconte/words.

Family Camping
North, Upper, and Lower Pines Campgrounds, Housekeeping Camp, and Curry Village are large and crowded in high season, and they can be noisy with road traffic and RV generators. Nevertheless, they are conveniently located for walking and biking to most public places and trailheads, and if your family is interested in taking advantage of the classes, interpretive hikes, and performances scheduled throughout the high season, a valley campsite or tent cabin may be your best choice. Children like the nightly campfires, too.

Some families like the quieter Wawona and Bridalveil Creek Campgrounds. Others head up the Tioga Road to White Wolf and Tuolumne Meadows Campgrounds, or hike into the wilderness to camp in solitude beside an alpine lake. It is absolutely necessary to make reservations for campgrounds throughout the park (800–436–7275; http://reservations.nps.gov). Some are booked up as much as a year in advance.

Family Camping Jamboree
(209) 379–2321
www.yosemite.org
Among the wide variety of fun, educational one-day and multiday courses and outings sponsored by the Yosemite Association is a multiday outdoor adventure course for families in Tuolumne Meadows High Country. Parents and kids camp, go on day hikes together, search for black bears and deer, look for wildflowers, and learn about Yosemite geology. There's a no-pressure feeling to this kick-back-and-get-to-know your-camp-neighbors program, while the kids play, learn, and relax a little themselves. No one has to cook or fuss—meals are included—leaving more time to walk the meadows or to take an optional Lembert Dome hike to Elizabeth Lake. Cost is $225 for each parent; kids are $125.

Happy Isles Nature Center
Shuttle stop 16, road marker V24
Named for a pair of small islands surrounded by rapids where the Merced River enters the valley, Happy Isles exists mostly for the children. Exhibits elucidate the natural features of the park, and the films, puppet shows, talks, and wildlife programs are designed specifically for kids. The Junior Ranger program is based here, and many guided hikes leave from Happy Isles, which is open in summer. Nearby you'll find short trails that focus on the area's four different environments: forest, river, talus, and fen.

If group activities are not your style, pick up Explorer Packs at Happy Isles and plan your own expeditions. Designed for investigation of Yosemite's rocks,

From late spring through early fall, midday temperatures in the park, particularly in the valley, may top 90 degrees, and the sun is intense at this elevation between 3,000 and 4,500 feet. Plan your young children's strenuous activities for times other than peak sun between late morning and mid-afternoon. Have them carry a daypack loaded with plenty of water, sunglasses, a hat, sunscreen, and insect repellent.

birds, trees, and flowers, each daypack has a theme such as "Rocking in Yosemite" or "Featuring Feathers," and each contains materials such as guidebooks, suggested activities, magnifying glasses, or binoculars.

Happy Isles is the trailhead for the famed John Muir Trail and for popular hiking routes to Vernal and Nevada Falls, Merced Lake, and Half Dome. Immediately west of Happy Isles is a two-acre fen, a rare ecosystem—a peat-forming wetland fed by moving groundwater—one of the few remaining in California. The fen is undergoing long-term restoration.

Junior Ranger Program

A variety of fun and educational activities are planned year-round for Junior Rangers, ages 7 through 13. June through August, there are workshops and guided walks and talks in Yosemite Valley, Wawona, Glacier Point, Hetch Hetchy, Tuolumne Meadows, and White Wolf. Winter programs are mainly in Yosemite Valley, although there's a daily snowshoe walk at Yosemite's Badger Pass. A self-guided *Junior Ranger Handbook* ($3.50), sold throughout the park or online at www.yosemitestore.com, helps kids follow the program. Besides personal interaction with National Park Service rangers, kids learn a lot about ecology, Native Americans, animals, birds, and forest lore. They can explore nature's mysteries and secret places in the park. For almost all of the activities, family members are welcome. Many families will choose something of interest to everybody, like an evening live theater performance, a walk hosted by a DNC guide or naturalist, a Yosemite Association program (www.yosemite.org), or one of the ranger programs. To preview these, look at what's been offered recently in *Yosemite Today* (www.nps.gov/yose/now/today.htm). Junior Rangers complete a number of activities, attend a ranger program, pick up a bag of litter, and then go to the visitor center or find a ranger to swear them in. The ranger presents them with a plastic Junior Ranger badge and a patch that some kids put on their scout sashes, backpacks, or hats.

It pays to ask about discounts for families. Open-air tram tours for sightseeing are exciting for young ones and discounted family pricing makes this way of seeing the park together both economical and easy on the driver and the environment. Yosemite Theatre performances also encourage families with specials and family rates.

Kids and Cameras

A special children's photo walk with a professional photographer, a Kodak Ambassador, starts from The Ahwahnee. It's a one-hour trek for ages 6 through 12; kids must have a parent or older sibling along. Check for schedules in *Yosemite Today* or with The Ahwahnee concierge desk. Children old enough to walk around the valley for a couple of hours and be relatively quiet are also welcome to tag along on the free camera walks based at the Ansel Adams Gallery.

Little Cubs Program

Children ages four to seven can have a happy learning experience too, much like a Junior Ranger. The *Little Cub Handbook* ($3.00), is available at Happy Isles, the visitor center, or online at www.yosemitestore.com. A fun teaching tool, the book

Free for Kids

Without spending a cent, you can keep your kids entertained all day, every day, in the park. (Check *Yosemite Today* for days, times, and locations of these activities and programs.)

- Watch the wranglers in action and pet the even-tempered mules at Yosemite Stables, the largest public stables in the western United States.
- It's free to peek into the bark houses in the Ahwahneechee Indian Village and to watch the frequent live demonstrations of traditional basket weaving, beadworking, acorn grinding, and Native American games.
- Your budding Rembrandts ages 10 and older can take advantage of free art classes at the Yosemite Art Center (details in the Events, Activities, and Tours Chapter).
- No charge to watch the award-winning film *Spirit of Yosemite,* shown several times daily at the visitor center.
- Children are fascinated by the costumed "inhabitants" of the Pioneer Yosemite History Center at Wawona. A blacksmith swings his hammer, a soldier stands guard with his rifle, and pioneer families cook traditional fare and care for their animals.
- Sign up for the free children's photo walk with a professional photographer; a parent or an older sibling must come along.
- Even toddlers kick up their heels at the Saturday night square dances outdoors at the Wawona Hotel. The dances are free for the whole family.
- Spend an hour listening to musician and historian Tom Bopp in the lobby of the Wawona Hotel. For no admission charge, he plays the piano and sings vintage Yosemite and camping songs several nights a week and shows slides on the history of Wawona.
- Free storytelling programs are held in various locations during the summer and in The Ahwahnee Great Lounge in the wintertime.
- Save a quiet hour or so for reading in the Children's Corner at the Le Conte Memorial.

covers various park features such as matching animals with their homes, taking a hike, learning about bears, and more. When they have attended a ranger program and completed the book, Little Cubs receive a patch and a Little Cub button.

Tenaya Adventure Club
Tenaya Lodge at Yosemite, Fish Camp
(877) 322–5492

Just outside the South Gate entrance to the park, kids five to 12 years old join counselors in a one-, two-, or three-day program that includes teepee building, rock climbing, hiking, snowshoeing, fishing, and archery. Sessions are from 11:00 A.M. to 3:00 P.M. and 5:00 to 9:00 P.M. daily, from late spring to early autumn. During the winter, the Tenaya Adventure Club entertains the kids on weekends and holidays. Cost is $65 per session for each child. Babysitting can be arranged for infants and children with advance notice.

Wawona
36 miles south of Yosemite Valley on Highway 41, 2 miles from the South Gate entrance to the park

Families with small children love Wawona for the riverside campground, for the fun

Kids staying with parents at The Ahwahnee, the Yosemite Lodge at the Falls, or Curry Village swim for free in the pools. If you're not checked in, there's a small charge of $2.50 for each swimmer. The Ahwahnee pool is open year-round; swimming at the Yosemite Lodge at the Falls or Curry Village is weather-dependent.

of the Mariposa Grove of Giant Sequoias tram ride, and the Pioneer Yosemite History Center, where costumed docents, including blacksmiths, reenact 19th-century life. Beaches and swimming spots are easily accessible on the south fork of the Merced River as it runs through Wawona.

On the other hand, the mezzanine of The Ahwahnee is a quiet hideaway for guests. A mother can lounge on the sofa with a cup of coffee—from the complimentary coffee, tea, and hot chocolate jugs behind her—and the morning newspaper while her children play games on the huge coffee table. See more about Wawona in the Wawona chapter.

Wee Wild Ones
(209) 372-1240
Just for kids ages six and under are the free 45-minute programs of stories, games, and fun surprises based on Yosemite-related themes such as wildlife and geology. In summer, Wee Wild Ones is offered two or three times a week in the early evening at outdoor amphitheaters at Yosemite Lodge at the Falls and Curry Village. The program moves indoors to The Ahwahnee's great fireplace in the winter. Parents, you must accompany your children, and you are encouraged to participate. See *Yosemite Today* for schedules and locations. Preregistration is not required.

OUTDOOR RECREATION

You can spend a lifetime in the great outdoors of Yosemite National Park, biking and swimming, mountain climbing, fly-fishing, riding horseback, and rafting down the Merced and the Tuolumne Rivers. It will take another lifetime or two to explore the national forests that completely surround the park. The advantage to recreation beyond the park is, number one, fewer people; number two, lower cost; and number three, a wider choice of activities, outfitters, and tour companies.

This chapter contains listings of the most popular sports and outdoor activities available in the park and in nearby areas—other than hiking and backpacking (which have their own chapter)—with a selection of tour and guide companies noted for their experience, safety, and local knowledge. In all cases, call around and ask a lot of questions, according to your individual needs, ages, fitness levels, budgets, and desires for either rip-roaring, death-defying excitement or a taste of the outback with all the comforts of home.

Within the surrounding Stanislaus, Sierra, Inyo, and Toiyabe National Forests and the Ansel Adams, John Muir, Hoover, and Emigrant Wilderness Areas, you'll find hundreds of miles of biking and horseback riding trails. Thousands of snow-fed streams, major rivers, and lakes comprise a mecca for anglers and campers. Sparsely developed, this vast wilderness region is surprisingly accessible with a little planning, map reading, and advice.

Mountain and rock climbers are in heaven in this part of the Sierra Nevada. The Sierra drops off on the east side of Yosemite, exposing steep, bare walls and spires, perfect climbing country. The Merced, Tuolumne, Stanislaus, American, Kings, and San Joaquin Rivers are world famous for white-water rafting; depending on the time of year and water flow, all ages can enjoy a guided raft trip.

Californians are avid mountain bikers, and although the biking trails in the park are limited to just over 12 miles, not far outside the park you can choose from gnarly, butt-kicking logging roads or easy, flat, paved paths, perfect for a family with small children.

The history of Yosemite is one of legendary mountain men and explorers who blazed the trails, made the first ascents, and discovered the alpine lakes that we enjoy today. With a little help from the dedicated, knowledgeable guides recommended herein, and with this book in your hand, make some history of your own.

BIKING

More than 12 miles of mostly flat, paved bikeways wind through the eastern end of Yosemite Valley, making this one of the world's most beautiful bike routes. Head out early in the morning, pack a lunch and bring water, tote your little kids in bike trailers, and explore the valley on two wheels. Most of the major natural and man-made attractions in the valley are accessible by bike.

Preserve your precious time in the park by bringing along a basic bike repair kit, a tire, and a tire pump. It's not a question of if you will get a flat in your lifetime, it's a question of when. And keep your eyes open for other bike traffic and walkers. In Yosemite, sightseers tend to stop in the middle of a trail or a road, gaze upward at some spectacular phenomenon of nature, and lose all common sense.

A biker pauses on Swinging Bridge over the Merced River, with Yosemite Falls nearby.
JOHN POIMIROO

Carrying Gear on Your Bike

• Handlebar bag: Make sure the bag allows access to your brakes and shifter barrel adjusters, and that it does not bend cables or affect the turning of the wheel.
• Backpack or camelbak: Focuses the bag weight on your body and not your bike. Do not strap on too tight, as it may restrict breathing. Chill your camelbak in the refrigerator before a hot ride and put some ice cubes in it.
• Seat bag: Fitting under the seat, this is a good place for tools and smaller gear.
• Butt pack: A good alternative to a backpack, as your back and chest remain free. It is also easily removed and can be carried when you stop to explore on foot.

You can rent six-speed bikes and baby trailers at Yosemite Lodge at the Falls in all seasons (209-372-1208, shuttle stop 8). Curry Village rents bikes April through October (209-372-8319, shuttle stop 13 or 21). Helmets are free, and all bikers under 18 years of age must wear a helmet. No mountain bikes are available, although you are welcome to bring your own. Bike rentals are $7.50 per hour, $24.50 per day. Stop in the visitor center or the main desk at your lodgings for Yosemite Valley bike trail maps. Strollers, pets, and all bicycles, including mountain bikes, are prohibited on unpaved pedestrian and hiking trails.

A nice, easy 2-mile route starts from Curry Village and goes past the stables and on to Mirror Lake. On the way back, stop at the stables and visit the friendly horses and mules. For a 5-mile ride round-trip, start from Yosemite Lodge at the Falls, go across the meadow and over the bridge toward the chapel, continue past Le Conte Memorial and on to Curry Village for an ice cream. Follow the signs to Yosemite Village to finish your loop around the valley.

Stop in at Yosemite Bicycle & Sport, 40120 Highway 41, Suite F, Oakhurst, (559) 641-2453, for information on single- and double-track trails and for good biking roads in the Sierra National Forest. The shop, which can assemble your preshipped bike, also offers rentals and a drop-off and pickup service for some breathtaking downhill rides above Fish Camp in the Goat Mountain area, outside of the southern section of the park. The Yosemite Bicycle Club operates from the same location, with weekday morning road and off-road mountain biking, and weekend tours.

Merced River Canyon
Highway 140 at Briceburg

Park at the BLM Visitors Center at the silver suspension bridge at Briceburg between Mariposa and El Portal. Bike 5 miles on the road along the river, to the Black Bridge and back. Along the way, stop at swimming holes and small beaches, July through September. There is a nice swimming hole under the Black Bridge, but do not swim in the spring when the water is high and fast.

On the north side of the Briceburg Bridge, drive to the right up the hill to the top and park at the first fire road leading right at the top of the grade. This is a great biking road making a 15-mile, rolling loop through an interesting stretch of terrain, with wide views of Yosemite and the canyon. To avoid getting off on other, less scenic fire roads, stop in at the Yosemite Bug Hostel, just up the highway, for a free map.

CLIMBING AND MOUNTAINEERING

Literally thousands of climbers from around the world flock to Yosemite every year to clamber and climb over everything from boulders to skinny, crackled spires to the massive walls of El Capitan and Half Dome. No other location in the lower 48 states offers this concentration of difficult, legendary ascents of sheer, vertical faces as Yosemite. Many avid rock jockeys work as park employees and in the restaurants and lodgings to support their addiction to climbing. Just ask around to hear some hair-raising tales of fearsome climbing routes with names like "Lurking Fear," "Squeeze Play," "Lost World," and "Realm of the Flying Monkeys."

Basking in the wildflowers and native grasses in El Capitan meadow, sightseers can watch the climbers on El Cap, Cathedral Rock, and Cathedral Spires. Although you can see some climbers with the naked eye, binoculars greatly enhance the experience (you can rent binoculars at your lodgings).

A good vantage point from which to see climbers is across from Yosemite Lodge at the Falls, near Camp 4 Campground. In the summertime, climbers are often active along the Tioga Road near Tenaya Lake and around Tuolumne Meadows.

Unconquerable until the first modern climbing techniques and equipment were designed in the 1950s, the 3,593-foot-high granite wall, El Capitan, was not summited until 1958, five years after the first ascent of Mount Everest. The first successful climber, Warren Harding, spent 45 days working his way up El Cap. The second ascent, a decade later, took less than a week. These days, "extreme" climbers make it in less than four hours, although the average, experienced climber takes three or four days.

See the Campgrounds chapter for some history about Camp 4, the legendary birthplace of American big wall climbing.

Did you know that the best way to fall, if you have to, is like a cat, landing on your feet and breaking a leg if necessary? John Dill, NPS Search and Rescue (SAR) has written, "Staying Alive," a wry, clear, and extremely detailed explanation of how Yosemite climbing incidents have happened and what can be done to prevent up to 80 percent of them. Take the warnings to heart and learn a lot about climbing, at www.nps.gov/yose/sar/climbsafe.htm.

Yosemite Mountaineering School and Guide Service (YMS)
Curry Village
(209) 372-8344 (summer),
(209) 372-8444 (winter)
Tuolumne Meadows
(209) 372-8435

The top-ranked mountaineering school in America, YMS is headquartered in what some claim is the world's premier rock-climbing area. Lessons and guided climbs are taught and led by some of the top climbers in the country, if not the world. Programs are offered for people of all abilities in Yosemite Valley during the spring and fall, and in Tuolumne Meadows each summer, including summer snow climbing. Winter mountaineering experiences are also available. Inquire at the Mountain Shop in Curry Village and at the Mountaineering School at Tuolumne Meadows, next to the gas station.

You can get a short rock climbing lesson, hire a guide to make a major ascent, or take a guided climb. All needed equipment is available to rent or purchase in the park. The school also offers Nordic skiing equipment and lessons as well as guided backpacking treks. Lessons include crack climbing, anchoring, leading/multipitch climbing, and self-rescue/aid climbing.

Go Climb a Rock

Due to the emergence of indoor climbing facilities nationwide in the last decade, rock climbing is a rapidly growing sport, and Yosemite is one of the best places in the world to learn and practice. With an experienced teacher and proper gear, it's easier than you may think. If you can climb a ladder, you can climb a rock. Rock climbing classes are conducted for beginning, intermediate, and advanced climbers, spring through fall in Yosemite Valley and at Tuolumne Meadows in the summertime. For some, you can just drop in at the scheduled time; for others, call ahead. The basic lesson provides hand-on experience and instruction on equipment, correct use of hand and footholds, belays, and rappels. All equipment is provided, except climbing shoes, which are available to rent. Prices for the comprehensive beginner's "Go Climb a Rock" session are $117 to $217 per person. The classes are limited to six, and with three or more participants, your group pays the cheapest rate. Call (209) 372-8344 or check price and program details on www.yosemitepark.com.

Southern Yosemite Mountain Guides
621 Highland Avenue
Santa Cruz
(800) 231-4575
www.symg.com

Experienced groups of climbers and guides have offered rock-climbing expeditions and climbing classes in the Ansel Adams Wilderness and Kings Canyon and Sequoia National Parks since 1991. They offer Rock Climbing Weekends (including gear, shoes, and all meals) for people of all abilities for $405 per person. You can opt for camping gear or stay at a variety of nearby lodgings. Five-day, four-night Rock Camp programs are an opportunity to learn and practice anchors, leading principles, AMGA standards for top ropes, advanced techniques, and multipitch systems. Cost is $795.

i

Legendary veteran climbers, such as Greg Couch, Royal Robbins, and others, sometimes give free talks in the Yosemite Lodge at the Falls Amphitheater, and the climbing film* Vertical Frontier *is also presented there. See* Yosemite Today *for days and times.

FISHING

The best stream fishing in Yosemite for brook, brown, and rainbow trout is in the Dana Fork and the Lyell Fork of the Tuolumne River. Fishing is also fine at Gaylor, Granite, May, Tenaya, Lukens, and Hardin Lakes. See more about these lakes in the Hiking and Backpacking chapter. Some of the very best fishing in the park can be had on the stretch of the Tuolumne River that is accessed from White Wolf Campground by a steep 7-mile trail.

Fishing is good in the Merced River from Vernal and Nevada Falls up to Merced and Washburn Lakes. As the lakes are easily accessible and very popular, better fishing is found above Washburn.

On the 7 miles of the Merced River in Yosemite Valley, more often than not, it is the skilled fly-fisher who is successful. The hordes of summer visitors who try their luck, including many kids, mostly catch fun and sunburn.

From Happy Isles, downstream through El Portal to the Foresta Bridge, it is catch-and-release only for native rainbow trout, and only artificial lures or flies with barbless hooks may be used. Bait is prohibited, in an attempt to control injury of fish swallowing hooks and to avoid introduction of foreign organisms into the river ecosystem.

i

Of interest to anglers and river rafters, flow levels for many California rivers and reservoirs are recorded daily at this number: (800) 952-5530.

Fishing in Yosemite

Fishing in Yosemite Valley has been a tradition for hundreds of years. The Southern Miwok were the first Native Americans in the area, and fishing was a source of food, rarely the pleasure that we enjoy today. When the first American tourists arrived in Yosemite, only one species of trout, the rainbow, was present. This beautiful fish is a joy to catch and still can be found in great numbers in the Merced River.

In 1926 the new paved Highway 140 from Merced promised a smooth, snow-free, all-season route into the valley, and a new fish hatchery was established at Happy Isles. Fishing was destined to become a premier sport in Yosemite as fish from the hatchery were added to the rivers and lakes in the High Country. The German Brown was stocked by the thousands and soon spread to every area of the Merced River. Since this introduction of nonnative fish into the parks, attitudes and ideas about natural resources and management within our national parks have changed and the stocking of the river was discontinued in 1948, with all stocking throughout the park discontinued in 1993 in order to let natural processes prevail.

Today, special rules and regulations have also been established. There is a strict catch-and-release policy for rainbow trout, but you can keep up to five browns per day or have 10 in your possession, representing several days of angling. This is to protect the native rainbow and weed out the introduced browns. Make sure you know and can identify each species of fish before setting out so you can help protect our native species of rainbow.

What you can expect from Yosemite trout is stealth and cunning. Only a patient angler will have great success, as the waters of the Merced River are cool and clear with little obstructing the fishes' view of you. Be as cautious as possible when approaching the water. Sit a spell to observe fish rising to the surface to feed. Even if you don't have a fishing pole, this can be a rewarding experience in itself.

Trout of the Merced River are not large by most standards. You can expect a fish of 4 to 6 or even 8 inches, but anglers still catch the occasional 12- to 14-inch fish. The record, set in 1932, is 27 inches and 12 pounds. I caught a brown of 17 inches but expect that to be one of the largest I will ever see.

—Leland Hales, a DNC naturalist guide

The best places to fish on the south fork of the Merced River in Wawona are upstream from the Wawona Campground, downstream from the Swinging Bridge, and in Big Creek—cross the golf course and walk about a half mile to Big Creek.

Trout season in Yosemite begins on the last Saturday in April and continues through November 15. All lakes and reservoirs in the Sierra are open for fishing year-round. Be sure to display your fishing licenses prominently on your clothing; get one-day, three-day, or all-season licenses and information at the Village Sport Shop or Wawona Store in summer, or at the (Curry Village) Mountain Shop in winter;

Best Places to Swim in Yosemite

- South Fork of the Merced River at Wawona, over the covered bridge and up the trail from the Pioneer Yosemite History Center
- Sandy bars between Clark's Bridge and Sentinel Beach in Yosemite Valley
- Tuolumne River at Tuolumne Meadows Campground
- Dog Lake, 1.5-mile walk from the east end of Tuolumne Meadows
- East end of Tenaya Lake, off the Tioga Road
- Swimming pool at The Ahwahnee, guests only
- Swimming pool at the Wawona Hotel, guests only
- Swimming pool at Curry Village, open to all
- Swimming pool at Yosemite Lodge at the Falls, open to all

you will need identification. Children under 16 are not required to carry a license.

Avid anglers know that some of the best fishing in the state is in the Bridgeport and June Lakes areas, not far from the East Gate of the park, on hundreds of miles of streams and in three dozen lakes. Below Bridgeport Reservoir, the East Walker River is top-notch for brown and rainbow trout fly-fishing. The reservoir itself is clogged with weeds and algae in the summertime and is fishable only in spring and fall.

Kirman Lake and Green Creek are two famous fishing spots. For the latest on where to go and what kind of flies and lures to use, go to Ken's Sporting Goods (258 Main Street, Bridgeport, 760-932-7707).

Many varieties of warm-water fish are caught in the lakes of the foothills surrounding the Oakhurst/North Fork area.

Here are some easily accessible, good places to fish outside the park.

Bass Lake
14 miles from Oakhurst off Highway 41 on Road 222
(559) 683-4665

At 3,400 feet, a large, developed recreational area surrounds a big lake with 16 species of fish, including trout, catfish, perch, black bass, and kokanee salmon. Camping, lodging, hiking trails, stores, and rentals of all kinds are available at Pines Village.

Eastman Lake
southwest of Oakhurst, via Grub Gulch Road
(559) 689-3255

In the lower foothills, this warm-water lake is open year-round and is California's first Trophy Bass Fishery. It's a good spot for bass, crappie, blue gill and sunfish, and brown and rainbow trout. The lake is not far from campgrounds, picnic areas, boat launch ramps, and sports shops, and is also home to a nesting pair of bald eagles. It can be hot and dry in midsummer and early fall.

Fish Camp Bridge
Highway 41

Park by the bridge and fish downstream, using flies and spinners, down to the campgrounds, about 3 miles. Fishing here is best in the early spring.

Hensley Lake
Southwest of Oakhurst off Highway 41 on the Fresno River
(559) 673-5151

This low-elevation lake harbors secluded coves great for bass, blue gill, crappie, and catfish. Amenities include a campground, picnic areas, two swimming beaches, hiking trails, and boat and water sports rentals.

June Lake Loop
See Outdoor Recreation in the East Gate Entrance chapter for information about excellent fishing for four trout species—brown, brook, cutthroat, and rainbow—on the June Lake Loop in the eastern Sierra.

Mammoth Pool Reservoir
40 miles east of North Fork
(559) 877-2218
On the San Joaquin River at 3,300 feet, this large trout lake has steep, rocky sides, so most fishing is by boat. In a lovely forest setting with mountains rising around the shoreline, this area includes boat ramps, picnic areas, and hiking trails. Visitors swim and camp here as well. The reservoir is closed May through June 16 to accommodate migrating deer.

Manzanita Lake
2 miles north of North Fork at Roads 222 and 226
(559) 877-2410
On Willow Creek, this small, very accessible lake is stocked with rainbow trout and is perfect for beginning anglers.

Merced River/Bagby/Lake McClure
Highway 49 or Highway 132 to Highway 49
Park at Bagby and fish downstream, following the trail on the old railroad bed, until the lake widens.

Merced River/El Portal
Highway 140
All along the Merced River at El Portal, there are many pools with good fly-fishing, especially in the fall. Parking is very accessible. Barbless hooks and catch-and-release rules are in effect. Take care when the water is running fast.

Merced River/Forest Road
Off Highway 41 at Fish Camp
From Fish Camp, take Forest Road up to Mount Hogan, about 7 miles; look for the Iron Creek trailhead, which descends about 2.5 miles to the Merced River. You can catch big fish here, including brown trout, particularly in the early spring.

Wilderness Fly-Fishing Outfitters

Frontier Pack Train
1012 East Line Street, Bishop
(888) 437-MULE
www.frontierpacktrain.com
In business for more than a decade, this company is staffed by locals who know the territory. They lead Golden Trout Pack Trips into the solitude of the beautiful Ansel Adams Wilderness on the east side of Yosemite National Park, guiding guests to the all-time best fishing spots. They set up camp at picturesque sites, take care of all the equipment, and cook incredible meals around the campfire. In recent years, Frontier was selected by the California School of Fly Fishing as its pack outfitter. Some of the top fishing waters on these trips are Crest Creek, Algers Lakes, Clark Lakes, and Thousand Island Lake at the headwaters of the San Joaquin River. It is not uncommon for guests to catch goldens from 12 to 16 inches in length.

Sierra West Adventures
(209) 588-1306
www.fishthesierra.com
This fishing guiding company covers 800 miles of moving waters and 20 still-water fisheries on the Sierra's western side, including the Merced River, which flows from Yosemite Valley through a rugged canyon to reservoirs. The same Tuolumne River that flows through Yosemite High Country provides fine fishing in its forks and feeders as it goes west. From the Emigrant Wilderness, the Stanislaus River flows into a drainage that delights anglers. The most popular trip, the multiday Sierra Sampler, runs year-round and offers a

variety of fishing waters and species, with meals, guides, and gear included. Cost is $380 per day.

Southern Yosemite Mountain Guides
621 Highland Avenue
Santa Cruz
(800) 231-4575
www.symg.com
During the summer months, the guides from this experienced company focus on fly-fishing in streams and lakes at 7,000 to 8,800 feet in elevation. Fly-Fishing Weekend trips run about $445 per person, in groups of two to four people, including breakfast and dinner and camping equipment; bring your own fishing gear or rent from them. After a full day of wade fishing, you return to the private camp for a relaxing campfire and fish tales.

A three-day fly-fishing school is also offered, including casting techniques, fly selection, reading waters, entomology, and more, all while fishing the Merced and Tuolumne Rivers. Evenings are spent learning to tie flies and relaxing at the lodge, which is the Yosemite Bug Rustic Mountain Resort (see the Arch Rock chapter for more about the Bug). Guides, equipment, and flies are included in the $545 per-person cost.

Yosemite Guides
P.O. Box 650, El Portal, CA 95318,
Yosemite View Lodge, Highway 140
(866) 922-9111, (209) 379-9111
www.yosemiteguides.com
From their base at El Portal, 2 miles from the Arch Rock entrance to the national park, experienced guides will take you on full-day or half-day expeditions to remote areas seldom seen or fished by park visitors and to little-known fishing holes along the Merced River and nearby tributaries. The cost for a full day is about $225 per person, including equipment, and $50 for each additional person. Half-days are $175. Groups are usually limited to three people, as personal attention is a top priority. Fishing guides with local knowledge will shepherd your party, providing all equipment, food, lodging, transport, and lots of instruction and TLC for beginning anglers.

GOLF

Wawona Golf Course
One of the only golf courses in a national park, the nine-hole Wawona Golf Course opened in June 1918 and was the first in the Sierra Nevada. Avid golfers find the 3,050-yard layout at Wawona a short, sweet golfing experience that enhances visits to the "quiet side" of Yosemite. The course begins in meadows alongside a stream, and once you set off into the narrow corridors of Douglas firs and ponderosa and sugar pines, a sense of sublime isolation ensues, at least until your ball bounces off one of the massive tree trunks. The most challenging hole is the seventh, a blind hole called the "Cathedral" with a frightfully narrow, uphill fairway bordered by incense cedars and pines. Watch out for strolling tourists, grazing deer, the occasional coyote, and even a bear, early in the morning. For more information, see the Wawona chapter.

HORSEBACK RIDING

In the Park

From spring through fall, the park service offers two- and four-hour guided rides, departing every day from stables at Yosemite Valley, Tuolumne Meadows, and Wawona. All-day rides, private rides, and wilderness pack trips can be arranged for a minimum of three people. Call ahead for reservations (209-372-8348 [Yosemite Valley], 209-372-8427 [Tuolumne Meadows], 209-375-6502 [Wawona]; www.yosemitepark.com). Costs are $51 for two hours and $67 for a half-day; all-day rides are $94.

You can also arrange to rent pack and saddle animals; this requires the services of a guide/packer, costing about $130 per day. And you can board your horse for $12 per day. Riders on all the trips must be at least seven years old and 44 inches tall, and weigh less than 225 pounds; helmets are mandatory and available free.

High Sierra Camps Saddle Trips
(559) 253-5674 (reservations), (209) 372-8348 (information)
www.yosemitepark.com

So popular as to be sold out well in advance, four- and six-day horseback trips between the High Sierra camps are led by experienced guide/packers. Groups of no more than 10 people depart from Tuolumne Meadows and move through spectacular alpine wilderness between 7,000 and 10,000 feet in elevation; you arrive at camp by midafternoon each day. Lodging is in tent cabins with beds, bedding, and meals provided. Personal belongings are carried on pack mules. Reserve as many months ahead as possible. See the Campgrounds chapter for descriptions of the High Sierra Camps.

Cost per person for the four-day horseback trip is about $732; for the six-day, about $1,155. A lottery is held annually for reservations; call in early November for a lottery application. Plan well ahead for your family to take this incredible wilderness trip—as long as everyone has done some riding before; children must be at least seven years old. This is the easiest, least physically demanding, most carefree way to see and experience the High Country.

Near the Park

Frontier Pack Train
1012 East Line Street, Bishop
(888) 437-MULE
www.frontierpacktrain.com

Ride into the spectacular Ansel Adams Wilderness on the east side of Yosemite National Park with guides who know the ropes, on a one-day or several-day trek.

One of their most popular trips is the four-day annual herding of 100 or so head of horses and mules between their winter headquarters and June Lake, which takes place in June. They also offer hiking with pack stock and wild horse tracking expeditions in the Inyo National Forest.

Your sleeping bag is all you need to bring. All campsite equipment and incredible meals around the campfire are provided.

Yosemite Trails Pack Station
P.O. Box 100, Fish Camp, CA 93623
(559) 683-7611
www.yosemitetrails.com

From Fish Camp near the South Gate entrance of the park, take a half-day ride to the Mariposa Grove of Giant Sequoias or shorter rides on scenic forest trails, for all ages, including young children. In the wintertime on holidays and some weekends only, horseback rides with snow on the ground are beautiful, bracing experiences.

RIVER RAFTING

In the Park

Born in the Sierra Nevada at 11,000 feet, the Merced River runs wild and free through Yosemite and into a deep canyon until it reaches the dam at Lake McClure, at the eastern edge of the Central Valley. Rafting on the Merced River where it runs through Yosemite Valley is a popular activity during the hot summer months, and that stretch of river is calm enough for first-timers and children. You can rent a raft for four to six adults, with a shuttle return or bring your own flotation device. (Each child must weigh at least 50 pounds to rent rafts in the park.) Nonmotorized vessels, such as kayaks, inner tubes, and blow-up toys, are permitted; each passenger must have a U.S. Coast Guard–approved life vest, which can be rented at the Curry Village Recreation Center, 209-372-8319.

The designated rafting area is between Stoneman Bridge (near Curry Village) and the Sentinel Beach picnic area, between the hours of 10:00 A.M. and

6:00 P.M. You can also raft on the South Fork of the Merced River in Wawona, between Swinging Bridge and the campground.

Make the most of your raft cruise by stopping along the way on sandbars or islands to swim, wade, picnic, or relax under a tree. Be prepared by having the family wear water shoes or sandals and swimsuits. And don't forget to bring hats, cover-ups, sunscreen, and plenty of water.

To protect the riverbanks in the park, embark and debark on sand or gravel bars. To avoid disappointment, it is a good idea to call ahead before you count on water sports, as access to the river is sometimes limited or banned due to water conditions or habitat restoration.

Near the Park

River rafting is very popular on 28 miles of the Merced River below the park between Red Bud (at the Foresta Bridge just west of El Portal) to Bagby, from early April through June when the rapids are high. Merced River whitewater is action-packed, with long wave trains and fast chutes, occasionally broken by a clear, glassy pool. This section of the river is rated Class III through Class V, and there is one mandatory portage, at North Fork Falls, about 6 miles east of Bagby.

The *Boating Trail Guide to the Merced River* is a good reference to have if you plan to raft on your own. It shows exactly where to put in and out of the river, locates campgrounds and public facilities, and also explains what to expect on various sections of the river. First-come, first-served campgrounds are available at the launch sites. A sunny hiking trail on the north bank is also shown on the map, following the river on an old railroad right-of-way. The map and trail guide brochure for this Federal Wild and Scenic River is free online at www.dbw.ca.gov/boattrails/merced.asp, or write to the California Department of Boating and Waterways, 2000 Evergreen Street, Suite 100, Sacramento, CA 95815-3888, (888) 326-2822, (916) 263-1331.

Water flow can change very quickly, so you are cautioned to check with the Merced River Canyon visitor information center in Briceburg before you debark, to get the daily prediction of flow conditions. All rafters wear life vests, and many wear wetsuits and carry changes of clothing to prevent hypothermia.

Both the Merced and Tuolumne Rivers are designated Wild and Scenic Rivers. The Tuolumne offers outstanding rafting for experienced rafters on an 18-mile stretch of nearly unceasing white water in an isolated canyon, with more than 25 major rapids, and massive wave trains, huge holes, and plunging rafters. The put-in sites are usually at Cherry Creek or at Lumsden near the Groveland Ranger Station, and for the scoot through the steep-walled canyon to Wards Ferry Bridge. As you must have a permit for rafting between May 1 and September 30, you might as well stop at the Ranger Station, as they issue the permits (Groveland Ranger Station, 9 miles east of Groveland; 24545 Highway 120, Groveland, CA 95321; 209-962-7825; www.fs.fed.us/r5/stanislaus/groveland). Three Forest Service campgrounds are located at the launch sites. A $15.00 fee is charged for reserving a rafting permit; for parties of 11 to 26 people, there is an additional charge of $2.00 per person. Permits issued on a nonreserved basis are free.

Due to the dependably raucous rapids, rated Class IV and V, rangers highly recommend that rafters on the Tuolumne River travel in teams of at least two boats; this is considered an advanced river run, for experts only. Several campgrounds, launching sites, public facilities, and hiking trails are shown on *The Boating Trail Guide to the Tuolumne River,* available free online at www.dbw.ca.gov/boattrails/tuolumne.asp, or at the Ranger Station.

For a relaxing, carefree river-rafting experience, book with an experienced rafting company. If you are traveling with children, ask the company about the best river and the best times of year for non-

Tuolumne River white-water rafting is world class and lots of fun. ZEPHYR WHITEWATER

scary raft trips. First-time rafters are less intimidated later in the summer, when the water flow lessens.

O.A.R.S.
P.O. Box 67, Angels Camp, CA 95222
(800) 346-6277, (209) 736-4677
www.oars.com
One of the oldest rafting companies in the country and possibly the most geographically diverse, O.A.R.S. has been in business for more than 30 years, guiding families, couples, individuals, and groups on the Merced, the Tuolumne, and many other rivers throughout California, Alaska, the western states, the Grand Canyon, and international destinations including Fiji and Peru. Besides rafting trips, they also have dory and kayak expeditions.

O.A.R.S. offers a wide variety of types of trips, from parent/child adventures, which include kids ages 4 to 13, to custom group charters and even gourmet food and wine raft trips. Day trips on the Merced River start at about $130 per person, and on the Tuolumne River, $205, with family discounts.

Sierra Mac River Trips
P.O. Box 264, Groveland, CA 95321
(800) 457-2580, (209) 532-1327
www.sierramac.com
For more than 40 years, Marty McDonnell and his crew have guided white-water rafting trips near Yosemite on the Tuolumne River, and Cherry Creek on the Upper Tuolumne.

McDonnell has guided thousands of people ages 5 to 75 safely down the rivers. Ask him about the unique California Roll, which takes place during every full moon throughout the summer, an 18-mile expedition on the roiling Tuolumne, complete with gourmet food, vintage winetasting, and campout under the stars.

Sunshine Rafting Adventures
P.O. Box 1445, Oakdale, CA 95361
(800) 829-7238
www.raftadventure.com
This company offers an easy introduction to self-guided river rafting by setting you up for a four- to five-hour expedition along the Lower Stanislaus River from Knights Ferry to Orange Blossom Park, a float trip popular with families (kids must be three or older). Bring a small ice chest, tennis shoes, a litter bag, bathing suits, sunscreen, hat, sunglasses with a cord, and no pets; a return shuttle is provided. Cost is about $49.00 per person, including raft, paddles, life vests, instructions, and a tasty deli lunch. You can also arrange for guided white-water rafting trips on the Stanislaus River, canoe and raft rentals, or a float trip further south, on the Kings River. Sunshine Rafting Adventures also offers camping and an RV park at Knight's Ferry.

The late May through early September Rail & Raft Trip is unique way to see the Sierra Nevada foothills from two perspectives. The Sierra Railroad and Sunshine Rafting Adventures operate a five-and-a-half- to six-hour hour combination that begins in Oakdale aboard the blue and gold Sierra Railroad Daylight Train. For the first two hours, the scenery of the Stanislaus River Valley passes by. Upon arrival in Knight's Valley, the float trip on the Stanislaus River begins, passing by scenic spots like Two Bluffs' volcanic landscape and dramatic Lover's Leap. As with the regular float trips, everyone ends up at Orange Blossom Park. Cost is $59; call (209) 848-2100; www.sierrarailroad.com.

Zephyr Whitewater Expeditions
P.O. Box 510, Columbia, CA 95310
(800) 431-3636, (209) 532-6249
www.zrafting.com
One of California's first-established rafting companies, in business since 1973, Zephyr commands one of the best safety records in the industry, due in part to their low-turnover, highly paid guides. Zephyr is also the largest river rafting company in the Yosemite area. They offer half-day to three-day white-water rafting trips on the Kings, Tuolumne, Merced, and American Rivers, all near Yosemite National Park. Cost ranges from $75 to $525, depending on the number of days. Wet suits, paddle jackets, and river use fees are included in trip fees (wet suits are not needed in midsummer). Ask about the 50-percent-off standby list. Depending on the snowpack and when the Merced River water begins running, an easy way to fit river rafting into a busy Yosemite National Park visit between April to July is to enjoy one of Zephyr's popular morning or afternoon half-day rafting trips. You'll get some rapids and stories to impress folks back home.

For the Yosemite Special, April through July, you park at Midpines, 45 minutes from Yosemite, and camp in tent cabins or in your tent in their private campground on the river, and combine a rafting day on the Merced River and two on the Tuolumne with an overnight visit to Yosemite. Zephyr offers group and family discounts, and a six-day white-water school in April.

TENNIS

Experience "love" on one of The Ahwahnee's outdoor tennis courts, tucked into a meadow beneath Royal Arches and within view of Yosemite Falls. Hotel guests seem to be occupied with sight-seeing and other activities, rather than tennis, so the courts are often empty.

Use of the tennis court at the Wawona Hotel is free to hotel guests and $2.50 per hour for visitors.

HIKING AND BACKPACKING

If you love to hike, at some point in your life you will make a pilgrimage to Yosemite, a fragment of wilderness so enthralling that simply walking in these mountains and valleys has inspired some people to stay for the rest of their lives and make it their life's work to preserve it.

In the national park, 840 miles of trails lie between 2,900 and 13,114 feet in elevation, from Yosemite Valley to the summit of Mount Lyell. From an easy stroll along the Merced River on the flat valley floor to a moderate climb to a waterfall, or several days of backpacking in the Tuolumne High Country, there are footpaths for every age and fitness level, even some wheelchair-accessible paths. Unless you hike in early spring, late fall, or winter, you will not be alone on the popular trails, although, with a little planning, map studying, and talking to park rangers, you can manage to find complete solitude. To avoid the crowds, set out as early as possible in the morning so at least your outbound route may seem as though you are the first person ever to have trod it. On a short walk in the valley or an all-day expedition, you will almost surely encounter rushing streams, creeks, and waterfalls, and riots of wildflowers.

Just a short drive up the Glacier Point Road will bring you to a wide choice of not-too-strenuous hikes with dazzling views. Other less-traveled trails are in the Hetch Hetchy and Wawona areas. At the west end of the Tioga Road, Crane Flat is a lovely complex of forest and wildflower meadows near trails in the Merced Grove and Tuolumne Grove of Giant Sequoias.

In midsummer when vehicles and people crowd the hot valley floor, hikers drive 45 miles up the Tioga Road to Tuolumne Meadows. Along the way, the elevation rises nearly 4,000 feet and the temperature drops dramatically near the summit of Tioga Pass at 9,945 feet. The road is normally open from late May or early June until the first big snowstorm, about November 1. Cross-country skiers and snowshoers use the road itself as well as some of the same trails.

Tuolumne Meadows is base camp for a vast network of trails into the High Country of alpine lakes and meadows, the rugged Merced and Tuolumne River canyons, and across mountains in the northern part of the park, above the tree line. The cross-Sierra John Muir Trail and the Pacific Crest Trail wind through the park here. The Tuolumne Meadows Trail itself and some other mostly flat, easy trails in this area are easy enough for little kids, although the high elevation may take the stuffing out of them.

Below the cliff walls surrounding Yosemite Valley, you'll find numerous footpaths that are mostly paved, flat, and easy. Wandering the valley on a get-acquainted tour, you can make a complete loop, about 13 miles, in a five- to seven-hour period. Bring plenty of water along and snacks or a picnic, or plan your valley ramble with meal stops at one of the many food outlets. The valley trails are quite close to the two main roads and the campgrounds, restaurants,

i

Do not "bushwhack." By staying on the trail and resisting the temptation to create your own shortcuts, you help maintain the trail system, the wildlife habitat, and the beauty of the wilderness.

and other public facilities; in fact, you can get no farther than a thousand feet from a paved road on the narrow valley floor.

On the eastern end of the valley, starting points for beautiful walks and hikes can be reached only by shuttle bus or on foot or bikes, such as the Happy Isles trailheads to Vernal and Nevada Falls, and Half Dome. In winter and early spring, nearly all of the trails in Yosemite Valley remain open; check the *Yosemite Today* tabloid for trail closings. Trail maps and hiking guides may be purchased at the several visitor centers, at information kiosks, the Village Store, the Village Sport Shop, and other retail outlets in the park. You can also order them by mail from the Yosemite Bookstore, P.O. Box 230, El Portal, CA 95318; (209) 379-2648; www.yosemitestore.com. For minutely detailed descriptions of all of the hikes in this chapter and many more throughout the park, take a look at the book *Yosemite National Park: A Natural-History Guide to Yosemite and Its Trails,* by Jeffrey P. Schaffer.

Although wilderness permits are not required for day hikes, in summer, the Yosemite Valley Wilderness Center is a great place to get advice and information on hiking trails, particularly in the High Country. The center is open 7:30 A.M. to 5:00 P.M., from April through late October (209-372-0200). This telephone number has hours of other Wilderness Center offices at Tuolumne Meadows, Hill's Studio (Wawona), Big Oak Flat, and Hetch Hetchy. Or, call (209) 372-0740, or check www.yosemite.org/visitor/wild.html. Permit reservation requests cost $5.00 per person and are nonrefundable.

Park ranger Scott Gediman advises hikers to take precautions when lightning threatens: avoid any high, exposed place, hilltops, mountaintops, and ridge tops; stay away from open water, lakes, or streams; seek shelter in the bottom of valleys; if lightning is close by, sit or squat on your backpack to insulate yourself from a lightning strike; and do not seek shelter under overhanging rocks or trees.

The following are primarily day hikes and easy walks, with some description of longer expeditions and backpacking trails.

HIKING

Yosemite Valley Trails

The "Map and Guide to Yosemite Valley," published by the National Park Service, is a wonderful, pocket-size key to valley hiking and biking trails, famous landmarks, picnic areas, and public facilities, plus an introduction to the common flora and fauna found in the valley; this is a great, basic resource, available for $2.50 at most retail outlets. The National Park Service website, www.nps.gov/yose/trip/hiking.htm, has descriptions of the features and lengths of the park's most popular trails.

You will see that the trails follow the river and the two main roads, veering away from the road, fortunately, in the less-developed western end of the valley. The running water seems to create its own microclimate and even a light, damp breeze, which is very cooling in the summertime. You will be tempted to stop, not only to snap photos but also to gaze into the water, watching the willows and evergreens reflected in the deep, clear pools, and an occasional trout flicker in the shadows. Several footbridges cross the river, making it possible to cut your hikes short, instead of making the entire loop from the upper east end of Tenaya

i

Dogs and other pets, bicycles, strollers, and motor vehicles are not allowed on Yosemite's unpaved hiking and walking trails. Dogs on their leashes may walk with their humans on about 12 miles of paved trails in Yosemite Valley and nowhere else in the park.

Canyon above Mirror Lake to Bridalveil Meadow on the west end.

Bridalveil Fall
Road marker V14, 3 miles west of Yosemite Village
You will get wet in the spring and early summer, when the lovely stream falls 620 feet in misty magnificence. It is a half-mile walk on a paved trail from the parking lot, and you can expect plenty of company in the high season. This is a great vantage point for photos of Cathedral Rock and El Capitan.

Cook's Meadow
Shuttle stops 9, 10
Allow at least 45 minutes for this 1-mile, self-guided interpretive trail beginning just outside the Valley Visitor Center. This is one of the largest and most beautiful Sierra meadows and has recently been restored as a natural habitat for flora and fauna. See more about Cook's Meadow in the Yosemite Valley chapter.

Half Dome
Shuttle stop 16, Happy Isles
Experienced, fit hikers make the pilgrimage to the top of Half Dome on a very strenuous, 17-mile round-trip from the valley floor, a 10- to 12-hour expedition involving a demanding elevation gain. Views of the surrounding mountain peaks from 4,733 feet above the valley are stupendous, and you can tell your grandchildren about it—or take them with you! To facilitate the last, scary 200 yards up the back of the dome to the summit, steel cable handrails are in place from late May to early October—don't look down!

Many people camp overnight in Little Yosemite Valley (a permit is required), conserving their strength, and make the final ascent the second day. Believe it or not, more than 500 people make the climb every day in the high season. As thunderstorms are not uncommon midyear, plan to set out by at least 6:00 A.M., and be heading down by early afternoon. If thunderclouds are visible, go another day.

Lower Yosemite Fall
Shuttle stop 6
Everyone in the Western Hemisphere, it seems, takes the half-mile, easy walk to the base of Yosemite Falls, the fifth highest waterfall in the world, consisting of upper and lower falls dropping 2,425 feet in two mighty cataracts. You get a lot of bang for your buck, as tons of water collide with the earth and flow into the Merced River. Late spring and early summer are the prime times to experience the thunderous boom and delightful, fizzy spray of the lower fall. By August, the fall is merely a beautiful mist. On moonlit nights in the spring, "moonbows" are unforgettable, unique sights at the base of the fall. A major expansion and improvement of the Yosemite Falls visitor area, including facilities, a new shuttle stop, and trails, with one flat and wheelchair accessible, was completed in 2005.

Mirror Lake
Shuttle stop 17
This is an easy, very popular half-mile walk on a paved path to a small lake named for its glassy reflection of Mount Watkins. A famous sight in the valley in decades past when it was a shallow, rockfall-dammed pool, now the lake is mostly a boggy meadow, best in spring and early summer when there is some water.

Among the live oaks and Douglas firs, dogwood blooms in creamy white clouds in the spring and maples flame in the fall.

For a moderately strenuous, 3.5-mile, one-way route to the rim of the valley, continue on to the little-used Tenaya Zig Zags/Snow Creek Trail, taking your time treading the 108 switchbacks to eye-popping views of Clouds Rest, Quarter Dome, and Half Dome. To see stunning images of Mirror Lake in its springtime glory, go online to http://yosemite.org/vryos/pages/views/mirror.htm.

Mist Trail to Vernal Fall
Shuttle stop 16, Happy Isles
The most popular hike in the valley, this 3-mile round-trip route begins on a paved,

Don't Worry, Be Prepared

- Practice using topographic maps and a compass, and have them in hand on the trail, even for day hikes.
- In the heart of the Sierra Nevada range, weather changes quickly. Always check weather conditions and forecasts and be prepared for sudden rain, snow, thunderstorms, a sudden drop or rise in temperature, and for an emergency bivouac. It may snow in June, and you can get seriously sunburned in March.
- Pack out every bit of trash. Dispose of human waste in a small hole at least 100 feet from water and trail.
- Let someone at your lodgings or in your group know where you are going and when you expect to return.

steep trail climbing 400 feet in elevation to the bridge and close-up views of Vernal Fall, which drops over a 317-foot cliff in a wide, mighty stream encircled by rainbows at its base. Bring a parka for the cold, drenching spray. There are rest rooms and a water fountain located here.

From here you can take the switchbacky, half-mile mountainside trail to the top of the fall, or climb 600 very steep granite steps carved into the cliff. Although children do make the trek, the wet, slippery steps take some care. This hike gives you the most scenery and thrills for the shortest distance. At the top, the sun shines on broad stone ledges where hikers bask after refreshing dunks in the freezing water of Emerald Pool.

In the wintertime when shuttles do not stop at Happy Isles, walk to the trailhead from Curry Village (about 15 minutes).

Nevada Fall
Shuttle stop 16, Happy Isles

Continue the Mist Trail to the trail for Nevada Fall, a 7-mile round-trip taking about six to eight hours total. This is a strenuous climb, with a 1,900-foot elevation gain. Past the top of Vernal Fall, you hike about 1.5 miles on switchbacks to the rim, then drop into a gully for the zinger view of Nevada Fall. From here, you can go on to Half Dome and Little Yosemite Valley, and even to Glacier Point on the Panorama Cliffs trail.

Upper Yosemite Fall
Shuttle stop 7, next to Camp 4 Campground

You gain 2,700 feet in elevation on this 3.6-mile expedition to reach a ledge above the tremendous upper fall. It takes six or more hours to make this strenuous hike up and back on the steep trail riddled with switchbacks. At a mile, Columbia Point is such a terrific panoramic vista point that many people call it a day and head back down. For those who stick it out, mist and spray from the fall help to cool their heels. Once on top, calm your vertigo and walk upstream a bit to explore the stream. Look for the path down to the pipe railings for a spectacular outlook on the cascades. Some hikers stay the night (permit required).

With more time and more energy, continue on another three-quarters of a mile to Yosemite Point to see the dramatic Lost Arrow Spire and view of the south rim of the valley.

Keep in mind that the higher in elevation your trail, the less oxygen is absorbed into your bloodstream, and the more you will huff and puff, the sooner fatigue will set in, and the more water you will need to carry. Take care to acclimate before a strenuous hike by arriving in the High Country a day or so before you plan to hike. If someone in your group begins to feel dizzy and/or nauseated, stop and rest; if they don't feel better in a short time, head back.

Glacier Point Road Trails

Glacier Point Road is open late May or early June to November. For winter skiing from Yosemite's Badger Pass Ski Area to Glacier Point, see the Yosemite in Winter chapter.

Dewey Point
Just west of Bridalveil Creek Campground, off Glacier Point Road
According to the time of year, this beautiful 7-mile, undulating but moderate loop trail may be bordered with sky-blue lupine, Indian paintbrush, or 6-foot-tall, rose-colored fireweed. Heading through a lodgepole pine forest, you cross a footbridge over the creek and bear left around McGurk Meadow, where mule deer graze in grasses sprinkled with shooting stars, corn lilies, and goldenrod. Beyond, beneath red and white firs, the waxy, brilliant red snowplant and pink coralroot may be thrusting up out of the duff. Crossings of tributaries of Bridalveil Creek are refreshing preambles to the shade of Jeffrey pine and huckleberry oaks, before the great reward, the 7,385-foot-high viewpoint of Bridalveil Fall and El Capitan. The easier way to return is to retrace your route, rather than looping back on the ridge trail. Or descend on Pohono Trail to the Wawona Tunnel and have someone pick you up.

Glacier Point Four-Mile Trail
Road marker V18, Southside Drive in the valley or at Glacier Point
Plan six to eight hours round-trip, or a half-day for one way up or down, taking the bus the other way. The Four-Mile Trail is actually nearly 5 miles, one-way, on a very steep, demanding route with 3,200 feet gain in elevation, to the top of Glacier Point. Dazzling views of the famous monoliths of the valley keep you going, interspersed with shady stretches among evergreens, firs, and pines, and a few snow patches until about mid-June.

You can take the bus from Yosemite Lodge at the Falls to Glacier Point and hike down the Four-Mile Trail to the valley. Or take it up, hike around, and take the bus down four hours later. Or don't hike at all—just enjoy the Glacier Point views without driving your car. To guarantee a seat, make reservations and/or purchase tickets up to seven days in advance (209-372-1240). Cost for the round-trip is $32.50 for adults; $26.00 for children. One way, it is $20.00 for adults; $12.00 for kids five and up.

Mono Meadow
2.5 miles east of Bridalveil Creek Campground, off Glacier Point Road
This eastbound trail drops a half-mile to Mono Meadow then continues on to the spectacular Mount Starr King View, with Half Dome and Clouds Rest, about 3 miles round-trip.

Ostrander Lake
1.3 miles past Bridalveil Creek Campground, off Glacier Point Road
This strenuous, 13-mile round-trip hike takes you to a bowl below Horse Ridge at 8,200 feet and Ostrander Lake, a popular destination in all seasons. You move through meadows and forestlands, crossing Bridalveil Creek (may be a challenge when waters are high in early summer). The last stretch before the lake is rather steep, but worth it. Your rewards are fabulous views of the Illilouette Creek basin with an array of domes plus Mount Hoffmann, Mount Starr King, and the Clark Range.

Walking the Four-Mile Trail is a great way to see Yosemite's vistas and waterfalls. JOHN POIMIROO

Fishing is good in the lake and camping is divine. (Perched atop a glacial moraine, Ostrander Hut is a cross-country skier's retreat in winter. See the Yosemite in Winter chapter.)

Panorama Trail
Glacier Point
Besides the usual heart-stopping views from Glacier Point, the first highlight of this downhill drop is Illilouette Fall, at about 1.5 miles. Continuing on the Panorama Cliffs, you ultimately reach Nevada Fall, where you can connect with the Mist Trail or the John Muir Trail down to the valley.

Sentinel Dome
6 miles east of Bridalveil Creek Campground, off Glacier Point Road
An easy, scenic 2.2-mile round-trip walk is a small price to pay for the 360-degree view from the top of Sentinel Dome. From here, you get a real perspective on the size of the park, looking out over hundreds of miles of wilderness topped by Half Dome, the Clark Range, Tenaya Canyon, and Cathedral Peak, among others.

The lightning-scarred Jeffrey pine on the rocky parapet was a landmark and a familiar photo op, until it fell in August 2003. At 8,122 feet, Sentinel Dome is a perfect example of exfoliated granite, the same type of formation as Royal Arches and many other Yosemite domes and rounded walls.

Taft Point
6 miles east Bridalveil Creek Campground, off Glacier Point Road
This 2.2-mile round-trip, moderate hike travels through a red fir and lodgepole pine forest. A lovely meadow leads to Taft Point, with dizzying views of Yosemite Falls, El Capitan, and the west end of the valley. Check out dazzling images of the Taft Point views online at http://yosemite.org/vryos/pages/views/taft.htm.

Wawona Trails

Alder Creek
0.5 mile up Chilnualna Falls Road
It is about 6 miles to Alder Falls through a pine forest and dry manzanita-covered slopes, into gullies, and over ridges to the 100-foot-high falls. Along the last part of the trek you will see railroad ties, remnants of when the Yosemite Lumber Company laid track to take out a timber harvest of a half billion board feet before 1930, including millions of board feet to construct the Hetch Hetchy dam. In 1930 John D. Rockefeller Jr. and the federal government bought the company's claim to park forestlands. Alder Creek is lovely and lush with vegetation.

Chilnualna Falls
0.7 mile east of Highway 41/Wawona Road, at end of Chilnualna Falls Road
This steep 8.2-mile loop through pines, cedars, and manzanita ends in a great reward—icy swimming holes and fabulous avalanches of water crashing over giant boulders. It takes about five hours, round-trip, along a creek and on switchbacks through a forest, with the last 3 miles fairly strenuous, uphill climbs. If you are not up for this, there is also a beautiful cascade about a quarter-mile from the trailhead. Take care when the water is high and boulders are slippery. From the main falls, you can hike to Bridalveil Creek Campground or to Chilnualna Lakes.

Mariposa Grove of Giant Sequoias
36 miles south of Yosemite Valley via Highway 41, 2 miles from the South Gate entrance to the park
On foot, cross-country skis, or snowshoes, the trail from the parking lot to the grove is 2 miles, one-way. Come early in the day to avoid the problem of a completely full parking lot; if no parking is available, you may need to park at the park entrance gate and take the free shuttle. Once in the grove, 8 miles of hiking trails wind through the magnificent upper grove, with a 1.8-mile

trail through the lower grove. For a small fee, you can take the open-air tram from the parking lot to the groves, hopping on and off at the various stopping points.

Swinging Bridge Loop
Behind the Pioneer Yosemite History Center, off Highway 41
Just under 5 miles, this is an easy stroll, best taken in spring or fall when summer vacationers are absent. Cross the covered bridge and walk east on the road, bear left at the fork at Camp Wawona, and go around the gate to the left toward the South Fork of the Merced River to the Swinging Bridge. Across the bridge, the trail continues left to a dirt road, crossing Chilnualna Creek, and connecting with Chilnualna Falls Road back to the Pioneer Yosemite History Center.

Wawona Meadow
Across from the Wawona Hotel off Highway 41, through the golf course to the parking area
Even little kids can manage all or part of this 3-mile, flat loop trail on an old dirt road beneath the shade of incense cedars and ponderosa pines, around magnificent Wawona Meadow. You are virtually guaranteed to see herds of grazing deer. The walk takes about an hour and a half and you will not be alone in the summertime, unless you set out very early in the morning.

Step carefully on the short paths into the meadow itself to avoid trampling the vegetation. You may see white star tulips, corn lilies, scarlet snow plant and pinedrops, lady's slipper orchids, and bright pink coralroot. In the spring, Western azalea burst into white clouds of bloom. Wawona's open meadows are popular with cross-country skiers in winter.

Tuolumne Meadows and Tioga Road Trails

Cathedral Lakes
Cathedral Lakes trailhead on Tioga Road
This gorgeous, moderate, 3.7-mile route passes granite domes before it reaches a spectacular lake at 9,595 feet, below Cathedral Peak. You can take a chilly swim here and fish for trout. Joining the John Muir Trail, this is a popular and dusty summertime path; be advised to hit the trail very early in the morning or early or late in the season.

Expect evergreens, a boggy, wildflowery meadow with snowy peaks mirrored in the water, and campsites. For more, hike 4.3 miles on to Sunrise Camp over Cathedral Pass for vistas of an incredible array of peaks and the Clark Range. You will encounter the headwaters of Echo Creek, amazing floral displays, and overlooks of southern Yosemite. Campsites are south of Sunrise High Sierra Camp.

At 10,911 feet high, bright and sheer Cathedral Peak is the most prominent summit of the jagged Cathedral Range, dominating the southern view from Tuolumne Meadows.

Clouds Rest
Highway 120 to Tenaya Lake
This is one of the most beautiful hikes on the planet. At 14 miles round-trip, this strenuous all-day trek starts at Tenaya Lake and ends on top of the world. You follow Tenaya Creek and other streams, drop through a forested area to lower, middle, and upper Sunrise Lakes, and climb out of Tenaya Canyon with breathtaking vistas all around, with sheer drops to the Yosemite River on one side and Little Yosemite on the other. Camp overnight for the sunrise of your life.

Along the way, you will see Tenaya Peak, Mount Hoffman, Tuolumne Peak, the Clark Range, and at the summit, the 9,926-foot-high Clouds Rest, the largest granite face in the park. Wildflowers are rampant—red-orange paintbrush, purple larkspur, scarlet penstemon, pale lavender aster, and more. Clouds Rest is just that—clouds frequently appear to be resting upon its summit, even when no clouds are visible anywhere else. It is the highest point visible from the Yosemite Valley floor.

Less ambitious hikers are happy to quit at Sunrise Lake, an 11-mile round-trip and a relatively easy walk; Sunrise High

Are You a PSR?

Rangers call them PSRs, possible search and rescues—park visitors who set out on day hikes in inappropriate clothing and with complete lack of knowledge of what they may encounter on the trail. Park rangers tell tales of hikers on the Yosemite Falls and Half Dome Trails wearing flip-flops, dress shoes, or even high heels; carrying beer instead of water; without hats in the summertime; without jackets in the winter; without maps when they get lost.

City folks with little or no outdoor experience may think of Yosemite as a kind of amusement park, rangers say, which it is not. For instance, one of the most popular footpaths in the park, the Yosemite Falls Trail, gains 2,700 feet in elevation, about the equivalent of a 270-story building—start this hike in your flip-flops at your peril.

The National Park Service Search and Rescue Team responds to nearly 200 incidents each year, half of them involving day hikers who had accidents on rugged cliffs, steep trails, and slippery rocks around waterfalls, among other places.

To avoid being a PSR, keep these tips in mind:

- Assess your abilities and limits. If uncertain, ask a ranger.
- Check weather conditions the day of your hike.
- Be prepared for storms in any month. Summer thunderstorms are common.
- Carry plenty of food and water.
- Stay on the trail.
- Use extreme caution in and around streams and waterfalls. Pay attention to all trail signs and heed the warnings.
- Wear safe, practical footwear and apparel.
- Carry a detailed map that you've studied beforehand, along with a written route description, and a compass or GPS.

Sierra Camp and more campsites are located here.

Depart for this hike in early morning to arrive at the summit by early afternoon and avoid afternoon thunderstorms in the summer. You can also hike to Clouds Rest from Happy Isles in the valley, an 11-mile uphill trek, one-way.

Dog Lake/Lembert Dome
Highway 120 to Lembert Dome parking area, road marker T32

It's a 2.8-mile, round-trip trek to the closest lake to Tuolumne Meadows and the warmest and shallowest of the chilly lakes at this altitude. A little steep at first, but easy enough for kids, the path meanders through a lodgepole forest and across granite slabs, across the face of Lembert Dome and a creek, then on to the lake, framed nicely by the evergreens. There's good swimming and fishing at the lake, and views of Mount Dana and Mount Gibbs. The lopsided dome shows how glaciers sculpted the landscape by moving up one side, causing rocks to crack off and create the steep side.

Elizabeth Lake
Tuolumne Meadows Campground
1 mile off Tioga Road, road marker T30, accessible by shuttle bus

From the campground, it's a moderate 2.4-mile, one-way hike to the scenic, subalpine Elizabeth Lake basin. On the way, you'll pass meadows fringed with lodgepole pines and lively Unicorn Creek before you reach the long meadow surrounding the lake, which sits at the foot of 11,000-foot Unicorn Peak. Bring a rod along for brook fishing and a camera for the wildflowers of Echo Creek—phlox, red heather,

Hikers between May Lake and Glen Aulin show their stuff in High Country. JOHN POIMIROO

and lupine. There are nice campsites and good fishing at Nelson Lake, about 3.5 miles farther on a rugged trail.

Gaylor Lakes and the Tarns
Just before the East Gate of the park on Tioga Road

Take an easy, quarter-mile walk to lovely alpine tarns reflecting snowcapped peaks, a scene of such beauty that photographers are often here at sunrise and sunset. Also from this trailhead, you can reach Gaylor Lakes basin, a 2-mile total round-trip, with a 1,000-foot elevation gain. On the timberline, the air is scintillating, alpine meadows are soft, and the view of Mount Lyell, the highest point in the park, and Tioga Peak, Mount Dana, and other monuments will make your day. The trail continues on a half mile to upper Gaylor Lake and on to Granite Lakes.

Glen Aulin
Highway 120 to 1 mile east of Tuolumne Meadows Visitor Center, near the stables

This 10.4-mile, moderately strenuous, very popular hike starts on what was once the old Tioga Road, built in 1883. It winds along a series of thrilling, crashing waterfalls into the Grand Canyon of the Tuolumne River, through lodgepole pines and past alpine meadows and granite domes. The Tuolumne Canyon separates the southern part of the park from the primitive northern wilderness of lakes, valleys, and mountains. You will see Lembert Dome rising 900 feet

That cold rushing water from snowmelt looks cool and refreshing, but resist the temptation to drink untreated water from lakes, waterfalls, rivers, creeks, and streams. Experts debate if and how much Yosemite National Park's water sources are affected, but testing has proven that air pollution from the Central Valley, sheep and cattle grazing, and careless backcountry visitors have contaminated the fabled pristine waters of the Sierra Nevada.

behind you, Fairview Dome, Cathedral Peak, and Unicorn Peak. Good swimming can be had just below Glen Aulin where the river spreads out, and there is a small sandy beach. On the river for the next mile or so, fishing is good and quite popular for rainbow and brown trout.

Harden Lake
Trailhead at White Wolf Campground, between Tuolumne Meadows and Yosemite Valley off Tioga Road, road marker T9

An easy, 5.6-mile round-trip trek from White Wolf Campground brings you to a pretty, fairly shallow, nine-acre lake at 7,600 feet that is popular for swimming in some of the park's warmest summer waters, and for just enjoying the view of the Tuolumne River Canyon. The trail meanders over and alongside the Middle Tuolumne River through groves of lodgepole pines, red firs, and aspens and over glacial moraine. Late summer sees the lake diminished greatly in size.

High Country Day Hikes

An environmental biologist and naturalist with a fascinating background in national park communications leads three days in a row of hiking from Tuolumne Meadows. On the way to Lyell Canyon, Glen Aulin, and Elizabeth Lake, among other spots, you will look for birds, identify wildflowers, and learn more about flora and fauna. The 5- to 11-mile hikes are moderately strenuous and a great introduction to some of the most spectacular areas of the park. Call (209) 379-2321 or go to www.yosemite.org for more information.

High Sierra Camps Guided Hikes
Trailhead at Tuolumne Meadows
(559) 253-5674

Plan to make your reservations early for the guided hikes between the five High Sierra Camps—these trips are very popular (see more about the camps in the Campgrounds chapter). The per-person cost for the five-day hike is $719.50, and for the week's trip, $1,027.00; it includes lodging, guide, and meals. This is a great way to introduce hikers, particularly a family, to the wilderness. You do not need to worry about maps or getting lost; about what to expect along the way; about meals or carrying sleeping gear; and you can take showers and enjoy a hearty meal every night.

The John Muir Trail

This is one of the most famous and most spectacular footpaths in the world. Established in 1938, the John Muir Trail begins at Happy Isles in Yosemite Valley, the threshold of 211 miles of unparalleled beauty. From the valley floor, it ascends to Tuolumne Meadows through the Sierra National Forest into Kings Canyon National Park and Sequoia National Park to the top of Mount Whitney, a hike that usually takes between three and four weeks.

The route rises into 12,000-foot-high passes, down through canyons created by glaciers, and affords access to dozens of azure alpine lakes. You take off northeast along the Merced River, through Little Yosemite Valley to Sunrise Lakes, past Tresidder Peak through the Cathedral Lakes basin to Tuolumne Meadows, joining the Pacific Crest Trail. The route turns south on the east side of the Cathedral Range through Lyell Canyon below Mammoth Peak to Donohue Pass. From here, it exits the national park and heads through the Ansel Adams Wilderness toward June

Don't Drink It

The Merced and Tuolumne Rivers and the lakes, streams, and ponds in Yosemite National Park are clear, cold, and fresh. However, you should take care to drink only tap water, bottled water, or properly filtered water, no matter where you are in the park, and this holds true throughout the Sierra. Carried by humans as well as domestic and wild animals, *Giardia lamblia* may contaminate the water.

An intestinal disease, *Giardia* will give you chronic diarrhea, agonizing cramps, and more lousy symptoms that remain indefinitely; only a doctor's prescription and care will cure you.

If you cannot carry water, use a *Giardia*-rated water filter or boil water for at least five minutes. Many campers favor the Katadyn filter, although it is expensive. The First-Need water purifier is reasonably priced and very effective; carry an extra filter with you. Iodine water purification pills kill most bacteria, but they do not always kill *Giardia*. Don't even brush your teeth with water that has not been treated.

Giardia-rated filters are on sale at the Wilderness Center and the Sport Shop in Yosemite Valley, at the Mountain Shop in Curry Village, at the Mountaineering Sport Shop at Tuolumne Meadows, and online at www.yosemitestore.com.

Lake and the Mammoth Lakes area in the central Sierra. The trail then recrosses the Sierra Crest at Island Pass and descends to Thousand Island Lake and separates from the Pacific Crest Trail, heading onward to Sequoia National Park.

The most popular segment of the John Muir Trail is from Happy Isles, just over 35 miles, one-way, to Donohue Pass.

For background and detail on exploring this trail, a good resource (though from the 1930s and the current trail is different) is *Starr's Guide to the John Muir Trail and the High Sierra Region*, by Walter A. Starr Jr. The Map-Pack of the John Muir Trail, which includes color topographic maps of the trail, is available from Tom Harrison Maps (800-265-9090, www.tomharrisonmaps.com). Detailed information about the trail is also available at www.pcta.org/about_trail/muir/over.asp.

Trailheads for the John Muir Trail have a daily quota from May 1 through November 1, meaning that a limited number of hikers are allowed to set off on the trail each day. At other times, you may self-issue a wilderness permit at Inyo National Forest ranger stations, or check in at the Wilderness Center in Yosemite Valley or at Tuolumne Meadows. From the Yosemite end, the Yosemite Association (209-372-0740, http://yosemite.org/visitor/wild.html) issues wilderness permits, including those for the sections of the John Muir Trail within the national park, at Wilderness Centers in the park, by phone, or online. For Inyo National Forest and the rest of the trail, check trail permit availability and get more information at www.fs.fed.us/r5/inyo/recreation/wild/permitres.shtml, or call (760) 873-2400.

Lukens Lake
Trailhead at White Wolf Lodge, between Tuolumne Meadows and Yosemite Valley off Tioga Road, road marker T9

All ages can manage this relatively easy, 4.6-mile round-trip route to a shallow lake with a grassy bottom, perfect for trout fishing and for midsummer swimming and lounging about. You walk across the Middle Tuolumne River and through forests of lodgepole and white pine, hemlock and fir. Be armed with mosquito repellent.

May Lake
Highway 120 past White Wolf, turn at road marker T21, 2 miles to parking area
Below 10,850-foot-high Mount Hoffman, beautiful May Lake is a fabulous day-trip destination, reached on an easy, 2.5-mile round-trip trail through forests and past dramatic granite outcroppings. You can spend the day, stay overnight in the backpackers' camp, or camp on your own; you must camp at least a mile from the lake. Many backpackers head on to the Ten Lakes basin or Glen Aulin. You can fish in May Lake, although swimming is not permitted. If you are up to it, hike up to the summit of Mount Hoffman for breathtaking views and the righteous feeling of looking down on the world from the geographical center of Yosemite. The 2-mile ascent gains about 1,500 feet.

Mono Pass
Trailhead 5.6 miles east of the Tuolumne Meadows Campground, road marker T37
You will gain about 1,000 feet in elevation on this relatively moderate, 8-mile round-trip hike through an interesting alpine area dotted with crumbling pioneer and miners' cabins from the late 1800s. Dana Meadows Creek, Parker Pass Creek, Spillway Lake, and, finally, Summit Lake are landmarks along the way as you trek through meadows and forests of whitebark and lodgepole pine. You may be surprised to encounter California gulls fishing on the lakes.

Mount Dana
Highway 120 at Tioga Pass/East Gate entrance to the park
It is only 5.8 miles round-trip, but a tough, almost 21 percent grade climb through the wildflowers to the summit of Mount Dana, at an elevation of 13,057 feet, the second highest peak in the park. From the top, the sweeping panorama of the Sierra Nevada crest, Mono Lake, and the Tuolumne Meadows area is the view of a lifetime. Unlike most of the Sierra, Mount Dana is reddish brown metamorphic rock. On the northeast side, look for a small glacier.

North Dome
Highway 120 at Porcupine Flat Campground
You can get to the north rim of Yosemite Valley on this 10-mile, moderately strenuous round-trip hike. At an elevation of 7,542 feet, massive, exfoliated North Dome dominates the north wall of Tenaya Canyon across from Half Dome, and above Royal Arches. While on the scene, look for the 5,947-foot-tall granite shaft called Washington Column.

Raferty Creek/Vogelsang High Sierra Camp
Highway 120 to Tuolumne Meadows
On the John Muir Trail, follow the Lyell Fork of the Tuolumne River through flower-filled meadows, ascending along Rafferty Creek to Tuolumne Pass, crossing creeks and streams, with two pretty little tarns at trailside. The destination is Vogelsang High Sierra Camp at the foot of Fletcher Peak on Fletcher Creek, not far from Fletcher Lake. The trip is nearly 15 miles, round-trip, and strenuous.

Soda Springs
Highway 120 to Lembert Dome parking area
Share the easy 1.5-mile round-trip trail with a throng in the summertime, but enjoy crossing Tuolumne Meadows and the Tuolumne River, which is a refreshing treat for the eyes and ears on a hot day. It's tempting to taste the carbonated mineral water at Soda Springs but there's almost certainly surface contamination. Take a peek at the ranger's residence at historic McCauley Cabin and exhibits in the Sierra Club's Parsons Memorial Lodge.

Tenaya Lake
31.9 miles east of Crane Flat, road marker T25 on Tioga Road
You park and nearly fall into the lake, it is so accessible to the Tioga Road. With easy accessibility comes popularity. The easy hike around the lake is just over 3 miles, and you can connect to the John Muir Trail and to Yosemite Valley.

Glaciers carved the lake's basin and left the surrounding, bare, glinting granite domes—bring your camera to shoot Polly Dome, Pywiack Domes, and other granite domes reflected in the dazzling deep blue; late afternoon is best for photos. Native Americans called this *Pywiack,* the "Lake of the Glistening Rocks."

Waterfalls of the Tuolumne
(866) 922-9111, (209) 397-9111
www.yosemiteguides.com
In one long day you will remember for a lifetime, hike on a forest trail along the Tuolumne River, where cascades and waterfalls make heavenly rest stops and foot coolers. Experienced guides spin tales of Yosemite history and explain geology, flora, and fauna. This is a moderately strenuous 7-mile hike that takes about seven hours, round-trip, and costs about $65 per person, including a hearty lunch and drinks.

Waterwheel Falls
Highway 120 to Tuolumne Meadows
One of many turbulent cascades on the river downstream from Tuolumne Meadows, Waterwheel is truly spectacular as huge jets of water explode up from the rocks into rainbows, a marvelous prize on an 8-mile, one-way hike or horseback ride from Tuolumne Meadows (3.5 miles from Glen Aulin High Sierra Camp). Along the way, you pass California Falls at the base of a high cliff; a nice swimming hole above where the river plunges over a cliff; and Le Conte Falls, before finally arriving at your destination. The falls are best from about mid-May through mid-July.

At the falls' base, you'll find more swimming holes, a small campsite beside a pool, and a larger site a little farther on by Return Creek.

Crane Flat Trails

Cascade Creek
From Highway 120, nearly 4 miles east of Crane Flat
An easy descent on an old road to beautiful Cascade Creek, where you can swim in the small pools in late summer and fall. Beside the creek are lovely dogwoods, willows, azaleas, and more trees—a perfect picnic site; 4.4 miles round-trip. To reach the trailhead, take the unpaved road to the east end of Tamarack Flat Campground.

Crane Flat/Tuolumne Grove of Giant Sequoias
Just north of the intersection of Big Oak Flat and Tioga Roads, near Crane Flat, Road marker O1
This 2-mile round-trip walk follows an old road, with a 600-foot change in elevation. You can wander around on 25 acres where ancient, giant sequoias are the main attraction. There is also a half-mile, signed nature trail.

El Capitan
From Highway 120, nearly 4 miles east of Crane Flat
This strenuous, 15-mile round-trip trek achieves the summit of El Capitan, a demanding climb with a spectacular reward—stupendous views of famous peaks, domes, and mountain ranges. The total hike over steep switchbacks is not for beginners. To reach the trailhead, take the unpaved road to the east end of Tamarack Flat Campground.

Merced Grove
3.5 miles north of Crane Flat off Big Oak Flat Road/Highway 120
Road marker B10
Take the 4-mile dirt road loop through the Moss Creek Valley to the magnificent grove of 20 giant sequoias. Both this trail and the one described above are among the least-trodden of any in the park. You can cross-country ski and snowshoe in both of the sequoia groves.

Spend a day on Glacier Point trails with park ranger Dick Ewart as he imparts orientation skills in his course, "Get Lost with a Ranger: Map and Compass for Beginners." A 30-plus-year veteran in the park, Ewart is an engaging, knowledgeable character, and his classes fill up every year. Cost is $80 including overnight camping (209-379-2321, www.yosemite.org).

Hetch Hetchy Trails

Laurel Lake
15-mile round-trip from O'Shaughnessy Dam

After ascending on the partly scenic, partly rugged, switchback Beehive-Vernon trail, an old road above the reservoir, your well-deserved destination will be 60-acre Laurel Lake, at 6,490 feet in elevation one of the lowest natural lakes in the park. This makes a nice overnight backpack with camping on the lakeside. Best camping is at the lake's outlet; you will find sites all along the lakeshore. Try fishing for rainbows—it's a challenge. Other places to stop and camp in this area are Lake Eleanor and Miguel Meadow, where a Park Service Ranger Station is headquarters for campers.

Poopenaut Valley Trail
Off Hetch Hetchy Road, 1.3 miles east of the Mather Ranger Station

Stop at the ranger station for precise directions, so as not to miss the tiny parking area on the road. This is an extremely steep, 2.4-mile round-trip hike down to what some believe is the best swimming on the Tuolumne River, which flattens out here. You can even dive off a 25-foot perch. Camp where the ridge meets the river.

Rancheria Falls
O'Shaughnessy Dam, at the north end of Hetch Hetchy Road

Tremendous views of the cliffs on the north wall of the reservoir are part of the reward on this moderately strenuous, 13.4-mile round-trip to Rancheria Creek and the beautiful falls, where some hikers throw off their clothes and jump into the cascades and pools. There is a popular campground at the falls, too, and pretty good fishing. Black bears around here like the fish and also like campers' food, so take care to properly store your provisions.

Wapama Falls/Tueeulala Fall
O'Shaughnessy Dam, at the north end of Hetch Hetchy Road

The best time of year for this 5-mile, round-trip, rather easy hike through a tunnel to both Wapama Falls and Tueeulala Fall is in the spring when the falls are full and the temperature is moderate. Midsummer and autumn can be brutally hot, and no swimming is allowed in Hetch Hetchy Reservoir. The 1,200-foot-high falls give you an idea of how spectacular the Hetch Hetchy Valley must have been before the dam was constructed. The footpath is bordered with live oak and bay trees and marvelous wildflowers, including purple and yellow harlequin lupine, and bright red columbine.

BACKPACKING

Hundreds of miles of backcountry trails thread through the magnificent northernmost reaches of Yosemite National Park, a backpacker's dream of solitude in a landscape lightly touched by man. One of Yosemite's first explorers in the 1800s, who blazed trails still used today, John Muir mused on how a ramble in the wilderness produces a feeling of liberation and deliverance from the perception of time. He wrote, "another glorious Sierra day in which one seems to be dissolved and absorbed and sent pulsing onward we know not where. Life seems neither long nor short, and we take no more heed to save time or make haste than do the trees and stars. This is true freedom, a good practical sort of immortality."

Nirvana in the arms of nature is definitely in the sky and clouds for hikers who take to the mountains of Yosemite with packs on their backs. One look at a map of the park reveals that most of the park is undeveloped wilderness distinguished by rugged, mountainous terrain and two major river valleys with hundreds of tributaries and streams. A number of trails, notably the John Muir Trail and the Pacific Crest Trail, connect with trails in the surrounding national forests.

The northwest section of the park, between Tuolumne Meadows and Crane Flat, on the north side of Tioga Road, is the area most favored by backpackers. Even isolated trails are well described in backpacking guidebooks, and there are a number of hike-in campgrounds; you can also camp on sites you discover yourself, taking care to leave no sign of your presence when you leave.

In-depth information from experienced hikers and mountaineers, maps, wilderness permits, and guidebooks are available at the Wilderness Center in Yosemite Village (209-372-0740).

A hiker's bus departs Yosemite Valley early each morning from July 1 to Labor Day, heading for High Country trailheads. The bus stops at Crane Flat, White Wolf Lodge, Tenaya Lake, and Tuolumne Meadows Lodge. You can debark and hike into the wilderness or snap a few photos at the stopping points then get off at Tuolumne Meadows Lodge for a walkabout and lunch, reboarding at 2:05 P.M. to arrive back at Yosemite Lodge just after 4:15 P.M. Round-trip cost is $23.00; for children, $11.50; one-way fares depend on your drop-off point. Reservations are advised; call (209) 372-1240 or sign up at Yosemite Lodge at the Falls, Curry Village, Village Store parking area activity desks, or the Valley Visitor Center. Backpackers can arrange in advance for return pickup.

Take care to prepare carefully for your backpack trip. Tip-top physical condition is a must if you want to enjoy yourself, keeping in mind that the higher the elevation, the more tuckered you will be. Check wilderness conditions at www.nps.gov/yose/now/conditions.htm. Set off armed with topographic maps and trail maps, a compass, and, always, raingear, even in the middle of the summer. Thunderstorms and unexpectedly damp weather, even snow, are not uncommon in the Sierra any month of the year.

If you are new to the area, consider hooking up with one of the experienced guides available through NPS, DNC, or one of the independent guiding companies, as listed below.

Wilderness Permits
Yosemite Association
(209) 372-0740
www.yosemite.org/visitor/wild.html

For all overnight trips into the Yosemite wilderness, you must obtain a permit (this is not necessary for day hikes). You can do this either by phone with a credit card, on the Web site, or in person; the fee is $5.00. The Wilderness Center in Yosemite Valley is open daily from 7:30 A.M. to 5:00 P.M., in summer only. Other places to get permits are Big Oak Flat at the park entrance, summer only; Tuolumne Meadows at the kiosk, summer only; the Hetch Hetchy park entrance; at Hill's Studio in Wawona; and in the wintertime, at the Valley Visitor Center. Wilderness Center hours change in winter.

Trailheads have quotas that are occasionally "sold out" in the high seasons of summer and fall; a maximum number of hikers may receive permits for some trails. You can make reservations 24 weeks to two days ahead: the nonrefundable $5.00 processing fee is charged. Half of the trailhead quota is available on a first-come, first-served basis the day of or one day prior to a given day.

Walk-In Camps

With a wilderness permit and a $5.00 fee, you may spend the night at walk-in backpackers' campgrounds at Hetch Hetchy, on the loop road near the O'Shaughnessy Dam trailhead; Camp 4 (primarily a

Bears in the Backcountry

Black bears and other wildlife recognize your backpack and smell your food and scented personal items. To avoid sharing your campsite with a bear or endangering your life, plan ahead and do this:

- Avoid hiking or camping alone—human activity and voices are stop signs for bears.
- Rent or buy National Park Service–tested, bear-resistant, portable food canisters at retail outlets in the park or at the Wilderness Center. Yosemite bears have learned that the containers are not worth investigating, even though they smell like food.
- At the trailhead, store all food properly. Do not leave your backpack unattended on the trail or in a campsite. Use installed devices such as metal storage boxes or poles or carefully hang food and other supplies using the counterbalance method.
- You are not at the top of the food chain in the Yosemite backcountry. Watch bears from a safe distance. Never, ever approach a bear, especially a cub, or try to feed it.
- If a bear enters your campsite, yell, clap your hands, and bang pots together. Throw small stones or pinecones from a safe distance. Stand together to present a more intimidating figure, but do not surround the bear.

climbers' camp), just west of Yosemite Lodge at the Falls; Backpackers Camp, beneath Royal Arches near the Sugar Pine Bridge in Yosemite Valley; and at the Backpackers Camp at Tuolumne Meadows. Here are two nicely located, walk-in camps (check before starting out, to verify where you are permitted to camp).

Cathedral Lakes Backpack Camp
John Muir Trail trailhead, off Highway 120 at Tuolumne Meadows
A 3.7-mile, mostly level hike gets you right into spectacular-view country on the way to a gorgeous subalpine lake, at an elevation of 9,595 feet, at the foot of Cathedral Peak. Campsites are in a boulder field near the lake; the coveted spots are on the east side. Photographers come here just to catch the reflections of the trees and the mountain in the glassy, emerald-green lake. It is a nice, short walk from here to Upper Cathedral Lake.

Lyell Fork Backpack Camp
Trailhead near the Lembert Dome parking area
As long as you have adjusted to the 8,500-foot elevation, this is an easy hike, 4 miles to the headwaters of the Tuolumne River. The trail follows along a stream with zowie mountain peaks above and lovely meadows beneath, to the headwaters of the Tuolumne River. The trout fishing is good here, and campsites are in a pine forest setting.

Backpacking Guides

Southern Yosemite Mountain Guides (SYMG)
621 Highland Avenue, Santa Cruz
(800) 231-4575
www.symg.com
Experienced, savvy, and supremely knowledgeable about the Sierra, the guides of

SYMG provide a true wilderness experience in Yosemite and Sequoia National Parks and the Ansel Adams Wilderness. Since 1991, hundreds of people have gone hiking, backpacking, horsepacking, rock-climbing, and fly-fishing with this company. From a day trip to a week in the outback, either camping or staying in a luxury inn, you can just relax and enjoy the glorious outdoors.

Yosemite Association Backpack Trips
P.O. Box 230, El Portal, CA 95318
(209) 379-2321
www.yosemite.org

A nonintimidating, comfortable, and fun way to take a first-time pack trip or introduce a child to backpacking is with an experienced, friendly naturalist-guide from the Yosemite Association. You learn about equipment, map, and compass; securing provisions from bears; and other backcountry techniques. Trip leaders talk about ecology, wildflowers, wildlife, geology, history, and other topics that help to make your trip not only educational, but unforgettable.

Hiking and camping take place in elevations from 8,600 to 11,000 feet in the Yosemite backcountry, so fitness is a must, even for hiking on mostly flat trails.

The association offers a wide variety of day-trip hikes and multiday expeditions for all ages and abilities.

Yosemite Mountaineering School and Guide Service Backpacking Tours (YMS)
(209) 372-8344
www.yosemitepark.com

The country's top headquarters for mountaineering and climbing, YMS offers half-day and full-day guided hikes and guided backpacking trips into the Yosemite backcountry with instruction in low-impact backpacking and camping techniques.

This is your opportunity to learn from some of the world's most acclaimed and experienced experts. Beginning backpackers learn wilderness skills such as map and compass use, food storage, animal safety, emergency shelters, stream crossing, and adverse weather survival, plus the use of equipment and much more. Breakfast, lunch, and dinner, while on the trail, and transportation to and from the trailhead are provided, as well as equipment such as tents, stoves, cooking gear, water filters, and wilderness permits. Sleeping bags and pads are available for rent, or you can bring your own.

Families can choose easy, level backpack trips to fishing and swimming lakes or challenging treks with an ascent of Mount Lyell; you can also arrange custom, private trips. The most popular trip, offered annually, is the four-day Tuolumne Meadows to Yosemite Valley backpack. You hike from Tuolumne to Booth Lake, cross Vogelsang Pass to Merced Lake, then head on down to Yosemite Valley. A rest day at Merced Lake gives a chance for day hiking, fishing, and swimming. Stronger participants may attempt a Half Dome ascent.

The three-day Mt. Lyell trek for hardy hikers starts with a fairly level hike of about 10 miles to a base camp below Mt. Lyell. On day two, you climb the tallest peak in Yosemite National Park.

Check www.yosemitepark.com for detailed information, including descriptions of the guides.

SHOPPING IN THE PARK

If you wish, you can arrive at Yosemite with just the clothes on your back and plan to purchase from park retail outlets all the gear, apparel, food, and accessories you might need for camping, hiking, fishing, taking photographs, swimming, reading, eating and drinking, and just about every other activity that can—legally—be enjoyed in the national park.

Now that your mind is at ease as to how much luggage to bring, look at it this way. Don't panic if you forget to pack a jacket, a best-seller, a swimsuit, or your favorite deodorant. Chances are very good that you will find what you need in the various stores and shops here. Most are clustered at Yosemite Village and at The Ahwahnee, at Yosemite Lodge at the Falls, and in Curry Village, all in the valley. In the Tuolumne High Country, at Wawona, and at a handful of other locations, you will find a much more limited selection of goods, although in the summertime at Tuolumne Meadows, a variety of outdoor recreation equipment is available.

As your time in Yosemite is precious, this description of retail outlets will come in handy for last-minute souvenir, postcard, guidebook, and seasonal apparel shopping. Expect high-quality items. Do not expect bargain prices.

---

i ***A few years ago, The Ahwahnee replaced its 66,000-square-foot Vermont slate roof with material from the same quarry. Salvageable pieces of slate from 1927 were "recycled" into plaques, coasters, clocks, mirror frames, key rings, magnets, and other furnishings, and are for sale at The Ahwahnee Gift Shop or at www.yosemitegifts.com/yosemite/ahwahneeslate.html.***

Ahwahnee Gift Shop
The Ahwahnee, shuttle stop 3
(209) 372-1409

Refurbished to showcase the hotel's historic decorative scheme and the park's natural and cultural history, the lobby shop displays a fine collection of Yosemite-related gifts and a large collection of guidebooks, calendars, postcards, art prints, and beautiful books of photography and history. You can purchase polo shirts, sweaters, purses, and Native American-inspired items such as Kachina dolls, rawhide drums, handcrafted silver jewelry, and pottery. "Native Critters" are fanciful figures decorated with fur, feather, and leather, with price tags in the hundreds.

When you fall in love with the hotel, take home a small sculpture of the building or china and glassware decorated with the distinctive Ahwahnee logo. Designed in 1929, the tabletop items are used in the restaurants today. The shop is open all year, 8:00 A.M. to 10:00 P.M.

For a preview of decorative accessories exclusive to The Ahwahnee Gift Shop, go to www.yosemitegifts.com/yosemite/ahwahneespirit.html.

Ahwahnee Hotel Sweet Shop
The Ahwahnee, shuttle stop 3
(209) 372-1271

Browse here for candy, snacks, sundries, cigars, magazines and newspapers, cold drinks, hotel logo merchandise, souvenirs, and postcards. You will also find an adequate selection of wines. Take your reading materials to nearby armchairs or out onto the patio. Or walk around to the south side of the hotel to a group of chairs and tables on a quiet terrace. The shop is open 7:00 A.M. to 10:00 P.M. year-round.

Buy Online

Get ready for your trip to Yosemite by obtaining guidebooks and maps at the Yosemite Association's online store: www.yosemitestore.com. This may be the most extensive collection of books available on Yosemite and the Sierra Nevada. Camping and hiking equipment can be ordered, too, from water filters to camp stoves and bear-resistant food containers. After your trip, shop on the Web site for Yosemite-logo apparel as well as music, posters, calendars, games, toys, and souvenirs to remind you and your family of your adventures in the national park.

The park concessionaire, DNC, also has a retail Web site, www.yosemitegifts.com, where National Park-logo items, climbing and hiking gear, guidebooks, and many more items are available. You can also call (209) 372-1354 or e-mail yosretail@dncinc.com.

Ansel Adams Gallery
Yosemite Village, shuttle stops 5 and 9
(209) 372-4413
This is the best gift shop in the park, bar none. Besides fine-art prints, photos, calendars, and posters, you will find handcrafted home accessories, Indian-motif silver jewelry, books for kids, and a terrific collection of fiction and nonfiction books in a serene, elegant atmosphere. The works of world-famous photographer Ansel Adams are perpetually on display and for sale here, along with images created by other notable photographers. Open 8:00 A.M. to 6:00 P.M. spring through fall, the gallery closes at 5:00 P.M. in the wintertime. For more information about the Ansel Adams Gallery, see the Yosemite Valley chapter.

Badger Pass Sport Shop
Yosemite's Badger Pass Ski Area
(209) 372-1333
Open during the winter season only, this store sells ski clothing, warm hats, sunglasses, sunblock, ski waxes, and ski- and winter-related apparel and gear. You can also get snacks, candy, film, and picnic foods.

Curry Village Gift Shop
Shuttle stop 20
(209) 372-8391
A grocery that stocks just about everything you might need for a day or a week of meals, this is also a general store selling some basic clothing, sundries, film, and souvenirs. Kids like the array of children's books, games, and toys; oenophiles are satisfied with the wine collection. The store is open 8:00 A.M. to 8:00 P.M. year-round.

Glacier Point Gift Shop
Glacier Point Road, road marker G11
(209) 372-8398
Hiking gear and apparel, astronomy- and geology-related gifts, summer clothing and film are on sale here, on top of the world. You can also outfit yourself with Yosemite-logo T-shirts and other apparel and pick up souvenirs, guidebooks, and maps. Snacks, beverages, and picnic foods are available, too. The shop is open spring to fall.

Habitat Yosemite
Yosemite Village, shuttle stop 2
(209) 372-8453
Bears in all forms crowd this small shop—

The next car you pass may have a Yosemite license plate. California residents can opt to pay extra to affix plates with Yosemite's panoramic vista from Tunnel View on their vehicle. For each license, $20 goes to support The Yosemite Fund's privately financed restoration projects in the park. Contact the California Department of Motor Vehicles, Special Processing Department, P.O. Box 932345, Sacramento, CA 94232-3450; (916) 657-7654.

stuffed, carved, and emblazoned on shirts, mugs, and crockery. Kids head to the children's corner for the books, toys, games, and backpacks designed just for the younger set. On sale are a variety of nature-oriented gift items and souvenirs, as well as Christmas ornaments. (The Yosemite Lodge at the Falls Nature Shop has similar merchandise.) The store is open 10:00 A.M. to 5:00 P.M. spring through fall.

Happy Isles Nature Center
Shuttle stop 16
(209) 372-0287

From 9:00 A.M. to 5:00 P.M. daily, spring through fall, families swarm the place, taking advantage of the ranger-led walks and talks and shopping for things-to-do stuff for the kids, educational toys and books, puzzles, bird calls, and compasses. Michael Elsohn Ross's *The Happy Camper Book,* complete with flashlight and rescue whistle, is a great choice, along with nature project and activity books for toddlers through middle-school kids. Everyone will enjoy *Sierra Campfire Yarns,* a book of tales, skits, and songs. The Star Light Binocular Astronomy Kit is a must for clear summer nights. The National Park Service has produced several games and educational toys, such as the park version of Monopoly and Yosemite playing cards.

Mountain Shop
Curry Village, shuttle stop 20
(209) 372-8396

State-of-the-art outdoor, camping, and mountaineering equipment is featured in this large store, with everything from backpacks, sleeping bags, parkas, ponchos, and tents to guidebooks, maps, freeze-dried food, nonstick cooking utensils, and water filtration systems. Shop here for hiking and climbing footwear; "Go Climb a Rock" T-shirts and caps; and ropes and accessories for mountain and rock climbing. Black Diamond and North Face are two of the top-quality brands offered.

Ordinary mortals who stay in hotels and drive, rather than walk, hike, or climb, will browse for seasonal apparel such as fleece vests, shirts, and jackets, summer sandals, and water bottles.

Even if your idea of outdoor recreation is watching a National Geographic special on TV, you may find the display cases of antique climbing gear of interest. Check out the posters by the entrance showing climbing routes for El Capitan and Half Dome.

The shop is open year-round 8:00 A.M. to 6:00 P.M. Outside the shop on the deck, you will likely encounter a gang of young climbers sharing stories of their adventures.

Mountaineering School and Sport Shop
Tuolumne Meadows, Highway 120 East/Tioga Road
(209) 372-8436

Mountaineering, climbing, hiking, and backpacking equipment and supplies are for sale in this headquarters for High Country adventurers, who often congregate here at the beginning and the end of each day during the summer season. Besides plenty of advice on where to boulder and climb, you can get stove fuel, rope, first-aid kits, sleeping bags, fishing gear, and more. A limited number of items are available to rent; you can buy or rent bear-proof food storage containers. The store is open seasonally, from early summer to early fall, according to the weather.

Where to Buy Groceries in the Park

- Crane Flat Store: a tiny convenience store, open spring to fall.
- Curry Village Camp Store: a small grocery and sundries market, open all year.
- Housekeeping Camp Store: a small convenience grocery store for campers, open spring to fall.
- Tuolumne Meadows Store: a general convenience store for campers, open spring to fall.
- Village Store, Yosemite Village: the only large, full-service supermarket in the park, with a butcher, good fresh produce, nice cheeses, and a good selection of wine.
- Wawona Store: a small grocery store and a U.S. Post Office.
- White Wolf Lodge: a tiny general store for campers in the summer.

Read more about the famous Yosemite Mountaineering School in the Outdoor Recreation chapter.

Tuolumne Meadows Store
Highway 120 East/Tioga Road
(209) 372-8428
At this small general store, open through the summer and into early fall, you will find basic groceries, snacks, souvenirs, hiking and camping supplies and equipment, guidebooks, maps, and apparel such as T-shirts, shorts, and sweatshirts. Gas at the station here is available 24 hours a day, seasonally, with your credit or ATM card.

Village Sport Shop
Yosemite Village, shuttle stop 4
(209) 372-1286
From camping gear to summer and winter clothing, fishing gear, guidebooks, maps, sunglasses, sunscreen, sun hats, and bicycle clips—you name it, they've got it for outdoor fun (except for climbing and mountaineering gear, which is found at Curry Village and Tuolumne Meadows). Come here for film, air mattresses, walking sticks, daypacks, fanny packs, and even baby backpacks. Open spring to fall, 8:30 A.M. to 6:00 P.M.

Village Store
Yosemite Village, shuttle stop 10
(209) 372-1253
A complete supermarket with fresh produce and a butcher shop, and not just that—you could literally arrive in any season with nothing but the clothes you're wearing (and maybe extra underwear) and outfit the whole family and feed them with what you find at the Village Store. You may find that prices are high compared to your grocery store at home. An ATM is nearby. Nice souvenirs and gifts, seasonal clothing, jackets, T-shirts, and bathing suits are for sale, as well as outdoor recreation equipment and toys for all seasons, including snow saucers. You will find reading material galore, from guidebooks to history and fiction, and Yosemite-related videos and DVDs. Cameras and film are on sale, and you can have film processed here. The store is open year-round, 8:00 A.M. to 8:00 P.M.

Wawona Golf Shop
Wawona Hotel, Highway 41
(209) 375-6572
This tiny but mighty golf central is especially convenient for visitors who neglect to bring along their golf gear—many folks have no idea there is a golf course in the national park. You can rent or buy top-

A check-cashing service is available year-round within the Yosemite Art Center in Yosemite Village, from 8:00 A.M. to 4:00 P.M. daily, closing at 2:00 P.M. some days. You may cash one check per day with a $100.00 limit, for a $5.00 fee.

quality clubs and pick up Yosemite-logo polo shirts as well as balls, socks, sweaters, jackets, and snacks. The shop is open seasonally, spring to fall, from 7:30 A.M. to 6:00 P.M.

Wawona Store and Pioneer Gift Shop
Pioneer Yosemite History Center
Highway 41
(209) 375-6574
A nice variety of handmade gifts and Americana is on sale, along with sundries, newspapers, magazines, guidebooks, posters, snacks, seasonal clothing, and jewelry. You can also buy basic groceries and deli items. The store is open spring to fall, 8:00 A.M. to 6:00 P.M.

Wilderness Center
Yosemite Village, shuttle stop 2
(209) 372-0740
Specific to hiking and climbing in the national park is a small inventory of maps and guidebooks and some excellent nature-related exhibits here. See more about the Wilderness Center in the Yosemite Valley chapter.

Yosemite Art Center
Yosemite Village, shuttle stop 2
(209) 372-1442
This is a small, well-stocked shop selling artists' materials and equipment, including top-quality watercolor paints and oils, brushes, paper, pens and pencils, and children's art kits. The store is open spring through fall.

Yosemite Bookstore
Valley Visitor Center
Yosemite Village, shuttle stop 4
(209) 372-0299
A major remodeling resulted in a beautiful new welcome center and bookstore to accommodate more than a million annual visitors. This is the place to shop for an extensive array of Yosemite Association and National Park Service guidebooks and maps, plus posters, books for children, and videos about the natural and human history of the park. The Valley Visitor Center is open 9:00 A.M. to 5:00 P.M. daily.

Yosemite Lodge at the Falls Gift Store
Shuttle stop 8
(209) 371-1205
A variety of Yosemite-related merchandise here includes T-shirts and sweatshirts, hats, souvenirs, guidebooks, and posters. This is a convenience store, too, selling snacks, beverages, picnic supplies and a few grocery items, film, sundries, newspapers and magazines, jewelry, and apparel. The store is open from 8:00 A.M. to 8:00 P.M. year-round.

Yosemite Lodge at the Falls Nature Shop
Shuttle stop 8
(209) 372-1438
The natural world is featured in large displays of sculpture, original photographs by some of Yosemite's leading professionals, and one-of-a-kind Native American-inspired art and jewelry. You will also find environment- and nature-oriented apparel, music, videos, wind chimes, home accessories, and books. The store is open 11:00 A.M. to 6:00 P.M. year-round.

Yosemite Museum Store
Yosemite Village, shuttle stop 5
(209) 372-0282
A small, fascinating collection of traditional Native American-style and -produced arts and crafts makes for a unique shopping opportunity in the park. You will find beadwork, leather items, beautiful jewelry, fine baskets, and books about Native American history and culture. The store is open 9:30 A.M. to 4:30 P.M.

ARCH ROCK ENTRANCE/ HIGHWAY 140

The lowest-elevation route into Yosemite National Park, Highway 140 heads from Merced in California's Central Valley east through rolling foothills and into the Wild and Scenic Merced River Canyon. Becoming the Central Yosemite Highway, it enters the park at the Arch Rock Entrance Station, at a modest 2,850-foot elevation.

On Highways 140 and 49 (the route parallel to Yosemite's west side that winds through California's Gold Rush Mother Lode region in the Sierra Nevada foothills), keep your eyes peeled for literally hundreds of species of resident and migrating birds. Only 5 percent of California's original four million acres of Central Valley wetlands exist today. More than one-third of the remaining wetlands are at the beginning of your route as you drive east in Merced County, where you can spot an astonishing number of birds along the roadside.

Approximately 45 minutes by car west of the Arch Rock Entrance Station, Mariposa is a picturesque old Gold Rush town in a county with fewer than 20,000 residents, no stoplights, no pretensions, and some very good reasons for you to stop along the way. The town of Mariposa is an antiques-lover's mecca, with a few places to stay and eat, an excellent regional visitor center, and two outstanding museums. Plan a couple of hours to do a walking tour of the 19th-century buildings and the antiques shops on the main street, but be sure you don't miss the Center Star emporium up Sixth Street and the shops at the top of Fifth Street. If you have limited time, first on your list should be the Mariposa Museum and History Center—one of the best in the Gold Country—and take a peek at one of the oldest county courthouses in the nation.

Mariposa County was home to the famous bandit Joaquin Murietta and the explorer John C. Frémont, who founded the town in 1847, just one year before the Gold Rush made it world famous. The first hard-rock gold mine of the 1849 Gold Rush, the Mariposa Mine, was discovered here by Kit Carson.

If you are in the mood for a picnic or just a lounge on the lawn, look for the Mariposa Park sign in midtown Mariposa and drive down, east off the main street, and up the hill to a nice, small park with grass, picnic tables, and play structures.

One of the best small art towns emerging in America, Mariposa is blooming with galleries and art-related activities; check out the annual calendar of events for opportunities to browse and buy locals' artworks and fine crafts at festivals and fairs (www.homeofyosemite.com). In 2004, an unused lot was transformed into the Mariposa County Art Park now enjoyed for picnics and outdoor concerts. In March, crowds roll into town for another type of art, the Mariposa Storytelling Festival, with folktales to tall tales entertaining kids and adults. For more information, call (800) 903-9936 or (209) 966-3155, or visit www.arts-mariposa.org/storytelling.html.

Since 1975, historic pioneer routes have been traced by the Mariposa County Pioneer Wagon Train, the annual June confab of wagons, horses, marchers, performers, and riders in Gold Rush– or pioneer-era costumes. The photogenic

---

i

Before exploring the art galleries of Mariposa County, learn more about local artists and see some of their works by going to www.yosemiteartists.org.

It's too easy to forget that the few businesses and towns near Yosemite National Park had a tumultuous and important history. Modern visitors have a tame and nostalgic version of the past at the Wawona Hotel and The Ahwahnee, but for some rip-roaring history, read the account of a 1905 Yosemite Stage(coach) holdup: www.mariposa research.net/holdup1905.html.

parade ends up at the fairgrounds for daylong events (209-966-3414 or 209-966-7081). Nationally recognized cowboy poets read to large crowds enjoying an old-fashioned barbecue and dance on Saturday night after the wagon train has rolled into the Mariposa County Fairgrounds. Stop in at the Mariposa Visitors Center for information on local museums and events and area camping, rafting, fishing, biking, hiking, horseback riding, and the national park. North of Midpines on Highway 140, the BLM Briceburg Visitors Center is occasionally open to provide literature and advice on local recreation.

The highway rolls on, gradually gaining elevation through the Merced River canyon, with mountainsides growing higher and more rugged as you approach the park. This is a pretty drive at any time of year, but spectacular sights await you when wildflowers blanket the hillsides in spring. California poppies begin the show in March, covering the landscape in great orange carpets so vast and so vivid they seem to have been painted by an artist. The Western redbud trees are a pink and magenta extravaganza.

Watch for the Merced River Trail for excellent walking and biking all along the north side of the river. White-water rafting is popular from early April through June when the rapids are high.

Just west of the park entrance, you may have trouble finding a town center in El Portal, which is really a few campgrounds, a couple of restaurants, a post office, a service station, and a grocery store. A huge flood in 1997 wiped out a string of tacky motels, which were replaced by nice, new units at the riverside Yosemite View Lodge and Cedar Lodge.

Entering the park, you pass beneath two monumental blocks of granite, which fell from the cliffs above—Arch Rock—a fitting approach to the breathtaking sight of the monoliths of Yosemite Valley. Giant boulders on both sides of the roadway and in the river are the result of a huge rockfall that took place in 1982. Meandering alongside the river, you will enter the valley between El Capitan and Bridalveil Fall.

ATTRACTIONS

California State Parks Mining and Mineral Museum
Mariposa County Fairgrounds, 1.8 miles south of Mariposa on Highway 49
(209) 742-7625
www.parks.ca-gov/?page_id=588

Within a replica of an 1890s mining complex is an extraordinary collection of more than 13,000 gems, minerals, rocks, and fossils. This is the official state collection, with some flashy highlights such as big nuggets of gold and mysterious meteorites, and the crystalline gold Fricot Nugget, weighing 201 ounces, the largest found during the Gold Rush. There is also a full-scale replica of a mine, an assay office, and a stamp mill. There is a mining tunnel connected to the museum, which allows visitors to see and experience what a miner's daily life was like. Among the merchandise offered at the gift shop are gemstone jewelry, gold samples, and guidebooks to gold-panning sites in the area. The museum is open daily 10:00 A.M. to 6:00 P.M. in the summer; October through April open 10:00 A.M. to 4:00 P.M., closed Tuesday. Cost is $3.00 for 16 and over.

Cascade and Wildcat Falls
Highway 140, 3.1 miles east of the Arch Rock entrance

Stop for a picnic at vivacious, photogenic Cascade Falls and walk west a few hun-

Panning for gold near Mariposa. MAXINE CASS

dred yards to Wildcat Falls, an even larger fall that is absolutely beautiful in the springtime when the mock orange, sunflowers, and spice bushes bloom.

Hornitos
At the intersection of Bear Valley Road and Hornitos Road, 15 miles west of Mariposa

The living ghost town of Hornitos was known as the wildest town in the west in the mid-1800s, with a population of 15,000 fortune seekers, 12 hotels, and 36 saloons and brothels. Bandito Joaquin Murietta came here often, creating legends of never-discovered escape routes. Today you will find a sleepy, tiny village of 75 residents. Photographers and history buffs explore the place, encountering original buildings, crumbling, vine-covered walls, and fragments of days gone by.

Mariposa County Arts Council Gift Shops and Art Galleries
5009 Fifth Street and 5022 A Highway 140, Mariposa
(800) 903-9936, (209) 966-3155
www.arts-mariposa.org

In one of the liveliest art communities in the state, the county Arts Council galleries show and sell the works of more than 40 local and regional professional artists. You will find the fine-art photography of well-known artist Howard Weamer and the stunning Yosemite- and nature-related paintings of Mark Gudmudsen. This is a great place to see museum-quality Native American and traditional crafts, pottery, sculpture, books, and ceramics. The shops also sell attractive cards and historic and contemporary posters and prints focusing on the Yosemite/Sierra foothills area, handmade jewelry, weavings, pine needle baskets, and more.

---

i *Gas is available in Mariposa, Midpines, and El Portal; there's no gas in Yosemite Valley.*

Mariposa County Courthouse
5088 Bullion Street, Mariposa
(866) 425-3366, (209) 966-5088

The oldest courthouse and oldest continually sitting Superior Court west of the Mississippi, this two-story, white clapboard building, with wooden pegs, square nails, and hand-planed lumber, was constructed in 1854. Mariposa County's seal and documents refer to itself as the "Mother of Counties," as it was declared a county even before California's admission to the Union as a state in 1850. The original boundaries encompassed one-fifth of California's territory. Since then, eleven counties have been carved out of the original. The courthouse, set among pines and topped by a massive clock tower, is between 9th and 10th Streets, 1 block east of Highway 140. County offices are downstairs while the main courtroom is upstairs. One Superior Court judge, J. J. Trabucco, never had a judgment overturned during his 1903–1938 tenure on the bench. Shipped around the Cape of Good Hope, the clock in the tower was brought from England and has been loudly tolling the hour since 1866. The courthouse is open weekdays from 8:00 A.M. to 5:00 P.M. Free guided tours are given Saturday 10:00 A.M. to 8:00 P.M. and Sunday, 10:00 A.M. to 4:00 P.M.

Mariposa Museum and History Center
Off Highway 140 near the north end of Mariposa, 12th Street at 5119 Jessie Street
(209) 966-2924

Children love this museum because many of the artifacts are located on or near the floor. More people-friendly than traditional museums where collections are laid out in glass display cases, this one groups the memorabilia in separate, elaborate settings, from a drugstore to a mining camp, a doctor's office, a child's cache of toys and dolls, a newspaper office, and a ranch house. Peek into Rattlesnake Ike's Saloon and the Bull Creek School and take a look at a huge array of photos of early days. The fabulous general store at the entrance is crowded with vintage merchandise from the Gagliardo store, once located in nearby Hornitos. You can see chunks of some of the gold found here in the 1850s, walk around outside among mining equipment—including a local landmark, the five-stamp mill—and a re-created Miwok village, and have a picnic at tables under the trees. The Smithsonian Institution named the Mariposa Museum and History Center one of the best small museums in America. It's open daily March through December, weekends in January, and closed in February. Cost is $3.00 for adults; children are free.

Sisochi Gallery
9486 Highway 140, 7 miles west of El Portal
(209) 379-2301
www.yosemitegold.com/nativeamerican/yngcontact.html
Stop here daily from 9:00 A.M. to 7:00 P.M. for a cold soda and to cruise the interesting little shop and gallery. Owner Letty Barry buys Native American pottery, rugs, baskets, and jewelry from tribes throughout the western states, and she is a book lover, so you will find a nice collection of history, art, and children's books. Don't miss the unique T-shirts depicting Native Americans in costume. Letty is also an expert on area Native American history. Next to the shop you'll find the trailhead for the famous Hite Cove wildflower trail. The Yosemite Association offers a botanist-guided day hike on the trail in March at the height of the blooming season (209-379-2321; www.yosemite.org).

VISITOR INFORMATION

The visitor center in Mariposa is chock-full of guidebooks and brochures. You can pick up maps, information, and advice on the entire county and the national park and buy yourself some souvenirs, too.

Mariposa County Visitors Center
P.O. Box 967, 5158 Highway 140, Mariposa, CA 95338
(866) 425-3366
www.homeofyosemite.com

ACCOMMODATIONS

PRICE CODE

A dollar sign ($) ranking indicates the average nightly rates for two adults. Unless otherwise noted, lodgings accept credit cards. Some bed-and-breakfast inns require two-night minimums.

$	$49–$75
$$	$76–$124
$$$	$125–$175
$$$$	$176 and up

Boulder Creek Bed and Breakfast **$$**
4572 Ben Hur Road, Mariposa
(800) 768-4752, (209) 742-7729
http://mariposa.yosemite.net/bcreek
Yummy German apple pancakes and fruit smoothies are on the complimentary breakfast menu at this pleasant, European chalet-style home with three nice guest rooms. Floor to ceiling windows look onto beautiful views of the Sierra foothills, and there are nearby walking trails and a hot tub. The park is just a half-hour drive from the inn.

Cedar Lodge **$$–$$$**
9966 Highway 140, El Portal
(888) 742-4371, (209) 379-2612
reservations@yosemiteresorts.us
www.yosemiteresorts.us
One of two, large, renovated motel complexes along the Merced River next to the highway, within 15 minutes of the Arch Rock entrance to the national park, this hotel offers lots of variety, including standard double rooms, suites, family units with kitchenettes, and very nice king rooms with double spa tubs. There is a large outdoor pool and an indoor pool, two restaurants, and a bar. Some rooms

have balconies or patios. Bus transportation into the park stops here. Kids love the 32 whimsical, larger-than-life, hand-carved wooden bears that are scattered around the property, and the on-site store is loaded with plush, carved, and porcelain bears. The front desk has a "bear map" to make it easier for kids to locate each one of the bears.

Little Valley Inn at the Creek **$$-$$$**
3483 Brooks Road, Mariposa
(800) 889-5444, (209) 742-6204
http://littlevalley.com

When the water's running in the creek, there's gold panning a few steps outside the private entrances to this inn's cabin rooms in the mixed oak and pine forest. This bed and breakfast-style inn is in Bootjack, 8 miles southeast of Mariposa along Highway 49 South. Guests can sit outdoors on private decks, listening to birds and the wind in the trees or walk a nature trail. There are Native American grinding stones nearby. All four rooms, the kitchen suite, and the separate cabin's Suncatcher Room have a private bath, satellite TV, heat, and air conditioning. Have a relaxed buffet breakfast in the inn's breakfast room or outside on the deck near a burbling fountain.

Poppy Hill Bed and Breakfast **$$-$$$**
5218 Crystal Aire Drive, Mariposa
(800) 587-6779, (209) 742-6273
www.poppyhill.com

This vintage home, restored and outfitted as a country inn, floats in an ocean of vivid, yellow-orange California poppies. Outdoor decks and a spa are the catbirds' seats for views of the meadows and rolling hills. The lush gardens attract many birds and butterflies and the occasional deer and fox.

The three guest rooms are spacious, with queen beds, down comforters, robes, private baths, and antique furnishings. The Poppy Room has a private sitting area overlooking the garden. A game alcove is shared by guests, and a refrigerator is stocked with complimentary soft drinks.

The full, complimentary breakfast may consist of puffed apple pancakes, croissant French toast, or a luscious egg dish, and beverages and hors d'oeuvres are served in the evenings.

American and European antiques and fine art decorate the parlor, which is complete with a wood-burning stove and a baby grand.

Rancho Bernardo **$$$**
2617 Old Highway South, Cathey's Valley
(877) 930-1669, (209) 966-4511
www.ranchobernardobnb.com

Nearby the highway about 15 minutes from Mariposa, this is a unique and convenient place to stay on the way to or from the national park. The bed-and-breakfast inn is on a 40-acre cattle ranch surrounded by rolling hills, sprawling oak trees, Chinese rock walls, natural springs, and grazing livestock. One of the two guest units, the Barn Suite, is a charming studio-apartment in the barn, with a queen bed and mini-kitchen. The horses bunk downstairs.

The separate guest house sleeps up to six people. In an airy, high-ceilinged, knotty-pine-paneled space is a loft, a small kitchen, a fireplace, pool table, wing chairs, and a sofa. Both units have plush bedding. Free videos are available.

Guests enjoy cookies and soft drinks in the afternoons, warm robes, and a sumptuous full breakfast each day.

Ask co-owner, Barney Lozares, about his days as a bull rider.

Restful Nest Resort **$$$**
4274 Buckeye Creek Road, Mariposa
(800) 664-7127, (209) 742-7127
www.restfulnest.com

On 11 acres of oak trees and meadows, a swimming pool, spa, and catch-and-release fishing pond are among the delightful amenities at this small, quiet bed-and-breakfast inn.

Guest rooms have queen beds, private entrances, and private baths. A separate guest house sleeping six has a wood-burning stove, a living room, bedroom, and bath. French is spoken by the hosts, Lois and Jon Pierre Moroni, who serve a full breakfast of freshly baked brioche, homemade sausages, and locally grown fruits. Fido is welcome, too!

Yosemite Bug Rustic Mountain Resort $-$$$
6979 Highway 140, Midpines
(866) 826-7108, (209) 966-6666
www.yosemitebug.com

Not far off the highway on 45 forest acres, accessed by a short gravel road, the "Bug" has evolved but not abandoned its beginnings as a lodge and hostel near the Merced River and within reach of Yosemite National Park. The resort is a complex of neat and newish motel units, rooms with private or shared baths, and dorm accommodations as well as tent cabins and tent campsites. All but the tent cabins and campsites are heated. The Bug has not abandoned backpackers—Hostelling International-licensed single sex, co-ed, or group dorm cabins with bunks are equipped with mattresses, pillows, linens, and blankets, and hostellers have access to their own kitchen. There are resident Bug pets, but your animals may stay during the less-frenetic season between September 15 to May 15 if they pass screening when you make reservations.

A casual cafe serves three meals a day and snacks, beer, wine, and locally roasted coffee. Folks in the know stop for a meal before making the last 25 miles to the national park. The Bug offers a Thanksgiving feast and a day of activities, including hikes, games, and music. The Christmas feast is popular, too. Long tables groan under the platters of fresh homemade holiday foods at very reasonable prices.

This is a favorite base camp for mountain bikers who enjoy nearby trails, including the Riverside Trail along the Merced River. You can rent snowshoes here in the winter to tromp around the forest or in the national park. The enthusiastic Bug staff will fill you in on where to find the local swimming hole and waterfall, mountain bike and hiking trails, and places to put in your river raft. Some rafting companies pick up passengers here.

The atmosphere here is young and social. The cafe is a gathering place for hanging out and reading, conversing, and eating. At day's end, guests congregate on comfy sofas by the wood-burning stove to play games or in-house instruments, or they sit out and relax on the glassed-in or outdoor decks. Kids are welcome. There is a small charge for Internet access, but for laptoppers, wireless access is free in the lobby. There's also a store with books, maps, limited groceries and outdoor necessities. In 2006, the Bug added a Health Spa, with Ayurvedic practitioners, two 10-person spring-water-filled hot tubs, a cedar hot rock sauna, a weight room, yoga classes, massage and other treatments.

Yosemite View Lodge $$-$$$
Highway 140, El Portal
(209) 379-2681

This two- and three-story motel with 335 units is the best place to stay near the Arch Rock park entrance, and the upscale, attractive accommodations make this a good alternative to the rather basic, and more expensive, Yosemite Lodge at the Falls in the valley. Desired rooms are those with balconies or patios overlooking the Merced River that storms by, crashing over huge boulders below a beautiful, forested hillside. The rushing sounds of the water will sing you right to sleep at night, and if you can't sleep, step outside onto your balcony to enjoy the sounds of nature. Deluxe rooms are spacious and attractive, with rustic mountain lodge-style furnishings and fully equipped kitchenettes with microwaves, refrigerators, toasters, coffeemakers, two-burner stoves, cooking equipment, and dishes. Refurbished rooms have flat-screen TVs, fireplaces, and separate seating areas with sofa beds, plus deep double whirlpool tubs and double showerheads. Nicely decorated standard rooms are set up with two double-size beds. Pets are welcome in some rooms.

Yosemite View Lodge in El Portal is near Yosemite National Park's Arch Rock Entrance.
JOHN POIMIROO

Three outdoor pools, a larger indoor pool, two small outdoor spas, one indoor spa, and nearby hiking and biking trails make this a place to linger. You can take bus transportation from the lodge into the valley for $4.50 or $9.00 round trip. The park entrance fee may be extra.

Two restaurants are located here, a pizza place and a quite good restaurant by the river serving breakfasts and dinners, with a cocktail lounge. Also on-site is a large convenience store and gift shop, where you can pick up basic food items, T-shirts and sweatshirts, camera supplies, guidebooks, toys, and touristy gifts.

Take a cruise through the lobby of the Yosemite View Lodge to see a collection of rare colorful advertising cards. The cards were first placed in cigarette packs, in the United States and Great Britain, in the late 1800s, and the "cigarette cards" are valued collectibles today. They portray subjects such as military equipment, sportsmen's and outdoor activities, historical buildings, and personalities. This huge collection dates from the early 1900s to the 1940s. Look for the cards sporting the signatures of Queen Victoria, Charles Dickens, and King George V.

RESTAURANTS

PRICE CODE

The prices following are based on the cost of two entrees from the dinner menu, not including appetizers, desserts, beverages, taxes, or gratuities.

$	$15 or less
$$	$16–$25
$$$	$26–$35
$$$$	More than $35

Café at the Bug **$–$$**
Yosemite Bug Rustic Mountain Resort
6979 Highway 140, Midpines
(866) 826-7108, (209) 966-6666
www.yosemitebug.com
This rustic cafe with a limited menu serves three hearty meals and snacks all day, with a special focus on vegetarian and Mediterranean items. Locals come out here from Mariposa and El Portal for the good food. You can sit outdoors in the summertime and have a beer by the fireplace in winter.

Castillo's **$–$$**
4995 Fifth Street, off Highway 140
Mariposa
(209) 742-4413
Come here for really good Mexican food and some less adventurous choices for breakfast, lunch, and dinner. Castillo's serves up big portions of everything, from Tostada Compuesta to veggie burritos and spicy *carne asada.* The locals love this place, so call ahead.

Charles Street Dinner House **$$–$$$**
5043 Highway 140 at Seventh Street
Mariposa
(209) 966-2366
www.charlesstreetdinnerhouse.com
The decor is funky, fun Old West, and even the waitstaff gets into the act with colorful costumes. On the menu (dinner only Monday through Saturday, with Sunday brunch) you'll find hearty American fare, including steak, rack of lamb, seafood, and chicken, all served with generous portions of soup, salad, and bread. Check out the wine list.

High Country Health Food
and Cafe **$–$$**
49'er Shopping Center, east end of
Mariposa on the north side
(209) 966-5111
Locals pack this casual cafe at lunchtime, munching on delicious veggie specialties, like "Lush Meadows" sandwiches and Bear Valley Burritos. There is fresh soup and quiche every day, and other goodies like Hornitos barbecued chicken, Chinese chicken salad, smoothies, and homemade desserts. In a hurry? You can get takeout, too. High Country Health Food and Cafe is open 9:00 A.M. to 3:00 P.M., with later hours for takeout and the store.

Red Fox Restaurant **$$–$$$**
5114 Highway 140 and 12th Street
Mariposa
(209) 966-7900
You can come in your jeans, but expect a luxurious dinner menu that includes rainbow trout, filet mignon, pasta with portobello mushrooms, and more. Lunches feature luscious salads, steak sandwiches, burgers, reubens, and omelettes, and it's open for breakfast.

Savoury's Restaurant **$$$**
5027 Highway 140, Mariposa
(209) 966-7677
Dinners are cheerful and elegant from 5:00 P.M. on, with 17 tables set in summer—including in an outdoor, vine-covered garden. Dining comes inside in winter with 11 cozy indoor tables. On the menu are pastas and vegetarian dishes, and specialties like nightly chive preparations, fresh seafood, roasted garlic cream scallops, chipotle pesto chicken, and filet mignon.

Yosemite View Lodge Restaurant and
Little Bear Pizza Parlor **$$–$$$**
11159 Highway 140, El Portal
(209) 379-2183
The closest restaurant to the Arch Rock entrance to the park, this very nice, casual restaurant and bar overlooking the Merced River serves everything from steak to grilled veggies, pasta, and fresh seafood, with homemade desserts. Besides traditional pizzas, parlor specialties include the Cowboy Pizza with barbecued chicken and red pesto sauce, the Garlic Chicken

Alfredo, and the Seafood Combo, with shrimp and crab. You can also order box lunches to go. Open daily 5:00 to 10:00 P.M.

OUTDOOR RECREATION

The Merced River rushes out of Yosemite National Park at Arch Rock, headlong into a canyon, and on to the San Joaquin Valley. Fishing, river rafting, camping, mountain biking, and hiking are among the popular outdoor pursuits.

Just west of El Portal on the east side of the river at Redbud are picnic tables, good fishing, and a launch site for raft floats down the river, plus a great, partially paved riverside biking and hiking road that runs above the river.

The riverside is accessible by car along a 6-mile Bureau of Land Management (BLM) road (the old Yosemite Valley Railroad grade) beginning at the Briceburg Visitor Center and ending at three BLM campgrounds. Beyond the campgrounds, only pedestrians, equestrians, and bicycles can continue along the ungroomed 18-mile river trail.

All along the Merced River in the El Portal area and at Briceburg, you'll find many pools with good trout fishing and prolific insect hatches, especially in the fall. Parking is easy. Barbless hooks and catch-and-release rules are in effect. Just take care when the river is at its roaring height in the spring and early summer.

Hiking

Hite's Cove Trail
Park across the road from Sisochi Gallery, 7 miles west of El Portal on Highway 140
Make a point to take this walk in March or April to see really eye-popping waves of wildflowers, starting with an incredible carpet of California poppies and then with purple and yellow lupine, magenta-colored spears of owl's clover, fabulous stalks of purple and pink Chinese Pagodas, magical purple and white shooting stars, and dozens more types of flowers. Don't be put off by the steep first few yards. The path becomes a gradual, rolling, climbing route high above the South Fork of the Merced River. Although not a difficult walk, the narrowness of the trail and the precipitous drop-off on one side makes this a poor choice for little kids. You get right into the flowers almost immediately, and after about 3.5 miles or so, you'll reach the remnants of an old mining town, Hite's Cove.

The abundance and variety of flora on this trail are so impressive that a book was written about it: *Wildflowers of the Hite's Cove Trail,* by Stephen Botti.

Merced River Recreation Area Visitor Center
Highway 140, Briceburg, 15 miles north of Mariposa
(916) 985-4474
www.ca.blm.gov/folsom/mercedriver rec.html
Open late April through Labor Day, the Bureau of Land Management Visitor Center operates here, next to the highway at the bridge. They offer maps and information on camping, fishing, and outdoor recreation in the area.

On an enchanted section of the Merced River, the old Yosemite Valley Railroad route winds beside the river, making a great biking and walking trail. Along the way, you'll find three nice campgrounds, available on a first-come, first-served basis. You'll have to walk a mile from the Visitor Center before you reach the first nice riverside beach. In midsummer and early fall, it can be very hot here.

Mountain Biking

Will Riskit Bike Club
Mariposa
(209) 742-5239, (209) 966-5139
Nonmembers are welcome to come along on biking expeditions on local scenic

Catch and Release

To successfully release your fish to grow and be caught again, keep it in the water as long as possible and handle it gently, with wet hands, without squeezing, keeping your fingers out of the gills. Use a barbless hook and remove it quickly. If deeply hooked, cut the leader and leave the hook in. Hold the fish in the water upright and move it forward and backward to run water through the gills, and when the fish begins to revive and struggle, release it immediately. To preserve the moment, have the camera ready ahead of time.

roads in the Mariposa area. Ray Solano and his fellow club members meet every six weeks to organize and schedule upcoming rides. Saturday rides and ride leaders are listed in the *Mariposa Gazette*. Everyone from beginners to racers join in, and it's a group dynamic where no one is left behind and everyone is matched to skill level with fellow riders. Riders peddle both road and mountain bikes, their own or a loaner (by calling in advance), 10 to 50 miles a ride, for a one- to three-hour workout. If you're under age 18, you'll need your parents' written permission to ride. Consistent Will Riskit riders pay a $10 annual insurance. Routes take riders along the Merced River, to Signal Peak, and to Buck Meadows and other spots in Yosemite National Park.

Yosemite Bug Rustic
Mountain Resort
6979 Highway 140, Midpines
(866) 826-7108, (209) 966-6666
bughost@yosemitebug.com
www.yosemitebug.com

Not far off the highway, accessed by a short gravel road, is a resort and hostel, which functions as an informal headquarters for mountain bikers. You can get advice for trails in the Stanislaus National Forest.

Biking trails near the "Bug" are popular nearly year-round, particularly the fire roads connecting the high, sunny Feliciana, Sweetwater, and Buckingham Mountains above Midpines. You can also ride along the Merced River on the Riverside Ride from Briceburg Bridge to the Black Bridge and back at a warmer 1,800-foot elevation.

Rafting

Class III–IV white-water rafting is very popular on 28 miles of the Merced River below the national park between Redbud (at the Foresta Bridge just west of El Portal) and Bagby. For complete information on river rafting, see the Outdoor Recreation chapter of this guidebook.

Lakes Recreation Area

In the Sierra Nevada foothills between Merced and Yosemite National Park, two meandering, warm bodies of water, Lake McClure and Lake McSwain, created by a dam on the Merced River, form a sprawling, multifaceted recreation area that is popular with houseboaters, water skiers, and campers nearly year-round (209-378-2521; www.lakemcclure.com). Activities and public facilities cluster around five marinas, at elevations of 400 to 1,000 feet, in pine and oak woodland settings. Summers are quite dry and very warm, with almost no rainfall. Daytime temperatures reach into the 90s and low 100s, perfect for swimming and lying on sandy beaches.

Lake McClure has more than 80 miles of shoreline and is abuzz in the summertime. All kinds of water craft and play equipment are available to rent at the marinas, including fishing boats, wave runners, and ski boats. As the weather is moderate year-round, you can rent houseboats and patio boats every month of the year (209-378-2441 or 877-736-8262). Swimming is primarily near the campgrounds.

For those who desire a quieter experience, with no waterskiing or houseboating allowed, the much smaller Lake McSwain is favored for its good trout fishing and swimming beach (209-378-2534).

Six hundred campsites are available at the two lakes and nearby, many with shade and RV hookups, and some campgrounds have hot showers and laundry facilities (for information, call 209-378-2521; 800-468-8889 for reservations).

The cooler the season, the better the fishing in the lakes for the stocked fish: trout, king salmon, bass, crappie, catfish, and shad.

For general information about the Lake McClure and Lake McSwain recreation area, call (209) 378-2521 or browse the Web site for details: www.lakemcclure.com.

BIG OAK FLAT ENTRANCE/ HIGHWAY 120 WEST

The Northern Yosemite Highway roughly parallels the flow of the Stanislaus and Tuolumne Rivers west from the Sierra Nevada. Starting from Modesto on Highway 108 at Oakdale, the highway joins Highway 120, until Highway 120 breaks off in the Mother Lode Gold Country to head east independently through Groveland and on to Yosemite National Park at the Big Oak Flat Entrance Station. As you start east from the Central Valley's agricultural spreads and ranches, along the roadside, you'll see booths selling the harvests of fruit and nut orchards and vegetable fields—almonds, apricots, peaches, walnuts, and more. Spring is a glorious time, when wildflowers cascade in great waves across the grasslands and in the riparian areas—vibrant blue lupine, golden poppies, and yellow mustard. At the Highway 108 junction, Mountain Pass Creek flows through a long meadow below Table Mountain. An annual spectacle of white meadow foam flowers streams across the grasses to the mountain.

A classic backdrop for countless western films, the prairies and low, rolling hills around Oakdale are cowboy country, where cattle ranches dot the landscape and there is an annual rodeo in April. Stop in Oakdale to stock up on locally produced foodstuffs such as cheese, almonds, and Hershey's candy.

Just east of Oakdale are popular fishing spots for rainbow trout, bass, and catfish. Canoers, kayakers, and white-water rafters head for Knights Ferry along the Stanislaus River, which also makes a nice picnic spot. There are museum displays, a historic covered bridge, and a traveler's information center.

When your vacation time allows it, consider taking an extra day or two for a side trip a short distance north on Highway 49, to the attractions in the Gold Rush towns of Sonora and Jamestown and the restored village at Columbia State Historic Park. Staying at an inn or hotel in this area is a convenient alternative when accommodations are booked up along Highway 120.

Farther along Highway 120, just 26 miles from the entrance to the national park, the little town of Groveland is a charmer, with a lineup of Gold Rush- and Victorian-era buildings. Founded in 1849, Groveland was originally called First Garrotte, a nod to the favored local method of execution. Travelers to Yosemite often stop here overnight to wander the wooden sidewalks, browse a couple of blocks of shops and galleries, and take a peek at the county museum. An absolutely beautiful, historic hotel is the main lodging and restaurant attraction, and you will find a handful of other inns and cafes from which to choose. You can pick up an excellent free map and guide, the *Highway 120 Corridor Business Directory and Historic Tour Map,* at various shops in town and at the Groveland Hotel.

Between the east end of Groveland and the park are some bed-and-breakfast inns, a motel, RV parks, and several campgrounds in the Stanislaus National Forest, where hiking, fishing, and river rafting are hugely popular.

Get road condition information by stopping at the Groveland Ranger Station, just east of town, to browse the excellent guidebook store and get maps and advice.

On Highway 120 at Bucks Meadows are the last lodgings and gas before the entrance to the national park. You can also get traveler's information, wilderness permits, trail maps, and guidebooks at the Big Oak Flat Information Station just inside the park entrance (209-379-1899).

ATTRACTIONS

Black Oak Casino
19400 Tuolumne Road North, 8 miles east of Sonora
Tuolumne
(877) 747-8777
www.blackoakcasino.com

Save your coins for almost 1,000 slot machines, video poker, and keno and your big bucks for blackjack, poker, and other table games. You can keep tabs on your favorite sports event on the seven flat-screen TVs in the bar and grab a meal in the casual cafe.

Cherry Lake
5 miles east of the Groveland Ranger District Office, go left on Cherry Lake Road
(209) 962-7825
www.fs.fed.us/r5/stanislaus/visitor/cherry.shtml

The 20-mile, paved road to Cherry Lake—sometimes called Cherry Valley Reservoir—is narrow, steep, and winding. Take it easy at 20 or 30 miles an hour. Your reward is great fishing, boating, hiking, horseback riding, swimming, and camping at the largest lake in the Stanislaus National Forest. Power boats are allowed. The area is generally open from late April through October, although the road is technically open year-round, barring winter conditions.

Forty-six sites in the campground are available on a first-come, first-served basis. RVs are limited to 22 feet in length. There are day-use boat launching sites and a designated swim area. Fishing in the lake and nearby lakes and streams is great for rainbow, eastern brook, and German brown trout.

Columbia State Historic Park
Off Highway 49, 3 miles north of Sonora, 14 miles south of Angels Camp
(209) 532-0150, (209) 588-9128
www.parks.ca.gov
Columbia California Chamber of Commerce
(209) 536-1672
www.columbiacalifornia.com

In the most perfectly restored and re-created Mother Lode settlement in the country, the 1850s come alive with costumed performers, horse-drawn vehicles, and the sights and sounds of the past. When gold was discovered here, the population exploded within a month from fewer than 100 to 6,000 people, and 150 saloons, gambling halls, and stores opened up. Many of the western false-fronts and two-story brick buildings with iron shutters remain, housing the shops, restaurants, and museums of today.

Storekeepers and wagon drivers, innkeepers and blacksmiths, street musicians and itinerant actors are encountered on the streets and in the restaurants and the theater. A horse-drawn stage clatters up and down the main street, which is free of auto traffic, while artisans demonstrate horseshoeing, wood carving, and other vintage crafts. You watch candles being dipped, take a horseback ride, and have a sarsaparilla at an old-fashioned ice cream parlor.

The town is crowded with visitors and hot during the summer, although pines and maples do shade the boardwalks. The mild months of spring and fall are the best times to visit. A lively schedule of festivals and special events is conducted all year, from the colorful Fireman's Muster in May, early June's Columbia Diggins 1852 gold rush encampment, and a "Glorious Fourth" celebration in July, to the Fiddle and Bango Contest in October. The two hotels in town put on such affairs as Murder Mystery Weekends, winemaker dinners, and a lamplight tour in December.

A living history reenactor makes the Gold Rush era come alive at Columbia State Historic Park. MAXINE CASS

Groveland Yosemite Gateway Museum
18990 Highway 120 (Main Street)
Groveland

Open 1:00 to 4:00 P.M. Thursday through Tuesday, the museum is a nice venue for displays of artifacts, photos, arts, and documents highlighting local pioneer families, the Gold Rush, birds and plants of the region, and even golf and fishing paraphernalia of the early 1900s. In the tiny shop, you can purchase history books, children's science and nature kits, jewelry, and souvenir items. On view are several films about Yosemite, the Old West, Hetch Hetchy, and the Mother Lode region.

Adjacent to the museum, the tree-shaded town park makes a nice rest stop. You can lounge on the lawns and have a picnic and let the kids blow off steam on the playground; there are restrooms here.

Jamestown
6 miles north of the Highways 120 and 49 junction
(209) 984-4616
www.jamestown-ca.com

Boomed and busted several times in the last 150 years, Jamestown—affectionately called Jimtown by residents—retains an anything-can-happen Wild West atmosphere from the days when it was just a cluster of tents on a dusty road. When the gold began to rush, saloons and dance halls were erected, then hotels and homes. Antiques and curio shops, saloons and restaurants line Main Street today. If you have not visited Jamestown for a few years, you will find attractive new cafes and boutiques offering higher-quality cuisine and more sophisticated, upscale inventory than before.

You can pan for gold right in town, take a ride on a steam train, and spend the night in a romantic Victorian-era hotel. If Jamestown looks familiar to you, it may be because parts of the movie *Butch Cassidy and the Sundance Kid* were filmed here.

Knights Ferry
12 miles east of Oakdale, off Highway 108

A mile off the highway, the tiny burg of Knights Ferry makes a fun stop. There is an 1852 general store where you can buy a few provisions, and you can get dinner Thursday through Sunday at River's Edge Restaurant at the Knights Ferry Resort. Fishing tackle and canoe rentals are available.

Knights Ferry Recreation Area
18020 Sonora Road, Knights Ferry
(209) 881-3517
www.spk.usace.army.mil/organizations/cespk-co/lakes/stanislaus.html

On the Stanislaus River, the Knights Ferry Bridge and Trail make a nice rest and recreation stop on the way to Yosemite National Park. An Army Corps of Engineers Stanislaus River Parks Information Center offers information and maps on where to camp and fish on the "Stan." This is a perfect place for grammar school-aged kids, who can touch stuffed wild animals and look into wildlife displays.

In 1849 William Knight established the first ferry across the Stanislaus River to facilitate the activities of the booming Gold Rush. A beautiful covered bridge replaced the ferry in 1863. The 360-foot-long covered bridge—which crosses the river near an old gristmill—is the longest one west of the Mississippi. Closed to vehicles, this is a scenic spot for photos.

You can poke around the ruins of the old settlement, including a flour mill and jail, and the park here has pretty picnic areas with barbecues. At the northeast end of the bridge, a hiking trail leads to sandy beaches and swimming and fishing holes. The walk is nice in spring and fall but hot and dry during the summer. Look for bedrock mortars, once used by Native Americans to grind acorns. The recreation area has rest rooms and is located off Highway 108.

Railtown 1897 State Historic Park
Fifth Avenue and Reservoir Road
Jamestown
(209) 984-3953
www.csrmf.org/railtown/default.asp
Plan a half-day here for all there is to see and do at this 20-acre exhibit of vintage steam locomotives and passenger cars, a roundhouse, and a store. Take a 40-minute train ride through the foothills or a two-hour "Twilight Limited," a sort of sunset cruise with refreshments, entertainment, and a barbecue dinner at the end. Trains operate weekends, April through October, on an hourly basis from 11:00 A.M. to 3:00 P.M., and there are special themed excursions on holidays.

Costumed conductors and workers are railroad and train lovers, and they are loaded with great stories and information. You can take a guided tour of the roundhouse generally a few minutes after the hour between 10:00 A.M. and 2:00 P.M.; call ahead to ensure tours are being offered the day of your visit. You'll see 100-ton locomotives and a blacksmith at his fiery task. Around the site are numerous photogenic artifacts from the many movies and TV shows that were shot here, including *Dodge City, High Noon, Back to the Future III, Petticoat Junction,* and *Wild Wild West.*

In the Depot Store is a huge collection of railroad- and train-related books and lots of fun things for kids, from games and toys to books and kits. This is a great place for a picnic at tables or on the lawns under the aspens and maples, within sight and sound of the exciting action on the track—whistles, bells, steam, and smoke. Admission to the park is free; small fees are charged for train rides and roundhouse tours. Open April to October, 9:30 A.M. to 4:30 P.M.; November through March, 10:00 A.M. to 3:00 P.M.

Rainbow Pool
14 miles east of Groveland on Highway 120
Park on either side of the bridge and walk down a short way to spectacular waterfalls on the South Fork of the Tuolumne River.

Driving time between Sacramento and the Big Oak Flat entrance to the National Park is about two-and-a-half hours. From there to Yosemite Valley is another half hour, about 25 miles on a winding mountain road, reaching 6,000 feet in elevation. The road is open year-round, although chains are required from time to time in the winter.

This is a lovely place, with picnic sites, restrooms, and a great swimming hole. A trail leads upstream to more swimming holes.

Sonora
10 miles north of the Highways 120 and 49 junction
(209) 533-4420
www.sonoraca.com
The "Queen of the Southern Mines," Sonora was once the largest city in the region, bustling with boisterous fortune seekers. Fistfighting, gun play, and even bear-horse fights were common on Washington Street. Today, the main street is as busy as ever, although the 49ers would be run over by the steady vehicle traffic. Along Washington for several blocks is a precious collection of 18th-century buildings, which now house shops, galleries, restaurants, and hotels. Visitors and residents get in the spirit of the Mother Lode by dressing in period costume for annual themed events like the Victorian Christmas Feast and Victorian Ball at the Sonora Opera Hall. You can purchase or rent beautiful Victorian and early Western apparel at Dragoons (68 South Washington Street, 209-588-1848), where you'll feel pampered in cowboy boots and hats, frock coats, fancy ball dresses, feathered hats, beaded purses, and fringed buckskin vests.

At the local museum (see the next entry) and around town, you can pick up a free map and guide—titled *Sonora: A Guide to Yesterday*—for a self-guided walking tour of the fabulous Victorian and Gold Rush homes and buildings. Highlights are the photogenic St. James Episcopal Church ("Red Church") at the west end of Washington Street, built in 1860, and the Street-Morgan Mansion, which stands across the street—one of the most elaborate Victorians in the Mother Lode.

Tuolumne County Museum and History Center
158 West Bradford Avenue
Sonora
(209) 532-1317
www.tchistory.org/museum.html
On a side street lined with tree-shaded, vintage cottages, the museum is housed in a former jail, a beautiful brick building with green iron shutters rebuilt in 1865 after a fire. The photo collection shows the early denizens of Sonora and Victorians in full regalia vacationing in Yosemite and riding in fabulous early motorcars and stages on the incredibly narrow, rugged, original roads into the national park.

A fascinating array of artifacts reflects the plight and the adventures of immigrants who trod and rode trails over the Sierra to California. Between 1840 and 1870, 250,000 people crossed the Sierra, including thousands on the Walker River-Sonora Trail, seeking their fortune and a new life on the western frontier. The museum shows fragments and illustrations of Conestoga wagons, items of domestic life, and a large collection of vintage handguns and rifles of the era. One notable rifle, an 1873 Winchester, was used to kill the county's last grizzly bear.

ACCOMMODATIONS

PRICE CODE

A dollar sign ($) ranking indicates the average nightly rates for two adults. Unless otherwise noted, lodgings accept credit cards. Some bed-and-breakfast inns require two-night minimums.

$	**$49–$75**
$$	**$76–$124**
$$$	**$125–$175**
$$$$	**$176 and up**

All Seasons Groveland Inn **$$$**
18656 Main Street, Groveland
(800) 595-9993, (209) 962-0232
www.allseasonsgrovelandinn.com
This century-old house was transformed into a lovely and unique inn, downtown on the main street. The five rooms each have private baths and are flamboyantly decorated with hand-painted murals and cushy fabrics and linens, whirlpool tubs, and gas fireplaces. One even has a waterfall. Each room has its own tiny refrigerator in the mini-kitchen, which is available to guests. Ask for a room at the back of the house.

The owners of this inn have a wonderful sister property, the All Seasons Sugar Pine Resort, which is in the community of Sugar Pine near Pine Crest Lake above Twain Harte. Jacuzzi tubs, steam rooms, fireplaces, and cozy lodge-style guest rooms make this a romantic place to stay (800-788-5212, www.allseasonssugar pineresort.com).

Alpenglo Bed & Breakfast at Manzanita Hill **$$$–$$$$**
19210 Highway 120, Groveland
(888) 534-2244, (209) 962-4541
innkeeper@manzanitahill.com, www.manzanitahill.com
At the top of a high hill with wonderful views of the foothills and distant mountains, this inn offers four nice bedrooms with private baths and patios. Two living rooms have fireplaces and cozy furniture. A bountiful gourmet breakfast is complimentary.

Camp Mather **$**
Off Highway 120, 15 miles from the Big Oak Flat entrance to Yosemite National Park
San Francisco Recreation and Parks Department
501 Stanyan Street, San Francisco
(415) 831-2715, (209) 379-2284
www.parks.sfgov.org
San Francisco residents have priority for reservations at this old-fashioned, long-established, very popular family camp in the High Sierra, at a cool eleva-

tion of 4,520 feet. Tent sites and 100 or so rustic cabins with covered porches sleep up to six people each. Hearty cafeteria-style meals are available for about $150 a week per person. Kids are perfectly safe to run around on their own, and counselors will also keep them busy with arts and crafts and other activities. There is horseback riding, bike riding, hiking, and swimming in the pool and Birch Lake. You can also fish in nearby streams and play softball and basketball. All ages get into the act at weekend dances and at campfire programs.

The season is short, from early June through most of August. Families can reserve for one week only; cabins and tent sites are assigned by lottery, with an application deadline in March. Cost is about $300 a week for a two-person cabin to $670 for the largest ones; tent sites start at about $120.

Evergreen Lodge **$$-$$$**
33160 Evergreen Road off Highway 120
Groveland
(209) 379-2606
info@evergreenlodge.com
www.evergreenlodge.com

A mile outside the park entrance at 4,500 feet in elevation and 8 miles from Hetch Hetchy Reservoir, Evergreen Lodge is surrounded by the Stanislaus National Forest. The year-round lodge complex has 50 fully furnished cabins and 18 restored original cabins of varying sizes and layouts. The main lodge was built in 1921, has a historic tavern, an indoor-outdoor restaurant serving contemporary cuisine, a general store, a recreation center and great room, and a meeting hall. Evergreen Lodge has an on-site professional guide service that leads trips to Yosemite National Park. No pets are allowed at the lodge.

Groveland Hotel **$$$-$$$$**
18767 Main Street/Highway 120 West
Groveland
(800) 273-3314, (209) 962-4000
reservations@groveland.com
www.groveland.com

This 1914 Queen Anne country inn is the Grande Dame of Groveland. The older section of the hotel, built in 1849, is the only adobe in the Sierra. The 17 guest rooms are luscious, with antiques and down comforters, robes, armoires, mahogany beds, and beautiful linens, plus suites with fireplaces, spa tubs, and featherbeds. Each room is a cozy, comfy nest with unique fabrics and lovely window coverings. Although most of the rooms are serene, a resident ghost favors the fanciful blue and white "Lyle's Room" and likes to move things around the room.

Guests enjoy a complimentary Innkeeper's Breakfast buffet. You can sit in a rattan settee or an armchair on one of the porches overlooking Main Street, or read a book beneath the evergreens on the back patio, where French lilac is redolent in the spring. See the description of their fine restaurant in the Restaurants section. Take a peek in the lobby, the bar, and the dining room to see the collection of fancy dolls, jewelry, hats, and other items for sale. Peggy and Grover Mosely; the resident dog, Rusty; and his counterpart, Miss Kitty, have made this destination inn an "experience," with a following and lots of press raves, so reserve well in advance, and check specials like packages including a free pass to Yosemite National Park and a tank of gas. In-room services include free high-speed wireless Internet access for humans, and a granny quilt, a two-bowl pet dish, and a treat for very welcome pets. Extra services include spa treatments, special bottles of wine or champagne, a dozen roses, or a combination. Peggy went to school with Elvis Presley, a proud tie with the Moselys' Tennessee roots.

Gunn House Hotel **$$**
286 South Washington Street, Sonora
(209) 532-3421
www.gunnhousehotel.com

Owners Mike and Shirley Sarno have completely transformed this two-story, adobe and brick, circa-1850 building on the main street of town. Eighteen rooms are now

Fruits of the Central Valley Tours and Tastes

Bloomingcamp Ranch and Bake Shop
10528 Highway 120, 2 miles east of Oakdale
(209) 848-8881
On your way to Yosemite, stock up on dreamy apple pies and tarts, fresh-pressed cider, apples, jams, dried fruits and nuts, and fresh-baked goods for the road. This is a good place to make a rest stop and picnic by the duck pond. Little kids will like the playground. The ranch is open daily from July through most of December.

Blue Diamond Growers Store
Modesto Nut and Gift Shop
4800 Sisk Road, Salida, 5 miles northwest of Modesto on Highway 99
(209) 545-6229
Watch a film of a day in the life of an almond grower and watch almonds being processed. Tastings are free. Open weekdays 10:00 A.M. to 5:00 P.M.; Saturday 10:00 A.M. to 4:00 P.M.

Hershey's Visitor Center
120 South Sierra Avenue, Oakdale
(209) 848-8126
Stop in for your chocolate infusion. You will find all of the varieties of Hershey's bars and candy specialties, gift baskets, Hershey souvenirs, and killer chocolate chip cookies. The place is open every day except Sunday from 9:00 A.M. to 5:00 P.M., and is open until 7:00 P.M. on Thursday.

Oakdale Cheese and Specialties
10040 Highway 120, Oakdale
(209) 848-3139
This gouda cheese factory and European bakery are operated by a couple from the Netherlands. You can watch cheese-making through windows and on video and tour the aging rooms. The factory is open daily from 9:00 A.M. to 6:00 P.M. Besides yummy cheese and bakery items, locally grown fruits, vegetables, and nuts are on sale. Kids like the farm-animal petting zoo and picnics by the ponds, which are inhabited by more than 100 koi fish.

luxurious retreats decorated with period wallpapers, beautiful antique furnishings, and luscious linens. All of the rooms are quite lovely; the quietest rooms are on the back side, such as the "Golf Room," a small charmer decorated in country club style with golf memorabilia. Larger rooms have king and queen beds and are inviting with comforters and piles of pillows. Some rooms have fireplaces and soaking tubs.

Wicker armchairs and rockers are waiting on the covered porches. A large heated swimming pool and stone patio lie under a canopy of oak trees. Overlooking the pool terrace, the breakfast room is cozy when a fire crackles in the stone fireplace and the antler chandeliers are aglow. Guests enjoy homemade fruit danish and coffee cakes, blueberry streusel muffins, incredible rugelach, and lemon cake, along with fresh fruits, cereals, juices, and accompaniments to the expanded continental breakfast.

Historic National Hotel $$$
18183 Main Street, Jamestown
(800) 894-3446, (209) 984-3446
www.national-hotel.com

A historic landmark built in 1895 on the main street of Jamestown, the hotel is a beauty. Nine cozy rooms are decorated with antiques and gorgeous Victorian-era wallpapers. Guests enjoy robes, excellent mattresses, and private baths, some with double showers. A unique feature is the romantic, deep-soaking, claw-foot tub, big enough for two, in a romantic Soaking Room, complete with fancy soaps, salts, towels, and music. An expansive buffet breakfast is included in the room rate.

On-site is an elegant dining room and a shady, vine-covered garden courtyard, where lunch, brunch, and dinner are among the best in town; and the wine list features great wines from seven Gold Country counties. Locals and visitors congregate in the Gold Rush Saloon.

Hotel Charlotte $$
18736 Main Street (Highway 120) Groveland
(209) 962-6455
www.hotelcharlotte.com

Most of the 10 guest rooms are on the second floor, with quilts, some antiques, whimsical touches, and country-style ambience. Many guests like to hug the large stuffed giraffe. Local artists' and photographers' work creates galleries along hallways and in rooms.

A little history of the hotel: Born in Genoa, Italy, in 1881, Charlotte DeFerrari emigrated with her family to the California gold fields when she was 16. She cooked for work crews and ranch hands, ultimately opened a restaurant, and in 1918 she built the hotel. Charlotte has been known to make her ghostly appearance in today's hotel from time to time. The hotel is now owned and operated by Lynn Upthagrove and her husband, Victor Niebylski, who is also the chef in the cafe (see the Restaurants section of this chapter).

Jamestown Hotel and Solomon's Landing $$-$$$
18153 Main Street, Jamestown
(800) 205-4901, (209) 984-3902
www.jamestownhotel.com

Built for the first time in 1858 and rebuilt in 1919, the hotel has eight guest rooms done up in simple Victorian style and each is unique. Rowdy Calamity Jane is actually quiet and comfortable at the back of the building. The Lotta Crabtree is a grand parlor room with a porch overlooking the town. The floral-themed Jenny Lind room has a spacious parlor and a door to a porch with wicker furnishings. Some rooms have whirlpool tubs.

Surrounded by etched-glass walls, Solomon's Landing dining room and bar is attractive and the food is excellent. Roasted game hen with three-citrus glaze and rack of lamb with demi-glaze are specialties, but the chef is known for fresh seafood preparations, including Salmon Rockefeller. In summertime, meals are served on an outdoor patio. Frequent wine tasting events pairing five wines with appetizers as well as occasional elegant winemaker dinners feature Gold Country vintages from nearby Calaveras County.

Yosemite Lakes NACO $
31191 Hardin Flat Road, Groveland
(800) 533-1001, (209) 962-0103
www.1000trails.com

This camping resort sits off a country road near hiking trails on the South Fork of the Tuolumne River, and offers yurts, cabins, hostel accommodations, and full RV hookups. This is a membership camping resort, with availability to nonmembers.

Yosemite Pines RV Resort $-$$
20450 Old Highway 120, Groveland
(877) 962-7690, (209) 962-7690
www.yosemitepines.com

With RV and tent sites (close together), cabins, yurts, a swimming pool, and a petting zoo, this is a nice place in the trees, located just 22 minutes from the park.

There is a tiny convenience store, propane, and firewood; restrooms and showers; and a laundry room. They also rent tents and RVs for on-site use. Your kids can sleep in a yurt and you can get a cabin with two bunks and a double-size bed.

Yosemite Westgate Motel $-$$$
7633 Highway 120, Buck Meadows
12 miles west of the Big Oak Flat
Yosemite National Park entrance
(800) 253-9673, (209) 962-5281
Just above the road, this simple two-story motel has a swimming pool and adjacent casual restaurant. Rooms have mostly queen-size beds, but some family units have tiny kitchens.

RESTAURANTS

PRICE CODE

The price is based on the cost of two entrees from the dinner menu, not including appetizers, desserts, beverages, taxes, or gratuities.

$	**$15 or less**
$$	**$16–$25**
$$$	**$26–$35**
$$$$	**More than $35**

Cafe Charlotte $
18736 Main Street, Groveland
(209) 962-6455
www.hotelcharlotte.com
A locals' favorite, located in the historic Hotel Charlotte, the cafe is smack in the middle of town. You can get hearty American comfort food and seasonal specialties for dinner Thursday through Sunday. Try the Mediterranean antipasto, the deep-fried calamari, Chicken Jerusalem, or a big, juicy steak.

Evergreen Lodge $-$$$
33160 Evergreen Road off Highway 120
Groveland
(209) 379-2606
info@evergreenlodge.com
www.evergreenlodge.com
Just 7 miles off Highway 120 on the way to Hetch Hetchy, the 1921 lodge with a plain, comfortable dining room serves sophisticated dinner as well as breakfast and lunch daily. The small store sells picnic items, ice cream, and milkshakes.

Groveland Hotel $$-$$$$
18767 Main Street/Highway 120 West
Groveland
(800) 273-3314
www.groveland.com
The beautiful Victorian Room is open year-round for dinner. Executive Chef Bobby Riviera changes the menu with the seasons and uses local produce on the menu whenever he can, creating a California seasonal cuisine. Specialties include roasted rack of lamb in an herb olive oil marinade and pan-seared duck breast with mashed garlic sweet potatoes and fried spinach. The ultimate in desserts is the spiced molten chocolate mountain cake that oozes chocolate from inside and is served with ginger-rum ice cream. Reserve well in advance, as Groveland's fine dining is limited.

The exceptional wine list has more than 500 labels and is more than 30 pages long, with an excellent representation of California vintages as well as wines from Australia, France, Chile, and Spain. *Wine Spectator* numbers are shown for each rated wine. Grover and Peggy Mosely, the proprietors, will show folks the underground wine cellar that was built by Chinese laborers in the 19th century. The Groveland Hotel hosts occasional winemaker dinners and wine-pairing events and offers a Wine Discovery the second and fourth Friday of every month, year-round. You will taste four wines while learning wine lore like the value of crystal glassware to the proper pre-sniff swirl. A full bar has expanded the little saloon's offerings.

May through September, you can dine in the patio courtyard while enjoying a Yosemite Courtyard Theater performance of Sierra Foothill historical plays or an Off-Broadway show, the musicianship of a jazz or big band group, or a country singer. Special events like the Valentine wine-and-chocolate festival are listed online. Peggy Mosely went to school with Elvis and shares a January birthday with The King—to celebrate, there's a party with an Elvis impersonator on the Saturday nearest his January 16 birthday. The Groveland Hotel also serves espresso to-go and can prepare a picnic lunch packed into your choice of a picnic basket or backpack.

Iron Door Saloon **$$**
18761 Main Street, Groveland
(209) 962-8904, (209) 962-6244
www.iron-door-saloon.com
Famous (or infamous) for more than a century, the Iron Door is said to be California's oldest continuously operating saloon, and it's well worth a stop, even if you only have a few minutes. The Wild West lives on in the atmosphere and the museum-like, rustic decor, featuring giant elk and buffalo heads, long rifles, and old photos of stagecoaches careening down the mountain roads into Yosemite. Two pool tables are tucked away in a nice, spacious room at the back. Lunch, dinner, and snacks are good and hearty. A weekly dinner-and-a-movie special includes pizza, salad, and dessert, and a feature film on the big-screen TV. Live weekend music tends to be country and western or blues and occasionally features such luminaries as Maria Muldaur and Eddie Money. Find some treats at the old-fashioned soda fountain at the general store. Wear your cowboy boots and belly up to the bar.

Pine Mountain Lake Golf and Country Club **$$**
19228 Pine Mountain Drive, Groveland
(209) 962-8620
www.pinemountainlake.com
Less than five minutes from town, the golf club is a nice place for lunch, dinner, or Sunday brunch. From the dining deck, the dining room, and the bar, you have wide forest views with glimpses of Yosemite peaks. If you are a golfer, ask about golf/restaurant packages. A big-screen TV keeps you posted on sports events, and there is live, local entertainment on many weekends.

River's Edge **$-$$**
10 miles east of Oakdale off Highway 120, Knights Ferry Resort
(209) 881-3349
You'll find a surprising choice of sophisticated fare at this casual place on the Stanislaus River. Sit on the riverside deck and enjoy Portuguese and Italian-influenced fare, from Thursday through Sunday.

Snowshoe Brewing Company **$$**
19040 Standard Road, Sonora
(209) 536-1445
www.snowshoebrewing.com
The former Pickering Lumber Company office building serves as one of two Snowshoe brewery restaurants in Gold Country. This Sonora location makes the special brews including Cutthroat Strong Ale (presumably named after the trout), Old Man Winter, Midnight Moon Oatmeal Stout, and five others ranging from pale ale to porter. The brewpub restaurant serves ribs and sandwiches, pizza, salads, appetizers, fresh soup, and hearty comfort food. The door behind the bar that's "Open 'til Whenever," leads to the building's original 1920s safe.

OUTDOOR RECREATION

Not highly developed due to rugged terrain and few access points, recreation on the Stanislaus River is headquartered at nine U.S. Army Corps of Engineers-maintained areas along 59 miles of the river; there are more than a dozen drive-in, boat-in, and walk-in campgrounds between Modesto and Knights Ferry.

---

i

A perfect swimming hole in Yosemite Creek, with sandy spots and shade, is found about 20 miles east of the Big Oak Flat entrance to the park, just off the Tioga Road.

Groveland Ranger Station
24545 Highway 120, 10 minutes east of Groveland
(209) 962-7825
www.fs.fed.us/r5/stanislaus/groveland/index.shtml
The Groveland Ranger Station is the place to get information on camping, hiking, rafting, fishing, and traveling in the Stanislaus National Forest and along the Tuolumne River.

This is where you get wilderness permits for overnight camping and rafting. Check out the excellent array of guidebooks and maps. Even when the facility is closed, you can locate campgrounds by looking on the big map posted outside. The rangers lead an annual wildflower walk to Pilot Peak on the Saturday closest to May 15. This is a very popular event, with limited space; make a reservation and bring your lunch and water.

Fishing

Cast for big rainbow trout in the rapids, riffles, and deep pools of the Stanislaus River between Goodwin Dam and Oakdale. Try for bass and catfish below Orange Blossom Bridge.

The fishing season on the Tuolumne River opens on the last Saturday in April, ending in mid-November. The river is stocked with salmon and rainbow and brown trout. To reach one popular riverside fishing spot, drive 10 miles east of Groveland, turn left on Ferretti Road, then go 5 steep, narrow miles on unpaved Lumsden Road; there is a boat launch. Or, you can drive 5 miles east of the ranger station, turn left on Cherry Lake Road, and go 5 miles to Early Intake.

Sierra West Adventures
(209) 588-1306
www.fishthesierra.com
This experienced company specializes in day trips and multiday walk-and-wade or float trips for fishing on the Tuolumne, Stanislaus, and Merced Rivers and on more than 20 still-water fisheries, including private waters. Guides will take you to the best spots for catching native trout, steelhead, salmon, and striped smallmouth, largemouth, and spotted bass.

Among other featured trips are the White Water and Fly Fishing Adventure, a three-day expedition involving fishing and rafting on more than 20 gorgeous miles of river.

Golf

Mountain Springs Golf Course
17566 Lime Kiln Road, Sonora
(209) 532-1000
www.mountainspringsgolf.com
Renowned architect Robert Muir Graves designed this championship 18-hole layout in the foothills. Six lakes and six dozen bunkers provide challenge, along with the distraction of zowie views from many holes. Ask about golf and lodging packages.

Pine Mountain Lake Golf and Country Club
19228 Pine Mountain Drive, Groveland
(209) 962-8620
www.pinemountainlake.com
Big greens and tree-lined fairways on this hilly, 6,351-yard layout are nicely maintained year-round. The rating is 70.6 and the slope 125. Check out the 475-yard, par 4, 11th hole. Facilities include a driving range, putting and pitching greens, a full-service pro shop, and a restaurant and bar (see under Restaurants in this chapter). This is a semiprivate course in a beautiful

---

i

Permits are required for backpacking, river rafting, and campfires in the Stanislaus National Forest. Permits are available at the Ranger Station, 10 minutes east of Groveland (209-962-7825).

residential development—you can buy a home on the golf course or a home with a personal hangar with direct access to the runway at the private airport. There's also an equestrian center, two tennis courts, and lake fishing for bass, trout, and catfish.

Twain Harte Golf Club
22909 Meadow Lane, Twain Harte
(209) 586-3131
Nine walkable holes in a pretty, wooded setting make this a good choice for beginners and for practicing your short game. Fairways are generally narrow and lined with many trees. On-site are a driving range, putting green, and small pro shop.

Hiking

Several hiking trails in the Stanislaus National Forest, in the Groveland area, and near the national park entrance are described in detail on the Groveland Ranger Station Web site (www.fs.fed.us/r5/stanislaus/groveland).

Crane Flat
Just inside the Highway 120 West entrance to the park, Crane Flat is a pretty, forested area at 6,192 feet, near the Tuolumne and Merced Groves of Giant Sequoias. From here, you either drive up the Tioga Road into the High Country, or head for Yosemite Valley. There are hiking trails and picnic sites nearby, and during the winter, this is a great place for cross-country skiing and snowshoeing.

Tuolumne River Canyon Trail
(209) 962-7825
This 6-mile, moderately strenuous hike at low elevation follows the south side of the Tuolumne River to the confluence of the Clavey River. See directions under "Fishing" and start half a mile downstream from the Lumsden Boat Launch. In the springtime, this is a beautiful area, awash in blue lupines, golden monkeyflowers, pink shooting stars, and globe lilies. California poppies carpet the steep cliffsides. Some of the wildlife you might see include golden eagles, wintering bald eagles, quail, coyotes, jack rabbits, mule deer, and sometimes river otters.

Horseback Riding

Mather Saddle and Pack Station
35250 "A" Mather Road, Groveland
(209) 379-2334
www.mathersaddleandpackstation.com
Breakfast rides, sunset rides along the Grand Canyon of the Tuolumne River, hay-wagon rides, and saddle and pack trips have been operated as a family business since 1929, at the city of San Francisco-owned Camp Mather near Hetch Hetchy. With friendly, experienced cowpokes, try a corral or meadow beginners ride for just $20 for kids and $23 for adults, or set off into the Yosemite backcountry for one day or several days of spectacular scenery and camp-out fun.

Pine Mountain Lake Equestrian Center
(209) 962-8677
www.pinemountainlake.com
Just outside Groveland, you and your children aged seven and up can take an easy, guided trail ride or climb on for special excursions like the Full Moon Trail Rides and the Tuolumne River Trail Rides. You can also get riding lessons here and sign the kids up for one-day horse camps.

Watersports

White-water rafters and kayakers love the 4 miles of surging rapids above Knights Ferry. Canoeists stick to the river below Knights Ferry. A California Department of Water Resources Web site gives up-to-date information on water conditions: http://cdec.water.ca.gov/riv_flows.html. For more information on river rafting, see the Outdoor Recreation chapter of this guidebook.

Lake Don Pedro
31 Bonds Flat Road, La Grange
(209) 852-2396
www.donpedrolake.com
At a low elevation northeast of Modesto, Don Pedro is a sprawling body of water with 160 miles of shoreline and several meandering arms. Summers are hot and dry, just perfect for waterskiing, sailing, wind surfing, and personal watercraft. Fishermen head to the northern, narrow end into the skinny arms of the lake, away from the noise and action. Fishing is good for bass, trout, salmon, crappie, bluegill, and catfish.

You can lounge on a sandy beach by the swimming lagoon on the south shore, at Fleming Meadows. Two full-service marinas provide every amenity, from boat rental to groceries, restaurants, gas stations, showers, and laundromats. Of the nearly 400 campsites located here, many have full RV hookups and are within view of the lake, enabling campers to moor their boats within eyesight of their campsites. Boat-in camping is allowed around most of the shoreline, and restroom and shower facilities are available.

SHOPPING

Along Highway 120, which runs right through the town of Groveland, several shops are well worth a visit. You can walk from one end of town to the other in 10 minutes.

Corner Critter
18743 Main Street
(209) 962-4438
www.crittercorneronline.com
Two irresistible corgis, Bubba and Sadie, warmly greet every customer who enters this cozy shop. In the wintertime they wear sweaters such as those on sale in the shop; you can also buy pet food, gifts, and supplies for dogs and cats. Bears of all descriptions are on display here, too, as well as USA-made windchimes, greeting cards, and seasonal home accessories.

Iron Door Store
18752 Main Street
(209) 962-6864
Across the street from the mother ship, the Iron Door Saloon, step in Easter through December, to browse a wealth of goods from camping supplies to blankets and throws; a wide jewelry selection; vivid, impressionistic paintings by Dharma Barsotti; and Miwok-style pine needle baskets. Among the one-of-a-kind items offered are Sioux pottery, decorated boxes from Poland, and Romanian stemware, proving that Groveland is a vortex for collectors. And where else in the world can you get a "Where the Hell Is Groveland?" T-shirt?

Jennifer & Co. Antiques and Collectives
18729 Main Street
(209) 962-7112
Just about everything in the shop is one-of-a-kind, from a large arrowhead collection and signed Norman Rockwell lithographs to turquoise and silver jewelry and Depression glass. Antiques lovers love the Roseville pottery, old bottles and insulators, vintage tools, radios, and Victrolas—plan to spend some time here.

Mountain Sage
18653 Main Street
(209) 962-4686
In the circa-1876 barn-red former home of one of the town's pioneer families, the Lavaronis, is a store and organic coffeehouse owned by a Lavaroni granddaughter and her husband. His vibrant color photography hangs in the small gallery. Her flair for store displays shows off high-quality outdoor gear, art, and nature-oriented gifts.

You will find camping accessories and seasonal outdoor clothing, books on hiking and nature, a map room, and fair trade handicrafts from around the world. Behind the store is a small nursery with plants, garden furniture and accessories, hammocks, and bird feeders.

Season's Gifts Home and Garden Decor
18687 Highway 120
(209) 962-5099
Shopkeeper Karen Edner fills her tiny space with fanciful gifts and decorative accessories: dolls, stuffed animals, cards, baby things, ceramics, and garden and Christmas ornaments. If a baby is due in your world, take a look at the soft, fringed, handmade baby blankets.

SOUTH GATE ENTRANCE/ HIGHWAY 41

A favorite time of the year in the Central Sierra is after Labor Day when traffic into the national park is light and the weather has cooled from the high 90s of midsummer to the 70s. Nights are delightfully crisp, and color is beginning to show in the maples, dogwoods, and oaks. Throughout the sparsely populated, lightly developed area south of Yosemite, you'll find rivers for fishing, lakes for swimming and camping beside, and the Sierra National Forest for hiking and exploration. A glance at a color-coded map of California shows a continuous expanse of green wilderness between Yosemite and Sequoia National Parks.

The main route to southern Yosemite, Highway 41 runs right through the small town of Oakhurst, with a population of about 15,000, a busy gateway to Wawona. Antiques- and art-lovers browse in the galleries and shops of the historic town, the southernmost of the Gold Rush boomtowns that sprung up in California in the 1850s. While you're here, visit the "Talking Bear" landmark in the center of Oakhurst, at Highway 41 and Road 426. It has provided a great photo op for nearly three decades. What does the bear say? He gives a brief history of the extinct California grizzly and asks for respect for forests and wildlife. Around town, you may notice the elaborate chain-saw sculptures of bears, pine trees, eagles, and other flora and fauna. The town also gives families a chance to load up on provisions on their way to summer vacations at Bass Lake and in the Sierra National Forest.

Oakhurst offers a lineup of motels, bed-and-breakfasts, and restaurants, plus a few surprises, like an opulent, five-star-rated French inn and some world-renowned resident artists. A vintage steam train, a magnificent sequoia grove, and a sprawling destination resort are all within a few minutes' drive. During the summer, when accommodations and campgrounds in Yosemite National Park are full, many people enjoy staying in Oakhurst, at Bass Lake, and at small resorts and campgrounds along the highway just outside the park.

Among the area's seasonal events, guests and locals enjoy the Oakhurst Mountain Peddler's Fair and the Golden Chain Theatre melodramas, complete with Grub Gulch Grannies and the Garter Girls. For more information, call (559) 683-7112, or visit the Web site: www.goldenchaintheatre.org.

South on Highway 41 in the mountains on the edge of the Sierra National Forest, you'll find the tiny, rustic community of Coarsegold, once populated by 49ers. Native Americans allegedly robbed the miners, which resulted in the Mariposa Battalion being ordered to enter Yosemite Valley and rout them out, which they did in 1851.

With a grocery store, a gas station, and a few shops with "treasures," North Fork—said to be in the exact geographical center of California—is the location of a major Native American museum and the launch pad on Beasore Road for travelers on the Sierra Vista National Scenic Byway, a spectacular backcountry driving route.

In the wintertime, Highway 41 is nearly always open into the national park. You can cross-country ski at Goat Mountain near Fish Camp. For snowmobiling, head for Beasore Road near Pine Village at Bass Lake.

Brook, brown, and rainbow trout are abundant in the mountain lakes and wild streams of the Central Sierra, and you can catch warm-water fish in the lakes of the foothills surrounding the Oakhurst/North Fork area.

ATTRACTIONS

Bass Lake
3.5 miles north of Oakhurst, off Highway 41 on Road 222, right 4 miles on Road 274 and on to Pines Village
Bass Lake Chamber of Commerce
P.O. Box 126
Bass Lake, CA 93604
(559) 642-3676
www.basslakechamber.com

The waters of this popular lake reach 78 degrees in the summer, when outdoor temperatures hover near 100. In the Sierra National Forest at 3,400 feet, Bass Lake is good for fishing in the spring and fall for trout, bass, catfish, and bluegill, and for water sports and camping all summer.

You can rent windsurfers and boats for canoeing, sailing, rowing, and waterskiing. At three small resort areas—Pines Village (800-350-7463, 559-642-3121; www.basslake.com, the most developed); Forks Resort (559-642-3737); and Miller's Landing (559-642-3633; www.millers landing.com)—you'll find shops, restaurants, groceries, and gas. Stay at the campgrounds or rent a house and enjoy the nearby hiking and cross-country ski trails. The visitor center is at the northwest end of the lake.

At Pines Village, the grocery sells a nice array of wooden sailboat models, little canoes, carved bears, and other mountain cabin accessories and souvenirs, plus sweatshirts and caps. Bullwinkle's Gifts and Antiques is a rambling emporium of new and old garden accessories, Gold Rush-era memorabilia, and locally made crafts and art (54331 North Shore Drive, 559-683-2018).

Hundreds of people flock to Bass Lake for annual events such as the Antique and Classic Wooden Boat Show and the Bass Lake Fishing Derby (both in May) and live Jazz on the Lake, which takes place during the summer.

***Bass Lake Queen II* Boat Tours**
Pines Resort Marina
(800) 350-7463, (559) 642-3121

Passengers onboard this canopied, barge-like boat seating 50 people enjoy a narrated, one-hour cruise on Bass Lake. Tours depart at 3:00 P.M. daily, Memorial Day to Labor Day; Saturdays in April, May, September, and October, weather permitting. Fees are $10.00 for adults, $6.00 for children.

---

i

For a small fee, campers can take showers at Miller's Landing at Bass Lake; at the High Sierra RV park in Oakhurst; and at Jones Store at Beasore Meadows.

Chukchansi Gold Resort and Casino
711 Lucky Lane, Coarsegold
(866) 794-6946
www.chukchansigold.com

About 30 miles south of Yosemite National Park in the historic little town of Coarsegold, a casino hotel is a big draw for thousands of visitors a year, especially on weekends. If Lady Luck is on your side, sidle up to one of 1,800 slot machines or try your skills at nearly 50 table games. Live concerts and entertainers, with audiences of more than 1,000 people, have featured such headliners as the Beach Boys, Wayne Newton, Wynonna, George Carlin, and Jay Leno.

Among seven themed restaurants are the California Market Buffet, a steakhouse, the 50s-style Deuces Diner, an Asian noodle bar, a traditional all-American cafe, an espresso/bakery cafe, and a big-screen TV sports bar.

All of the 192 rooms and Jacuzzi suites, tricked out with mountain lodge decor, have nice sunrise or sunset views of the southern Yosemite region.

Coarsegold

A historic community at the southern tip of the Mother Lode on Highway 41, this little town makes a nice half-day stop on the way to Yosemite. In 1851, at the height of the Gold Rush, the population topped 10,000 people. Today, a few hundred live here. The tiny mountain community is done up for tourists in Native American themes and offers antiques and curio shops and places to eat. The big Peddler's Fairs take place on Memorial Day and Labor Day weekends.

In the Coarsegold Historic Village (35300 Highway 41, 559-683-3900; www.coarsegoldhistoricvillage.com) on weekends, artisans demonstrate their works, from a blacksmith to a saddlemaker, leather- and woodworkers, and others.

Inanna's Gift Studio-Gallery & Creative Arts Gallery (35463 Highway 41, 559-683-7529; www.inannasgift.com), is open daily for changing gallery shows and a wide variety of arts classes such as working with clay, mosaic, beading, pine needle baskets, knitting, preschooler storytelling, and a drumming circle. Owner Jane Senn hosts a First Thursday Open House each month, a great chance to meet local Sierra region artists.

Fresno Flats Historical Park
1 mile east of Oakhurst on Road 427
(559) 683-6570
www.fresnoflatsmuseum.org

Jails, schools, barns, wagons, buggies, and a furnished home were moved from all over the county to re-create this Western town from the region's early timber and ranching era. You can ramble around on your own anytime, or check in at the museum and gift shop to ask about guided tours. There are outdoor concerts on weekends, a playground, picnic tables, barbecues, and horseshoe pits, making this a busy hometown park. Admission is free.

Gallery Row
40982 Highway 41, on the north end of Oakhurst
(559) 683-3375

In the southern Yosemite area is a confluence of artists and lovers of the visual arts. Do save some time to browse the exceptional art galleries in Oakhurst. You may be surprised at the level of expertise and the nationally known reputations of the artists who live and work here. The complex of top-notch galleries at Gallery Row is a place to start.

The Grimmer Gallery (559-658-2104; www.grimmergallery.com) features the stunning watercolor paintings of Caryl and Jerome Grimmer and Michael Hodgson, fascinating raku pottery, Terry Reed's miraculous wood carvings, and more. In the National Park Arts Center are the works of Mark Gudmundsen, a painter of vibrant, realistic national park scenes (559-683-4308; www.nationalparksart.com). You can see him in person, working in the lobby of the Tenaya Lodge on weekends. Timberline Gallery (559-683-3345; www.sierratel.com/timberline) features the works of nearly 25 nationally known artists—from potters to watercolorists—and the incredible wood carvings made by Calvin Lyster.

The Stellar Gallery (559-658-8844; www.galwest.com/stellargallery) displays the fine images of several artists, including famous Yosemite photographer David Ashcraft. Stephen Stavast creates magical, 3-D images of stones and other natural elements in his super-realistic paintings. Stavast himself is often found at work in his Stavast Studio/Gallery (559- 683-0611; www.stavaststudiogallery.com).

Madera Wine Trail
(800) 733-8068
www.maderavintners.com

On your way to Yosemite National Park, consider a couple of hours of winery touring. Within a short distance of each other just off Highway 99, nine wineries in the Madera Viticultural Area (an official appellation) open their doors to visitors, and they get together to put on annual special events: the Wine and Chocolate Weekend in February, the Spring Wine Trail Adventure in June, and the Holiday Spirit Wine Trail Weekend in November. Each of these events features not only wine tasting but also live music, art, and food pairings.

Wineries of note are Ficklin, which makes fabulous vintage port in the Portuguese tradition (www.ficklin.com), and Quady, a specialist in dessert wines (www.quadywinery.com). At Quady, when you are in a romantic mood, try the Essensia, made from orange muscat grapes, and Elysium, a luscious concoction pressed from the black muscat variety.

The vintner's association will send a brochure, wineries map, and schedule of events, or check online.

Miami Motorcycle Trails
Bass Lake Ranger District
57003 Road 525, North Fork
(559) 877-2218

Just off Highway 41 north of Oakhurst, the Miami Trails are 60 miles of marked ATV, motorcycle, and dirt bike routes in a mixed pine forest at 3,600 to 4,800 feet in elevation. Camping is available nearby. For a free trail map, stop by the Yosemite Sierra Visitors Center in Oakhurst, that also acts as a Sierra National Forest Ranger Office to issue permits.

Detailed descriptions of several other trails for off-road vehicles are found on the Sierra National Forest Web site, www.fs.fed.us/r5/sierra/recreation/activities/ohv.shtml.

Nelder Grove of Giant Sequoias
10 miles north of Oakhurst off Highway 41, take Sky Ranch Road/Road 632 for 6 miles
(559) 877-2218

Loggers in the 1800s were not able, with the equipment available then, to cut the largest sequoias in this magnificent grove of big trees, although they did take down hundreds of smaller trees. In a forest of pine, fir, and incense cedars, 106 old-growth sequoias remain in the Sierra National Forest, with the largest concentration in the Upper Nelder Creek Grove. The Shadow of the Giants National Recreation Trail is a 1-mile, easy, self-guided trail along the banks of Nelder Creek, leading to the Bull Buck giant sequoia in Nelder Grove. At 99 feet around, the Bull Buck is thicker at the base than the world's largest tree—the General Sherman in Sequoia National Park—but is 30 feet shorter and slimmer at the top.

The biggest and most beautiful trees are at the far end of the trail loop.

Oakhurst River Parkway
Oakhurst Community Park
http://orptrail.org

An easy, 3-mile walking trail just off the main street of Oakhurst meanders past Fresno Flats Historical Park, the Fresno River, China Creek, and Oak Creek—the water flows in late winter, spring, and early summer. Beginning at the Community Park just off Civic Circle, the trail makes a great stopping point on the way to southern Yosemite. You can stroll along the water and watch ducks, beavers, red-winged blackbirds, and other wild creatures and have a picnic or a barbecue in the small, grassy park.

Sierra Mono Museum
33103 Road 228 at Mammoth Pool Road/Road 225, North Fork
(559) 877-2115
www.sierramonomuseum.org

Owned and operated by the Mono Indians, this major exhibition displays Native American artifacts, basketry, and beadwork as well as a grizzly bear, a mountain lion, elk, moose, antelope, wolves, and other wildlife. Open Tuesday through Saturday 9:00 A.M. to 3:30 P.M., call ahead before driving up here, as sometimes the museum is closed. Admission is $3.00 adults, $1.00 kids. In early August, the Sierra Mono Indian Fair Days and Pow Wow is held here, featuring traditional dances, crafts, and games.

The Mono, Miwok, and Chukchansi tribes call the southern Sierra their home, and many of them are artisans whose works are displayed and sold in shops and at fairs throughout the region.

Are you an art lover? On your way to southern Yosemite, plan to stop in the lively art community of Oakhurst for Sierra Art Trails in October. You will be able to visit the studios of artists and fine craftspersons, watch them work, and get to know them. A special preview exhibit will be on display a few weeks in advance. For information, call (559) 658-8343 or (559) 683-5551; www.sierratrails.org.

Sierra Vista Scenic Byway
(559) 683-4636
www.byways.org/browse/byways/2300
Part of the National Scenic Byway System, this little-traveled, 82.7-mile route meanders through the Sierra National Forest from North Fork to the exit point on Highway 41, passing Nelder Grove. The drive takes about five hours without stops, which you will want to make, for vista points, short hikes, picnics, and photo-snapping; a portion of the road is unpaved, but drivable by most vehicles. Take the easy, ⅕-mile hike to Fresno Dome viewpoint to see panoramic vistas. The Byway is a seasonal route, generally open from June through October; some of the forest roads are blocked by snow during the winter. Call ahead to check road and weather conditions.

Wagner's Store at Mammoth Pool is the only place to get gas and is not open during the winter (209-841-3736). Restroom facilities are found at campgrounds along the way.

Wassama Roundhouse State Historic Park
On Highway 49 near Ahwahnee
(559) 822-2332
This is one of only two or three authentic ceremonial Indian roundhouses surviving in the state that are open to the public. The oak-shaded grounds are interesting, with Native American grinding stones used to grind acorns, as well as other artifacts, and you can picnic here. The park is open daily for a small fee. Also here is a sweat lodge, used for cleansing and religious purposes, and a cemetery. Often on weekends there are demonstrations of basketry, acorn preparation, beadwork and hand games, and occasionally dances. Your visit to the roundhouse will be greatly augmented if you manage to get here while guides and artisans are on site; call ahead.

Yosemite Mountain Sugar Pine Railroad
56001 Highway 41, between Oakhurst and Yosemite
(559) 683-7273
www.ymsprr.com
If you have children, plan to spend a couple of hours here riding the train, picnicking, and enjoying the beautiful forest. An 84-ton, vintage Shay locomotive—the largest ever built for a narrow-gauge track—pulls open passenger cars carved from huge logs 4 miles through forestlands into Lewis Creek Canyon. It's exciting to climb aboard at the tiny station while steam rolls out from under the huge engine and black smoke belches into the sky. A conductor spins tales of when the railroad hauled timber out of the Sierra.

From mid-May to early October, a couple of nights a week, a "Moonlight Special" evening train excursion ends with a steak barbecue and live music around a campfire. The Sugar Pine Trio has been entertaining families for nearly two decades with tunes from the Old West. Watch out for masked horsemen, who are known to stop trains searching for passengers' loot! The railroad is open daily from March to October. Special outdoor melodrama performances, combined with the Moonlight Special, are scheduled in the late summer. There is a restaurant and a small inn on the property and a gift and sandwich shop and the Thornberry Museum in a 140-year-old cabin. Get a fun preview of the train whistles, bells, brakes, and other exciting noises and see a few photos of the trains by going to www.ymsprr.com/sightsnsounds.html.

Yosemite Mountain Sugar Pine Railroad rolls through Lewis Creek Canyon.
TENAYA LODGE AT YOSEMITE

Yosemite Sierra Visitors Bureau
41969 Highway 41, Oakhurst
(559) 683-4636
www.yosemitethisyear.com
At the north end of Oakhurst on the east side of the Southern Yosemite Highway, as Highway 41 is known here, this very pleasant visitors center provides information on lodging, campgrounds, and road conditions. Staffers help visitors with brochures listing the region's attractions and events. Maps, guidebooks, and postcards are for sale. A 24-hour phone kiosk is available to help late arrivals locate lodging and services. The bureau's Web site has its complete page-by-page visitors guide online. You can even hear the pages turning!

ACCOMMODATIONS

PRICE CODE

A dollar sign ($) ranking indicates the average nightly rates for two adults. Unless otherwise noted, lodgings accept credit cards. Some bed-and-breakfast inns require two-night minimums.

$	**$49–$75**
$$	**$76–$124**
$$$	**$125–$175**
$$$$	**$176 and up**

Apple Blossom Inn **$$–$$$$**
44606 Silver Spur Trail, Ahwahnee
(888) 687-4281, (559) 642-2001
www.appleblossombb.com
Twenty miles from the South Gate entrance to the national park, on five acres

in an organic apple orchard overlooking the Oakhurst Valley, this commodious country-style inn offers three very pretty, comfy rooms, a Jacuzzi on the sundeck, and a sitting room with a wood-burning stove. The complimentary full breakfast may include strawberry French toast, apple pancakes, homemade coffee cakes, or fancy egg dishes.

Bass Lake Rentals **$$-$$$**
P.O. Box 349, Bass Lake, CA 93604
(559) 642-3600
www.basslakerealty.com
Bass Lake Rentals rents out almost 100 or so very nice, privately owned cabins and houses; about half have lake views or are on the lake. All properties are completely equipped and furnished, and can be rented by the night or weekly, generally Saturday to Saturday.

Big Creek Inn **$$$-$$$$**
1221 Highway 41, Fish Camp
(559) 641-2828
www.bigcreekinn.com
This bed-and-breakfast inn, the closest to the South Gate entrance to the national park, Big Creek lies in a beautiful spot right on the creek, which will lull you to sleep as it bubbles by. In three luxurious rooms are king, queen, or two double beds; soaking tubs; gas fireplaces; and private balconies, depending on which room you book. See the Web site for photos. Anything but fussy, the decor is light, airy, and uncluttered, and the rooms are well soundproofed. A sumptuous full breakfast is served in the dining room. With a day's notice you can have massages, facials, and body wraps in your room.

Chateau du Sureau **$$$$**
48688 Victoria Lane, Oakhurst
(559) 683-6860
www.chateausureau.com
It is nothing short of astonishing that this luxurious inn exists anywhere, let alone in the laid-back little town of Oakhurst. Expect featherbeds, French iron balconies, Oriental rugs, antique furnishings, bubbling fountains, glorious gardens, and more opulence and finery—Robert DeNiro, Kevin Bacon, and friends love the place. Museum-like interiors are adorned with fine art, gilded mirrors, even hand-painted ceilings, and huge bouquets of fresh flowers. In the 2,000-square-foot, two-bedroom villa, you have your own butler, silk-and-satin bedding and draperies, lavish marble bathrooms with oversize Jacuzzi tubs and steam showers, fireplaces, antiques, and private outdoor spaces. The whole spectacular estate is sometimes booked for weddings. A posh Spa du Sureau (559-683-6193) provides treatments for guests daily, from 9:00 A.M. to 7:00 P.M.

The five-star-rated restaurant here, Erna's Elderberry House, presents classic European cuisine and a stunning wine list.

Ducey's on the Lake **$$$**
Pines Village, Bass Lake
(559) 642-3131
www.basslake.com
This two-story mountain lodge with lovely rooms and suites overlooks the lake and is in the same building as the excellent Ducey's restaurant. Guests enjoy swimming in the beautiful, big lakeside pool and relaxing in the outdoor Jacuzzis and sauna. A large marina sits right in front, and vacationers can rent personal watercraft, water skis, party barges, and fishing boats.

Rooms are quite nice, and beam-ceilinged king-size suites are spacious and deluxe, with double whirlpool tubs and separate showers, sitting areas with sofa beds, wood-burning fireplaces, wet bars with microwaves and refrigerators, and private decks overlooking the lake and the forest beyond—a place to settle in. Ask about packages that include meals.

The Forks Resort **$$-$$$**
39150 Road 222, Bass Lake
(559) 642-3737
www.theforksresort.com
Families return here year after year for their summer vacations in cabins on the

southwest corner of the lake. Conveniently grouped together are a general store selling groceries and fishing and camping gear, a marina renting patio and fishing boats, and a casual, '50s-style cafe serving three meals a day. The cabins are actually spacious houses in the trees, most with lake views. They are completely outfitted with everything you might need for a day or a week—just arrive with your clothes.

The Homestead **$$$**
41110 Road 600, Ahwahnee
(800) 483-0495, (559) 683-0495
homesteadcottages@sti.net
www.homesteadcottages.com
On 160 wooded acres, these beautiful adobe and stone cottages are spacious and romantic, with kitchens, fireplaces, and privacy. Larry and Cindy Brooks make sure guests are pampered, with satellite TV, air-conditioning, and on-site massages. Check the Web site for the details and photos of the various amenities. You also can stable your horses here and get maps and advice for nearby trails.

Hounds Tooth Inn **$$-$$$**
42071 Highway 41, 3 miles north of Oakhurst
(559) 642-6600
www.houndstoothinn.com
One of the nicest places to stay in the area, Hounds Tooth Inn offers 12 rooms in a Victorian-style house, each with private baths and outside entrances. Some rooms have spas and fireplaces. Guests enjoy a complimentary full breakfast and wine bar. You may have a room with a window seat and wingback chairs, or a sofa, a wicker rocker, or a wet bar and microwave. The separate cottage has a king-size spa, fireplace, kitchenette, and private patio. Check the Web site for seasonal and midweek special discounts.

Narrow Gauge Inn **$$-$$$$**
48571 Highway 41, Fish Camp
(888) 644-9050, (559) 683-7720
www.narrowgaugeinn.com
Four miles from the South Gate entrance to the national park, this charming, 26-room mountain inn is adjacent to the Yosemite Mountain Sugar Pine Railroad. Nice, spacious, country-style rooms have private baths and balconies; one has two bathrooms and a claw-foot tub. On the forested grounds are a small heated swimming pool, hot tub, and creekside nature trails. Your dog is welcome, too!

Owl's Nest Lodging **$$**
P.O. Box 33, Highway 41
Fish Camp, CA 93623
(559) 683-3484
owlsnest@sti.net
www.owlsnestlodging.com
Although near the highway, it is quiet at night in these nice, two-story cabins. You can rent a tiny cabin for two with basic amenities and no kitchen, or bigger places that sleep six, one with a fireplace.

The Pines Resort **$$$**
P.O. Box 109, Pines Village
Bass Lake, CA 93604
(800) 350-7463, (209) 642-3121
www.basslake.com
A complex of 84 rustic, condominium-style chalets is very near the lake, The Pines Resort offers guest options that include kitchens and fireplaces. Guests also enjoy the resort's tennis courts, large swimming pool, small playground, and laundry.

Tenaya Lodge at Yosemite **$$$-$$$$**
1122 Highway 41, Fish Camp
(888) 514-2167, (877) 322-5492
www.tenayalodge.com
In a sun bowl surrounded by forested mountains, this 244-room, destination resort hotel is just a five-minute drive from the South Gate entrance of the national park. You can hike, bike, take a sleigh ride, cross-country ski, snowshoe, and horseback ride right from the lodge. The variety of guided tours and outdoor recreation made available through the lodge is amazing. The Guest Experience Center in the lobby will sign you up for a variety of

Renowned artist Mark Gudmundsen can be seen in the lobby of the Tenaya Lodge at Yosemite, painting his unbelievably lifelike, photo-realistic paintings of national park landmarks and vistas.

guided expeditions, from an easy morning nature hike, an evening flashlight walk in the forest, or a 5.5-mile guided hike or bike ride to a waterfall for a picnic. You can rent mountain bikes, take a climbing class, and have a family photo taken in a scenic location. Transportation into Yosemite National Park is available. Make the most of your stay here by calling the center in advance to make reservations for tours and events (888-514-2167, #2).

Annual events at the lodge range from outdoor concerts to wine dinners, and the New Year's Eve Gala. Ask about special seasonal packages, such as Winter Fun that includes lift tickets at Yosemite's Badger Pass, and snow play equipment rentals and special programs. The Weekend Snowshoe includes a night's lodging, snowshoe rentals, and a fun bonfire party with s'mores and hot beverages. The Summer and Fall Fun include all the activities you can cram into 24 hours, from hikes and horseback riding to climbing, biking, fly-fishing, and evening entertainment. One recent fall offering is Geocaching Sierra Style, a GPS treasure hunt by bike or hiking. Check the Web site for off-season discounts.

The two-story atrium lobby and the restaurants have a casual yet luxurious feeling, decorated with Native American artifacts and cushy, upscale, Western-style furnishings. The fitness center and spa offers steam, sauna, whirlpools, a nice array of workout equipment, and a staff of therapists for massage and other health and beauty treatments.

Kids 5 to 12 years old join Tenaya Adventure Club counselors in a one-, two-, or three-day program that includes teepee building, rock climbing, hiking, snowshoeing, fishing, and archery. Babysitting can be arranged for toddlers. Kids love the huge indoor and outdoor swimming pools, the big playground, and the Snow Play area (saucers are available).

Spacious and attractive, the rooms have many amenities, including ironing boards, coffeemakers, and Nintendo; some have two double beds and sitting areas with sofa beds, and there are huge suites for special occasions and for small meetings. Most of the rooms have wonderful forest and mountain views, and you can open the windows to smell the pines. Some ground-floor rooms are available for guests and their dogs; special doggy amenities include dog beds.

Among a plethora of special events, barbecue evenings start with a horse-drawn wagon ride to the cookout, with campfire singing and marshmallow roasting with cowpokes.

Tin Lizzie Inn **$$$$**
Fish Camp
(866) 4T-Tours (488-6877)
www.driveamodelt.com

A luxurious new inn in a pine and cedar glen lies just 2 miles from the south entrance to the national park. Done up with Victorian furnishings and antiques, original light fixtures, and stained glass, the inn is a dream realized for owners David and Sheran Woodworth, who also own Yosemite T-Tours, the Model-T touring company described later in this chapter in the "Auto Touring" section.

The Tin Lizzie Suite encompasses the entire second floor of the inn and is complete with a fireplace, robes, fine linens, and the use of a real Model T; plus a full gourmet breakfast on the balcony and late afternoon high tea in the parlor. The inn is open in July, David says, "until the weather becomes uncomfortable."

Yosemite's Four Seasons **$$-$$$$**
7519 Henness Circle,
Yosemite National Park
(800) 669-9300, (209) 372-9000
www.yosemitelodging.com

Near the South Gate entrance to the

national park, Yosemite's Four Seasons offers rooms, studios, homes, and apartments to rent, all running the range from simple to luxurious. You can sleep under ruffles in a canopied bed, bask in an indoor Jacuzzi, play pool, watch a 35-inch TV screen, or sit by a stone fireplace.

Yosemite Gateway Inn **$-$$$**
40530 Highway 41, Oakhurst
(800) 780-7234, (559) 683-2378

You would never know from the highway that more than 122 nice motel units in this Best Western are scattered across the hillside in a parklike setting, with oak trees, lawns, gardens, and hidden glades. Some two-bedroom family units have kitchenettes. Most of the rooms have two double- or queen-size beds. There are indoor and outdoor swimming pools and spas, a casual restaurant and a bar with fireplace, a barbecue and picnic area, a guest laundry, and a playground. The higher up the hill, the quieter your room will be. Above the muraled lobby, the gift shop features garish ceramics and expensive pinecones.

RESTAURANTS

PRICE CODE

The price is based on the cost of two entrees from the dinner menu, not including appetizers, desserts, beverages, taxes, or gratuities.

$	**$15 or less**
$$	**$16–$25**
$$$	**$26–$35**
$$$$	**More than $35**

Castillo's Mexican Restaurant **$**
49271 Golden Oak Loop, Oakhurst
(559) 683-8000

Castillo's offers terrific tacos and homemade Mexican food. It's a full-bar cantina, too—try the blackberry margaritas! The sister restaurant in Mariposa is at 4995 Fifth Street, a block off Highway 140.

Ducey's on the Lake **$$-$$$$**
Pines Village, Bass Lake
(559) 642-3131
www.basslake.com/dining.html

Overlooking the lake, Ducey's on the Lake's dining room looks like a cross between a gleaming yacht and a hunting lodge, with stone accents and wood paneling, brass trim, vintage ski equipment, great old photos, and game heads on the walls. Ask for a comfy booth. The dinner menu includes several types of steaks, rack of lamb, and a luscious prime rib of pork, plus crab cakes, lobster, and more fresh seafood. On the sunny deck, have grilled chicken, salads, burgers, fresh fish, or pasta for lunch. Try the traditional American breakfast or eggs Benedict, French toast, or an omelette.

Every Friday evening from Memorial Day to Labor Day, enjoy live jazz outdoors and fireworks.

Erna's Elderberry House **$$$-$$$$**
48688 Victoria Lane, on the south end of Oakhurst
(559) 683-6800
www.elderberryhouse.com

Rich, red walls, upholstered banquettes, French tapestries, and flickering candles create an elegant, romantic atmosphere for the French and California cuisine menu and fabulous wine list. When weather permits, you can enjoy the terrace and the view. Daily specials may include lobster and house-cured sturgeon salad, lamb in smoky red wine sauce, beef tenderloin with apple-brioche pudding, or veal stuffed with morels. Breakfast, lunch, and dinner feature seasonal specialties prepared by one of the most acclaimed chefs in California. Erna's daughter, Renée-Nicole Kubin, is an award-winning sommelier and previously cellar master of Charlie Trotter's. She adds to the restaurant's stellar wine list, which includes many hard-to-find "cult" wines, and she is on hand for special wine and food events. Erna and her distinguished chef conduct three-day cooking schools for small groups twice a year.

Mountain House Restaurant $-$$
Highway 41 at the Bass Lake turnoff at Road 222
(559) 683-5191
A real family-oriented, casual place in a mountain setting, Mountain House Restaurant serves burgers and steaks, sandwiches, salads, chicken, and fish. Wash it down with a choice of drinks ranging from espresso to microbrews. In a hurry? Pick up takeout or box lunches. The restaurant is open for breakfast, lunch, and dinner.

Narrow Gauge Inn $$$$
48571 Highway 41, Fish Camp
(888) 644-9050, (559) 683-7720
www.narrowgaugeinn.com
The Victorian Era and the Old West come together in this rustic dining room and the Buffalo Bar, which is cozy when fires burn in the stone fireplaces. On the menu is all-American comfort food such as venison from deer raised by local Mono Indians, elk, several cuts of steak, pasta, seafood, and chicken, plus elaborate appetizers and salads. This is an excellent restaurant, a little pricey for families. Closed for the winter and early spring; call ahead for weekend and summertime reservations.

Sierra Meadows Country Club $$
46516 Opah Drive, just west of Oakhurst off Highway 49, Ahwahnee
(559) 642-1343
www.sierrameadows.com
A pleasant place to be on a sunny day for sandwiches, hot dogs, and soup for lunch. Call ahead to get a table on the deck overlooking the golf course.

Southern Californians approach Yosemite National Park from Fresno on Highway 41. Expect an eight-hour drive from Los Angeles. When the snow flies, consider heading north to Merced and entering the park via Highway 140, the "All-Weather Highway."

Sierra Restaurant $-$$$
Tenaya Lodge at Yosemite, 1122 Highway 41, Fish Camp
(888) 514-2167
In an upscale, relaxed atmosphere with a fireplace and views of the surrounding forest, the Sierra Restaurant at the Tenaya Lodge serves three meals a day. Big breakfast buffets are very popular, and there is often a wait on weekends. The dinner menu may offer grilled honey and thyme-crusted rabbit loin, steak, or fresh seafood, paired with a notable wine list. The popular winemaker dinners are held in a beautiful banquet room overlooking the mountains.

Jackalopes Bar and Grill is a cozy spot with a fireplace, serving microbrews, burgers, wood-fired pizzas, and sandwiches; you can also sit outside by the fire ring. A casual coffee shop, The Parkside Deli, opens at 7:00 A.M. and serves snacks, sandwiches, espresso drinks, and deli takeout.

Todd's Cookhouse Bar-B-Que $$
40713 Highway 41, #5, Oakhurst
(559) 642-4900
www.toddscookhousebbq.com
Todd Leaf won Kraft Foods' Barbecue Sauce Flavor Search Contest in 1999, and the sauce became a best seller. Todd's boasts "real Southern-style smoked bar-b-que," cooked on a blend of live oak, hickory, and local Fresno fruitwoods. Beef brisket, Memphis-style pulled pork, Cajun sausage, chicken wings, and the mandatory ribs are on his very reasonably priced menu.

Yosemite Coffee & Roasting Company $$
40879 Highway 41, Oakhurst
(559) 683-8815
www.yosemitecoffee.com
The smell of roasting coffee beans will lure you to this coffee spot. From 6:30 A.M., folks are getting a cup of brew and sandwiches, housemade soups, smoothies, and later, beer and wine. Breakfast can include a bagel, burrito, or breakfast sandwich. In the evenings, enjoy one of the

four-shot espresso specialty coffees or another drink while listening to karaoke on Thursday and live music including rock 'n roll and Delta blues on Friday and Saturday; and learn to jitterbug at the Sunday afternoon Dance Party.

OUTDOOR RECREATION

Auto Touring

Yosemite T-Tours
(866) 4T-Tours (488-6877)
www.driveamodelt.com

More than any other car, the Model T Ford put Americans on the road. Very likely, it was the first car your grandparents owned. Now you can drive an original Model T runabout (roadster) or touring car for the day or for several days, just like the early visitors to Yosemite. Based near the southern gate of Yosemite, this company will give you a short driving lesson (you shift with your feet . . .), fix you up with a luscious picnic lunch in a wicker basket and a satellite phone, and suggest scenic backroads for your road trip into the past. Not an inexpensive adventure (day rental is about $400), Model T touring is a romantic, photogenic experience of a lifetime and a memorable way to see the national park. Some of the perfectly restored cars are spacious enough for four people—tops down on the runabouts and touring cars! Model A fans who want to drive "a more modern car"—Maria Shriver's recent choice—are in luck! Owner David Woodworth, for whom a retirement dream became both a business and a labor of love, maintains these 1928–1929 vehicles and the Model T fleet in top working condition.

Yosemite T-Tours also offers guided small group tours of Yosemite and group or individual Model T touring on the Central Coast of California, around Cambria and Hearst Castle.

Fishing

Warm-water fishing is good for bass and kokanee salmon in foothills lakes. Bass Lake is the largest, with the most development. Just north of North Fork, Manzanita Lake is stocked with rainbows and has a nice picnic area. Big Creek and Willow, Fish, Rock, Chiquito, and Granite Creeks are roadside streams stocked with rainbow trout in the summer. See more about fishing in the Outdoor Recreation chapter.

Old Corral Grocery and Tackle Shop
1.5 miles off Highway 41, 41872 Road 222
(209) 683-7414

For fishing enthusiasts on their way to Bass Lake and the streams and rivers in the Sierra National Forest, this is the most complete tackle shop in the region. You can get everything from live worms to crickets, and rent or buy rods and reels. Pick up your fishing licenses and picnic fare here, too; the shop is open daily, 8:00 A.M. to 8:00 P.M.

Boating and Water Sports

Bass Lake Water Sports and Marina
Pines Village, Bass Lake
(800) 585-9283, (559) 642-3200
www.basslakeboatrentals.com

This full-service marina rents just about every type of warm-water watercraft you can imagine: Jet Skis; patio, ski, and fishing boats; canoes, kayaks, bananas, and tubes. You can take ski lessons and hire a boat driver, or cruise the lake at your leisure in a party barge. The marina is open 8:00 A.M. to 8:00 P.M. daily in the summer.

The shop here sells snacks, boat parts, ski gear, summer clothing, souvenirs, and fishing equipment. In the winter, you can rent snowmobiles here, too.

Hensley Lake
South of Oakhurst off Highway 41
(559) 673-5151
www.spk.usace.army.mil/organizations/cespk-co/lakes/hensley.html
Hensley Lake is a low-elevation, warm-water fishery for bass, blue gill, crappie, catfish, and rainbow trout in winter. The 55-site Hidden View Campground (877-444-6777; www.reserveusa.com), picnic areas, a swimming beach, boating on the lake, and hiking trails are other draws. Boat and water sports equipment rentals are available.

Miller's Landing Boat Rentals
Bass Lake
(559) 642-3633
www.millerslanding.com
On the southeast edge of Bass Lake, Miller's rents a wide variety of watercraft in the summer. There is a general store and small cafe here, a half dozen very nice cabins, and a few rustic cabins to rent, too.

Golf

Sierra Meadows Country Club
46516 Opah Drive, just west of Oakhurst off Highway 49, Ahwahnee
(559) 642-1343
www.sierrameadows.com
Formerly the Ahwahnee Golf Club, now open year-round as the centerpiece of a residential development, semi-private Sierra Meadows is a nicely maintained, 18-hole layout on sensuously rolling fairways roaming between towering valley oaks and pines; 70.5 rating, 138 slope. Greens are small and fast. There are a driving range, putting green, chipping area, nice pro shop, large clubhouse with a pleasant restaurant and bar, and swimming pool, too. Collared shirts are required for golfers.

Greens fees range from the $25 twilight rate to $49 on weekends, including cart, with discounts for the walking golfer.

Hiking

Goat Mountain Trail
Spring Cove Campground and Fork Campground at Bass Lake
(559) 683-4665
For nonstop views of Bass Lake and the Sierra Nevada, hike 4 strenuous miles one-way to the summit and the fire lookout. You can cut the distance and the degree of difficulty of this beautiful trail in half by starting at one campground, leaving a car at the other, and turning back where the two trails meet on the way up. Cross-country skiers and snowshoers frequent these trails, too. Mountain bikers roar 7 miles downhill on a gnarly single track.

Lewis Creek National Recreation Trail
5 miles west of the South Gate entrance to the national park, off Highway 41
(559) 683-4665
From the highway parking area, walk 0.25 mile south on the trail to 100-foot-high Corlieu Falls, then 1.8 miles north to Red Rock Falls, through dogwood, azalea, and pines along Lewis Fork Creek, passing near the historic Madera Sugar Pine Lumber Company flume. The creek is stocked with trout and is popular with anglers.

Way of the Mono Trail
Along Road 222 at Bass Lake
This nice, easy, half-mile trail passes through a variety of vegetation where plaques explain Western Mono history, hunting, and gathering. You pass an acorn grinding area over a seasonal creek and get great views of the Sierra and Bass Lake. The trail begins between the Forks Resort and the California Land Management Office.

Mountain Biking

Since off-road cycling is not allowed in the national park, many cyclists come to the southern Yosemite area to ride the many wilderness trails, country roads, and old railroad grades. The Sierra Vista National Scenic Byway, which starts in North Fork, is a popular route, as is the ride around Bass Lake. Bring your own bikes or rent equipment at local shops.

Winter Sports

A few minutes drive south from Fish Camp, Goat Mountain (www.fs.fed.us/r5/sierra/recreation/wintersports/goat.shtml) is a favorite cross-country skiing area. And on Beasore Road, near Pines Village at Bass Lake, you can drive on the paved road to the snow line to ski, snowshoe, and snowmobile.

Whisky Snowmobile Trail above North Fork is a 35-mile, marked snowmobile route through a forest following existing roads.

Yosemite Snowmobile Company rents snowmobiles at Pines Village at Bass Lake and offers guided tours, December through February (800-585-9283).

Guides

Southern Yosemite Mountain Guides
621 Highland Avenue, Santa Cruz (with an office at Bass Lake)
(800) 231-4575
www.symg.com
Experienced local guides lead backpacking trips in the southern Sierra, the Ansel Adams Wilderness, and Kings Canyon and Sequoia National Parks. They offer rock climbing, mountain biking, and fishing tours, too. All equipment and provisions are provided.

Yosemite Bass Lake Fishing Adventures
Ducey's Dock, Pines Village
(559) 642-3200
Perfect for beginners, this is a three-hour morning excursion to hot fishing spots with a savvy local guide in a comfortable patio boat. Price includes equipment rental, bait, instruction, and drink.

Yosemite Trails Pack Station
P.O. Box 100
Fish Camp, CA 93623
(559) 683-7611
www.yosemitetrails.com
For all ages, this experienced company conducts guided half-day horseback trips into Mariposa Grove, and shorter rides around other parts of Wawona. Beginners enjoy the one- or two-hour group rides on a flat road through the forest in the area adjacent to the Tenaya Lodge at Yosemite.

The wintertime sleigh rides and winter trail rides are absolutely beautiful in a snowy forest. In the summer, two gorgeous Belgian draft horses pull a big wagon down historic Jackson Road to a "cowboy camp" for a Western barbecue and campfire sing-along.

You can arrange with the pack station for a guided wilderness pack trip, and they will also transport you and your supplies into Yosemite's backcountry and drop you off; then they come back, pack up your camp, and lead you out, all on horseback.

EAST GATE ENTRANCE/ HIGHWAY 120 EAST

Between the eastern edge of Yosemite National Park and the desolate desert expanse of the Great Basin, the Eastern Sierra comprises some of the most dramatic landscapes in the world. Three wilderness areas and two national forests border the national park on the eastern side. The Tioga Road descends from the East Gate entrance to the park at 9,945 feet at the crest of the Sierra Nevada through Lee Vining Canyon, in a distance of just 12 miles, to Mono Lake at 6,382 feet. Like a milky blue sapphire, the lake gleams at the bottom of the shallow depression of 25-mile-wide Mono Basin, bordered by rolling volcanic uplands, a stunning and unusual "moonscape" due to its unique geologic history.

In the quiet here east of Yosemite National Park, sparkling streams skip past wildflowery meadows and hidden canyons to gather in jewel-colored lakes, many accessible by vehicle, and more within day-hike range. The region is a summer paradise for anglers, campers, and hikers.

Dozens of lakes are stocked annually, and some weekly, with rainbow, eastern brook, brown, and cutthroat trout—the fishing is legendary. Exclusive to the lakes and streams from southern Inyo County to northern Mono County are the unique and delicious Alpers trout, which are locally hand-fed and raised on the Alpers Owens River Ranch and stocked in the lakes. Not handy with a fly rod? Look for Alpers trout on local restaurant menus.

The small town of Lee Vining is centrally located for anglers, campers, hikers, and travelers between Los Angeles and Reno. You can find a motel room, good meals, supplies, and outdoor recreation equipment.

A green, meadowy vale surrounded by high peaks on one side and low, desert hills on the other, the Bridgeport Valley lies below Matterhorn Peak and the rugged Sawtooth Mountains and is the starting point for backcountry trips into the Hoover Wilderness. Known more than a century ago as "Big Meadows" for its wide-open range and grasslands, the county seat of Bridgeport was settled in the 1850s by farmers and cattlemen. The little town is a good overnight stopping point on the way into the park—which is about 45 minutes away—and is a busy headquarters for anglers.

Fall is a great time to explore the area, when the mountainsides and canyons glow golden with aspens. Along Highway 120, which accesses Yosemite National Park, dense aspen groves in Lee Vining Canyon burst into streams of brilliant gold in October. U.S. Highway 395 between Bridgeport and Lee Vining runs along above the Virginia Creek gorge, where aspens are massed across the hillsides, before the landscape flattens out into the Mono Basin. In Lundy Canyon—just north of Lee Vining and Mono Lake—anglers head for Mill Creek and hikers discover waterfalls amid blazing autumn color.

Sightseers shouldn't miss the scenic June Lake Loop drive, a close-up look at the otherworldly tufa towers of Mono Lake, and wandering around Bodie State Historic Park ghost town.

---

i

During snowy winters in the Eastern Sierra, many businesses and some side roads are closed. From late fall through early spring, always call ahead. For current weather and road conditions on the Highway 395 corridor, call (800) 427-7623 or go online to www.monolake.org/visiting/roadinfo.htm.

MONO LAKE

Reflecting the clouds and the sky like a mirror, the dense, milky-looking waters of Mono Lake are two and a half times saltier than an ocean and sit at an elevation of 6,382 feet. Ringed by mountains and volcanoes, the lake is actually a volcanic crater; the two black-and-white islands are volcanic domes. At least 760,000 years old, this is one of the oldest continuously existing lakes on the continent.

Bizarre-looking tufa—say *too-faa*—towers and knobs of porous rock line the shoreline. Formed from calcium bubbling from freshwater springs up through the carbonate-rich waters, the towers are made of limestone that builds up around the spring openings. Some of these tufa towers are 30 feet high. No flora grows on the edges of the lake on the lava spires. Sierra streams flow in, but until recently, none could flow out.

Microscopic algae survive in the seemingly barren environment, providing food for brine shrimp and brine flies, which are eaten by about a million nesting and migratory birds and waterfowl—nearly 100 species—including 85 percent of the California gull breeding population.

To see some of the largest tufa towers up close and do some bird watching, take the easy, flat South Tufa trail on your own, or go with a naturalist on a free group tour. Wear a hat and sunscreen, and bring binoculars and water. Tours depart the South Tufa parking lot several times a day during summer and one time a day on winter weekends, 5 miles east of US 395 on Highway 120. A $3.00 per-person fee is charged (760-647-6595 or 760-647-3044).

You can launch kayaks and canoes at Navy Beach, just beyond the South Tufa area, and a dirt road follows much of the edge of the lake. In all cases, before exploring check in with the staffers in the Mono Lake Committee Visitors' Center, as conditions and access may change. Interpretive Mono Lake Boat Tours are offered by Tioga Lodge (888-647-6423). For more information, call (760) 647-6595, (760) 647-6629, or check at the Visitors' Center.

The lake looks as it does because the city of Los Angeles, hundreds of miles to the south, has been diverting water from the Mono Basin since 1941, lowering the lake by 45 vertical feet, cutting the remaining volume of water in half, and doubling its alkalinity and salinity. After years of lawsuits, the diversion has ceased and the lake is again growing, very slowly. Streams are moving into and out of the lake, cottonwoods and willows are taking hold again, though it remains too salty for fish to appear.

Mono Basin National Forest Scenic Area Visitors Center
US 395, 0.5 mile north of Lee Vining
(760) 647-3044
www.fs.fed.us/r5/inyo

Take a look at the dioramas and exhibits that introduce the natural and human history of Mono Basin, watch a 20-minute film, *Of Ice and Fire: A Portrait of the Mono Basin,* get involved in the interactive activities, and browse the art galleries and the bookstore. Get information here on a variety of guided walks and talks, and buy maps, guidebooks, and wilderness permits. Kids will zero in on the children's books, games, and toys.

The view from the terrace is of nearly the entire lake—bring your binoculars!

Mono Lake Committee Visitors Center and Lee Vining Chamber of Commerce
Corner of US 395 and Third Street, Lee Vining
(760) 647-6595, (760) 647-6629
www.monolake.org

Interpretive displays recount the history of this organization's efforts to save Mono Lake, a lobbying and legal campaign that has finally resulted in the cessation of water diversion and a chance to restore the lake to its natural state. Some interesting things are on sale here—books, jewelry, souvenirs, and art related to the region.

A canoe tour led by a Mono Lake Committee guide passes Mono Lake's tufa columns.
JOHN POIMIROO

Get information here on a variety of guided walks and talks and peruse the excellent, large selection of maps, guidebooks, history books, and children's books and games. You can also check your e-mail here and browse the Internet. Next door, grab a burger at Bodie Mike's Barbecue; down the street, get espresso drinks.

ATTRACTIONS

Ansel Adams Gallery
Mono Inn, US 395, 4 miles north of Lee Vining
(760) 647-6581
Owned by the family of the legendary photographer of Yosemite and the West, Ansel Adams, and operated by his granddaughter, this sophisticated gallery and gift shop, open from May to fall, is likely the most rewarding in the entire area for the collector interested in fine art and fine crafts. Interpretive items relate to the region's natural history, and there is an exceptional collection of books, handcrafted home accessories, Native American crafts, jewelry, and art. Ansel Adams' legendary images of Yosemite are on view and for sale, from $20 prints to calendars and cards, and individually reproduced, matted, and framed prints.

Bridgeport
(760) 932-7500
www.bridgeportcalifornia.com
US 395 runs right through the tiny town of Bridgeport, which lies in an idyllic valley surrounded by the dramatic Sawtooth Range. Along the roadway are several motels and casual cafes, a lovely bed-and-breakfast inn, an excellent restaurant in a Victorian house, and a few historic attrac-

tions, making this a place to linger for a day or so. The ultimate photo op is the Mono County Courthouse, as tall, as pristine white, and as fancy as a wedding cake. Built in 1880, the courthouse is still in use today.

For fishing gear, advice, and a nice selection of guidebooks, maps, souvenirs, and fishing-related gifts, stop in at Ken's Sporting Goods at 258 Main Street. Next door to Ken's at the General Store, pick up groceries, toys, and deli foods. You can park your RV overnight at the Bridgeport Reservoir on the edge of town and rent a fishing boat here. The shoreline is a nice place to be at the end of the day, to watch the sun warm the jagged mountain ranges with a rosy glow.

Fishing is king in these parts, with Robinson and Buckeye Creeks, the East Walker River, and Twin Lakes (which holds the state record for brown trout), the most popular fishing destinations near Bridgeport. Boating, camping, hiking, and rock climbing are also popular at Twin Lakes.

Bridgeport fills up annually for the Fourth of July Celebration, the Bridgeport Rodeo, and Founder's Day. For information about outdoor recreation and sights throughout the region, stop in at the Humboldt-Toiyabe National Forest ranger station (760-932-7070) on the south end of town.

Creekside Spa and Fitness Center
Double Eagle Resort
(760) 648-7004
www.doubleeagleresort.com

In a spectacular mountain setting by Ron's Pond, this full-service spa and fitness center is a major draw for resort and day guests. It offers a menu of more than 40 body and beauty treatments in a spacious, luxurious facility, including a two-level fitness area with exercise equipment and classes in yoga, aerobics, and Pilates led by professional trainers. The spa offers guided outdoor activities, such as the forest labyrinth meditation walk; tai chi and yoga on the Eagle's Nest platform; nature walks, hikes, and biking. Winter walks, ice climbing seminars, guided snowshoeing, and more winter recreation is scheduled when the snow flies. June Mountain Ski Area is close by.

i

Just before reaching the north end of June Lake, notice the enormous erratic, a boulder known as "Balanced Rock." Estimated to weigh about 100 tons, it was created eons ago by glacial activity.

Ask for a spa brochure or check the Web site to choose from the wide variety of treatments, such as the Symphony Duo Massage and the Sierra Sports Massage, shiatsu, reflexology, seaweed wraps, body treatments, hydrotherapy, facials, and more.

A fabulous 60-foot indoor swimming pool and whirlpool with glorious mountain views from the window walls and a spacious sun deck are major features of the Creekside Spa. For a $20 day fee, guests may use the indoor pool, whirlpools, steam rooms, showers, and attend scheduled fitness center classes. The Creekside Corner Bar serves smoothies, espresso drinks, beer, wine, sandwiches, and snacks.

June Lake Loop
Highway 158, off US 395
(760) 648-7584
www.junelakechamber.org

In a serene alpine setting at the base of June Mountain and Carson Peak, about 20 miles from the Tioga Pass entrance to the national park, the village of June Lake has a few restaurants and shops, and a population of 600. This is the heart of the June Lake Loop, a 15-mile scenic route meandering past June, Gull, Silver, and Grant Lakes, all known for excellent fishing.

The lakes are stocked with fish throughout the year, and at five marinas you can rent fishing boats, float tubes, fishing gear, paddleboats, and kayaks. A plethora of campgrounds, cabins, and RV parks are busy with vacationers, spring through fall.

At the south end of June Lake, at Oh Ridge, there is a campground, a playground, picnic sites, and a nice swimming beach. At Gull Lake, look for a grassy park at the lakeside, where a nice playground, picnic and barbecue sites, and tennis courts make this a great family recreation area. You can also rent fishing and paddleboats at the small marina here. Picnic tables are found in lovely spots under the aspens on the shores of Silver Lake, not far from the road.

From the June Lake Chamber of Commerce, you can get a good map showing the best fishing spots on the June Lake shoreline and streams (760-648-7584).

Aspen groves put on a glorious show all along Highway 158 in the fall, and winter snows promise excellent downhill skiing at June Mountain ski area (760-648-7733). Snowboarding, ice climbing, snowmobiling, and cross-country skiing are also popular.

Lee Vining Canyon Scenic Byway
Highway 120, between the East Gate entrance and US 395
(760) 647-3040

This 12-mile route drops from Tioga Pass through the spectacular and rugged Lee Vining Canyon to Mono Lake, connecting the spare landscape of the Great Basin with the snowcapped peaks, alpine meadows, and tarns of the Sierra Nevada. You get incredible views of Mono Lake, the line of Mono Craters, and the eastern range of the White Mountains. Stop along the way to picnic, fish, or swim at Tioga Lake.

Lee Vining Schoolhouse Museum
1 block east of US 395, Lee Vining
(760) 647-6461

This museum, in a circa-1925 schoolhouse, displays pioneer and Gold Rush artifacts, photographs, and mining equipment and is run by a friendly volunteer staff. Open May to October, Thursday through Sunday, noon to 8:00 P.M.

Mono County Museum
2 blocks west of the Mono County Courthouse, Bridgeport
(760) 932-5281

In the sweet little Bridgeport Elementary Schoolhouse, built in 1880, are exhibits of fine Paiute baskets and other Native American artifacts, mining and farming equipment, photos, and more relics from 19th-century Mono County. Across from the museum in Bridgeport City Park is a very nice playground, lawns, and a picnic area. The museum is usually open from May to some time in October, from 10:00 A.M. to 5:00 P.M.

Panum Crater
5 miles south of Lee Vining on US 395, then 3 miles east on Highway 120
(760) 647-3044

One in a group of 21 volcanic cones just south of Mono Lake, which form the youngest mountain range in North America, the crater is easy to explore on a 1-mile hike to the top of the pumice ring, with wide views of the Sierra, Mono Lake, and the Mono craters. Take advantage of the guided tours during the summer.

Saddlebag Lake
Off Highway 120, 2.4 miles from the East Gate entrance of the national park, take the dirt road 2.5 miles
www.saddlebaglakeresort.com

At 10,087 feet, this is the highest lake in the state that can be reached by public road. The mostly unpaved road is fine for most vehicles, except large RVs, if you take it slow. You can take a water taxi tour around the lake, and/or the boat will drop you off near trailheads into the Twenty Lakes Basin of the Hoover Wilderness, a region favored by hikers, backpackers, and photographers (see later in this chapter). The 5-mile trail passes Lake Helen as well as jagged Z Lake and four-pronged Shamrock Lake.

The round-trip boat ride is about $9.00, plus extra fees for backpacks and dogs. As boat access to the basin trails is limited by the Forest Service, on some weekend days boat passage may be sold out early in the day, although you can always hike 2 miles around the lake to the trailheads.

Fishing in the basin lakes is very good, and in Saddlebag Lake for brook, brown, and rainbow trout.

The 20-site Saddlebag Lake Campground is a good headquarters for anglers and hikers on a first-come, first-served basis. The scenery is fabulous; the campsites are close together and primitive.

The small store and restaurant here is run by a jovial couple, Richard and Carmen Ernst, who will sell you fishing gear, rent you a boat, and fix you up with a juicy hamburger, a sandwich, or slices of homemade pie and cake. Chairs around the big stone fireplace are popular on chilly days. The store is open 7:00 A.M. to 7:00 P.M.

The road and the area are generally accessible mid-June through October. The Mono Lake Visitors' Center can tell you when Saddlebag Lake opens and closes (760-647-3044).

Tioga Lake
Off Highway 120, 2 miles from the East Gate entrance
(760) 647-3044

This beautiful subalpine lake just below the roadside makes a nice stop for a picnic or a walk on an easy, flat trail. You can also camp here, and the fishing is good (see the Campgrounds chapter, and "Fishing" in this chapter). From the north end of the lake, look back to Mammoth Peak. Taken very early in the morning, your photographs will look as though you hiked for days into the outback. Park just beyond the lake to access the Nunatak Nature Trail, a short, easy path leading to two lovely mountain tarns.

Twenty Lakes Basin

The main trailhead for Twenty Lakes Basin is at Saddlebag Lake (see earlier in this chapter). Twenty azure lakes and stunning alpine scenery are accessed by a 5-mile hiking trail in the Hoover Wilderness area of Inyo National Forest, just north of Tioga Pass. Walking through groves of whitebark pine and centuries-old junipers at an elevation of about 10,000 feet, with a dramatic backdrop of granite peaks, you will encounter clear streams and small glaciers on your way to the lovely lakes, habitat of the elusive golden trout. Sierra daisy and alpine goldenrod sprout in the meadows in spring and summer. The basin gets fewer hikers than in the national park, although in high season as many as 200 people may be in the area each day. Unmarked, undeveloped campsites are scattered around the lakes. Remember that you need a wilderness permit to camp overnight; get one at the Mono Basin Ranger Station, a half-mile north of Lee Vining (760-647-3044).

ACCOMMODATIONS

PRICE CODE

A dollar sign ($) ranking indicates the average nightly rates for two adults. Unless otherwise noted, lodgings accept credit cards. Some bed-and-breakfast inns require two-night minimums.

$	**$49-$75**
$$	**$76-$124**
$$$	**$125-$175**
$$$$	**$176 and up**

Boulder Lodge **$-$$$**
1 mile east of June Mountain Ski Area
Highway 158, June Lake
(800) 458-6355, (760) 648-7533
www.boulderlodge.net

Boulder Lodge overlooks June Lake with a variety of well-maintained accommodations, from motel rooms to suites and fireplace cabins with one or more bedrooms, including one with five bedrooms and three bathrooms. The lodge also has a nice indoor swimming pool, hot tub and sauna, game room, and tennis courts. Ask about ski packages.

The Cain House **$$-$$$**
340 Main Street, Bridgeport
(800) 433-2246, (760) 932-7040
info@cainhouse.com,
www.cainhouse.com

Seven elegantly decorated Victorian-style rooms have private baths and queen- or king-size beds, quilts, and down comforters. Once owned by the largest landowner in Bodie during the Gold Rush, this country house is a cross between a European-style inn and a Western farmhouse. An avid rock climber and backpacker, co-owner Chris Gohlich teaches elementary school in town. His wife, Marachal, returned a decade ago to her hometown of Bridgeport from a career at glitzy hotels and resorts. Expect a luscious, full breakfast (think about fresh berry pancakes, French country omelettes, cinnamon French toast, and breakfast burritos) and complimentary afternoon wine and cheese. Before heading out, relax awhile in the backyard or on the front porch in an Adirondack chair, and watch the world rush by.

Take care to make reservations well in advance, as more than half of the guests at Cain House are returnees during the late April through October season. If you are unable to gain occupancy here, ask about a vacancy at the plain and very clean Silver Strike Motel next door, which is also owned by the Gohlichs.

Double Eagle Resort and Spa **$$$$**
5587 Boulder Drive, Highway 158, June Lake
(760) 648-7004
www.doubleeagleresort.com

This resort sits at the base of 11,000-foot Carson Peak not far from June Lake and offers spectacular views of granite mountain peaks and waterfalls. In an aspen, juniper, and pine forest on Reverse Creek, the resort has luxury suites, each with two king- or queen-size beds, a rustic stove, whirlpool tub, and mini bar, with a private deck overlooking Ron's Pond. Two-bedroom knotty pine-paneled cabins furnished in alpine lodge style are nestled among towering pines. Wood-burning stoves lend atmosphere, while TVs, fully equipped kitchens and private decks make the cabins comfortable.

Beginning anglers get fly-casting lessons and practice their skills on Ron's Pond; you can rent and buy top-notch fishing gear here, too. The resort proprietor, Ron Black, knows every lake and stream in the area and will give you the inside scoop on where to fish, bike, hike, and horseback ride in the area. Resort guests also have the privilege of fishing on the private Black's Trophy Pond, a stunning little body of water filled by Rush Creek. Alpers trout up to about 12 pounds are caught by humans, while great blue herons, eagles, osprey, the occasional bobcat, and brown bear fish here, too.

Resort guests and visitors luxuriate in the on-site Creekside Spa and Fitness Center (see under Attractions in this chapter) and the Eagle's Landing Restaurant and Saloon (see under Restaurants in this chapter). Throughout, the resort buildings are decorated with gold mining-era artifacts and antiques.

In the wintertime, picturesque Horsetail Falls creates a frozen curtain for ice climbing. Skiers head up the road to the June Mountain Ski Area. Ron's Pond freezes over and ice skating ensues, complete with music, a bonfire, and mugs of hot chocolate. White lights sparkle in the aspens from November to February, and a huge Christmas tree gleams on the restaurant deck.

Book your reservations well in advance for summer and for all weekends and holidays because this is a popular destination. Numerous weddings are held at the resort, too, which fills the guest rooms and cabins. Ask about seasonal packages.

In the spa shop are warm-up, sports, and workout clothing, spa products, candles, and gift items.

Hunewill Circle H Guest Ranch $$$$
P.O. Box 368
Bridgeport, CA 93517
(760) 932-7710 (summer),
(775) 465-2201 (winter)
www.hunewillranch.com

In a glorious meadow setting at about 6,500 feet, at the foot of the Eastern Sierra near Bridgeport, cowpokes on this 26,000-acre cattle ranch have been ridin' and ropin' since 1861. Since the 1930s, paying guests have returned year after year for authentic ranch vacations—most stay for a week. They share the place with 1,200 cows, 120 horses, 60 sheep, 35 llamas, 4 pigs, and several dogs.

Anglers also headquarter here for expeditions to nearby streams and lakes. Horseback riding is the main activity at the ranch, along with campfire sing-alongs, hayrides, horseshoes, barn dances, cattle roping, and more down-home, fun activities. You can also fly-fish on a large pond—catch and release only—which is stocked with good-size rainbows, and fish from a float tube. The ranch "rests" the fish on Tuesday, when no angling is permitted. Child care is available, as well as riding lessons, personal fitness training, and massage several times a week. Intermediate and advanced riders gather in September and November for popular cattle drives.

Guests stay in two dozen two-room, two-bath cabins, each with a porch for just sittin'. Hearty meals are taken family-style in the Victorian ranch house. The ranch is open to guests from late May to mid-October.

Lake Front Cabins $$-$$$$
P.O. Box 98, 2716 Boulder Drive (Highway 158), June Lake, CA 93529
(800) 648-6835, (760) 648-7527
www.junelake.com/lodging/lakefront

Across the road from June Lake, you'll find housekeeping cabins with one or two bedrooms and equipped kitchenettes, all built around a grassy common area with picnic tables, lawn chairs, gas barbecues, and a fire pit. There are also motel rooms with and without kitchen facilities, condominiums, and a two-bedroom house. Open year-round, this is a busy place just 500 feet from the June Lake marina, where you can rent or launch boats.

Lundy Lake Resort $-$$
P.O. Box 550, Lee Vining, CA 93541
(626) 309-0415

At 7,800 feet in elevation, this mile-long, absolutely beautiful lake is stocked with German brown and rainbow trout. The Fish and Game department plants more than 26,000 rainbows throughout the season. Small eastern brookies are caught in the beaver ponds and the creek above the lake. You will see anglers out in small boats, on the shore near the dam, and across from the boat dock. At the end of the road, a tiny, very rustic resort caters to avid fishing fans who just love the rough-around-the-edges cabins, clean mobile homes, and the basic RV and tent sites. The resort is usually open from the last weekend of April to November 1, weather permitting.

Even if you do not fish, take the short drive to the end of the lake and walk or bike along the quiet road above the lake, which is surrounded by aspen groves and high, stark, alpine mountainsides. Fall color and spring wildflowers are wonderful sights to see.

Lundy Lake is 5 miles off US 395, just north of Lee Vining, on a good, paved road.

Silver Lake Resort $$-$$$
P.O. Box 116
June Lake, CA 93529
South of Lee Vining on Highway 158
(760) 648-7525
www.silverlakeresort.net

The oldest resort in the eastern Sierra, rustic, charming Silver Lake Resort has been operating continuously since 1916 on the shores of a gorgeous lake. Nearly 20 small, nicely and simply furnished housekeeping cabins lie in an aspen grove by Alger Creek, with a duck and trout pond adding to the ambience.

Stop here to rent a fishing boat or a canoe and to stock up on provisions at the general store or pick up a few gifts and souvenirs in the gift shop. Do not fail to have a hearty breakfast or lunch in the tiny, lakeview cafe—sandwiches, burgers, and slices of pie are huge. Take a look at the wonderful old photographs of vacationers in the '20s, '30s, and '40s and the amazing fish trophies on the knotty-pine walls. Look for the rosy-toned, 9-pound, 12-ounce brook trout, caught in 1932, which still holds the state record. Today, it is not unusual for anglers to catch 6- to 9-pound Alpers trout in the lake.

The resort is open from the last week in April through mid-October. The cabins sleep two to eight people and have full kitchens with basic cooking gear and dishes, propane heaters, and bed linens and towels. Cabin rentals range from about $95 to $235 per night (cabin #5, called Creek House, is a nice one, near the rushing creek). You can also park your RV here for $25 per night or $156 a week and get full hookups and use the showers, the laundry room, and the barbecue area. Adjacent to the resort is a Forest Service campground in a wide-open flat area near the road; see the Campgrounds chapter for more information.

The lovely wooded setting beneath dramatic cliffs and great fishing in the lake make the resort a very popular vacation destination. Call well in advance for reservations, even a year in advance for midsummer and weekends.

Tioga Lodge **$$**
54411 US 395, 2.5 miles north of Lee Vining
(888) 647-6423, (760) 647-6423
www.tiogalodge.com
Transported to the current site on the highway late in the 19th century from the historic gold-mining town of Bodie, the white wooden clapboard buildings of today's lodge and restaurant are a charming sight on the roadside. Fresh-looking, country-style rooms, some with sitting areas, have handmade aspen log bedsteads or iron beds. The Joseph Walker Mountain Man Room has a pine bed, a long rifle, and an elk's head. Views of Mono Lake and the mountains are stunning, you'll find an excellent restaurant onsite, and you can board a 90-minute Mono Lake Boat Tour here.

Tioga Pass Resort **$$-$$$$**
P.O. Box 7, Lee Vining, CA 93541
reservations@tiogapassresort.com
www.tiogapassresort.com
Guests return year after year to this, their favorite wilderness lodge, located on the highway 2 miles outside the East Gate of the national park near beautiful lakes and streams, good fishing, and fabulous hiking. You can walk to Ellery Lake and Tioga Lake, and drive on a dirt road 2 miles to Saddlebag Lake and launch your fishing boat.

The cabins have kitchens, are big enough for small families, and can be rented on a weekly basis. They tend to fill up for July and August up to two years in advance; rates range from about $875 a week. The resort also has four motel units. A casual restaurant serves three hearty meals a day while a little grocery store sells fishing and outdoor equipment and clothing.

At 9,641 feet, the summer season at the resort begins on the Fourth of July, and the place is popular with cross-country skiers, who sometimes ski as late as April.

Virginia Creek Settlement **$-$$**
US 395, 5 miles south of Bridgeport
(760) 932-7780
www.virginiacrksettlement.com
Stay in your own RV or tent or stay in a "tent town" unit that sleeps four people, or a log cabin with knotty-pine walls, iron beds, and Old West false fronts, just made for cowpokes. Bedding is available or you can bring your own. There are restrooms, hot showers, picnic tables, fire rings, and a rustic restaurant serving American food. Above the dining room is a nice suite with a queen-size and twin beds. The fishing is

Bodie State Historic Park

This is a real ghost town, with 10,000 ghosts from the Gold Rush boom here in 1877. More than $38 million worth of gold and silver was taken from Bodie mines, but by 1888, the boom busted and everyone left town, leaving more than 170 spooky and fascinating wooden buildings, including dozens of saloons, churches, homes, stables, stores, and bunkhouses. Walk through the graveyard, the streets, and the open buildings, where some of the miners' faded belongings remain. This is the most authentic, untouched, unrestored 1800s town in the West. There are no services out here, no souvenir shops, just one restroom and a small museum open only in the summer. Bring your own food and water. You will find self-guiding tour brochures; ask about the guided Standard Consolidated Mill tour or the Historic Mining District Tour. Free history talks are given daily at the Methodist Church.

From Lee Vining, drive 20 miles north on US 395 to Highway 270 and turn east for 13 miles; the last 3 miles of the road are dirt, but good enough for most vehicles. The park is open 8:00 A.M. to 7:00 P.M. daily through Labor Day; a small admission fee is charged. For more information call (760) 647-6445; www.parks.ca.gov.

good along beautiful Virginia Creek. These are the closest accommodations to Bodie.

RESTAURANTS

PRICE CODE

The price is based on the cost of two entrees from the dinner menu, not including appetizers, desserts, beverages, taxes, or gratuities.

$	**$15 or less**
$$	**$16–$25**
$$$	**$26–$35**
$$$$	**More than $35**

Bridgeport Inn **$$–$$$**
US 395, 205 Main Street, Bridgeport
(760) 932-7380
http://thebridgeportinn.com
This white clapboard inn was a stage stop in the 1870s. Locals are loyal patrons for the Bridgeport Inn's all-American breakfasts, lunches, and dinners, including the famous prime rib, steaks and chops, charbroiled chicken, and pasta. Charbroiled sandwiches are on the lunch menu. The wooden bar that spills onto the porch facing Main Street, is filled with antiques. Toss a few quarters in the jukebox in the adjacent parlor to hear '50s and '60s hits. The Bridgeport Inn is open year-round.

Carson Peak Inn **$$–$$$**
June Lake Loop, Highway 158, between Gull and Silver Lakes
(760) 648-7575
www.horseshoecanyon.net/cpi_main.htm
Locals love this barn-red dinner-only place for the surf-and-turf, filet mignon, prime rib, trout, and Alaska king crab legs. Portions are huge and the food is hearty and good.

Creekside Corner Bar **$**
Double Eagle Resort, Highway 158
June Lake
(760) 648-7004
www.doubleeagleresort.com
Inside the Creekside Spa at the Double Eagle Resort, this is the place for fresh fruit smoothies, juices, espresso drinks, herbal teas, sandwiches, snacks, beer, and wine.

Eagle's Landing Restaurant $$-$$$$
Double Eagle Resort, 5587 Boulder Drive, Highway 158, June Lake
(760) 648-7004
www.doubleeagleresort.com

Step through an elaborately carved wood and glass door into a charming mountain lodge atmosphere warmed by a big stone fireplace, wood carvings, pine planks, log beams, and racks of antlers. Relax in a big booth and enjoy the cliff-side and forest views while perusing the top-notch wine list. The dinner menu features prime rib, several types of chicken, osso bucco, ribs, halibut, salmon, and pastas. Do try the famous Alpers trout appetizer, The Angler, for fish smoked here at the resort.

For breakfast, choose from traditional breakfast fare: pancakes, big bowls of fresh fruit, French toast, or burritos. Sunday brunch is popular.

For lunch, chicken wraps, fish tacos, and the smoked Alpers trout club are big-city choices, along with country-style burgers and sandwiches.

The Eagle's Nest Saloon is small, cozy, and friendly.

Hays Street Cafe $
21 Hays Street, Bridgeport
(760) 932-7141
ww.haysstreetcafe.com

On the south end of town, locals and visitors flock here for big American breakfasts of platter-size blueberry pancakes and buttermilk biscuits and gravy. Sandwiches—hot, cold, and hearty—are on the menu for lunch. Do not miss the homemade carrot cake. Owners Jeff and Arleen Mills keep the cafe open year-round.

Mono Inn Restaurant $$-$$$
US 395, 6 miles north of Lee Vining
(760) 647-6581
www.monoinn.com

Some say this is the best restaurant on US 395. Rustic in an elegant sort of way with Arts and Crafts-style decor and Stickley furniture from the 1920s, the dining room has a fireplace, an outdoor deck, and a fabulous view of Mono Lake. Hearty California cuisine may include Atlantic salmon, American bison, steaks, lamb shanks, grilled quail, lobster Alfredo, sautéed bay scallops, and quesadillas. Don't miss the chocolate pecan pie. The wine list is top-notch, and microbrew aficionados like the Mammoth Brewing Company's beer of the month. The restaurant is open for dinner only 4:30 to 9:00 P.M., May through October. Take care to make reservations in advance, and arrive with an open mind, as seating and service is slow; there is a small bar, and you can relax with a cocktail and a lake view in the upstairs Lake Room's Ansel Adams Gallery.

Restaurant 1881 $$$-$$$$
362 Main Street, Bridgeport
(760) 932-1918
www.restaurant1881.com

In a lovingly restored, pretty, white Victorian house, fishermen with three-day beards and travelers find surprisingly sophisticated cuisine. Signature dishes include rack of lamb in a crispy pistachio crust; local Alpers trout with mushrooms, pinenuts, and a chive leek sauce; and Chateaubriand with black truffle butter and a cabernet glaze. You can also order simpler dishes such as plain ol' cowboy steak and pasta with veggies.

Owned by Bridgeport native Erinn O'Connell, the dinner house is quite popular; reservations are advised.

Silver Lake Cafe $-$$
South of Lee Vining on Highway 158, June Lake Loop
(760) 648-7525
www.silverlakeresort.net/Cafex.html

Settle in with the locals for a hearty breakfast and lunch in a casual, knotty-pine-paneled place with lake and aspen views and vintage photos on the wall. Try the giant "El Gordo," the "Carson Camp Special" three-egg omelette, flapjacks, or biscuits and gravy. On the lunch menu are homemade chili, big and juicy burgers, High Sierra roast beef dips, veggie specials, salads, and more.

Tioga Gas Mart and Whoa Nellie Deli $
22 Vista Point Road, at the intersection of US 395 and Highway 120
Lee Vining
(760) 647-1088
This is not your grandfather's gas station. They don't fool around here with food. Try the juicy Cowboy Steak Sandwich, a 10-ounce rib eye with red wine herb butter on a French roll; an Angus hamburger; barbecued chicken; cilantro pesto pizza; lobster taquitos; fish tacos; or buffalo meatloaf. The place opens at 7:00 A.M. for cowboy steak and eggs and other breakfast choices. Sit at a booth indoors or on the terrace for a wide view of Mono Lake. Choose a bottle of wine from the top-notch selection, and try a mango margarita or a glass of the Mammoth Brewing Company's best.

While you're at it, you can buy gifts and souvenirs here, as well as camping and fishing licenses and supplies, guidebooks, posters, and maps. Motorcycle groups, locals, tour buses, and tourists congregate here from morning until night, noshing and enjoying the fabulous views of Mono Lake from the dining terrace. On summer weekends, live music keeps the party going.

Outside is a handy courtesy phone board for making lodging reservations along US 395 and on the June Lake Loop.

Although gas is available 24 hours, daily, the market and deli restaurant is open seasonally from May to October.

Tioga Lodge $$-$$$
54411 US 395, 2.5 miles north of Lee Vining
(888) 647-6423, (760) 647-6423
Take your choice of seats on the outdoor patio, in the garden overlooking Mono Lake, or in the dining room of this old lodge. Breads and pastries are baked on-site daily. The menu includes traditional American comfort food, and such fancy stuff as baked brie, pecan pork, seafood pasta, and New York steak. The saloon feels nice and old, with a wood ceiling, a sand floor, and Western movie posters on the stone walls. The lodge is open for dinners and for breakfast on weekends.

In the mood for a long weekend of leaf peeping? Every autumn, aspen, cottonwood, and willow put on a dazzling show of gold, orange, and russet in the Eastern Sierra along US 395. For a map and description of best routes and places to see fall color, call (800) 845-7922 for the **Eastern High Sierra Fall Color Guide.**

Virginia Creek Settlement $-$$
Highway 120, 25 miles north of Lee Vining, 5 miles south of Bridgeport, at US 395
(760) 932-7780
www.virginiacrksettlement.com
Enjoy Italian specialties and American comfort food—steak, chicken, pasta—in this rustic, roadhouse environment. The homemade pizza, like Gorgonzola and garlic, is memorable. The building was once a boardinghouse for gold miners and has rooms above the restaurant.

OUTDOOR RECREATION

Fishing is the main attraction for many people in the Eastern Sierra, in numerous subalpine lakes; in the East Walker River, which empties into Bridgeport Lake; and the Owens River. A glance at a topographic map will reveal dozens of rivers and streams draining eastward from Yosemite National Park. June Mountain is ground zero for downhill skiing and snowboarding. The region also offers ice climbing and cross-country skiing opportunities, although trails are generally ungroomed. The Mono County Tourism/Film Commission (800-845-7922, www.monocounty.org) has detailed information on fishing and four-season activities.

Fishing

If you love trout fishing, you probably already know about the Eastern Sierra, where many lakes, rivers, and creeks are regularly stocked with rainbows, brooks, and German browns. You can fish from shore or rent a boat at one of many marinas at Rock Creek, Silver Lake, Gull Lake, June Lake, Twin Lakes, and Grant Lake, to name a few. The Walker and the Owens Rivers are legendary for their superb trout fishing, and Lee Vining, Rush, and Mill Creeks are excellent. For every bit of equipment you could possibly need for fishing, and for maps and current information on what's biting where, stop in at Ernie's Tackle and Ski Shop in June Lake, 2604 Highway 158; (760) 648-7756; http://erniestackleandski.com, or Ken's Sporting Goods in Bridgeport, 258 Main Street; (760) 932-7707; www.kenssport.com.

Here are some of the top fishing lakes:

Bridgeport Reservoir: Just northeast of town, the fishing is good here and on the East Walker River, which feeds the lake.

Ellery Lake: Near the East Gate entrance to Yosemite National Park, this is a 50-acre lake inhabited by native brooks and browns, and stocked with rainbows. You will find easy access to the shoreline and a campground below the highway.

Gull Lake: "The Brooky Hole" to the left of the marina is a favorite spot for boat fishing. You can rent a fishing boat, canoes, and paddleboats here. A small campground is located in a shady strip between the lakeshore and the highway.

Get maps and campground information and obtain wilderness permits at the Humboldt-Toiyabe National Forest Ranger Station located on US 395, just south of Bridgeport (760-932-7070). While you are here, browse the excellent array of guidebooks, regional history books, and children's books and games.

June Lake: Fish from the shore of this deep, glacier-fed lake along the highway near Boulder Lodge, at the beach area at the east end, and near the reeds on the west end of the lake.

Lee Vining Creek: Fish along the campground access road. More than 40,000 catchable fish are planted in the creek annually. See Lee Vining Canyon in the "Hiking" section of this chapter.

Lundy Lake: Try near the dam and across from the boat dock. You can camp among the aspens and pines below Mill Creek, take a housekeeping cabin, or park your RV at the rustic resort.

Rush Creek: The popular stretch of this creek lies between Silver Lake and Grant Lake, near submerged boulders and trees.

Saddlebag Lake: See "Attractions" in this chapter.

Silver Lake: Fish near the parking lot at the south end of the lake, rent fishing boats if you desire, and float around the southeast shoreline. See more in the "Accommodations" section of this chapter.

Grant Lake: The best spots are where Rush Creek enters the north end of the lake at the narrows by the marina, and at Sheepherder's Bay. Water-skiers love this place in the summertime, and there is a basic campground with RV sites and a small marina with boat rentals.

Tioga Lake: Park near the campground on the road and fish along the western shore; thousands of catchable rainbows are stocked. See "Attractions" in this chapter.

Twin Lakes: Troll for big browns or fish from the shore along the road and near the inlet to Lower Twin Lake. At Upper Twin Lake, a 26-pound, 8-ounce brown trout set the state's record as the largest caught. Nearby Robinson and Buckeye creeks are popular fishing spots.

Alpers' Owens River Ranch
15 miles south of Lee Vining off US 395, 4 miles east on Owens River Road
(760) 648-7334

At the upper end of Long Valley, 2 miles of the Owens River meander through the broad meadows of this 100-year-old

family-owned ranch, where private river access is made available to guests for catch-and-release fishing for Alpers trout, raised here in the hatchery. This part of the river is slow moving and clear, with many rainbows and brown trout. You can stay here in housekeeping cottages that sleep up to 10 people; you can also buy fishing tackle, beer, and a few groceries.

Hiking

Paved and unpaved trails are found along the streams and around the many lakes of the Eastern Sierra. Here are canyons and trails with easy access that reward the hiker with glorious views. One caution: Most trails are well over 6,700 feet above sea level.

Lee Vining Canyon

Dense aspen groves are quivering columns of green in the spring and summer, turning dazzling gold in October. Off Highway 120, just west of the junction with US 395, watch for the sign to Moraine, Boulder, and Aspen campgrounds. Running west about 2.5 miles is a very quiet, very pretty paved road, where you can walk or bike, dipping down to the beautiful, rushing Lee Vining Creek to picnic, wade, cast a line, or nap in the shade. See the Campgrounds chapter for campgrounds along the creek here.

Lee Vining Creek Trail

Meander along the cool riparian corridor of Lee Vining Creek with a naturalist, learning about flora, fauna, Native American history, and current restoration projects. The easy, 3-mile guided walk takes about one-and-a-half hours and occurs Wednesday and Saturday mornings at 9:00 A.M. through Labor Day; check first with the Mono Basin Visitor Center (760-647-3044).

Meet about 50 yards south of the Best Western motel units on the east side of the highway in Lee Vining; the end of the trail is at the Visitor Center. To walk on your own, ask for a self-guiding pamphlet. Follow the trail down to the tree-shaded banks of the stream.

Lundy Canyon

Seven miles northwest of Lee Vining off US 395, take Lundy Lake Road to the end, to the small fishing resort. Ask for directions where to drive on the rough dirt road past the store to the trailhead. From here, it is a rather strenuous, beautiful trail up through aspen groves to streams and waterfalls. Some hikers shuttle a car to Saddlebag Lake and make the tough 7-mile, steep hike to the Twenty Lakes Basin above Saddlebag Lake.

Nunatak Tarns Nature Trail

About a half mile east of the Tioga Pass/East Gate entrance to Yosemite National Park, parking is at the trailhead for a very easy, flat, paved, pretty, half-mile loop trail that winds around several alpine tarns. This is a popular, developed footpath with interpretive signs, a few benches, and one picnic table; you can lay a blanket beside one of the tarns for a rest or a picnic. It is unusual to find a paved trail outside the park; this one works for strollers and wheelchairs.

Parker Lake Trail

From US 395, turn onto the June Lake Loop, Highway 158, at the north junction. Watch for the sign to Parker Lake, and take that road about 2 miles to the sign for the trailhead. Do not let the steep rise at the beginning scare you, as it flattens out alongside Parker Creek and winds through lovely meadows and forests. Continue past the Silver Lake sign to Parker Lake for a 4-mile round-trip.

Rush Creek Trail

Behind the RV park at Silver Lake Resort on the June Lake Loop is the trailhead to a pretty footpath that climbs up a couple of miles to great views of Agnew Lake and Gem Lake in the Ansel Adams Wilderness, and the surrounding landscape.

Ice-skate with the locals all winter on the June Lake Loop and on Gull, Silver, and June Lakes; rent skates in the town of June Lake. You can also skate on the pond at the Double Eagle Resort where skates are also available.

Yost Lake/Fern Lake Trail

About a mile south of Silver Lake on the June Lake Loop on Highway. 158, wander through the pines about 1.5 miles to a fork. The right trail is a steep, strenuous, 0.7 mile to Fern Lake, while the left trail is a moderately difficult 2.3 miles to Yost Lake.

Mountain Biking

An excellent brochure and map show a variety of mountain bike routes off US 395. The Panorama, Hartley Springs, and East Craters Loops are near June Lake. Obtain the brochure by calling (888) 466-2666 or by requesting it online at www.visitmammoth.com/activites/mtnbikingfr.html.

Winter Sports

The four-season Mammoth Lakes region is outside the scope of this title's Yosemite National Park gateway communities, although Mono County's population and economic development are concentrated here. In winter, Mammoth Mountain draws heavily from Los Angeles and Southern California. Find out more at (800) 626-6684, www.mammothmountain.com.

SKIING AND SNOWBOARDING

June Mountain Ski Area
US 395, 20 miles north of Mammoth Lakes on the June Lake Loop
(888) 586-3686, (760) 648-7733
www.junemountain.com

Two 10,000-foot peaks, Rainbow and June Mountains, afford dazzling views of the Sierra for skiers and snowboarders at this lively ski resort, beloved by those who prefer fewer people, shorter lift lines, and a more relaxed atmosphere than larger ski areas. Seven lifts, including two high-speed quads, take skiers to tackle 2,600 vertical feet of descent. Black diamond skiers love the steep chutes and bowls, while intermediates glide on wide, rolling trails and beginners enjoy the gentle slopes.

Snowboarders rave about the extensive terrain development. Pay up your medical insurance, hold your breath, and try the two terrain parks, the Superpipe, and two jib parks, one on the summit. With one of the best snowboarding complexes in the west, June Mountain has hosted several U.S. Snowboard National Championships.

A staff of PSIA-certified ski instructors teaches all ages. Kids ages 4 through 12 get a lift ticket, gear rental, and lessons for about $70. The adult beginners package is about $10 more.

Motels and a wide variety of cabins, condos, and houses are available to rent, year-round, near the ski area; check www.junemountain.com/lodging for accommodation details. US 395 and the June Lake Loop Road are nearly always open, even in midwinter; call (800) 427-7623 for road conditions.

CROSS-COUNTRY SKIING AND SNOWSHOEING

Nordic skiing is enjoyed around the June Lake Loop, and there are numerous signed and groomed and unsigned, ungroomed trails in the region. The Mammoth Lakes Winter Recreation Map shows ski and snowmobiling trails in the June, Mono, and Mammoth Lakes areas. Obtain it by calling (888) 466-2666, or request it online: www.visitmammoth.com.

A free, guided cross-country ski tour is conducted on weekends in the South Tufa area of Mono Lake. Meet at the South Tufa parking lot, 5 miles east of US 395 on Highway 120. Call for information: (760) 647-3044, (760) 647-6595.

Cross-country skiing is excellent around Dundelberg Peak for all skill levels, and you have access, from here, to skiing in the Hoover Wilderness. Get here by parking at Conway Summit, 11 miles south of Bridgeport on US 395, and skiing out Virginia Lakes Road (760-932-7070).

Obsidian Dome, on the west side of US 395, south of June Lake and just north of Deadman Summit, is a favorite skiers' destination. Marked trails are groomed in the Inyo National Forest.

You can also ski, snowshoe, and snowmobile to Bodie State Historic Park. Five miles south of Bridgeport off US 395, turn onto Bodie Road and drive until you reach snow.

BACKCOUNTRY TOURING

The experienced ski tour guides from Sierra Mountain Center and June Mountain's Back Country Adventure Zone will lead you on one-day or several-day skiing expeditions, including snow camping and/or ice climbing if you wish. Spring skiing can be glorious, with shirt-sleeve temperatures, easygoing corn snow, and stupendous Sierra vistas: Rock Creek Canyon, Davis Lakes, Agnew Meadows, across the slopes of San Joaquin Ridge to Clark Lakes, and many more routes. Retaining a professional guide service is the best way to make these trans-Sierra trips, as the services arrange for any necessary permits and food and lead you safely to the most spectacular locations (Sierra Mountain Center, 760-873-8526, www.sierramountaincenter.com).

SNOWMOBILING

You can rent snowmobiles from DJ's Snowmobile Adventures (760-935-4480, www.snowmobilemammoth.com) at Smokey Bear Flats, which is located off US 395, about 3 miles north of the US 395/Highway 203 junction. Groomed trails meander across 500 acres of wide-open flats and rolling hills with spectacular views of the Sierra and Mount Morrison. The combination of snowmobiling in this open area, and a good tubing and sledding hill nearby, make this a favorite winter play area for families.

For great views of the Bridgeport Valley from your snowmobile, park at Conway Summit, 11 miles south of Bridgeport on US 395, and drive your snowmobile west on Virginia Lakes Road (760-932-7070).

For a gorgeous, full-day expedition, rent snowmobiles at the June Lake Junction, ask for directions to the Shady Rest Winter Trailhead, and ride 20 miles all the way to Mammoth on a marked trail.

Guides and Outfitters

Double Eagle Resort and Spa
5587 Boulder Drive, Highway 158, June Lake
(760) 648-7004
www.doubleeagleresort.com

On half-day, full-day, or multiday trips, experienced fishing guides will lead you to excellent fishing spots on private waters and lakes and streams in the area, including Black's Pond, just a half mile from the resort, and on the East Walker River. You can also learn the basics of fly-fishing right here in the resort, and fly casting and hooking Alpers trout on Ron's Pond. Private lessons include gear, and no license is required. A one-hour lesson is $60 per person.

Frontier Pack Train
1012 East Line Street, Bishop
(888) 437-MULE
www.frontierpacktrain.com

From age six and up, everyone will enjoy an hour-long horseback ride through meadows and sagebrush and along Rush Creek. Trail rides depart several times a day, and the cost is $25 per person.

You can also spend a half day riding to the top of Parker Bench for zowie views of Mono Lake and the craters. Or take a daylong trek into the Sierra backcountry to beautiful Gem Lake for fishing, swimming, or sitting under a pine tree; this ride leaves at 7:30 A.M. and returns about 5:00 P.M.; cost is $85 per person.

Savvy local guides also lead pack trips into the beautiful Ansel Adams Wilderness to great hidden fishing waters. They set up camp at picturesque sites, take care of all the equipment, and cook incredible meals around the campfire. In recent years, Frontier was selected by the California School of Fly Fishing as its pack outfitters. It also offers photographic safaris and a four-day wild mustang adventure into the Inyo National Forest. Some of the most popular trips are the June Lake and Black Lake Horse Drives, where dudes and cowpokes drive more than 100 head of horses and mules.

Leavitt Meadows Pack Station
7386 Highway 108, Bridgeport
(530) 495-2257
www.leavittmeadows.com
This experienced company offers a variety of trips and services involving horseback riding in a spectacular part of the Toiyabe National Forest around Sonora Pass and in the Hoover Wilderness. Families enjoy the half-day ride to Lane and Roosevelt Lakes, the West Walker River, and Leavitt Falls and the scenic, two-hour ride along Secret Lake Ridge.

You can ride to a base camp at beautiful Fremont Lake or to Walker Meadows, where a complete camp is set up with spacious tents, tables and chairs, portable showers, and comfort stations. All meals are provided. From here you can ride during the day, fish, hike, or just hang out in the wilderness.

For longer forays, you can ride a Pack Station horse, accompanied by a guide and pack animal with your gear, to a location of your choice—a trail or a campsite—and arrange to be picked up there or at the end of the trail.

Sierra Mountain Guides
P.O. Box 446, June Lake, CA 93529
(760) 648-1122
www.themountainguide.com
A climber for more than three decades, Doug Nidever is a past chief guide for the Yosemite Mountaineering School, said to be the best of its kind in the country. He has guided numerous major ascents, and his specialties are ski touring, technical ice climbing, and winter mountaineering. Adventurers in the Eastern Sierra hire Doug and his experienced guides for rock and ice climbing; winter mountaineering, camping, and survival; winter peak ascents; avalanche courses; backcountry ski tours; and guided hikes.

Swimming

June Lake
This is the best—not to mention the warmest—place for swimming all summer. From Lee Vining, drive 10.5 miles south to Highway 158, turning west to June Lake; go right on June Lake Road to Pine Cliff Road, then left to the Oh Ridge Campground and down to the beach; keep going to the last parking lot. There are restrooms and picnic tables here.

Mono Lake
For a unique experience, try swimming in the very salty Mono Lake, where you will float right on top, just like in the Dead Sea. Don't try this if you have open cuts or wounds. From Lee Vining, drive 5 miles south to Highway 120, go east 5 miles to the South Tufa Reserve Road, then bear right to Navy Beach.

RELOCATION

We live on the toes of the feet of a giant. We who live in communities along the gateway routes into Yosemite National Park may not visit the park often, but for most of us, it defines who we are: people of the foothills, our economy largely affected by the dollars that iconic park tourism generates. When the giant that is the park experiences a change of master plan, a decrease in federal funding, or a record Merced River flood as in 1997, or when it builds or takes down visitor lodging or changes a mode of transportation, it affects us.

We often look to California's Central Valley for higher education and medical care, but the region around Yosemite has all we could want for recreation—in our backyards or a short drive away. Many of us left the urban scene in the San Francisco Bay Area, its southern extension in Silicon Valley, or even more distant Los Angeles for a lifestyle that is less stressful and less congested, with cleaner air and more dramatic seasons. Some of us have family roots in the foothills that date back a century or so, perhaps even to California's 1849 Gold Rush. Native Americans may have the deepest roots of all. Many of us are young retirees looking to relocate to an area where the economy isn't exactly booming, but our city-earned savings can be invested in a larger house on acreage that we never could find in the urban areas where we pursued careers. Some of us just enjoy the quiet and isolation that our rolling hills, green forests, blue lakes, swift rivers, and glacier-carved mountains provide. We like to say that in our small towns, everyone knows you, your parents, your children, and even your pets by name.

The stars are bright on a clear night. Below about 4,000 feet on the western side of the park, in Tuolumne, Mariposa, and Eastern Madera Counties, we are above Central Valley fog and mostly below the snow level. For our neighbors who live in the snow zone, there's a wintertime landscape of deep snow and crisp air, and a corresponding knowledge of how to build a fire in a wood-burning stove to have heat when the electricity goes down. In summer and fall our thunderstorms build up like mighty white marshmallows. Newcomers from the coast can't get over our warm summers and lack of coastal fog and wind. Some permanent residents started out by living here in summer, perhaps in a cabin along a lake, and later moved here permanently. The most successful are likely to have visited our counties multiple times and have lived here through at least one full winter and enjoyed the challenge.

Those of us who live on the east side of Tioga Pass in Mono County live near the East Gate entrance to Yosemite National Park but embrace a different lifestyle. We are cut off from crossing the park on Highway 120 East by the annual November-to-May closure of Tioga Pass. The front range scenery of sheer mountain upsweeps along U.S. Highway 395 emphasizes our self-sufficient nature. Mono County residents look north, south, and east to the state of Nevada for provisions and resources.

Yet we all share a love of awe-inspiring scenery, countryside, and what we like to call good rural living. Many of us envision ourselves with a home on perhaps five acres, with neighbors nearby, though maybe not in sight. Our Realtors, usually independently owned franchises of major nationwide names in real estate, sell property and homes in several foothill counties. We tell friends to come and drive around the area, identify the most appealing town or rural area, and then

Ever thought of working and living in Yosemite National Park? No one owns or leases property or housing in the national park, but the park concessionaire, Delaware North Companies Parks & Resorts at Yosemite, Inc., has company-subsidized housing and meal plans for employees, deducted from their checks. Salary grade and tenure determine an employee's housing. Tent cabins are the most rustic. Wooden cabins and dormitory units are where most employees live. Management rates single-family housing. Cost for your nominal rent includes all utilities. To view employment opportunities, check under Jobs at www.yosemitepark.com, contact DNC Parks & Resorts at Yosemite, Inc., Human Resources at P.O. Box 578, Yosemite National Park, CA 95389, or call (209) 372-1236.

walk into a local real estate office and interview the real estate agents on their inventory and areas of expertise and interest before looking at property or homes. There is enough competition to sell local real estate to provide a choice of a realty company and agent.

In our towns, we generally like to keep government local; few of our gateway route communities on either side of the Sierra Nevada are incorporated. Our housing developments allow space between homes. We like having schools close by and teachers we have met.

Our spirit comes from a community of individuals who are more at home running a small business than in working for big business. Our ancestors were miners, lumber mill workers, ranchers, government workers, and entrepreneurs. Mining and mills are gone. Rock and forest natural-resource use and processing are highly regulated. Cowboys still work cattle ranches in the less hilly areas. Various levels of government and the hospitality industry, especially our hotels, motels, and restaurants, employ a large number of workers.

Because our towns serve as gateways, portals, doorsteps, or Yosemite National Park's front yards, we revel in our hometown atmosphere and plan frequent getaways to relax, whether by fishing, rafting, swimming, hiking, horseback riding, or hang gliding. We admit that relocation here has its challenges—city types will quickly learn the nuances of television and radio reception, septic tanks or sewers, and fire access. We'll make it easier by beginning this chapter with an introduction to the county, communities, and sellers of real estate along each park gateway route. Then we'll tell you about health care, education, retirement, fire and road safety, and a little about our houses of worship. Welcome to our four-gateway, four-county region of mountains, hills, valleys, and rural communities, best characterized in Tuolumne County promotional brochures as "The Great Unfenced."

REAL ESTATE

Arch Rock Entrance/ Highway 140

MARIPOSA COUNTY

There's no stoplight in Mariposa County, no incorporated area, and no business licensing in this rural county of small communities, small farms, and ranches, where 40 percent of the roads are gravel. A 10 percent transient occupancy tax on hotel bed nights provides a significant chunk of the county budget. The town of Mariposa, with the oldest courthouse still in use west of the Mississippi River, is the county seat and main population center, with 2,500 residents.

Mariposa County's current population is about 18,500 and average family income hovers around $31,000. A county general plan took effect in late 2005 that will maintain low density by "building out" over many years to accommodate no

Colorful fall foliage frames Yosemite Falls. JOHN POIMIROO

more than 50,000 residents. The plan mandates that the county's average home, built on a five-acre parcel, cannot, with a few exceptions, be further subdivided. Local expectations are that large lots, a limited housing inventory, and restricting the population density could create a highly desirable area for those seeking to settle here. One-third of current residents are self-employed as shop owners, small businesspeople, contractors, and consultants who telecommute from home offices. Mariposa County and its school district, the National Park Service, and California Division of Forestry are major employers. With the 2005 opening of the University of California campus in Merced, 35 miles from Mariposa, university staff and educators are moving to this relaxed country setting where locals boast of their "elbow room." The Mariposa Board of Realtors Web site (www.mariposabor.com) provides the county's Multiple Listing Service online.

MARIPOSA COUNTY REAL ESTATE

A single-family dwelling on that five-acre lot will cost from $350,000 to $400,000. Custom-built homes can be constructed in six months, at prices from $150 per square foot. In less than 60 days, a buyer can have a five-acre home site bulldozed, secure permits, and locate a modular home on the property. Making the lifestyle transition from a million-dollar home on a 60-foot lot to a home at one-third the price with substantial acreage also comes with a learning curve: instead of sewer service, septic tanks are used in about 80 percent of county homes. Wells are the water source for everyone except the residents of Mariposa town and two rural subdivisions. Shoveling snow can be a shock and pine trees inhibit showy flower gardens. Virtually no apartments or condominiums are available in Mariposa County and the acute demand for housing creates a scarcity of homes for rent.

Century 21 Sierra Gold
4989 Highway 140, Mariposa
(800) 655-5175, (209) 966-5354
www.c21sierragold.com
Word-of-mouth referrals generate 75 percent of Century 21 Sierra Gold's business, says broker/owner Gene Mickel of the half-century-old Mariposa company he owns with his wife, Kay. Their staff of 10 Realtors work regular hours seven days a week and personally answer phone calls. Between them, the Realtors have more than 175 years of cumulative experience in "country" real estate. Since the Mickels bought the real estate company they worked for in 1987, helping newcomers move quickly from city life to country living is what their staff does best, says Gene. Sierra Gold agents tour new owners around, invite them to community functions, and get them involved with their new community. "Our company motto," says Mickel is, "Above the fog, below the snow, and delightfully behind the times."

Big Oak Flat Entrance/ Highway 120 West

TUOLUMNE COUNTY: GROVELAND, SONORA, JAMESTOWN

Two-thirds of Yosemite National Park is found in Tuolumne County, and the western stretch of Highway 120 is open year-round for park access. Gold Rush history lives in our main streets' architecture and small businesses. Tourists search with nostalgia for the region's past glories, and residents new and old value heritage, preferring a lifestyle we feel is close to the way it used to be.

Groveland is along Highway 120 in the lower Sierra Nevada foothills, east of the edge-of-the-Central Valley town of Oakdale, the self-proclaimed "Cowboy Capital of the World." A brief stretch of Highway 120 in our Great Unfenced county crosses Highway 49, the north-south route through California's Gold Country. Sonora, the Tuolumne County seat and its largest city with more than 4,600 of the county's 57,000 residents, perches at an elevation of 1,796 feet on Highway 49, about 20 miles north of Groveland. Incorporated in 1851, Sonora is a major population center in the heart of Gold Country, the Mother Lode.

Retirees and former residents are attracted to Groveland, Sonora, and Gold Country by the region's open spaces, trees, and clean air, a healthy environment in a hometown atmosphere. Our voter registration rate is 50 percent above California's average, and our violent crime rate is well below state statistical averages.

Once heavily dependent on gold and rock mining and timber, Tuolumne County's economy is in transition to Gold Country, Yosemite National Park, and national forest tourism; the health care industry; and technology businesses. Government employs nearly one-third of our workforce. Up to 10 percent of the county's workforce is unionized, comprised of most of the teachers and some retail employees. Retirees 55 years and up represent 35 percent of our population. Our children most often go to more urban areas for higher education and return between the ages of 45 and 55 years with young families. They are returning to a small-town atmosphere specifically to enroll their own children in good, locally administered schools.

TUOLUMNE COUNTY REAL ESTATE

More than 78 real estate offices and more than 330 active agents cover Tuolumne County, where the median housing price is $397,000 (in 2005). Offices and agents primarily work from Groveland and Sonora locations. New residents having homes built can expect lots of personal attention from their contractors, who typically are only working on a few houses at once. Dwellings run the gamut from a mountain cabin on one-half acre to an upper-end home in town, a foothill ranch, or a million-dollar lakeside property.

Join the Newcomer's Club of Tuolumne County for the first three years of residence in Groveland, Sonora, or one of the county's other Gold Country communities. At September through May monthly dinner meetings, speakers from community organizations talk about what's out there. Picnics, holiday brunches, ladies' lunch, card groups, and golf all help newcomers or returning former residents integrate into foothill living. Membership is $20 per year. For information check the Web site, www.tcnc.org or e-mail tcncinfo@tcnc.org.

Coldwell Banker Mountain Leisure Properties
(800) 659-5263
www.mtnleisure.com

18687 Main Street, Groveland
(209) 962-5252 (real estate)
(800) 962-4765, (209) 962-4396 (rentals)

5065 Highway 140, Mariposa
(209) 742-7000

6430 Greeley Hill Road, Greeley Hill
(209) 878-3456

Land sales were half of Mountain Leisure Properties's gross sales of $60 million in 2005, notes broker/owner John Stone. He has 32 Realtors working in four offices (the Lake Don Pedro/Grange office is outside the scope of this title) of the company he has owned since 1965. Operations cover three Yosemite gateway counties, from Groveland in Tuolumne County and Mariposa in its county to Oakhurst and beyond in Eastern Madera County. Stone himself deliberately sticks to commercial property sales so as not to compete with his agents. Small offices in multiple locations, each with a manager and an in-office trainer, are Stone's strategy. Since 1965 his agents have sold some properties as many as 10 times, following a pattern where a client often will first rent a cabin, later buy a second home on a cabin site, and eventually purchase a conventional home. Telecommuters moving to the foothills are the company's latest specialization, says Stone. "Relocation is our specialty; it's what we do."

Prudential California Realty
www.pcr1.com
133 Old Wards Ferry Road, Suite G, Sonora
(209) 533-3333

22920 Twain Harte Drive, Twain Harte
(209) 586-1107
After becoming PCR licensees in mid-2002, the two Tuolumne County offices have grown quickly, boasting 40 agents by late 2005. The company handles relocation, commercial, residential, land, investment, and retirement property.

Sugar Pine Realty, GMAC
www.sugarpinerealty.com

19520 Hillsdale Drive, Sonora
(209) 533-4242

5008A Main Street, Coulterville
(209) 878-0499

18727 Main Street/Highway 120, Suite A
Groveland
(209) 962-7765

18223 Main Street, Jamestown
(209) 984-2087

23012 Joaquin Gully, Twain Harte
(209) 586-9777
Sugar Pine Realty was founded in 1977, and 65 real estate agents now work out of eight offices, including 8 in the Yosemite foothill region. Emmett Brennan, broker/owner, says he doesn't compete for sales with his Realtors, who average 10 years with the company. Sales dollar volume increased 20 percent from 2004 to 2005. "In Tuolumne County, we have pockets of population," he says, "so our offices grow as part of the neighborhood." Sugar Pine specializes in residential property, with expertise in IRS 1031 tax-deferred property exchange and working with land subdivisions building out in West Tuolumne County.

South Gate Entrance/ Highway 41

EASTERN MADERA COUNTY: OAKHURST, BASS LAKE, COARSEGOLD, NORTH FORK, FISH CAMP, WAWONA, YOSEMITE WEST

Rural, mountain atmosphere is simply the best living in the world for many residents of Eastern Madera County along Southern Yosemite Highway 41, the Southern gateway. There are even residents who may never have been to Yosemite National Park or rarely visit, even though they may work in hotels, restaurants, or shops that cater to park visitors. We like our recreation, fishing on Bass Lake, and our access to wide-open spaces.

Ranchers from Coarsegold have been driving cattle into high country across the Sierra Nevada each spring for generations, then driving the cattle west again in the fall. The North Fork lumber mill closed in 1994, and that community, with the Mono Indians' cultural center, is working toward a new future. There is talk of incorporation around the major population center, Oakhurst, with about 12,800 residents—10 percent of Madera County's population—but mostly, we like a sense of relative isolation. Many of us lived the urban lifestyle, have had enough of government, and want to live a peaceful existence in a home we have built in the middle of five acres. We'll leave our retreat once a week or so to shop in Oakhurst, where the downtown is never jam-packed. We're glad there are a couple of supermarkets there but would never want 15 to choose among. For medical services except urgent care, we go to Madera or Fresno in the Central Valley. Prescriptions can be filled at one of four Oakhurst pharmacies, but winter snow may mean that pharmaceutical deliveries are late.

There's a pioneer spirit here. Bears in yards are common, mountain lions are spotted, coyotes can be heard howling at night, and everyone uses a bungee cord to secure garbage cans from raccoons and bears. Thunderstorms cause Oakhurst Basin cable service to go out periodically, and in the mountains satellite television is a plus. When cable or power goes out, there's KTNS-AM from Oakhurst, which uses solar power to broadcast emergency information, and a network of amateur radio (ham) operators. Septic systems, well water, pumps, propane for fuel, and backup generators are a way of life in our mountains, along with summer wildfires. Oakhurst's talk of possible incorporation also brings up the growing need for sewers, public water sources, and other infrastructure improvements the area may need in the future.

When the Chukchansi Gold Resort & Casino, owned by the (Native American) Picayune Rancheria, opened in Coarsegold in mid-2003, our version of Las Vegas became the area's major employer, with 1,200 employees. Tenaya Lodge at Yosemite, just outside the park, the USDA Forest Service, the National Park Service, and Raley's and Von's supermarkets in Oakhurst employ many of the rest of our citizens. Dentists, doctors, attorneys, accountants, and retail shops are the backbone of a thriving service industry.

Park-induced tourism goes full throttle from June through August, idles during shoulder months April to May and September to October, and suffers significantly from January through early April from the lack of a major ski area and the public misconception that Yosemite National Park is closed in winter. While our hotels, motels, and restaurants remain open, the ebb and flow of park tourism affects us all. We use our time off to fish and get into the outdoors that drew us here and welcome four seasons of weather and independent living.

EAST MADERA COUNTY REAL ESTATE

Newer arrivals tend to be people who are more than 50 years old, have visited the area, and are considering buying a parcel of two-and-a-half acres to build on. For an average of $220,000, a conservative price for a condominium in Los Angeles or San Francisco, newcomers find they can semi-retire in a single-family dwelling with a job in the hospitality industry or a small start-up business, with a dramatic decrease in overhead costs. Mobile homes start at $135,000, and apartment rentals in a tight Oakhurst market range from $550 to $1,200 per month.

Home & Ranch Magazine (Wild Pete Publishing, 888-222-6677, www.wildpete.com), based in Coarsegold, publishes a guide to those searching for an East Madera County broker or real estate.

Century 21 Ditton Realty
(800) 350-1155, (559) 683-7653
www.yosemiterealestate.com

40307 Highway 41, Oakhurst
(800) 350-1155, (559) 683-7653

54299 Road 432, Bass Lake
(800) 350-1155, (559) 642-1636

32011 Meadow Ridge Road, Coarsegold
(800) 266-8700, (559) 683-8700

27955 Yosemite Springs Parkway
Yosemite Lakes Park
(800) 972-7901, (559) 868-4412

54511 Road 200, North Fork
(559) 877-4352

Owner Brad Ditton is local. He was born and reared in Yosemite Valley in the national park, and today he lives in Coarsegold. Tradition lives in the Oakhurst office's Victorian-era building with a landmark Talking Bear statue out front. The largest real estate company in Eastern Madera County operates out of five offices with 50 Realtors. One-stop shopping includes in-house loan and escrow departments and a relocation coordinator.

If you are considering relocating in California, check www.dre.ca.gov, the California Department of Real Estate's user-friendly Web site. From home-buying tips to real estate law, terms, and jargon, and a Kids Korner to help youngsters make the move, this site makes it easier to decide where to start and what to look for in one of the country's most active real estate states.

The company sells ranches, homes, land, and commercial investment property. In addition to selling Bass Lake Resort properties, the company manages 100 Bass Lake vacation cabins.

Coldwell Banker Dan Blough & Associates
Relocation Division (in Fresno, CA)
(800) 488-2957
www.cbdanblough.com
Oakhurst and Coarsegold are among eight Dan Blough offices serving Eastern Madera County, the Central Valley, and California's Central Coast. Local office Realtors refer all relocation inquiries to the company's relocation division, where corporate clients and other transferees are assisted with area tours, home finding, home marketing, rentals, school information, and newcomer packages.

Pine Tree GMAC Real Estate
www.pinetreegmac.com

40366 Highway 41, Oakhurst
(800) 350-3387, (559) 683-7477

29850 Yosemite Springs Parkway, Suite B, Coarsegold
(800) 226-3387, (559) 658-7477

Highway 140 at Highway 49 North Mariposa
(800) 266-7402, (209) 742-7653
Three offices, 20 Realtors, and dedication to quality service are what Pine Tree agents say their 25-year reputation is built on. After a property sale, the real estate agent follows up with a questionnaire for both buyer and seller and stays in touch long after the property purchase. Professional rental property management of Yosemite Lakes Park homes is a specialty for this real estate company primarily focused on Eastern Madera County.

East Gate Entrance/ Highway 120 East

MONO COUNTY: LEE VINING, MONO LAKE, BRIDGEPORT, JUNE LAKE, CROWLEY LAKE, MAMMOTH LAKES

Wide-open spaces? Mountains? Winter snow? Mono County, on the eastern side of the Sierra Nevada, is literally a world apart from the gateway communities on the western side of Yosemite National Park. Two-thirds of the county's 12,000-some residents live in or close to Mammoth Lakes, the country's third most popular ski resort area. It hosts 1.5 million visitors a year. The all-season resort, 25 miles south of Highway 120 East/US 395 junction at the small settlement of Lee Vining, known for an eclectic mixture of facilities, 35 lifts and 185 ski trails, was purchased in late 2005. New owners plan to build boutique and major-name hotels, trendy restaurants, entertainment, and new residential development by the end of the decade, focusing even more of the county's employment market here. Mammoth Lakes, or Mammoth, as everyone here calls it, is a favorite Los Angeles getaway. The weather-determined seasonal closure of Tioga Pass from approximately November through May forces current residents to look south to Mammoth Lakes for hospital care, educational, and child care resources, and the main high school.

Some of us who work in Mammoth live along a nearby 10-mile stretch of US 395 called Crowley Lake or Long Valley. Ours is a bedroom community without tourism; we have jobs in government, management, or facility maintenance.

Bridgeport, our county seat in the north welcomes tourists but provides only basic services: California Highway Patrol, county sheriff, firefighting services, the county health department, and a health clinic. Emergency medical evacuation is by air to Washoe or Nevada, or we drive 70 miles northeast to Gardnerville, Nevada.

Mono Lake, our namesake natural wonder with its tufa formations and bird populations along with glistening recreational lakes on the June Lake Loop, is a magnet for those seeking nature's majesty. Small communities live at the lakes' edges. Mono City, with fewer than 200 inhabitants, has an artists' community that includes potters.

MONO COUNTY REAL ESTATE

If we have a choice, most of us choose to live in the hills, a sort of sophisticated hillbilly lifestyle, on a less luxurious level than Mammoth residents. Mammoth Lakes's median home price in late 2005 is $785,000, reflecting the resort's popularity with well-off Californians from coastal areas of the state. Property values should increase with the resort's development. With two-thirds of Mono County's population within 10 miles of Mammoth, most county real estate is handled by Realtors based in Mammoth Lakes.

Coldwell Banker Mammoth Real Estate
3293 Main Street, Mammoth Lakes
(800) 266-6966, (760) 934-2562
www.mammothrealestate.com

Repeat business, 70 percent of total sales, is a major factor for this 37-year-old realty. Proximity to Schat's Bakery next door means that customers, both buyers and sellers, get treated to coffee and fresh doughnuts by the 35 full-time agents who work in the Mammoth Lakes office, each with an average of 15 years of experience selling in the Mammoth market.

HEALTH CARE

You're moving to the foothills or maybe even to the mountain altitudes. Above about 4,000 feet in Yosemite National Park and its gateway communities, you'll be faced with living in snow and with the health challenges that altitude and cold winters present. If you're active in rock or mountain climbing, kayaking, or rafting, you may find yourself in an emergency room or seeking out an orthopedic sports medicine specialist more often than most residents. Aging presents its own health challenges, such as a need for nearby cardiac care.

As part of checking on services in the community and county where you're considering relocation, ask lots of questions of everyone you meet in your new town. Where do they go? What services and specialties do they rely on? When there's an emergency, where is the nearest emergency room? When and how is someone medevaced to facilities in California's Central Valley or, for Mono County, to urban areas in Nevada? The following major health care facilities serve their communities in comprehensive and distinctive ways.

Yosemite Medical Clinic
9000 Ahwahnee Drive, ¼ mile west of The Ahwahnee, Yosemite National Park
(209) 372-4637

This private, for-profit clinic serves the 1,200 National Park Service and concessionaire employees working in the national park, as well as the medical needs of the park's several million annual visitors. Tenet HealthSystem Medical, Inc. affiliate, Doctors Medical Center of Modesto, will operate the clinic under contract until 2010.

From roots as a U.S. Army field hospital in 1851 and subsequent operations in converted army barracks, the need for a serious medical center in the park became apparent when the all-weather, year-round Mariposa-Yosemite Road opened in 1925. The Lewis Memorial Hospital, named for a former park superintendent, became permanent in 1929 with a $50,000 congressional grant for a 12-bed facility. In 1975 the hospital became a clinic with family practice and urgent care.

Those in need find a four-bed emergency room, six triage rooms, and two crash carts. The facility may have clinic status, but it functions as an emergency room 24 hours per day, 365 days a year. "Everything a big-city ER sees, we do, too," says clinic manager Sean Pence. Common problems presented include acute mountain sickness, heart attacks, strokes, diabetic injuries, and asthma attacks. Many patients are treated for falls, rock climbing injuries, rattlesnake bites, and wild animal-petting bites from park denizens like raccoons and squirrels. Rabid animals are always a concern. Fainting from a combination of altitude, dehydration, and drinking alcohol after physical activity is the most common condition treated. For injuries it can't treat, the clinic acts to stabilize, then arranges for helicopter medevac or 24-hour paramedic ambulance service to the nearest equipped facility. In winter season, usually from December to March, Advanced Life Services are also provided at the A-frame ranger hut at Yosemite's Badger Pass Ski Area.

A family nurse practitioner and physician's assistant are full-time staff. Doctors under contract work in the park for 7 to 10 days at a time. A certified physical therapist is on staff; an acupuncturist and a Mariposa County psychiatrist hold sessions once a week; and the clinic has X-ray and laboratory services. Pence cheerfully admits that everyone working at the clinic is overqualified with such special training as a certified emergency nurse, mobile intensive care nurse, advanced cardiac life support, basic trauma life support, and pediatric advanced life support. All staff are CPR certified.

YMC is a teaching clinic for medical residents from all over the country, eager for exposure to a wide range of emergencies, illnesses, and nature-inflicted damage. The clinic also trains National Park Service employees in medic and EMT training and provides CPR and first-aid training to Yosemite Valley residents and seventh-graders at the Yosemite Valley School. Daily scheduled clinic hours are 8:00 A.M. to 6:00 P.M., although a wait at the clinic won't be as long as it could be at an urban facility. The YMC accepts some health insurance plans, Medicare, MediCal (California State Medicaid), and cash. There is also an independent dental clinic in the park.

Mariposa County
John C. Fremont Healthcare District
5189 Hospital Road, Mariposa
(209) 966-3631
www.jcfremonthospital.com

Mariposa County's residents are served by a full-service public, nonprofit medical center in the county's main population base. The 34-bed hospital provides 18 beds for general acute care and 16 for skilled nursing. From its origins more than a half century ago in 1951, this institution now boasts the only MRI and CT scanner in the foothill area and teleradiology for immediate reading of X-rays. Air ambulances use the facility's heliport. Twenty-one specialty physicians on staff augment care in 24-hour emergency room operations and two rural health clinics. Certified nursing assistant and home health aide classes are offered, in support of 24-hour-a-day, seven-day-a-week Home Health Services, Private Duty, and Hospice services. Hospice staff and 10 volunteers provide in-home hospice care, short-term respite care, and bereavement counseling. One hospice patient at a time can receive care in the hospital's George King Radanovich Room.

Tuolumne County
Sonora Regional Medical Center
1000 Greenley Road, Sonora
(209) 532-5000
www.sonorahospital.org

This is the largest and newest-built medical complex in the region, with roots back to 1957 as Sonora Community Hospital. The 72-bed, faith-based, nonprofit hospital is known for its birth center and emergency care. Sonora Regional Medical Center is an Adventist health facility, though community service takes precedence over the operator's religious traditions. There are no religious, spiritual, or denominational restrictions for patients. Serving Tuolumne County, South Calaveras County, and North Mariposa County, the medical center's cardiac, cancer, and surgical services use state-of-the-art technology comparable to urban medical centers. It boasts the only cardiac catheterization lab in the Sierra foothills. More than 30,000 annual visits can be handled by the emergency department's 14 exam rooms, and a facility helipad accommodates trauma patients. The hospital operates skilled nursing services and one transitional care unit. A 44,000-square-foot medical office in two facilities attached to the hospital is home to 16 physicians, the Sonora Regional Cancer Center, and a community pharmacy. Outreach includes affiliation with 14 primary-care clinics in the region.

Tuolumne General Hospital
101 Hospital Road, Sonora
(209) 533-7100
www.tghospital.com
This 79-bed, Tuolumne County-owned, nonprofit hospital is as proud of being the first California hospital to offer doctors "managed care"—in 1856—as it is of ultramodern video/electronic teleconferencing with the University of California, Davis, for emergency care and other consultations. The full-service hospital accepts all insurance and provides emergency services, inpatient and outpatient surgery, medical-surgical, intensive care, acute psychiatric services, long-term care, adult day health care, and lab services. The hospital oversees operation of two Sonora medical clinics: Family Health and Wellness (adjacent to TGH) and Mother Lode Medical Center (Cedar Road). A TGH-affiliated Visiting Nurse Association serves the Medicare-certified Hospice of the Sierra, (209) 533-6800.

Eastern Madera County
Community Medical Center
48677 Victoria Lane, Oakhurst
(559) 683-2992
Operated by Community Medical Centers, this Highway 41 facility acts as a rural health clinic. Radiology and medical services are offered. The Community Living Center-Oakhurst (40131 Highway 49; 559-683-2244), run by the same corporation, is a 64-bed skilled nursing facility.

Kaiser Permanente
Oakhurst Medical Offices
40595 Westlake Drive, Oakhurst
(800) 262-6663
www.kaiserpermanente.org
This HMO's members have Oakhurst access to adult medicine, pediatrics, an allergy clinic, pharmacy, and poison control, but no urgent care at this facility. Inpatient and other services are available in Central Valley locations.

Mono County
Mammoth Hospital
85 Sierra Park Road, Mammoth Lakes
(760) 934-3311
www.mammothhospital.com
Mammoth Hospital and its 11 Sierra Park Clinics form the Southern Mono Healthcare District. The nonprofit special district governmental entity based in Mammoth Lakes serves the entire county population as well as Mammoth resort's 1.5 million annual visitors. Since the late 1990s, the hospital's 15 beds, emergency room, and clinics have seen patient-served numbers increase from 8,000 to 45,000 patient visits per year.

While the facility, built in 1978, always tended to ski injuries and visitors' mishaps and emergencies, the newer specialty clinics mean that Mono County residents now "go local" for many services, including delivery of babies. Twenty-three physicians are on the hospital staff. Sierra Park

Clinics include family dental (760-924-4007), internal medicine (760-924-4001), family medicine (760-934-2551), pediatrics (760-924-4000), women's health services (760-934-4044), and surgery (760-924-4014). There is a family medicine clinic in Bridgeport (760-932-7011), operated as a satellite specialty care facility. Hospital expansion of the emergency room, operating room, imaging department, and labor/delivery unit will be complete in late 2006. The Sierra Park Orthopedic and Rehabilitation Therapy (SPORT), a 13,000-square-foot, two-story facility a few blocks from Mammoth Hospital, provides services crucial in an activity-oriented resort: orthopedic and neurology clinics (760-924-4084); a physical and rehabilitation therapy clinic and a human performance laboratory (760-934-7302).

Doctors and staffers are expert in dealing with altitude sickness, a problem for some visitors. For care of patients it can't treat, like some cardiac cases, premature babies, and severely broken bones, Care Flight operates a 24-hour air(plane) ambulance medevac service to other hospitals. There are cancer patient and grief recovery support groups. Mammoth Hospital Foundation provides lodging, mileage, and a meal allowance for cancer patients who must travel beyond the area for treatment, with community outreach.

EDUCATION

California's academic accomplishments are world-renowned. The University of California system has generated many Nobel laureates. The state universities are respected, and local two-year community college systems are extensive. Yet in the Yosemite gateway communities, attaining higher education has often meant looking elsewhere in the state. Columbia College, a two-year community college in Sonora (Tuolumne County), and the Oakhurst Center of the State Center Community College District were notable exceptions. Foothill community youth traditionally looked to Modesto or Fresno for higher education; area higher education was enhanced with the fall 2005 opening of the University of California, Merced.

For undergraduates, Sierra foothill and Mother Lode traditions remain strong in the number of one-school districts with small student complements. California funds nonsectarian, local school district-approved charter schools, organized by parents, teachers, and community leaders. Homeschooling is permitted in California, and one of three alternative schools supervised by the Mariposa County Unified School District has about 90 students homeschooling in the Independent Learning School.

Religion-affiliated schools include the Mother Lode Adventist Junior Academy in Sonora, Victory Baptist Christian School in Mariposa, the Oakhurst Seventh-Day Adventist School and Gateway Christian School in Oakhurst, and Summit Christian High School in Ahwahnee. Most have student populations of fewer than 100. The Sierra Waldorf School (19234 Rawhide Road, Jamestown, Tuolumne County; 209-984-0454; www.sierrawaldorf.com) offers elementary schooling to 170 students, with the 1875 Rawhide Schoolhouse as the assembly hall-classroom. Current lists of preschools, day care centers, and private day care providers are available from county or local chambers of commerce.

Mono County's Eastern Sierra Unified School District (231 Kingsley Street, Bridgeport; 760-932-7443; www.esusd.org) encompasses approximately 930 students from a 2,600-square-mile area including Lee Vining and Bridgeport. The district provides transportation for 90 percent of its scholars. Eastern Sierra Academy in Bridgeport forgoes high school athletics but emphasizes high-tech in its renowned academic program (760-932-7161, http://esaonline.org).

University of California, Merced
5200 North Lake Road, Merced
(209) 724-4400
www.ucmerced.edu
The campus of the University of California in Merced opened for the fall 2005 school year with its first 1,000 undergraduates and 55 professors on former Central Valley farmland. Classrooms and other buildings were still under construction. UC Merced is the tenth University of California campus in the state, the first one opened since 1965. Initially, nine majors are being offered and Sierra foothill communities hope it will give their students access to a school closer to home. No one should expect mountains, lakes, or other scenic wonders here, although buildings' sustainable environmental features such as energy efficient lighting, fine-tuned control of utilities, and water-tank cooling to offset sometimes sizzling outside temperatures help the modern, "green" feel of the campus architecture. Yet, the Merced campus's relative proximity to Yosemite, Sequoia, and Kings Canyon National Parks, and the national forests and wildernesses make it easy for student researchers—and future graduate students—to do fieldwork close to their home base and laboratories. UC Merced's plans will accommodate a student body of 25,000.

Columbia College
11600 Columbia College Drive, Sonora
(209) 588-5100
www.columbia.yosemite.cc.ca.us
One of two public community or junior colleges in the 4,000-square-mile Yosemite Community College District, Columbia College claims a student population that hovers around 3,800. Campus buildings near the town of Sonora surround lakelike 4.5-acre San Diego Reservoir in the midst of a 280-acre hardwood forest. Columbia College has been around since 1968, offering two-year academic associate degrees with full accreditation or vocational certificates for mountain community youth. Vocational programs include fire technology, forestry technology, and watershed management. Athletic programs offer intercollegiate women's volleyball and men's basketball. Columbia College is proud of its two-bedroom, three-to-four-occupant student apartments, one of only a handful of California community colleges with on-campus housing.

The University of Nevada, Reno's Good Neighbor Policy, detailed at www.ss.unr.edu/records/pdf/forms/res:appl_gn.pdf, offers reduced out-of-state tuition fees to neighboring states' high school or community college graduates of counties including Mono County. Call Elizabeth Maile, (775) 784-4700, ext. 2046.

State Center Community College District Oakhurst Center
40241 Highway 41, Building G, Oakhurst
(559) 683-3940
www.oakhurstcenter.com
This two-year community college center offers nearly 460 East Madera County students 75 day and evening academic and vocational courses. Facilities include computer and science labs.

Cerro Coso Community College: Eastern Sierra Center Mammoth
101 College Parkway, Mammoth Lakes
(760) 934-2875
www.cerrocoso.edu/escc/mammoth
This Mammoth Lakes-based community college is one of the Kern Community College District Cerro Coso Community College campuses. The Mammoth campus serves students as far south as Death Valley with day, evening, and online courses. Its first 1997 building, Edison Hall, houses the Mammoth Ski Museum and Beekley International Collection of Skiing Art & Literature. A 20,000-square-foot learning center houses 11 classrooms, two computer labs, and offices. A number of courses target local needs like fire technology. Sierra College cites Microsoft founder Bill Gates's accolade that Cerro Coso is a pioneer in online education to

convey the importance of online resources to such a geographically dispersed student base. Its online campus division (888-537-6932, http://cconline.cerro coso.edu) offers 12 degrees, more than 100 online courses, and serves students without standard on-campus attendance requirements. Sierra College's nursing program is California's first to be completely online (except for required clinical time).

Going to School in Yosemite National Park

Children of parents working for the National Park Service, the concessionaire, and, in El Portal, the park support community usually attend school in the park, as children have for more than 125 years. Weather, rock slides, and snowy road conditions make it impractical for many students to consider a daily trip to school in Mariposa or Oakhurst, the major towns closest to park gates. California school budgets have had funding cut, and the small-scale park schools struggle to maintain facilities, fund art, music, and physical education programs, and provide special education teachers. U.S. Congressional testimony indicates that some park parents choose to relocate to other assignments to find full-resource schools, and some parents in Wawona choose home-schooling.

The **Yosemite Valley School** (209-372-4791; www.home.inreach.com/yvschool) has close to 55 students in grades K through 8, within three class units. Children have all the advantages of the park—the natural world is all around them, and programs like the national parks' Artist in Residence program provides unique exposure to some subjects. YVS has a sister school in Japan, and both schools measure and send weather information. The one-room, one-teacher **Wawona School** educates a maximum of 20 grade K-through-6 students. **Yosemite National Park El Portal Elementary School** teaches about 50 elementary-age children. In 1997 **Yosemite Park High School** opened in the same building (9670 Rancheria Flat Road; 209-379-2414); it has one room with a kitchen, an office, and eight computer stations. Both El Portal schools are administered by the Mariposa County Unified School District with a single principal. A **Yosemite Valley day care center** (209) 372-4819, for NPS, concession, and park contractors' children operates during the week.

Madera County Office of Education
28123 Avenue 14, Madera
(559) 673-6051
www.maderacoe.k12.ca.us

Mariposa County Office of Education
Mariposa County Unified School District
5082 Old Highway North, Mariposa
(209) 742-0250
www.mariposa.k12.ca.us

Mono County Office of Education
37 Emigrant Street, Bridgeport
(760) 932-7311
www.monocoe.k12.ca.us

Tuolumne County Office of Education
175 South Fairview Lane, Sonora
(209) 536-2000
www.tuolcoe.k12.ca.us

RETIREMENT

Age 50? AARP solicits membership from mature adults beginning their sixth decade. Lighthearted women join the Red Hat Society's many Sierra foothill chapters at that milestone birthday or up, relieving feminine aging angst with tea parties, purple dresses, and elaborate red hats. Social Security *may* raise the retirement age, but for right now, reduced benefits can be claimed at age 62. So-called senior discounts call attention to good values in restaurants and stores. In 2000 the U.S. Census recorded that 13 percent of the population was 65 years old or more; almost 5 million Californians are over age 60; by 2010, 20 percent of Californians will be past 60.

Among the Yosemite gateway counties, even in Mono County, with two-thirds of its population living in or near Mammoth Lakes resort, the over-60 age group was 12 percent of the population in the 2000 U.S. Census. In Mariposa County, 23 percent of the population was over 60; in Tuolumne County, 24 percent. Statistics are only the echo of a trend that Realtors watching inquiries, phone calls, and walk-ins confirm. Recreation, a rural lifestyle, a slower pace of life, and real estate selling at a much lower price than many retirees sell houses for make retirement here attractive. Senior services may span multiple counties in the region.

For an excellent summary of the services and legal issues affecting golden-age California residents, there is a free State Bar of California report and reference guide, *Seniors & the Law: A Guide for Maturing Californians,* available online at www.calbar.ca.gov/state/calbar/calbar_home.jsp.

The **California Department of Aging** (800-510-2020 in California; 800-677-1116 for callers outside California; www.aging.state.ca.us) coordinates federal, state, and local programs for seniors, including the Area Agencies on Aging. CDA predicts an increasing senior population in the Yosemite gateway counties through 2030, when the Baby Boomer generation begins to reach 85 (now the life expectancy of an average American male).

By mandate and need, the Agencies on Aging keep track of health care, nutrition programs, senior transportation options, legal resources for seniors, senior center activities, and senior volunteer opportunities. If you are retirement age and considering moving to one of the Yosemite gateway communities, contact the local county's Agency on Aging, local community's Chamber of Commerce, and the nationwide **Eldercare Locator** (800-677-1116; www.eldercare.gov) for lists of current senior and retirement resources—and fun group activities and volunteer groups within reasonable distance from wherever you may choose to live.

Area 12 Agency on Aging (Mariposa and Tuolumne Counties)
13975 Mono Way, Suite E
Sonora
(800) 510-2020, (209) 532-6272

Mariposa County Community Services Department
5246 Spriggs Lane, Mariposa
(209) 966-5315
Community meetings are held at this Mariposa facility, which offers transportation to seniors and to veterans needing VA facility access, and provides meals for seniors.

Tuolumne County Senior Center
540 Greenley Road, Sonora
(209) 533-2622
Lunch, classes, talks, support groups, counseling, and a lounge are enjoyed by a number of seniors. Meals on Wheels are prepared and delivered by the senior center.

Senior Lounge & Boutique
201 South Stewart Street, Sonora
(209) 532-7890
Seniors can stop by for coffee, chat, classes, organized activities, and free blood pressure checks.

Fresno-Madera Area Agency on Aging
2085 East Dakota Street, Fresno
(800) 510-2020, (559) 453-4405
www.fmaaa.org
Fresno County and a large part of Madera County are in the relatively populous Central Valley, and citizens there have access to more senior service locations. In Eastern Madera County, several senior centers offer activities, nutritious meals, and social contact for many local residents.

Coarsegold Community Center
35610 Highway 41, Coarsegold
(559) 683-1443

North Fork Center
North Fork Town Hall
Highway 41, 56442 Road 200, North Fork
(559) 877-2653

Oakhurst Senior Center
Road 425B/49111 Cinder Lane, Oakhurst
(559) 683-3811

Inyo-Mono Area Agency on Aging
568 West Line Street, Bishop
(800) 510-2020, (760) 873-6364
www.inyocounty.us/imaaa/
A care planner can do a senior home condition assessment, create a care plan, and arrange for caretakers and respite workers. Physically limited seniors who cannot ride the Inyo Mono Transit bus can be escorted, and an escort is also provided for medical appointments in Southern California or Reno, Nevada. The joint county agency operates seven senior centers, all at some distance north (Walker), south (Bishop is the closest), or southeast (Benton) of Lee Vining, the community closest to the park's east entrance. Activities may include birthday parties, art classes, and bingo, as well as health screening and help with income taxes.

California Advocates for Nursing Home Reform
650 Harrison Street, 2nd Floor
San Francisco
(800) 474-1116, (415) 974-5171
www.canhr.org
With the state of California's blessing, this advocacy group lists and monitors the performance of more than 1,400 skilled nursing facilities (SNFs) in the state, and "assisted living" or residential care (board and care) facilities for the elderly (RCFEs). You can also check with the county Agencies on Aging and the major hospital and health care centers for facilities and references.

NEWSPAPERS

Residents may subscribe to a major newspaper published outside of the Yosemite gateway community, including the *San Francisco Chronicle, Sacramento Bee, Modesto Bee,* or *Fresno Bee,* as wider-reaching sources of information. The Yosemite foothill area and Mammoth have their own full-service community papers:

Mammoth Times
(760) 934-3929
www.mammothtimes.com
The "Eastern Sierra's #1 Newspaper" publishes on Thursday.

Mariposa Gazette
(209) 966-2500
www.mariposagazette.com
This is California's oldest continuously published weekly newspaper, published on Wednesday. Most Mariposa residents also subscribe to the *San Francisco Chronicle* or *Sacramento Bee.*

The Sierra Star
Oakhurst
(559) 683-4464
www.sierrastar.com
Looking for property as well as news and information about Eastern Madera County? This newspaper, publishing each Wednesday and Friday, also produces the *Sierra Home Advertiser.* Catch up on local news and events in this community-oriented paper, published since 1957.

The Union Democrat
Sonora
(209) 572-7151
www.uniondemocrat.com
The masthead trumpets, "The leading newspaper of the Mother Lode since 1854." Tuolumne County's newspaper of record publishes weekdays except some holidays. It covers everything from news to real estate and periodically publishes a "Know It All" section (available online)

with lists and contact information for government, social service, health care, education, clubs, and interest groups.

SAFETY AT HOME AND ON THE ROAD

Ask any of our neighbors, and they will say that wildfire is our greatest challenge with Mother Nature. Precautions include seeking appropriate property and structure insurance, stocking emergency kits and larders, and clearing forest and brush from a perimeter around our homes. One of the proudest traditions of the Sierra Nevada, and one of the most crucial, is being a firefighter. When you consider moving here, ask whether the fire department is permanent or volunteer. Is there access to your property? Veteran firefighters warn of problems maneuvering vehicles and equipment into box canyons, and hillside locations can slip if after-fire rainfall loosens the soil. Ask how you can get involved as a volunteer firefighter, or join a local chapter of the watchdog and policy group, the California Fire Safe Council (www.firesafecouncil.org).

Winter snow presents its own challenges. Vehicles should have chains, and everyone living in mountain communities should know how and if their roads get plowed (most national forest roads are not plowed) and the road condition phone number, (800) 427-ROAD (7623); www.dot.ca.gov/hq/roadinfo. That Web site also indicates mountain pass closures and when and where chains are required.

Department of Motor Vehicles
(800) 777-0133
www.dmv.ca.gov/dmv.htm
Some California DMV offices are open on Saturday. A driver may use any DMV office in the state.

Bishop (serves Mono County):
473 South Main Street, Bishop

Madera (serves Eastern Madera County):
1206 West Maple Street, Madera

Mariposa:
5264 Highway 49 North, Mariposa

Sonora:
885 Morningstar Drive, Sonora

HOUSES OF WORSHIP

From burying 49er gold miners who died of typhoid when their diggings were contaminated by flooding rivers to marrying congregants, the Yosemite gateways' churches and places of worship have functioned at the heart of their communities' spiritual and social lives for decades. A few, like National Register of Historic Places listee St. Joseph Catholic Church, Rectory, and Cemetery in Mariposa, have functioned for more than a century. We count a wide range of Christian denominations: mainstream Catholic, Episcopal, Lutheran, Methodist, and Baptist; charismatic; Bible-based; independent; Unitarian; Assemblies of God; Church of Christ; the Church of Jesus Christ of Latter-day Saints; Christian Scientist; Four Square; Jehovah's Witnesses; Nazarene; Seventh-Day Adventist; and Pentecostal. The Mother Lode Jewish Community serves Tuolumne and Calaveras Counties, and there are Baha'i Faith meeting and study groups in several areas.

Yosemite Chapel (Yosemite Community Church) offers nondenominational services on Thursday and Sunday. Roman Catholics attend Sunday mass in the Yosemite Valley Visitor Center Theater. Not everyone who lives here is affiliated with a church or place of worship, but local clergy are usually prominent in our communities, and we are proud of our heritage of beliefs that lets us worship as we please.

CHAMBERS OF COMMERCE

Mariposa County Chamber of Commerce
5158 Highway 140
Mariposa, CA 95338
(209) 966-2456
www.mariposa.org

Tuolumne County Chamber of Commerce
222 South Shepherd Street
Sonora, CA 95370
(209) 532-4212
www.tcchamber.com

Highway 120 Chamber of Commerce
18583 Highway 120, Suite A
Groveland, CA 95321
(209) 962-0429, (800) 449-9120
www.groveland.org

Oakhurst Area Chamber of Commerce
49074 Civic Circle Drive
Oakhurst, CA 93644
(559) 683-7766
www.oakhurstchamber.com

Bass Lake Chamber of Commerce
P.O. Box 126
Bass Lake, CA 93604
(559) 642-3676
www.basslakechamber.com

Coarsegold Chamber of Commerce
P.O. Box 815
Coarsegold, CA 93614
(559) 642-2262
www.coarsegoldchamber.com

North Fork Chamber of Commerce
The Chamber Building
Old Mill Office Building
57839 Road 225
North Fork, CA 93643
(559) 877-2410
www.north-fork-chamber.com

Mono County Tourism
(800) 845-7922
www.monocounty.org

Mono County, California
www.monocounty.ca.gov

Bridgeport Chamber of Commerce
P.O. Box 541, Main Street
Bridgeport, CA 93517
(760) 932-7500
www.bridgeportcalifornia.com

June Lake Chamber of Commerce
P.O. Box 2
June Lake, CA 93529
(760) 648-7584
www.junelakechamber.org

Mono Lake Committee Information Center
Lee Vining Chamber of Commerce
P.O. Box 29
Lee Vining, CA 93541
(760) 647-6595, (760) 647-6629
www.monolake.org/chamber
www.leevining.com

Mammoth Lakes Visitors Bureau
P.O. Box 48
Mammoth Lakes, CA 93546
(888) 466-2666, (760) 934-2712
www.visitmammoth.com

INDEX

Z

ABOUT THE AUTHORS

Karen Misuraca is a travel and outdoor writer based in Sonoma, in the heart of California's Wine Country. When not exploring the High Sierra, kayaking on the California coast, or golfing, she writes travel books and contributes articles to a variety of publications, including *Alaska Airlines* and *Horizon Air* magazines, *Distinction,* TravelClassics.com, and others. She is the author of *Backroads of the California Wine Country, The 100 Best Golf Resorts of the World, The California Coast, Our San Francisco, Quick Escapes San Francisco,* and *Fun with the Family in Northern California.* Karen has written about golf in Spain, waterborne safaris in Africa, and adventure travel in Central America and Vietnam. She is accompanied on some of her journeys by her three daughters, a lively contingent of grandchildren, and her partner, Michael Capp, an international broker of architectural products. More information about Karen is available at www.karenmisuraca.com.

Maxine Cass enjoys trekking with cameras and a notebook into the less-crowded natural places on the planet. Between writing and illustrating books on California, San Francisco, and the Pacific Northwest, Western Canada, Florida, and Mexico, the San Francisco–based photojournalist and author also covers the business and leisure sides of travel for publications around the world. Maxine's San Francisco books include *It Happened in San Francisco, Time for Food: San Francisco,* and *A AAA Photo Journey to San Francisco.* Born in Palo Alto on the Stanford University campus, she has lived in San Francisco, Los Angeles, and Santa Barbara; studied medieval history; served as a West Africa Peace Corps volunteer in Senegal; and remembers a beautiful summer on a Greek island when she traveled for the first time and learned to love the journey as much as the destination. Maxine recently added yoga to her passions for walking, hiking, biking, gardening, and photographing the world's wonders.

© MAXINE CASS